U0032268

《論語》之於中國人，就像聖經之於基督教世界的人們，是人類共同的文化寶藏，世界上最重要的思想經典。

讀論語學英語&

The Analects of Confucius

【論語中英文譯注讀本】

理雅各（James Legge）英譯　林宏濤 譯注

| 英譯者簡介 |

理雅各（James Legge, 1815-1897）

英國倫敦會（London Missionary Society）來華教士，於傳教之餘翻譯中國典籍近二十種，自港返英後，潛心研究漢學，成為中國學術研究之權威。他翻譯的《*The Chinese Classics*》是國際漢學之定本。全集凡五卷，第一卷論語、大學、中庸；第二卷孟子；第三卷尚書；第四卷詩經；第五卷春秋左傳。

除了四書五經之翻譯研究以外，另著有*The Nations of Chinese Concerning God and Spirit* (1852)；*The Life and Teachings of Confucius* (1867)；*The Life and Work of Mencius* (1875)。

| 譯注者簡介 |

林宏濤

台灣大學哲學系碩士，德國弗來堡大學博士研究。

譯著有：《鈴木大拙禪學入門》、《啓蒙的辯證》、《菁英的反叛》、《詮釋之衝突》、《體會死亡》、《美學理論》、《法學導論》、《愛在流行》、《隱藏之泉》、《神在人間》、《眾生的導師：佛陀》、《南十字星風箏線》、《神話學辭典》、《與改變對話》、《死後的世界》、《正義的理念》等作品。

前言

前言

　　《論語》是孔子和學生們的言行紀實。《漢書・藝文志》：「論語者，孔子應答弟子、時人及弟子相與言而接聞於夫子之語也。當時弟子各有所記，夫子既卒，門人相與輯而論纂，故謂之《論語》。」學者考訂《論語》應是在戰國初年編輯成書。至於撰述者是誰，則眾說紛紜，朱子《論語序說》：「程子曰：論語之書，成於有子曾子之門人，故其書獨二子以子稱。」無論如何，《論語》確定成於許多人之手，而且年代前後相去三、五十年。王充《論衡・正說》：「初，孔子孫孔安國以教魯人扶卿，官至荊州刺史，始曰論語。」應是《論語》之名的由來。在漢代，論語有四種版本：《古論》二十一篇、《齊論》二十二篇、《魯論》二十篇、《張侯論》二十篇。現在通行的《論語》是張侯論。何晏在《論語集解》序裡說：「漢中壘校尉劉向言魯論語二十篇，皆孔子弟子記諸善言也。太子太傅夏侯勝、前將軍蕭望之、丞相韋賢及子玄成等傳之。齊論語二十二篇，其二十篇中，章句頗多於魯論。琅邪王卿及膠東庸生、昌邑中尉王吉皆以教授。故有魯論，有齊論。魯共王時，嘗欲以孔子宅為宮，壞，得古文論語。……安昌侯張禹本受魯論，兼講齊說，善者從之，號曰張侯論，為世所貴。」今本《論語》分二十篇，凡四百九十八章，一萬六千言。前十篇為《上論》，九篇以記錄孔子的談話為主，〈鄉黨篇〉則敘述孔子的日常生活；《下論》中八篇仍為孔子言行，〈子張篇〉則記錄孔子弟子的談話，而〈堯曰篇〉則有頗多可疑之處。

　　關於《論語》的著作不勝其數，程樹德《論語集釋》引述的作品就有六百八十種。其中比較重要的有：魏何晏的《論語集解》，除了他自己的注解

以外，還收錄孔安國、馬融、包咸、王肅諸家之解說，《十三經注疏》裡的《論語注》就是這部書；梁皇侃的《論語義疏》，博採各家之說，「博極群書，補諸書之未至，爲後學所宗」；宋邢昺之《論語注疏》，以何注爲本，「剪皇氏之枝蔓，而稍傅以義理」，是漢學到宋學的轉折點；朱熹之《論語集注》，著重義理的詮釋，清朝考試取士則規定以朱注爲本；劉寶楠及恭冕父子合著之《論語正義》，總結各家研究成果，保留漢魏古注，並且發揮乾嘉學風，注重文字訓詁、史實考訂和義理闡發，「可謂能集自漢至清經學家論語注釋之大成焉。」蔣伯潛評說：「論語注本，以何晏等之《論語集解》爲最古，朱熹之《論語集注》爲最精，劉寶楠之《論語正義》爲最博。」至於《論語》之語譯注解，則有楊伯峻《論語譯注》、錢穆《論語新解》、毛子水《論語今註今譯》、謝冰瑩等《新譯四書讀本》。

　　《論語》之於中國人，就像聖經之於基督教世界的人們，經過歷史長河的洗鍊，已經成爲人類共同的文化寶藏，世界上最重要的思想經典。近三百年來，《論語》先後譯爲世界各國語言，義大利教士利瑪竇（Matteo Ricci）於十六世紀末把《四書》譯爲拉丁文，爲最早的翻譯，可惜已經失傳；另外還有其他教士先後以拉丁文翻譯傳世；《論語》最早的法文譯本在一六八八年於巴黎出版，譯者爲伯洪（J. de la Brune）；其他如德文、義大利文、荷蘭文、俄文、英文譯本，都陸續出現。英譯的時間雖然比較晚，著作卻是最多。本書採用之英譯本，是英國教士理雅各（James Legge）《中國經典》（*The Chinese Classics*）的第一卷，包括《論語》、《大學》、《中庸》，一八六一年於香港出版。

　　理雅各是世界著名的漢學家，他在中國經典的翻譯以及學術研究的成就，使他位列世界名人。理雅各爲英國蘇格蘭人，生於一八一五年，年輕時進亥伯利神學院（Highbury Theological College）研究神學，其後加入倫敦會

（London Missionary Society）。一八三九年偕妻子來華傳教，擔任香港英華書院校長。一八四八年開始致力於中國學術之研究，擬定計畫翻譯四書五經並出版，是為《中國經典》共五卷，全集凡五卷，第一卷《論語》、《大學》、《中庸》；第二卷《孟子》；第三卷《尚書》；第四卷《詩經》；第五卷《春秋左傳》。另外也翻譯《竹書紀年》、《易經》、《道德經》、《高僧傳》以及《莊子》等著作。除了翻譯研究以外，理雅各著有《中國人之神鬼觀》（*The Notions of Chinese Concerning God and Spirit,* 1852）、《孔子生平及其學說》（*The Life and Teachings of Confucius,* 1867）、《孟子生平及作品》（*The Life and Work of Mencius,* 1875）。一八七三年，理雅各返英，一八九七年去世，那時候他還在翻譯《楚辭》。

理雅各的英譯《論語》，不僅考訂訓解詳盡，在翻譯上的研究也成為日後中國經典翻譯之範式；關於理雅各之翻譯研究，請參考閻振瀛《理雅各氏英譯論語之研究》。

《讀論語學英語》是以《論語集解》、《論語義疏》、《論語注疏》、《論語集注》和《論語正義》的注釋為藍本，並且比較蔣伯潛、楊伯峻、錢穆、毛子水、謝冰瑩等學者的語譯，既收錄比較各家之解說和考證，也從現代世界意義的角度去詮釋文本。在英譯方面，則加以字詞解釋並討論翻譯的問題；讀者從英文翻譯回頭來理解《論語》，會有另闢蹊徑的感覺。例如說，「仁」在《論語》裡有許多不同的意義，而無論注解或語譯都很少突顯這點；在英譯裡，我們可以看到「仁」有 benevolence（慈愛）、perfect virtue（完美的德性）、the virtue proper to humanity（人類特有的德性）、true virtue（真正的德性）等不同的譯名，方便我們了解孔子在不同情境裡所談的「仁」。

目　錄

學而第一

———— ❦ 第一章 ❦ ————

子曰：「學而時習之，不亦説乎？有朋自遠方來，不亦樂乎？人不知而不愠，不亦君子乎？」

語譯　孔子說：「學過的東西時時溫習，不是很高興嗎？好友從遠方來，豈不是很快樂的事嗎？人家不知道我的學問才識，我也不怨恨，不就是有德的君子嗎？」

注釋　①**子**　夫子。《集解》：「馬曰：子者，男子之通稱，謂孔子也。」②**說**　同「悅」。③**愠**　含怒意。④**君子**　成德之名。

解說　「學」者，學為人也。朱注：「學之為言效也。人性皆善，而覺有先後，後覺者必效先覺之所為，乃可以明善而復其初也。」《集解》：「王曰：時者，學者以時誦習之。」則是注重記誦之學。「習」可以說是「複習」或「實踐」。讀書能夠時常溫習，學到的道理能夠實踐，心裡有所體會，自然就會感到快樂。「人不知而不愠」，在〈憲問篇〉裡也說：「君子病無能焉，不病人之不己知也。」做學問是為了自己，管別人知不知道做什麼？

———— ❦ 第二章 ❦ ————

有子曰：「其為人也孝弟，而好犯上者，鮮矣；不好犯上，而好作亂者，未之有也。君子務本，本立而道生。孝弟也者，其為仁之本與？」

語譯　有子說：「做人能夠孝順父母、尊敬兄長，卻喜好冒犯長上，恐怕很少有這種人吧。不喜好冒犯長上，而喜歡作亂，更不會有這種人。君子專心致志在根本的事情，打好根基，自然就會生成仁道，而孝悌應該就是仁道的根基吧？」

注釋　①**有子**　孔子的學生，姓有名若。②**鮮**　少。③**與**　同歟，語助詞。

解說　朱注：「善事父母為孝，善事兄長為弟。」威權時代都過了，哪裡還有「犯上」的禁忌呢？不是這樣的。儒家認為，家庭倫理是社會秩序的基礎力量。家庭如果能夠父慈子孝、兄友弟恭，社會相對的也會安定和諧。在瀕臨瓦解的現代社會結構裡，這個道理更加值得人們深思。

Chapter 1

1.1. The Master said, "Is it not pleasant to learn with a constant perseverance and application?

1.2. "Is it not delightful to have friends coming from distant quarters?

1.3. "Is he not a man of complete virtue, who feels no discomposure though men may take no note of him?"

注釋　the Master: 夫子，是指孔子；perseverance: n. 堅忍、不屈不撓；application: n. 專心致志；quarter: n. 地區；discomposure: n. 心慌不安。

解說　perseverance 是指努力完成艱難的事，application 是指勤奮專注，用來解釋「時習之」相當貼切。a man of complete virtue，德性完整的人，指的就是「君子」，意譯自朱熹的「君子，成德之名」。君子也譯爲 superior man，是泛指在上位者。

Chapter 2

2.1. The philosopher Yu said, "They are few who, being filial and fraternal, are fond of offending against their superiors. There have been none, who, not liking to offend against their superiors, have been fond of stirring up confusion.

2.2. "The superior man bends his attention to what is radical. That being established, all practical courses naturally grow up. Filial piety and fraternal submission! -- are they not the root of all benevolent actions?"

注釋　filial: adj. 做人子女的；fraternal: adj. 做兄弟的；offend: v. 冒犯；superior: n. 長輩或上級；stir up: 煽動，惹起；confusion: 混亂；bend one's attention to: 專注於；radical: 根本的；practical course: 實踐之道；filial piety: 孝順；fraternal submission: 友愛；benevolent: 仁慈的。

解說　注意這裡的君子譯爲 superior man，指的是爲政者。「仁」這個字在這裡譯爲 benevolent actions，「仁」並不只是特定的外在行爲，而是指每個人都

———————————— ❊ 第三章 ❊ ————————————

子曰：「巧言令色，鮮矣仁！」

語譯　孔子說：「說討人喜歡的話，裝出奉承的表情，這種人很少有仁德的。」

注釋　①**巧言**　好聽而騙人的話。②**令色**　用媚人的態度去奉承別人。③**鮮**　很少。

———————————— ❊ 第四章 ❊ ————————————

曾子曰：「吾日三省吾身：為人謀而不忠乎？與朋友交而不信乎？傳不習乎？」

語譯　曾子說：「我每天反省自己三件事：為別人做事有不盡心嗎？和朋友交往有不誠實嗎？老師教的東西有放著不溫習嗎？」

注釋　①**曾子**　孔子的弟子，名參，字子輿。②**傳**　老師傳授的東西，又解為「專」，記述老師的話。

解說　曾子反省的三件事都是待人接物的道理。朱注：「尹氏曰：曾子守約，故動必求諸身。」這裡的「習」同樣也可以解釋為實踐的意思。

———————————— ❊ 第五章 ❊ ————————————

子曰：「道千乘之國：敬事而信，節用而愛人，使民以時。」

語譯　孔子說：「治理有千輛兵車的諸侯之國，處理政事謹慎認真，對人民信實無欺，節省財支而愛護百姓，在農閒的時候才役使民力。」

注釋　①**道**　同「導」，治理的意思。②**千乘之國**　乘是兵車的意思。春秋時代以作戰時的兵力衡量國家的強弱。千乘之國在當時已經不算是大國了。③**敬事**　工作態度很認真。④**時**　指農閒的時候。《集解》：「包曰：作使民必以其時，不妨奪農務。」

有的良知良能，所以也有人譯作 humanity、benevolence、goodness、perfect goodness，或是直接音譯爲 jen，以強調這個字在英語裡沒有直接對應的名詞。

─────── ❀ **Chapter 3** ❀ ───────

The Master said, "Fine words and an insinuating appearance are seldom associated with true virtue."

注釋 insinuating: adj. 諂媚的、奉承的；appearance: n. 表情；associate with: 聯想，關係到；virtue: 德性。

─────── ❀ **Chapter 4** ❀ ───────

The philosopher Tsang said, "I daily examine myself on three points: -- whether, in transacting business for others, I may have been not faithful; -- whether, in intercourse with friends, I may have been not sincere; -- whether I may have not mastered and practiced the instructions of my teacher."

注釋 transact business for: 爲人辦事；faithful: adj. 守信、忠實的；intercourse with sb.: 和人交往；sincere: adj. 誠摯的；master: v. 精通，熟練；instruction: n. 教導。

解說 「習」在這裡譯爲 master and practice。

─────── ❀ **Chapter 5** ❀ ───────

The Master said, "To rule a country of a thousand chariots, there must be reverent attention to business, and sincerity; economy in expenditure, and love for men; and the employment of the people at the proper seasons."

注釋 chariot: n. 戰車；reverent: adj. 恭敬的；sincerity: n. 誠懇、言行一致；economy: n. 節約；expenditure: n. 開支；employment: n. 雇用。

解說　這裡談到治理國家的三個原則：政令推行要謹慎鄭重，否則就容易朝令夕改；國家財政要「節以制度，不傷財，不害民」，否則就流於橫征暴斂；國家工程徵用民力，不要在農忙的時候，才不會招致民怨，這點在古代農業社會特別重要。這三個原則看似簡單，其實蘊意深遠。朱注：「程子曰：此言至淺，然當時諸侯果能此，亦足以治其國矣。聖人言雖至近，上下皆通。此三言者，若推其極，堯舜之治亦不過此。若常人之言近，則淺近而已矣。」

———————— ❊ 第六章 ❊ ————————

子曰：「弟子入則孝，出則弟，謹而信，汎愛眾，而親仁。行有餘力，則以學文。」

語譯　孔子說：「弟子在家要孝順父母，出外要尊敬長輩，言行謹慎信實，博愛大眾，親近有仁德的人。如此還有餘力的話，再去學習詩書六藝。」

注釋　①汎　廣也。②文　朱注：「文指詩書六藝之文。」

解說　所謂「學不躐等」，儒家的學說是實踐重於知識，所以強調為人處世的具體規範是做學問的基礎。朱注：「程子曰：『為弟子之職，力有餘則學文，不修其職而先文，非為己之學也。』尹氏曰：『德行，本也。文藝，末也。窮其本末，知所先後，可以入德矣。』洪氏曰：『未有餘力而學文，則文滅其質；有餘力而不學文，則質勝而野。』」

———————— ❊ 第七章 ❊ ————————

子夏曰：「賢賢易色，事父母能竭其力，事君能致其身，與朋友交，言而有信。雖曰未學，吾必謂之學矣！」

語譯　子夏說：「如果能夠重視妻子的品德，而不重容貌，盡心盡力侍奉父母，獻身盡職地為君王做事，和朋友交往說話信實，這樣的人，雖然自謙說沒什麼學問，我也要說他是學習過了。」

注釋　①子夏　孔子弟子，姓卜名商。②賢賢　上一個賢字是動詞，尊敬的意思，下一個賢是名詞，有賢德的人。③易　改易，也有不重視的意思。④

—————————◆ **Chapter 6** ◆—————————

The Master said, "A youth, when at home, should be filial, and, abroad, respectful to his elders. He should be earnest and truthful. He should overflow in love to all, and cultivate the friendship of the good. When he has time and opportunity, after the performance of these things, he should employ them in polite studies."

注釋　broad: adj. 戶外的；respectful: adj. 謙恭有禮 [to, toward]；earnest: adj.認眞；truthful: adj. 誠實；overflow: v. 溢出、氾濫；cultivate: v. 培養；opportunity: n. 機會；performance: n. 完成、履行；polite studies: 教養的研習。

解說　to overflow in love to all 是字面的翻譯「讓愛流向每個人」，簡單的說，就是 to love all；polite studies「學文」，這裡的「文」指的不只是文學，而是所有成爲君子的技藝，也就是禮、樂、射、御、書、數「六藝」。

—————————◆ **Chapter 7** ◆—————————

Tsze-hsia said, "If a man withdraws his mind from the love of beauty, and applies it as sincerely to the love of the virtuous; if, in serving his parents, he can exert his utmost strength; if, in serving his prince, he can devote his life; if, in his intercourse with his friends, his words are sincere: -- although men say that he has not learned, I will certainly say that he has."

注釋　withdraw: v. 移開、抽回 [from]；exert: v. 發揮、運用；utmost: adj. 最大限度的；devote: v. 奉獻。

讀論語學英語
The Analects of Confucius

致其身 朱注：「委致其身，謂不有其身。」獻身職守，不爲自己著想的意思。

解說 關於「賢賢易色」有不同的解釋，朱子說：「賢人之賢而易其好色之心。」宋翔鳳《樸學齋札記》說：「賢賢易色，明夫婦之倫。」也就是指夫妻的關係，而和其後的父子、君臣、朋友的關係對應，似乎比較合理。這裡的「學」不是指知識性的學問，而是道德修養。

———— ❋ 第八章 ❋ ————

子曰：「君子不重則不威，學則不固。主忠信。無友不如己者。過則勿憚改。」

語譯 孔子說：「君子如果不莊重就沒有威嚴，所學也不會堅固。要以忠信爲第一原則，沒有不如自己的朋友。有過錯就不要怕改正。」

注釋 ①重 厚重。②威 威儀。③憚 畏難也。

解說 莊重不是指虛僞的道貌岸然，如果是那樣，就流於假道學了。人只要踏踏實實地做學問，自然就會流露出令人尊敬的風範，「問渠哪得清如許，爲有源頭活水來，」就是這個道理。「無友不如己者，」朱注：「無，毋通。禁止語辭也。」解釋爲不要和不如自己的人做朋友。然而這是無法普遍化的命題，每個人都不跟不如自己的人交朋友，結果很可能是每個人都交不到朋友。《正義》：「不如己者即不仁之人。夫子不欲深斥，故祇言不如己而已。」也就是說不要和沒有仁德的人做朋友。這都是從消極面去說的。如果解釋爲「我的朋友沒有不如我的」，意指懂得欣賞朋友的長處而拿他們做榜樣，甚至感到榮耀，是不是更積極的態度呢？

———— ❋ 第九章 ❋ ————

曾子曰：「慎終追遠，民德歸厚矣。」

語譯 曾子說：「盡禮盡哀辦理父母親的喪事，誠敬追思祖先，如此社會的風俗才能夠淳厚。」

注釋 ①慎終追遠 朱注：「慎終者，喪盡其哀。追遠者，祭盡其敬。」

解說 儒家強調喪葬祭祀，是要人們不忘本，而不是做表面功夫。

解說　「賢賢易色」或譯爲 treat the worthy as worthy without strain（很輕鬆自然地把賢人當作賢人去對待），和上下文不合。

Chapter 8

8.1. The Master said, "If the scholar be not grave, he will not call forth any veneration, and his learning will not be solid.

8.2. "Hold faithfulness and sincerity as first principles.

8.3. "Have no friends not equal to yourself.

8.4. "When you have faults, do not fear to abandon them."

注釋　grave:adj. 嚴肅、認眞；call forth: 引起；veneration: n. 尊敬；solid: adj.堅固的；principle: n.原則；equal to: 相等；fault: n.過錯；abandon: v. 放棄、戒除。

Chapter 9

The philosopher Tsang said, "Let there be a careful attention to perform the funeral rites to parents, and let them be followed when long gone with the ceremonies of sacrifice; -- then the virtue of the people will resume its proper excellence."

注釋　ceremony: n. 典禮；sacrifice: n. 獻祭；resume: v. 恢復。

---※ 第十章 ※---

子禽問於子貢曰：「夫子至於是邦也，必聞其政，求之與？抑與之與？」子貢曰：「夫子溫、良、恭、儉、讓以得之。夫子之求之也，其諸異乎人之求之與？」

語譯　子禽問子貢說：「夫子到每個國家，總會聽人說到該國的政事，是他自己要求的還是別人主動告訴他的呢？」子貢說：「夫子是以他的溫和、良善、恭敬、節制和謙讓去得知的。就算是求得的，也和別人的求法不同吧！」

注釋　①**子禽**　孔子弟子，姓陳名亢字子禽。②**子貢**　孔子弟子，姓端木，名賜，字子貢。③**與**　同歟。④**其諸**　語助詞。

解說　儒家強調淑世的理想，因此孔子到任何國家，都會關心那裡的政治良窳。而因為孔子的德性，使得那裡的人們都樂於告訴他。子貢的話語裡也流露出學生對老師的孺慕之情。

---※ 第十一章 ※---

子曰：「父在，觀其志；父沒，觀其行；三年無改於父之道，可謂孝矣。」

語譯　孔子說：「父親在的時候，做兒子的不能自專，要看父親的志向；父親過世後，該看他的行為。居喪三年裡能不改他生前所為，算是孝順了。」

注釋　①**沒**　歿，死去的意思。②**行**　去聲。

解說　這裡的「道」，不只是作為而已，而應該說是「擇善而從」。

---※ 第十二章 ※---

有子曰：「禮之用，和為貴。先王之道斯為美，小大由之。有所不行，知和而和，不以禮節之，亦不可行也。」

語譯　有子說：「禮的應用以順乎自然最為可貴。先王之道的優點就在這裡，無論大事小事都是恰如其分。但是這不是任何情況都適用的，如果只求和氣

❋ **Chapter 10** ❋

10.1. Tsze-ch'in asked Tsze-kung saying, "When our master comes to any country, he does not fail to learn all about its government. Does he ask his information? or is it given to him?"

10.2. Tsze-kung said, "Our master is benign, upright, courteous, temperate, and complaisant and thus he gets his information. The master's mode of asking information, -- is it not different from that of other men?"

注釋　not to fail to: 一定；benign: adj. 溫和、親切；upright: adj. 正直；courteous: adj. 有禮貌；temperate: adj. 有節制；complaisant: adj. 和藹；mode: n. 方式、做法。

❋ **Chapter 11** ❋

The Master said, "While a man's father is alive, look at the bent of his will; when his father is dead, look at his conduct. If for three years he does not alter from the way of his father, he may be called filial."

注釋　bent: n. 喜好、性向；alter: v. 更改。

❋ **Chapter 12** ❋

12.1. The philosopher Yu said, "In practicing the rules of propriety, a natural ease is to be prized. In the ways prescribed by the ancient kings, this is the excellent quality, and in things small and great we follow them.

12.2. "Yet it is not to be observed in all cases. If one, knowing how such ease should be prized, manifests it, without regulating it by the rules of

而不考慮禮的本意，那也是行不通的。」

注釋　①**和**　從容不迫之意。②**斯**　此也，指發乎自然的禮。

解說　「和爲貴」，朱注：「蓋禮之爲體雖嚴，而皆出於自然之理，故其爲用，必從容而不迫，乃爲可貴。」意思是說禮節要順乎自然。《中庸》：「喜怒哀樂之未發謂之中，發而皆中節謂之和。」指的是合乎節度，也就是說禮以恰到好處最可貴。也可以解釋爲「和諧」的意思。但是如果只是追求和諧而忘記禮的本意，也是不可以的。《集解》：「馬曰：人知禮貴和，而每事從和，不以禮爲節，亦不可行也。」

———————————— ✣ 第十三章 ✣ ————————————

有子曰：「信近於義，言可復也；恭近於禮，遠恥辱也；因不失其親，亦可宗也。」

語譯　有子說：「與人約定的事，得先求合理，才可能履行承諾；對人恭敬，也要合乎禮，才不致遭致羞辱。如果他親近的是值得接近的人，也就可以尊敬他們。」

注釋　①**義**　朱注：「事之宜也。」②**復**　履行的意思。③**因**　依靠。④**宗**　尊敬的意思。

解說　這裡說到很具體的道德問題。承諾的事必須是正當的，否則只是硜硜之信，仍然站不住腳；對人恭敬也得合乎禮法，不然就顯得曲意承歡，反而被人家看輕。〈泰伯篇〉說：「恭而無禮則勞。」就是這個意思。「因不失其親，亦可宗也，」朱注：「所依者不失其可親之人，則亦可以宗而主之矣。此言人之言行交際，皆當謹之於始而慮其所終，不然，則因仍苟且之間，將有不勝其自失之悔者矣。」就是說如果他親近的人都是值得接近的，也就可以尊敬他們。楊伯峻則解釋爲「依賴關係深（或家族）的人，也就可靠了」。

———————————— ✣ 第十四章 ✣ ————————————

子曰：「君子食無求飽，居無求安，敏於事而慎於言，就有道而正焉，可謂好學也已。」

propriety, this likewise is not to be done."

注釋　propriety: n. 禮節、規矩；prize: v. 珍視；manifest: v. 表現、顯露；regulate: v. 管制。

解說　「禮」這個字在中文裡含意甚廣，不只是「儀式」（ritual）或「典禮」（ceremony），還包括普遍的行為規範，英語裡很難找到完全對應的字，英譯者以「義者事之宜」的觀念來翻譯「禮」，即 the idea of what is proper，名詞為 propriety。natural ease 即朱子所說的「從容不迫」。

※ **Chapter 13** ※

The philosopher Yu said, "When agreements are made according to what is right, what is spoken can be made good. When respect is shown according to what is proper, one keeps far from shame and disgrace. When the parties upon whom a man leans are proper persons to be intimate with, he can make them his guides and masters."

注釋　agreement: n. 約定；shame: n. 恥辱（因他人的鄙視而感到恥辱）；disgrace: 恥辱（因為失去他人的尊敬而感到羞恥）；lean: v. 依賴 [upon]；intimate: adj. 親近 [with]。

解說　「義」在這裡譯為 what is right，通常會譯為 righteousness（正當、正義）。

※ **Chapter 14** ※

The Master said, "He who aims to be a man of complete virtue in his food does not seek to gratify his appetite, nor in his dwelling place does he seek the appliances of ease; he is earnest in what he is doing, and careful in his

語譯　孔子說：「君子對飲食不求飽足，對居處不求安適，工作勤奮而說話謹慎，求教於有德者，以匡正自己的行為，這樣就可以說是好學了。」

注釋　①**無求**　不勉強去求。②**就有道而正焉**　就，親近。正，匡正。

解說　朱注：「不求安飽者，志有在而不暇及也。」生活的安逸不是君子立身的目的。

―――――※ 第十五章 ※―――――

子貢曰：「貧而無諂，富而無驕，何如？」子曰：「可也。未若貧而樂，富而好禮者也。」子貢曰：「詩云：『如切如磋，如琢如磨。』其斯之謂與？」子曰：「賜也，始可與言詩已矣！告諸往而知來者。」

語譯　子貢說：「窮人能夠不諂媚，有錢人能夠不驕傲，這種人怎麼樣？」孔子說：「可以了。但是不如貧窮卻還是樂於道，有錢還知道要謙虛好禮。」子貢說：「《詩經》說：『像雕琢骨、角、玉、石那樣，不斷地切磋琢磨。』也是這樣的意思吧？」孔子說：「賜啊，像這樣才可以和你談詩了。告訴你一些，你就能體會到其他的道理。」

注釋　①**諂**　卑屈也。②**驕**　矜肆也。③**切磋琢磨**　都是雕塑的動作，即：切割、銼刻、雕削、磨光。朱注：「言治骨角者，既切之而復磋之；治玉石者，既琢之而復磨之；治之已精，而益求其精也。」④**往**　已經說過的。⑤**來**　還沒有說到的。

解說　修身之道不只是遵守倫理規範，而且要樂在其中。

―――――※ 第十六章 ※―――――

子曰：「不患人之不己知，患不知人也。」

語譯　孔子說：「不要怕別人不知道我，怕的是自己不知道別人。」

注釋　①**患**　憂慮。②**不己知**　不知道自己。

解說　求學是為了心裡有所領悟，別人知不知道並不重要。反過來說，如果自己不能知道別人，那就無法明辨是非，反倒要擔憂了。

speech; he frequents the company of men of principle that he may be rectified: -- such a person may be said indeed to love to learn."

注釋　gratify: v. 滿足；appetite: n. 食欲；dwell: v. 居住；appliance: n. 設備；ease: n. 安逸、舒適；rectify: v. 糾正。

❋ Chapter 15 ❋

15.1. Tsze-kung said, "What do you pronounce concerning the poor man who yet does not flatter, and the rich man who is not proud?" The Master replied, "They will do; but they are not equal to him, who, though poor, is yet cheerful, and to him, who, though rich, loves the rules of propriety."

15.2. Tsze-kung replied, "It is said in the Book of Poetry, 'As you cut and then file, as you carve and then polish.' -- The meaning is the same, I apprehend, as that which you have just expressed."

15.3. The Master said, "With one like Ts'ze, I can begin to talk about the odes. I told him one point, and he knew its proper sequence."

注釋　pronounce: v. 斷定、表示意見；flatter: v. 阿諛奉承；cheerful: adj. 開朗快樂；file: v. 用銼刀去銼；carve: v. 雕刻；polish: v. 磨光；apprehend: v. 了解；ode: n. 頌詩；sequence: n. 後續的結果。

❋ Chapter 16 ❋

The Master said, "I will not be afflicted at men's not knowing me; I will be afflicted that I do not know men."

注釋　afflicted: adj. 苦惱。

爲政第二

———— ✤ 第一章 ✤ ————

子曰：「為政以德，譬如北辰，居其所而眾星共之。」

語譯　孔子說：「以德行來治理國家，自己就會像北極星一樣，在一定的位置，其他星辰都拱繞著它。」

注釋　①北辰　北極星。從地球望去，北極星似乎是不動的。②共　同拱，拱繞的意思。

解說　朱注：「德之為言得也，行道而有得於心也。……為政以德，則無為而天下歸之，其象如此。程子曰：『為政以德，然後無為。』范氏曰：『為政以德，則不動而化、不言而信、無為而成。所守者至簡而能御煩，所處者至靜而能制動，所務者至寡而能服眾。』」他以道家無為而治的說法去解釋這段話，其實孔子所說的「德」指的是道德人格，有別於道家的定義。《四書證義》說：「既曰為政，非無為也。政皆本於德，有為如無為也。」

———— ✤ 第二章 ✤ ————

子曰：「詩三百，一言以蔽之，曰『思無邪』。」

語譯　孔子說：「詩經三百篇，用一句話概括地說，就是真誠。」

注釋　①詩三百　《詩經》共三百零五篇。②蔽　概括。③思無邪　思是語助詞，無邪，真誠。

解說　「思無邪」語出《詩經》〈魯頌‧駉篇〉。朱注：「凡詩之言……其用歸於使人得其情性之正而已。……程子曰：『思無邪者，誠也。』」古人總是以道德教化的觀點去解釋《詩經》，或許孔子只是說，《詩經》裡都是真情流溢的作品。

———— ✤ 第三章 ✤ ————

子曰：「道之以政，齊之以刑，民免而無恥；道之以德，齊之以禮，有恥且格。」

語譯　孔子說：「用政法來領導人民，以刑罰來整飭他們，那麼人們只求免於處

⚜ **Chapter 1** ⚜

The Master said, "He who exercises government by means of his virtue may be compared to the north polar star, which keeps its place and all the stars turn towards it."

注釋　exercise: v. 執行。

⚜ **Chapter 2** ⚜

The Master said, "In the Book of Poetry are three hundred pieces, but the design of them all may be embraced in one sentence 'Having no depraved thoughts.'"

注釋　embrace: 包含；depraved: adj. 墮落的、卑鄙的。

解說　「思無邪」在這裡譯為 having no depraved thoughts，把「思」當作名詞，
　　　解釋為「思想」。

⚜ **Chapter 3** ⚜

3.1.　The Master said, "If the people be led by laws, and uniformity sought to be given them by punishments, they will try to avoid the punishment, but have no sense of shame.

3.2.　"If they be led by virtue, and uniformity sought to be given them by the

罰，並沒有羞恥心。如果以德行去感化百姓，以禮制來規範他們，那麼人們既有羞恥心，而且心悅誠服。」

注釋 ①道 同導，教導的意思。②齊 整飭。③免 苟免。④格 朱注：「至也。言躬行以率之。……一說格正也。書曰：格其非心。」也可以解釋爲歸服或嚮往。

解說 孔子認爲以嚴刑峻法去維持社會秩序，只能做到人民的外在服從，唯有道德教化才能真正移風易俗。

※ 第四章 ※

子曰：「吾十有五而志於學，三十而立，四十而不惑，五十而知天命，六十而耳順，七十而從心所欲，不踰矩。」

語譯 孔子說：「我十五歲時便立志向學，到三十歲時人格真正成熟，四十歲時通達事理而沒有疑惑，五十歲時得知天命，六十歲時能夠完全明白所聽到的一切，七十歲的時候，心裡想什麼就做什麼，任何念頭都不會踰越法度。」

注釋 ①有 又也。②立 朱注：「有以自立。」③不惑 朱注：「於事物之所當然，皆無所疑。」④天命 生而爲人的責任和使命。朱注：「天命，即天道之流行而賦於物者，乃事物所以當然之故也。」⑤耳順 《集解》：「鄭曰：耳聞其聲而知其微旨。」朱注：「聲入心通，無所違逆，知之之至，不思而得也。」

解說 這段文字經常被引用，孔子固然自述爲學進德的各個階段，也在告訴學生既不要躐等躁進，也不可以怠墮推諉。三十而立，原來指的是嫻熟於禮制的規範，在這裡解釋爲人格的成熟。「命」這個字有許多意思，可以是指命定或命令，而對於儒家而言，則是指生而爲人的道德責任。「耳順」是說可以不假思索地判斷是非真僞。

rules of propriety, they will have the sense of shame, and moreover will become good."

注釋　uniformity: n. 整齊畫一；avoid: v. 逃避；punishment: n. 處罰；shame: n. 羞恥。

解說　以 led by laws 來翻譯「道之以政」，還不足以說明「政」的意思，或譯為 govern the people legalistically。uniformity sought to be given them by punishment，則是從字面去翻譯「齊」這個字，其實可以直接說 control them by punishment。「格」，become good，則是取自朱注「格正」的意思。

※ **Chapter 4** ※

4.1.　The Master said, "At fifteen, I had my mind bent on learning.

4.2.　"At thirty, I stood firm.

4.3.　"At forty, I had no doubts.

4.4.　"At fifty, I knew the decrees of Heaven.

4.5.　"At sixty, my ear was an obedient organ for the reception of truth.

4.6.　"At seventy, I could follow what my heart desired, without transgressing what was right."

注釋　bent: adj. 專注於、決心去做 [on, upon]；firm: adv. 穩固；decree: n. 命令；obedient: adj. 順從的；organ: n. 器官；reception: n. 接受；transgress: v. 踰越、脫離。

解說　「立」譯為 stand firm（站得穩），也是直譯，無法彰顯原義；「天命」在英語裡也沒有直接對應的名詞，這裡譯為 the decrees of Heaven，把「天命」解釋為位格神的命令，不很恰當；而「耳順」的「耳」直譯為 ear，太過拘泥字面意義。

————— ❀ 第五章 ❀ —————

孟懿子問孝。子曰：「無違。」樊遲御，子告之曰：「孟孫問孝於
我，我對曰『無違』。」樊遲曰：「何謂也？」子曰：「生，事之
以禮；死，葬之以禮，祭之以禮。」

語譯　孟懿子問孔子怎樣才算孝順。孔子說：「不要違背禮節。」有一次，樊遲
　　　為孔子駕車，孔子告訴他說：「孟孫問我孝道，我告訴他說，不要違背禮
　　　節。」樊遲說：「這是什麼意思？」孔子說：「父母健在時，以禮侍奉他
　　　們。過世後，以禮安葬，以禮祭祀。」

注釋　①**孟懿子**　魯國大夫，姓仲孫，名何忌，懿是諡號，父親是孟僖子仲孫
　　　貜，過世前囑咐孟懿子要跟隨孔子學禮。②**無違**　不要違禮。③**樊遲**　名
　　　須，字子遲，孔子弟子。④**御**　為孔子駕車。⑤**孟孫**　即仲孫。

解說　從本章到以下各章節，可以看到孔子如何因材施教，對於「孝」的問題有
　　　不同的解釋。

————— ❀ 第六章 ❀ —————

孟武伯問孝。子曰：「父母唯其疾之憂。」

語譯　孟武伯問孔子怎樣才是孝順，孔子說：「父母親總是擔心子女的身體（所
　　　以做子女的要照顧好自己的身體）。」

注釋　①**孟武伯**　孟懿子的兒子，名彘，諡號為武。②**其**　指子女。

————— ❀ 第七章 ❀ —————

子游問孝。子曰：「今之孝者，是謂能養。至於犬馬，皆能有養；
不敬，何以別乎？」

語譯　子游問孔子孝道的問題，孔子說：「現在所謂的孝，只是扶養父母就行
　　　了。但是人們也會養狗和馬；如果對父母沒有敬愛的心，那和養狗養馬有
　　　什麼不同？」

注釋　①**子游**　姓言名偃，字子游，吳國人，孔子弟子。②**是謂能養**　是，「只
　　　是」的意思。

Chapter 5

5.1. Mang I asked what filial piety was. The Master said, "It is not being disobedient."

5.2. Soon after, as Fan Ch'ih was driving him, the Master told him, saying, "Mang-sun asked me what filial piety was, and I answered him, -- 'not being disobedient.'"

5.3. Fan Ch'ih said, "What did you mean?" The Master replied, "That parents, when alive, be served according to propriety; that, when dead, they should be buried according to propriety; and that they should be sacrificed to according to propriety."

注釋　disobedient: adj. 不服從的、反抗的；bury: v. 埋葬。

Chapter 6

Mang Wu asked what filial piety was. The Master said, "Parents are anxious lest their children should be sick."

注釋　anxious: adj. 擔憂、掛慮；lest: conj. 擔心會……。

Chapter 7

Tsze-yu asked what filial piety was. The Master said, "The filial piety nowadays means the support of one's parents. But dogs and horses likewise are able to do something in the way of support; -- without reverence, what is there to distinguish the one support given from the other?"

注釋　support: n. 扶養；reverence: n. 敬意；distinguish: v. 區別 [from]。

解說　「至於犬馬，皆能有養，」也有人解釋說，狗能看家，馬能載人，都算是養人，但是對人並不會心存敬意。

＊ 第八章 ＊

子夏問孝。子曰：「色難。有事，弟子服其勞，有酒食，先生饌，曾是以為孝乎？」

語譯　子夏問孔子怎樣才是孝順。孔子說：「最難的是和顏悅色地侍奉父母親。有事情的時候，由年輕人操勞，有酒飯的時候，年長的人先吃，這難道就算是孝順嗎？」

注釋　①**色難**　和顏悅色是很困難的事。②**饌**　飲食。③**曾**　乃也，難道。

解說　色難，朱注：「謂事親之際，惟色為難也。」《集解》：「包曰：色難者，謂承順父母色乃難為。」也就是說，討父母親歡心是很難的事。酒食，「食」唸作「似」。朱注：「程子曰：告懿子，告眾人者也。告武伯者，以其人多可憂之事。子游能養而或失於敬，子夏能直義而或少溫潤之色。各因其材之高下，與其所失而告之，故不同也。」可以總結以上論「孝」諸章。

＊ 第九章 ＊

子曰：「吾與回言終日，不違如愚。退而省其私，亦足以發。回也，不愚。」

語譯　孔子說：「我整天和顏回講學，他既沒有反對意見也沒有問題，像個笨蛋似的。等他離開後，我考察他和同學私下的討論，卻也能有所發揮，可見顏回實在不笨。」

注釋　①**不違**　朱注：「意不相背，有聽受而無問難也。」②**退**　回去。③**私**　私下討論。④**發**　闡發。

解說　「退而省其私」，《集解》：「孔曰：察其退還與二三子說繹道義。」朱注：「愚聞之師曰：『顏子深潛純粹，其於聖人體段已具。其聞夫子之言，默識心融，觸處洞然，自有條理。故終日言，但見其不違如愚人而已。及退省其私，則見其日用動靜語默之間，皆足以發明夫子之道，坦然

❋ **Chapter 8** ❋

Tsze-hsia asked what filial piety was. The Master said, "The difficulty is with the countenance. If, when their elders have any troublesome affairs, the young take the toil of them, and if, when the young have wine and food, they set them before their elders, is THIS to be considered filial piety?"

注釋 countenance: n. 臉色、表情；elder: n. 長輩；troublesome: adj. 麻煩的、困難的；to take the toil of: 辛苦工作。

❋ **Chapter 9** ❋

The Master said, "I have talked with Hui for a whole day, and he has not made any objection to anything I said; -- as if he were stupid. He has retired, and I have examined his conduct when away from me, and found him able to illustrate my teachings. Hui! -- He is not stupid."

注釋 objection: n. 反對意見；retire: v. 離去；conduct: n. 品行、行為；illustrate: v. 闡明。

由之而無疑，然後知其不愚也。』」各家都說本章是在稱讚顏回聞言即解的才學，其實從言談間也可以窺見孔子的教學方法，他在私底下會去關心學生是否了解老師說的話，而不只是憑著課堂裡的表現去評斷學生。

———————※ 第十章 ※———————

子曰：「視其所以，觀其所由，察其所安。人焉廋哉？人焉廋哉？」

語譯　孔子說：「先看他所做的事，再了解他的動機，考察看看是不是他心裡喜歡的，這樣的人怎麼掩藏得住呢？」

注釋　①以　為也，所做的事。②由　從也，做事的動機。③安　樂也，心之所樂也。④人焉廋哉　焉，何也。廋，藏匿。

解說　《集解》：「孔曰：觀人終始，安所匿其情。」「安」也解釋為「意之所止。」楊伯峻別譯為：「考查一個人所結交的朋友；觀察他為達到一定目的所採用的方式方法：了解他的心情，安於什麼，不安於什麼。」

———————※ 第十一章 ※———————

子曰：「溫故而知新，可以為師矣。」

語譯　孔子說：「溫習以前學過的知識，能有新的體會和發現，就可以做別人的老師了。」

注釋　①溫　溫習。

解說　朱注：「溫，尋繹也。故者，舊所聞。新者，今所得。言學能時習舊聞，而每有新得，則所學在我，而其應不窮，故可以為人師。」知識視野的拓展，是從已知的領域歸納綜合，而得到新的領會和啟發。

———————※ 第十二章 ※———————

子曰：「君子不器。」

語譯　孔子說：「君子不像器皿一樣，只有一種用途。」

注釋　①器　器具。

─────── ✤ **Chapter 10** ✤ ───────

10.1. The Master said, "See what a man does.

10.2. "Mark his motives.

10.3. "Examine in what things he rests.

10.4. "How can a man conceal his character? How can a man conceal his character?"

注釋　mark: v. 留心、注意；motive: n. 動機、目的；rest: v. 依靠、寄託；conceal: v. 藏匿；character: n. 人格、品行。

─────── ✤ **Chapter 11** ✤ ───────

The Master said, "If a man keeps cherishing his old knowledge, so as continually to be acquiring new, he may be a teacher of others."

注釋　cherish: v. 珍愛；acquire: v. 習得。

解說　如果「溫」解釋爲溫習的話，譯爲 review 或 revise 會比較好。

─────── ✤ **Chapter 12** ✤ ───────

The Master said, "The accomplished scholar is not a utensil."

注釋　accomplished: adj. 有才能或專長的；scholar: n. 學者；utensil: n. 家庭用品。

解說　君子在這裡譯爲 the accomplished scholar（有才能的學者）。

解說　朱注：「器者，各適其用而不能相通。成德之士，體無不具，故用無不周，非特爲一才一藝而已。」用現代的語言說，就是要做個整全的人；在知識分工的社會裡，不拘一格的通才教育可以提高個人競爭力，是很重要的。

———— ❋ 第十三章 ❋ ————

子貢問君子。子曰：「先行其言，而後從之。」

語譯　子貢問孔子，怎樣才算是君子。孔子說：「君子在沒說以前先做，做到了然後再說。」

注釋　①**先行其言**　行於未言之前。②**而後從之**　言之於已行之後。

解說　《集解》：「孔曰：疾小人多言而行之不周。」子貢這個人能言善道，所以孔子特別提醒他要微言篤行。

———— ❋ 第十四章 ❋ ————

子曰：「君子周而不比，小人比而不周。」

語譯　孔子說：「君子待人忠信而不偏私。小人結黨營私而不知道要忠信。」

注釋　①**周**　忠信也。②**比**　阿黨也，比音必。

———— ❋ 第十五章 ❋ ————

子曰：「學而不思則罔，思而不學則殆。」

語譯　孔子說：「只知道讀書而不會思考，那就懵懵懂懂而沒有收穫；只會空想而不讀書，會不切實際而有危險。」

注釋　①**罔**　無所得也，或解釋爲誣罔，受騙的意思。②**殆**　危而不安，或解釋爲疲殆。

解說　這是很重要的讀書方法。讀書不求理解思考，終究只是死記；而自己枯坐冥想，也不會有什麼結果。

—※ **Chapter 13** ※—

Tsze-kung asked what constituted the superior man. The Master said, "He acts before he speaks, and afterwards speaks according to his actions."

注釋　constitute: v. 構成。

—※ **Chapter 14** ※—

The Master said, "The superior man is catholic and not partisan. The mean man is partisan and not catholic."

注釋　catholic: adj. 寬大的、一視同仁的；partisan: adj. 有黨派觀念的。

解說　「周」在這裡譯為 catholic，也可以譯作 broad-minded。

—※ **Chapter 15** ※—

The Master said, "Learning without thought is labor lost; thought without learning is perilous."

注釋　labor lost: 白費力氣；perilous: adj. 危險的。

───────────── ❋ 第十六章 ❋ ─────────────

子曰：「攻乎異端，斯害也已！」

語譯　孔子說：「把不同於你的說法當作異端去攻擊，那是有害處的。」

注釋　①**攻**　攻擊。②**斯**　連接詞。③**也已**　語助詞。

解說　許多人把「攻」字解釋爲鑽研的意思，也就是說，鑽研異端學說是有害的。楊伯峻譯爲：「批判那些不正確的議論，禍害就可以消滅了。」這麼解釋會不會流於黨同伐異的偏見呢？如果解釋爲求同存異，或許更能表現孔子的寬容精神。

───────────── ❋ 第十七章 ❋ ─────────────

子曰：「由！誨女知之乎？知之爲知之，不知爲不知，是知也。」

語譯　孔子說：「由啊，我告訴你如何求知吧！知道的就說知道，不知道的就說不知道，這才是眞正的知識。」

注釋　①**由**　姓仲名由，字子路，孔子弟子。②**誨**　教誨　③**女**　同汝。

解說　許多人強不知以爲知，結果只是證明自己的無知。能夠明白自己知識的限制，是很重要的人生智慧。希臘哲學家蘇格拉底所說的「無知之知」，也是這個道理。

───────────── ❋ 第十八章 ❋ ─────────────

子張學干祿。子曰：「多聞闕疑，愼言其餘，則寡尤；多見闕殆，愼行其餘，則寡悔。言寡尤，行寡悔，祿在其中矣。」

語譯　子張想學做官。孔子說：「多聽別人說，有疑問的地方就加以保留；其餘的也要謹愼地說，便能減少錯誤。多看別人做事，把覺得不妥的地方擱置一旁，其餘的也要謹愼去做，這樣就能減少懊悔。說話少過失，行事少後悔，祿位就在這裡頭了。」

注釋　①**子張**　姓顓孫，名師，字子張，孔子弟子。②**干祿**　干，求也，求取官祿。③**闕**　空也，擱置的意思。④**尤**　過失。⑤**殆**　指心有未安者，覺得不妥的意思。⑥**悔**　悔恨。

⋇ **Chapter 16** ⋇

The Master said, "The study of strange doctrines is injurious indeed!"

注釋　injurious: adj. 有害的。

解說　意譯爲「鑽研異端是有害的」。

⋇ **Chapter 17** ⋇

The Master said, "Yu, shall I teach you what knowledge is? When you know a thing, to hold that you know it; and when you do not know a thing, to allow that you do not know it; -- this is knowledge."

注釋　hold: v. 認爲、相信。

⋇ **Chapter 18** ⋇

18.1. Tsze-chang was learning with a view to official emolument.

18.2. The Master said, "Hear much and put aside the points of which you stand in doubt, while you speak cautiously at the same time of the others: -- then you will afford few occasions for blame. See much and put aside the things which seem perilous, while you are cautious at the same time in carrying the others into practice: then you will have few occasions for repentance. When one gives few occasions for blame in his words, and few occasions for repentance in his conduct, he is in the way to get emolument."

解說　不只是做官，做人也是如此，言行謹慎，就可以避免過失和悔恨。

———————————— ❖ 第十九章 ❖ ————————————

哀公問曰：「何為則民服？」孔子對曰：「舉直錯諸枉，則民服；舉枉錯諸直，則民不服。」

語譯　魯哀公問孔子說：「怎樣才能讓老百姓服從？」孔子回答說：「舉用正直的人在邪曲的人之上，百姓就會服從。舉用邪曲的人在正直的人之上，百姓就不會服從。」

注釋　①**哀公**　魯國君王，姓姬名蔣，定公之子，「哀」是其諡號。②**錯**　放置。③**諸**　之於。④**枉**　邪枉之人。

解說　朱注：「錯，捨置也，諸，眾也。」亦通。

———————————— ❖ 第二十章 ❖ ————————————

季康子問：「使民敬、忠以勸，如之何？」子曰：「臨之以莊則敬，孝慈則忠，舉善而教不能，則勸。」

語譯　季康子問說：「怎樣才能讓人民尊敬且忠於執政者，又能夠相互勸勉？」孔子說：「執政的人要以認真的態度面對百姓，他們自然就會尊敬你。自己要孝順父母親，慈愛百姓，他們就會忠於你。提拔好人，教育能力差的人，民眾自然就會相互勸勉了。」

注釋　①**季康子**　魯國大夫，姓季孫，名肥，康是其諡號。他是當時的權臣。②**以勸**　以，連接詞，而也。勸，勸勉。③**臨之以莊**　上對下曰臨。莊，態度莊重。

解說　朱注：「臨民以莊，則民敬於己。孝於親，慈於眾，則民忠於己。善者舉之而不能者教之，則民有所勸而樂於為善。」孔子始終認為，為政者必須以身作則，百姓才會心悅誠服；以賢舉才，普及教育，人民才有相互勸善的目標。從現代的意義去看，選舉和教育是公民權的必要條件，也是實現自由民主社會的重要基礎。

注釋　with a view to: 為了某個目的；official: adj. 公務的、官方的；emolument: n. 薪俸；put aside: 挪開；stand in doubt of: 懷疑；cautiously: adv. 謹慎地；afford: v. 給予；occasion: n. 理由；blame: n. 責難；repentance: n. 悔恨。

※ **Chapter 19** ※

The Duke Ai asked, saying, "What should be done in order to secure the submission of the people?" Confucius replied, "Advance the upright and set aside the crooked, then the people will submit. Advance the crooked and set aside the upright, then the people will not submit."

注釋　duke: n.（小國的）君主、公爵；submission: n. 服從；advance: v. 拔擢、晉陞；upright: adj. 正直；set aside: 擱置、捨棄；crooked: adj. 心術不正的。

※ **Chapter 20** ※

Chi K'ang asked how to cause the people to reverence their ruler, to be faithful to him, and to go on to nerve themselves to virtue. The Master said, "Let him preside over them with gravity; -- then they will reverence him. Let him be filial and kind to all; -- then they will be faithful to him. Let him advance the good and teach the incompetent; -- then they will eagerly seek to be virtuous."

注釋　reverence: v. 尊敬；faithful: adj. 忠實的；nerve oneself to: 發奮去做；preside: v. 管理；gravity: n. 認真、嚴肅；incompetent: adj. 無能力的；eagerly: adv. 熱切地；seek: v. 試圖。

———————— ✤ 第二十一章 ✤ ————————

或謂孔子曰:「子奚不為政?」子曰:「書云:『孝乎,惟孝友于兄弟。』施於有政,是亦為政。奚其為為政?」

語譯　有人問孔子說:「先生為什麼不從政呢?」孔子說:「《尚書》說:『真正的孝啊,是孝順父母而且友愛兄弟。』把這個風氣影響在政治上去,也算是從政了,又何必要做官呢?」

注釋　①或　有人。②奚　何也。③施　推而行之。

解說　「孝乎惟孝、友于兄弟。」出自偽古文《尚書》〈君陳〉篇。《正義》引包慎言《論語溫故錄》說:「白虎通云:孔子所以定五經何?孔子居周末世,王道陵遲,禮義廢壞,彊淩弱,眾暴寡,天子不敢誅,方伯不敢問,閔道德之不行,故周流冀行其道。自衛反魯。知道之不行,故定五經以行其道。」這時候應該在哀公十一年後。孔子沒有從政,有其難言之處,所以對他這麼說。

———————— ✤ 第二十二章 ✤ ————————

子曰:「人而無信,不知其可也。大車無輗,小車無軏,其何以行之哉?」

語譯　孔子說:「人沒有信用,我不知道他還能做什麼。就像是大車沒有安橫木的輗,小車沒有安橫木的軏,怎麼能夠使車子走動呢?」

注釋　①大車　牛車。②輗　轅端橫木以縛軛。輗音倪。③小車　兵車。④軏　轅端上曲鉤衡。軏音越。

———————— ✤ 第二十三章 ✤ ————————

子張問:「十世可知也?」子曰:「殷因於夏禮,所損益可知也;周因於殷禮,所損益可知也;其或繼周者,雖百世可知也。」

語譯　子張問孔子:「可以預知十個朝代以後的事嗎?」孔子說:「商朝因襲夏朝的禮制,有所增減的部分,現在仍可以知道。周朝因襲商朝的禮制,有所增減的部分,現在仍可以知道,那麼如果將來有繼周朝而起的朝代,就

❄ **Chapter 21** ❄

21.1. Some one addressed Confucius, saying, "Sir, why are you not engaged in the government?"

21.2. The Master said, "What does the Shu-ching say of filial piety? -- 'You are filial, you discharge your brotherly duties. These qualities are displayed in government.' This then also constitutes the exercise of government. Why must there be THAT -- making one be in the government?"

注釋　address: v. 對某人講話；engaged in: 從事於；discharge: v.履行；display: v. 顯示。

❄ **Chapter 22** ❄

The Master said, "I do not know how a man without truthfulness is to get on. How can a large carriage be made to go without the crossbar for yoking the oxen to, or a small carriage without the arrangement for yoking the horses?"

注釋　truthfulness: n. 誠實；get on: 過日子；crossbar: n. 橫木；yoke: v. 套上軛；ox: n. [pl. oxen] 公牛；arrangement: n. 配備。

❄ **Chapter 23** ❄

23.1. Tsze-chang asked whether the affairs of ten ages after could be known.

23.2. Confucius said, "The Yin dynasty followed the regulations of the Hsia: wherein it took from or added to them may be known. The Chau dynasty has followed the regulations of Yin: wherein it took from or added to them may be known. Some other may follow the Chau, but though it should be at the distance of a hundred ages, its affairs may be known."

算是一百個朝代，也可以預見到。」

注釋 ①**世** 朱注：「王者易姓受命爲一世。」就是朝代的意思。②**因** 因襲。③
損益 增減。

解說 子張問孔子社會政治體制的因襲變革問題。孔子回答他說，從過去的歷史
經驗裡可以知道未來發展的原則。

———————————— ✣ 第二十四章 ✣ ————————————

子曰：「非其鬼而祭之，諂也。見義不為，無勇也。」

語譯 孔子說：「不是自己應該祭祀的鬼神而去祭祀他們，那就是諂媚。遇到應
該做的事卻不去做，那就是怯懦。」

注釋 ①**諂** 求媚也。

解說 古代人死叫作鬼，通常是指自己的祖先。那時候的祭祀有浮濫不合禮制的
現象，孔子是針對時弊而說的。

注釋　affair: n. 形勢、時局；age: n. 歷史時期；dynasty: n. 朝代；regulation: n. 規
　　　定。

 **Chapter24**

24.1. The Master said, "For a man to sacrifice to a spirit which does not belong to him is flattery.

24.2. "To see what is right and not to do it is want of courage."

注釋　spirit: n. 鬼魂、亡靈；be want of: 缺少。

▶八佾第三

———— ✣ 第一章 ✣ ————

孔子謂季氏八佾舞於庭:「是可忍也,孰不可忍也?」

語譯 季氏在自己的前庭使用八佾舞,孔子評論說:「如此僭越的事都可以容忍,還有什麼事不可以容忍的呢?」

注釋 ①**季氏** 指季平子,也就是季孫意如。②**八佾** 天子之樂,八人一排,共八排,六十四人;諸侯之樂是三十六人;卿大夫是十六人。③**忍** 容忍。

解說 朱注:「季氏以大夫而僭用天子之樂,孔子言其此事尚忍為之,則何事不可忍為。」在這裡「忍」字解釋為「敢去做」,也就是說,這種事都敢做了,還有什麼做不出來的呢?

———— ✣ 第二章 ✣ ————

三家者,以雍徹。子曰:「『相維辟公,天子穆穆』,奚取於三家之堂?」

語譯 魯國孟孫、叔孫、季孫在撤祭品的時候,也唱雍詩。孔子說:「雍詩有言:『助祭的是諸侯,天子儀容肅穆莊重。』這句話如何用在三家的廟堂上呢?」

注釋 ①**三家** 魯國大夫孟孫、叔孫、季孫。②**雍** 《詩經》〈周頌〉裡的篇名。③**徹** 祭祀後撤掉供物。④**相維辟公** 相,助祭的意思;辟公,指諸侯,辟音必。⑤**穆穆** 容貌莊嚴;朱注:「穆穆,遠深之意。」⑥**奚** 何也。

解說 天子宗廟之祭,歌雍詩以徹,而魯國權臣竟然僭禮使用。孔子便引用雍詩裡的話來諷刺他們說,當他們在唱到這句詩的時候,是否覺得很突兀呢?

———— ✣ 第三章 ✣ ————

子曰:「人而不仁,如禮何?人而不仁,如樂何?」

語譯 孔子說:「人如果沒有仁心,即使有禮制,又能如何呢?人如果沒有仁心,即使有音樂,又能如何呢?」

注釋 ①**如** 奈也、如何、如之何。

---------------- ❊ **Chapter 1** ❊ ----------------

Confucius said of the head of the Chi family, who had eight rows of pantomimes in his area, "If he can bear to do this, what may he not bear to do?"

注釋　head: n. 領袖、家主；row: n. 排；pantomime: n. 默劇；area: n. 庭院；bear: v. 容忍 [+ to do/+ doing]。

---------------- ❊ **Chapter 2** ❊ ----------------

The three families used the Yung ode, while the vessels were being removed, at the conclusion of the sacrifice. The Master said, "'Assisting are the princes; -- the son of heaven looks profound and grave'; -- what application can these words have in the hall of the three families?"

注釋　vessel: n. 容器；remove: v. 移開；conclusion: n. 終結；assist: v. 輔助； profound: adj. 深遠的；grave: adj. 嚴肅認眞的。

---------------- ❊ **Chapter 3** ❊ ----------------

The Master said, "If a man be without the virtues proper to humanity, what has he to do with the rites of propriety? If a man be without the virtues proper to humanity, what has he to do with music?"

注釋　proper to: 特有的；rite: n. 禮儀。

解說　「仁」譯爲 virtues proper to humanity（人類特有的德性）。

解說　這句話非常重要。所有社會規範都必須回歸到個人的道德自覺，如果沒有仁人愛物的心，那麼這些規範都是徒託空言。

※ 第四章 ※

林放問禮之本。子曰：「大哉問！禮，與其奢也，寧儉；喪，與其易也，寧戚。」

語譯　林放問孔子禮的本質是什麼。孔子說：「問得好！就一般的禮而言，與其奢侈鋪張，寧可儉樸；至於喪禮，與其著重形式的細節，寧可內心哀戚。」

注釋　①**林放**　魯國人。②**易**　治也，嫻熟各個細節。

解說　林放看到當時社會的繁文縟節，懷疑是否失其本意，所以問孔子禮的本質是什麼。「大哉問」也可以解釋為「這個問題太大了」，所以孔子就具體的禮儀問題回答他。過奢或過儉都不合禮，但是在取捨的時候，還是選擇節儉比較好；只注重形式或是只感到哀戚也是不合禮的，但是相較之下，還是內心的哀戚比較重要些。

※ 第五章 ※

子曰：「夷狄之有君，不如諸夏之亡也。」

語譯　孔子說：「異邦雖然有個君主，還不如中國沒有君主。」

注釋　①**夷狄**　泛指異族。②**諸夏**　指中國諸侯之國。

解說　在當時的中國，北方有狄，東方有夷，西方有戎，南方有蠻。這句話是說，異族雖然有個主政的君王，但是沒有禮樂教化，而中國雖然諸侯分據，至少禮義不廢。朝代自有興亡盛衰，重要的是文化和歷史的傳承要能夠相續不斷。朱注：「程子曰：夷狄且有君長，不如諸夏之僭亂，反無上下之分也。」也就是說，連夷狄都還有個國君，不像中國亂得不像話。這個解釋也不錯，憑什麼夷狄就比不上中國呢？

※ 第六章 ※

季氏旅於泰山。子謂冉有曰：「女弗能救與？」對曰：「不能。」

──────────────── ❖ **Chapter 4** ❖ ────────────────

4.1. Lin Fang asked what was the first thing to be attended to in ceremonies.

4.2. The Master said, "A great question indeed!

4.3. "In festive ceremonies, it is better to be sparing than extravagant. In the ceremonies of mourning, it is better that there be deep sorrow than in minute attention to observances."

注釋　attend: n. 注意；ceremony: n. 儀式；festive: adj. 節慶的；sparing: adj. 節儉的；extravagant: adj. 奢侈的、浪費的；mourning: n. 喪事；minute: adj. 微細的、瑣碎的；observance: n. 慣例。

──────────────── ❖ **Chapter 5** ❖ ────────────────

The Master said, "The rude tribes of the east and north have their princes, and are not like the States of our great land which are without them."

注釋　rude: adj. 野蠻的、沒有教養的。

──────────────── ❖ **Chapter 6** ❖ ────────────────

The chief of the Chi family was about to sacrifice to the T'ai mountain. The

子曰：「嗚呼！曾謂泰山不如林放乎？」

語譯　季氏要去祭泰山。孔子對冉有說：「你不能阻止這件事嗎？」冉有回答說：「不能。」孔子說：「唉，難道泰山的神明還不如林放知禮嗎？」

注釋　①旅　祭祀的名稱。②泰山　在魯國，古代只有天子才能祭祀泰山。③冉有　孔子弟子，姓冉名求，字子有，當時為季氏家臣。④弗能　不能。⑤救　阻止，朱注：「謂救其陷於僭竊之罪。」

解說　意思是說，泰山的神明也不會接受這種僭越的祭禮。

────────── ❋ 第七章 ❋ ──────────

子曰：「君子無所爭，必也射乎！揖讓而升，下而飲，其爭也君子。」

語譯　孔子說：「君子沒有什麼可爭的。如果有的話，那就是在比射的時候吧！但是也要相互作揖，然後登堂比射，射完後又相互作揖走下堂，勝的人讓敗的人飲酒，這樣的競爭，可以說是君子之爭。」

注釋　①射　射箭比賽。②揖讓而升　朱注：「大射之禮，耦進三揖而後升堂也。」③下而飲　朱注：「謂射畢揖降，以俟眾耦皆降，勝者乃揖不勝者升，取觶立飲也。」

解說　勝的人少喝酒，所以說是君子之爭。

────────── ❋ 第八章 ❋ ──────────

子夏問曰：「『巧笑倩兮，美目盼兮，素以為絢兮。』何謂也？」子曰：「繪事後素。」曰：「禮後乎？」子曰：「起予者商也！始可與言詩已矣。」

語譯　子夏問說：「『笑容甜美，酒渦微動，秋波流盼，嫵媚迷人，粉白的底子繪以五彩顏色，更加的美麗。』請問這是什麼意思？」孔子說：「先有白色的底子，然後再加上五彩的顏色。」子夏說：「那麼是不是說，先有仁心，然後才有禮？」孔子說：「卜商，你真是能發揮我的意思啊！像這樣就可以和你談論詩了。」

Master said to Zan Yu, "Can you not save him from this?" He answered, "I cannot." Confucius said, "Alas! will you say that the T'ai mountain is not so discerning as Lin Fang?"

注釋　alas: int. 唉；discerning: adj. 有辨識力的。

───────────────── ⁂ **Chapter 7** ⁂ ─────────────────

The Master said, "The student of virtue has no contentions. If it be said he cannot avoid them, shall this be in archery? But he bows complaisantly to his competitors; thus he ascends the hall, descends, and exacts the forfeit of drinking. In his contention, he is still the Chun-tsze."

注釋　contention: n. 競爭、爭論；archery: n. 箭術、射藝；bow: v. 鞠躬；
　　　complaisantly: adv. 彬彬有禮地；competitor: n. 競爭對手；ascend: v. 登上；
　　　hall: n. 大廳；descend: v. 走下來；exact: v. 強迫；forfeit: n. 處罰 [of]。

解說　君子在這裡譯為 student of virtue，取自「尚德之人」的意思。

───────────────── ⁂ **Chapter 8** ⁂ ─────────────────

8.1. Tsze-hsia asked, saying, "What is the meaning of the passage -- 'The pretty dimples of her artful smile! The well-defined black and white of her eye! The plain ground for the colors?'"

8.2. The Master said, "The business of laying on the colors follows the preparation of the plain ground."

8.3. "Ceremonies then are a subsequent thing?" The Master said, "It is Shang who can bring out my meaning. Now I can begin to talk about the odes with him."

注釋　①**倩**　臉頰的酒渦很美的意思。②**盼**　眼睛很美。③**素**　畫畫時的底粉。④
絢　五彩的顏色。⑤**繪事後素**　先著底粉再繪彩。⑥**起**　啓發。

解說　這幾句詩出自《詩經》〈衛風·碩人〉第二章，但是沒有「素以爲絢兮」
　　　這句話。前兩句在形容美人容貌，下一句話卻在說繪畫，子貢便問孔子是
　　　什麼意思。孔子回答說：「繪事後素。」意思是說，如果沒有美麗的容
　　　貌，再怎麼化妝也是沒有用的。

———— ❖ 第九章 ❖ ————

子曰：「夏禮，吾能言之，杞不足徵也；殷禮，吾能言之，宋不足
徵也。文獻不足故也，足則吾能徵之矣。」

語譯　孔子說：「夏朝的禮制，我能說個梗概，可惜夏的後代杞國不足於驗證；
　　　商朝的禮制，我也能說得出來，可惜商朝的後代宋國沒辦法驗證。那是他
　　　們沒有足夠的典籍和賢者，如果足夠的話，便能驗證我所說的了。」

注釋　①**杞**　周之封國。周武王的時候，賜封夏朝的後代在杞國。②**徵**　驗證。③
宋　商朝後裔的封國。④**文獻**　文指典籍，獻指賢者。

———— ❖ 第十章 ❖ ————

子曰：「禘自既灌而往者，吾不欲觀之矣。」

語譯　孔子說：「禘祭的禮，從第一次獻酒以後，我就不想看了。」

注釋　①**禘**　古代極爲隆重的儀式，王者每五年在太廟舉行大祭。禘音帝。②
灌　以酒灑地上，以迎祖先。朱注：「灌者，方祭之始，用鬱鬯之酒灌
地，以降神也。」

解說　本段是慨嘆魯國的祭祀非禮，從「灌」以後，就沒有什麼誠意，他也就看
　　　不下去了。

———— ❖ 第十一章 ❖ ————

或問禘之說。子曰：「不知也。知其說者之於天下也，其如示諸斯
乎！」指其掌。

注釋 passage: n. 段落；dimple: n. 酒渦；artful: adj. 巧妙的；well-defined: adj. 輪廓分明的；plain: adj. 樸素的、沒有花紋的；business: n. 事情；to lay on: 塗抹；subsequent: adj. 後續的；to bring out: 發揮，闡明。

解說 「禮」在這裡譯為 ceremonies，指涉的範圍似乎稍嫌狹隘，或譯作 manners。

※ **Chapter 9** ※

The Master said, "I could describe the ceremonies of the Hsia dynasty, but Chi cannot sufficiently attest my words. I could describe the ceremonies of the Yin dynasty, but Sung cannot sufficiently attest my words. They cannot do so because of the insufficiency of their records and wise men. If those were sufficient, I could adduce them in support of my words."

注釋 describe: v. 描述；sufficiently: adv. 充分地；attest: v. 證實；record: n. 紀錄；adduce: v. 引證。

※ **Chapter 10** ※

The Master said, "At the great sacrifice, after the pouring out of the libation, I have no wish to look on."

注釋 pour out: 倒出去；libation: n. 奠酒；have a wish to: 想要；look on: 旁觀。

※ **Chapter 11** ※

Some one asked the meaning of the great sacrifice. The Master said, "I do not know. He who knew its meaning would find it as easy to govern the kingdom as to look on this" -- pointing to his palm.

語譯　有人問孔子關於禘祭的禮制。孔子說：「我不知道，知道的人來治理天下，會像把東西擺在這裡這麼容易。」說著指自己的手掌。

注釋　①**不知也**　《集解》：「孔曰：答以不知者，為魯諱。」②**說**　禮制、理論。③**示**　同「置」，擺放的意思。也有解釋為「視」。

解說　禘是天子之禮，魯國行禘禮，已經是僭越了，而孔子不願明講，所以說不知道。

※ 第十二章 ※

祭如在，祭神如神在。子曰：「吾不與祭，如不祭。」

語譯　「祭如在」的意思是：祭祀祖先的時候，就像祖先在那裡受祭。孔子說：「如果我不能親自參加，那麼就等於沒有祭祀。」

注釋　①**與**　音預，參與。

解說　「祭如在」，《集解》：「孔曰：言事死如事生。」

※ 第十三章 ※

王孫賈問曰：「與其媚於奧，寧媚於竈，何謂也？」子曰：「不然，獲罪於天，無所禱也。」

語譯　王孫賈問說：「與其討好屋子西南隅的神，寧可討好竈神，這是為什麼？」孔子說：「不對，如果是得罪了上天，禱告也沒有用。」

注釋　①**王孫賈**　衛國大夫，周朝王者孫。②**與其媚於奧，寧媚於竈**　當時俗諺，媚，親近、討好的意思。朱注：「室西南隅為奧。竈者，五祀之一，夏所祭也。凡祭五祀，皆先設主而祭於其所，然後迎尸而祭於奧，略如祭宗廟之儀。如祀竈，則設主於竈陘，祭畢，而更設饌於奧以迎尸也。故時俗之語，因以奧有常尊，而非祭之主；竈雖卑賤，而當時用事。喻自結於君，不如阿附權臣也。」

解說　王孫賈用這句俗諺暗示孔子要討好他。孔子回答說，假如做了傷天害理的事，巴結誰都沒有用。

注釋　palm: n. 手掌。

解說　「禘」譯為 great sacrifice（大祭），或譯作 quinquennial sacrifice（每五年舉行一次的祭典）。

⁂ **Chapter 12** ⁂

12.1. He sacrificed to the dead, as if they were present. He sacrificed to the spirits, as if the spirits were present.

12.2. The Master said, "I consider my not being present at the sacrifice, as if I did not sacrifice."

注釋　present: adj. 在場。

⁂ **Chapter 13** ⁂

13.1. Wang-sun Chia asked, saying, "What is the meaning of the saying, 'It is better to pay court to the furnace then to the southwest corner?'"

13.2. The Master said, "Not so. He who offends against Heaven has none to whom he can pray."

注釋　to pay court to: 諂媚；furnace: n. 爐灶；offend: v. 違反 [against]。

解說　pay court to the furnace，討好爐灶，很難理解什麼意思，譯為 pay court to the god of furnace (or hearth)，似乎比較清楚，同樣的，「奧」譯為 the god of the hall 比較好。

---※ 第十四章 ※---

子曰：「周監於二代，郁郁乎文哉！吾從周。」

語譯　孔子說：「周朝的禮制以夏商兩代為根據，禮樂文物真是美盛！我主張用
　　　周朝的制度。」

注釋　①監　察看、比較。②郁郁　文物美盛。③文　文物，指典章制度。

解說　周朝考察夏、商二代之禮而有所損益，所以更加完備。

---※ 第十五章 ※---

子入大廟，每事問。或曰：「孰謂鄹人之子知禮乎？入大廟，每事
問。」子聞之曰：「是禮也。」

語譯　孔子到了周公廟，每件事都要問人。有人便說：「誰說這個鄹邑的年輕人
　　　知道禮？到周公廟來，什麼事都要問人。」孔子聽到了就說：「這就是禮
　　　啊！」

注釋　①大廟　大音太，魯國祭祀周公之廟。②鄹　音鄒。魯國邑名。孔子的父親
　　　叔梁紇曾經做過鄹邑大夫。

解說　《集解》：「孔曰：雖知之，當復問，慎之至也。」意思是說，凡事謹慎
　　　就是禮的精神。莊述祖認為孔子這句話是反詰魯祭不合禮，而應讀為「是
　　　禮也？」（難道這就是禮嗎？）

---※ 第十六章 ※---

子曰：「『射不主皮』，為力不同科，古之道也。」

語譯　孔子說：「『比箭的時候不一定要射穿箭靶』，這是因為每個人力氣大小
　　　不同，這是古代的規矩。」

注釋　①射不主皮　是鄉射之禮。朱注：「古者射以觀德，但主於中，而不主於
　　　貫革。」②科　等級。

解說　孔子說，古代比箭時，只求射中目標，而不是猛力貫穿箭靶。這也是感嘆
　　　當時禮的精神蕩然無存。

❉ **Chapter 14** ❉

The Master said, "Chau had the advantage of viewing the two past dynasties. How complete and elegant are its regulations! I follow Chau."

注釋　to have the advantage of: 佔優勢；elegant: adj. 優雅。

❉ **Chapter 15** ❉

The Master, when he entered the grand temple, asked about everything. Some one said, "Who say that the son of the man of Tsau knows the rules of propriety! He has entered the grand temple and asks about everything." The Master heard the remark, and said, "This is a rule of propriety."

注釋　remark: n. 評論。

❉ **Chapter 16** ❉

The Master said, "In archery it is not going through the leather which is the principal thing; -- because people's strength is not equal. This was the old way."

注釋　principal: adj. 主要的。

———————— ❖ 第十七章 ❖ ————————

子貢欲去告朔之餼羊。子曰：「賜也，爾愛其羊，我愛其禮。」

語譯　子貢要省掉每月告朔獻祭的羊。孔子說：「賜啊！你愛惜那隻羊，我卻愛惜那種禮。」

注釋　❶告朔　告音谷，朔，每月一日。朱注：「告朔之禮：古者天子常以季冬，頒來歲十二月之朔於諸侯，諸侯受而藏之祖廟。月朔則以特羊告廟，請而行之。」或解釋爲天子每月頒告朔於諸侯。❷餼羊　朱注：「餼，生牲也。」告朔禮的供物，殺而未烹。餼音係。

解說　幽王之後，不告朔於諸侯。而魯有司，循例供羊。朱注：「子貢蓋惜其無實而妄費。然禮雖廢，羊存，猶得以識之而可復焉。若併去其羊，則此禮遂亡矣，孔子所以惜之。」其實子貢也不是吝於祭獻，而是認爲這種名存實亡的制度可以廢除了。

———————— ❖ 第十八章 ❖ ————————

子曰：「事君盡禮，人以為諂也。」

語譯　孔子說：「根據臣子的禮節爲君主做事，別人反而說他是在諂媚。」

解說　孔子感嘆當時的人不知道事君之禮

———————— ❖ 第十九章 ❖ ————————

定公問：「君使臣，臣事君，如之何？」孔子對曰：「君使臣以禮，臣事君以忠。」

語譯　魯定公問說：「國君該如何使喚臣子，而臣子又該如何服事國君？」孔子回答說：「國君應該依禮來使喚臣子，臣子要忠心服事國君。」

注釋　❶定公　魯定公，名宋，昭公之弟，哀公之父。

解說　《集解》：「孔曰：時臣失禮，定公患之，故問之。」

⁂ **Chapter 17** ⁂

17.1. Tsze-kung wished to do away with the offering of a sheep connected with the inauguration of the first day of each month.

17.2. The Master said, "Ts'ze, you love the sheep; I love the ceremony."

注釋　inauguration: n. 正式開始。

⁂ **Chapter 18** ⁂

The Master said, "The full observance of the rules of propriety in serving one's prince is accounted by people to be flattery."

注釋　flattery: n. 恭維、巴結。

⁂ **Chapter 19** ⁂

The Duke Ting asked how a prince should employ his ministers, and how ministers should serve their prince. Confucius replied, "A prince should employ his ministers according to the rules of propriety; ministers should serve their prince with faithfulness."

注釋　employ: v. 任用。

---------------------------※ 第二十章 ※---------------------------

子曰：「關雎，樂而不淫，哀而不傷。」

語譯　孔子說：「〈關雎〉這篇詩，說到快樂的地方不會流於放蕩，說到感傷的
　　　地方也不會太痛苦。」

注釋　①**關雎**　雎音居。《詩經》篇名。②**淫**　過度而失當的意思。朱注：「樂之
　　　過而失其正者也。」③**傷**　朱注：「傷者，哀之過而害於和者也。」

解說　「淫」指的是「過度」，而不是淫慾。

---------------------------※ 第二十一章 ※---------------------------

哀公問社於宰我。宰我對曰：「夏后氏以松，殷人以柏，周人以
栗，曰使民戰栗。」子聞之曰：「成事不說，遂事不諫，既往不
咎。」

語譯　魯哀公問宰我該種什麼社樹。宰我回答說：「夏朝用松樹，商朝用柏樹，
　　　周朝用栗樹，意思是要人民戰慄害怕。」孔子聽到了就說：「已經做了的
　　　事就不要再解釋了，已經完成的事也不能再諫阻，已經過去的事不便再追
　　　究了。」

注釋　①**宰我**　孔子弟子，名予，字子我，魯國人。②**社**　祭祀土地神的地方。朱
　　　注：「古者立社，各樹其土之所宜木以為主也。」

解說　古時候「栗」字通「慄」，宰我列舉三代的社樹後，告訴哀公要使人民恐
　　　懼才有威嚴，孔子責備他曲解立社樹的本意，告訴他說過的話是無法挽救
　　　的，要他以後謹言慎行。

---------------------------※ 第二十二章 ※---------------------------

子曰：「管仲之器小哉！」或曰：「管仲儉乎？」曰：「管氏有三
歸，官事不攝，焉得儉？」「然則管仲知禮乎？」曰：「邦君樹塞
門，管氏亦樹塞門；邦君為兩君之好，有反坫，管氏亦有反坫。管
氏而知禮，孰不知禮？」

❊ **Chapter 20** ❊

The Master said, "The Kwan Tsu is expressive of enjoyment without being licentious, and of grief without being hurtfully excessive."

注釋　be expressive of: 表現；licentious: 放縱；grief: n. 悲傷；hurtfully: adv. 有害地；excessive: 過度的。

解說　「樂而不淫，哀而不傷」或譯為 passionate without being sensual, plaintive without being morbid（熱情而不耽於官能，悲傷而不病態），似乎是過度解釋。

❊ **Chapter 21** ❊

21.1. The Duke Ai asked Tsai Wo about the altars of the spirits of the land. Tsai Wo replied, "The Hsia sovereign planted the pine tree about them; the men of the Yin planted the cypress; and the men of the Chau planted the chestnut tree, meaning thereby to cause the people to be in awe."

21.2. When the Master heard it, he said, "Things that are done, it is needless to speak about; things that have had their course, it is needless to remonstrate about; things that are past, it is needless to blame."

注釋　about: prep. 在周圍；altar: n. 祭壇；sovereign: n. 君王；pine: n. 松樹；cypress: n. 柏樹；chestnut: n. 栗樹；be in awe: 敬畏；needless: adj. 不必要；course: n. 過程、發展；remonstrate: v. 勸諫；blame: v. 責備。

❊ **Chapter 22** ❊

22.1. The Master said, "Small indeed was the capacity of Kwan Chung!"

22.2. Some one said, "Was Kwan Chung parsimonious?"

22.3. "Kwan," was the reply, "had the San Kwei, and his officers performed no double duties; how can he be considered parsimonious?"

語譯　孔子說：「管仲的器量眞是狹小！」有人問說：「是不是因爲他太節儉呢？」孔子說：「管仲收了人民許多市租，他的家臣從不兼職，怎麼能說是節儉呢？」又有人問說：「那麼管仲知禮嗎？」孔子說：「國君在門外設置屏風，管仲也有。國君設宴招待外國君主時，在正堂有放酒杯的坫，管仲在宴客時也有。如果說管仲懂得禮節，那麼誰不懂呢？」

注釋　①**管仲**　姓管，名夷吾，字仲，齊國大夫。②**器小**　器量狹小。③**三歸**　市租。④**官事不攝**　攝，兼職。⑤**樹塞門**　樹，樹立。塞門，屏風。⑥**反坫**　反者還也，致也。坫，音店，築土爲之，形如土堆。在兩楹之間，兩國君王相會，喝完酒後，把酒杯放回到坫上，稱爲反坫。

解說　關於「三歸」有許多解釋，有說是娶三個老婆、有三個家、築了個三歸臺，或者是三牲禮，這裡根據楊伯峻的解釋，說爲「市租」。

※ 第二十三章 ※

子語魯大師樂。曰：「樂其可知也：始作，翕如也；從之，純如也，皦如也，繹如也，以成。」

語譯　孔子告訴魯國樂官關於音樂的道理說：「音樂是可以了解的。開始的時候，各種樂器同時合奏。接著繼續演奏，音調和諧，節奏分明，相續不絕，直到樂曲結束。」

注釋　①**大師**　即太師，樂官。②**翕**　音系，合奏的意思。③**從之**　從同「縱」，樂聲揚開。④**純**　和諧。⑤**皦**　明白，指節奏分明。⑥**繹**　相續不絕。⑦**如**　語助詞。

※ 第二十四章 ※

儀封人請見。曰：「君子之至於斯也，吾未嘗不得見也。」從者見之。出曰：「二三子，何患於喪乎？天下之無道也久矣，天將以夫子爲木鐸。」

語譯　衛國儀邑的邊防官要見孔子。孔子說：「有賢人來我們這裡，我從沒有不和他見面的。」隨從的弟子帶他去見孔子。他出來以後，對孔子的弟子們說：「各位何必憂心你們的老師丟官呢？天下失去正道很久了，上天要請

22.4. "Then, did Kwan Chung know the rules of propriety?"

22.5. The Master said, "The princes of States have a screen intercepting the view at their gates. Kwan had likewise a screen at his gate. The princes of States on any friendly meeting between two of them, had a stand on which to place their inverted cups. Kwan had also such a stand. If Kwan knew the rules of propriety, who does not know them?"

注釋　capacity: n. 度量、包容力；parsimonious: adj. 小氣、吝嗇；screen: n. 簾幕、屏風；intercept: v. 遮斷；gate: n. 大門；stand: n. 支架；invert: v. 倒轉、倒置。

解說　反坫譯為 a stand on which to place their inverted cups（倒置酒杯的支架），把「反」解釋為「倒著放」，似乎有誤。

───────── ❧ **Chapter 23** ❧ ─────────

The Master instructing the grand music master of Lu said, "How to play music may be known. At the commencement of the piece, all the parts should sound together. As it proceeds, they should be in harmony while severally distinct and flowing without break, and thus on to the conclusion."

注釋　commencement: n. 開始；piece: n. 一首曲子；proceed: v. 繼續；harmony: n. 和諧；severally: adv. 各自；distinct: adj. 獨特的、清楚的。

───────── ❧ **Chapter 24** ❧ ─────────

The border warden at Yi requested to be introduced to the Master, saying, "When men of superior virtue have come to this, I have never been denied the privilege of seeing them." The followers of the sage introduced him, and when he came out from the interview, he said, "My friends, why are you distressed by your master's loss of office? The kingdom has long been without the principles of truth and right; Heaven is going to use your master as a bell with its wooden tongue."

你們老師做為教導人民的木鐸。」

注釋　①**儀封人**　儀，衛國邑名。封人，掌封疆之官。②**請見**　「見」音現。③**從者見之**　「從」音縱。「見」音現。④**喪**　失去官位。⑤**木鐸**　銅質木舌之鈴。宣布政令時，搖鈴召集大眾。

—————— ❖ 第二十五章 ❖ ——————

子謂韶，「盡美矣，又盡善也。」謂武，「盡美矣，未盡善也。」

語譯　孔子談到韶樂時說：「樂曲美極了，內容也很純正。」談到武樂則說：「樂曲固然很美，但是內容還不夠純正。」

注釋　①**韶**　舜時的舞樂。②**武**　武王時的舞樂。③**盡美矣，又盡善也**　朱注：「美者，聲容之盛。善者，美之實也。」

解說　《集解》：「孔曰：韶，舜樂也。謂以聖德受禪，故盡善。武，武王樂也。以征伐取天下，故未盡善。」還是以道德標準去品評藝術。

—————— ❖ 第二十六章 ❖ ——————

子曰：「居上不寬，為禮不敬，臨喪不哀，吾何以觀之哉？」

語譯　孔子說：「在上位的人不寬容，行禮時不恭敬，弔唁時不哀戚，這種人我拿什麼來觀察他呢？」

注釋　①**為禮**　行禮。②**臨喪**　到有喪事的人家去。

注釋　border: n. 邊界；warden: n. 管理人；request: v. 請求；introduce: v. 引見；privilege: n. 特權、殊榮；sage: n. 聖哲；distress: v. 使苦惱；wooden: adj. 木質的；tongue: n. 舌頭。

解說　木鐸直譯為 a bell with its wooden tongue，無法理解其寓意，譯為 tocsin（警鐘）或許比較好。

✦ Chapter 25 ✦

The Master said of the Shao that it was perfectly beautiful and also perfectly good. He said of the Wu that it was perfectly beautiful but not perfectly good.

✦ Chapter 26 ✦

The Master said, "High station filled without generosity; ceremonies performed without reverence; mourning conducted without sorrow; -- wherewith should I contemplate such ways?"

注釋　high station: 上層階級；generosity: n. 寬大；mourning: n. 喪事；sorrow: n. 悲傷；wherewith: 以什麼方法；contemplate: v. 仔細思考。

里仁第四

───────※ 第一章 ※───────

子曰:「里仁為美。擇不處仁,焉得知?」

語譯　孔子說:「居住的地方要風俗仁厚才好。如果選擇住在沒有仁厚風俗的地方,怎麼能算是聰明呢?」

注釋　①**里**　《集解》:「鄭曰:里者民之所居,居於仁者之里,是為美。不處仁者之里,不得為知。」「里」可以解釋為動詞「居住」的意思,或解釋為居於仁道。②**處**　居也。③**知**　同智。

解說　選擇有好鄰居的居住環境,才是好的。這自然是很具體的生活問題。不過也可以解釋為以仁為安身立命的處所,那麼即使在陋巷裡,也是怡然自得。

───────※ 第二章 ※───────

子曰:「不仁者,不可以久處約,不可以長處樂。仁者安仁,知者利仁。」

語譯　孔子說:「沒有仁德的人,沒辦法長久處於窮困,也不能長久處於安樂。有仁德的人會安於仁,而有智慧的人,則知道仁的好處。」

注釋　①**約**　窮困。

解說　朱注:「不仁之人,失其本心,久約必濫,久樂必淫。惟仁者則安其仁而無適不然,知者則利於仁而不易所守,蓋雖深淺之不同,然皆非外物所能奪矣。」這就是後來孟子所說「富貴不能淫,貧賤不能移,威武不能屈」,只是由孔子說來,更是如沐春風。

───────※ 第三章 ※───────

子曰:「唯仁者能好人,能惡人。」

語譯　孔子說:「只有仁者,才能公正地喜歡人的善,厭惡人的不善。」

注釋　①**好**　音浩。喜歡。②**惡**　音務。討厭。

解說　這裡是說只有仁者才能無私地評判他人的善或不善。

❖ **Chapter 1** ❖

The Master said, "It is virtuous manners which constitute the excellence of a neighborhood. If a man in selecting a residence do not fix on one where such prevail, how can he be wise?"

注釋　constitute: v. 構成；excellence: n. 卓越；residence: n. 住處；fix on: 決定；prevail: v. 盛行。

解說　比較以下的翻譯：The Master said: "It is the moral character of a neighborhood that constitutes its excellence, and how can he be considered wise who does not elect to dwell in moral surroundings?"

❖ **Chapter 2** ❖

The Master said, "Those who are without virtue cannot abide long either in a condition of poverty and hardship, or in a condition of enjoyment. The virtuous rest in virtue; the wise desire virtue."

注釋　bide: v. 居住、忍受；condition: n. 條件、狀況；poverty: n. 貧窮；hardship: n. 困境。

❖ **Chapter 3** ❖

The Master said, "It is only the truly virtuous man, who can love, or who can hate, others."

※ 第四章 ※

子曰：「苟志於仁矣，無惡也。」

語譯　孔子說：「如果人能夠真心向善，也就不會做什麼壞事。」

注釋　①苟　朱注：「誠也。」

解說　「無惡也」，不會做壞事。朱注：「其心誠在於仁，則必無為惡之事矣。
楊曰：『苟志於仁，未必無過舉也，然而為惡則無矣。』」楊伯峻譯為
「總沒有壞處」。

※ 第五章 ※

子曰：「富與貴，是人之所欲也，不以其道得之，不處也；貧與
賤，是人之所惡也，不以其道得之，不去也。君子去仁，惡乎成
名？君子無終食之間違仁，造次必於是，顛沛必於是。」

語譯　孔子說：「富貴是人人都想要的，但是如果方法不正當，君子是不會接受
的；貧賤是人人厭惡的，但是如果方法不正當，君子是不會想要去擺脫
的。君子拋棄了仁德，如何成就他的名聲呢？君子沒有一頓飯的時間忘記
仁德，倉促匆忙的時候要固守仁德，顛仆困頓的時候也要固守仁德。」

注釋　①惡乎成名　惡音烏，何也。②終食之間　一頓飯的時間，形容片刻之
時。③違　離開。④造次　匆忙。⑤顛沛　跌倒，指遇到困境。

解說　畢沅說：「古讀皆以不以其道為句。」所以讀為「不以其道，得之不處也
……不以其道，得之不去也。」這樣比較通順。

Chapter 4

The Master said, "If the will be set on virtue, there will be no practice of wickedness."

注釋　be set on: 打定主意；wickedness: n. 邪惡。

Chapter 5

5.1.　The Master said, "Riches and honors are what men desire. If they cannot be obtained in the proper way, they should not be held. Poverty and meanness are what men dislike. If they cannot be avoided in the proper way, they should not be avoided.

5.2.　"If a superior man abandon virtue, how can he fulfill the requirements of that name?

5.3.　"The superior man does not, even for the space of a single meal, act contrary to virtue. In moments of haste, he cleaves to it. In seasons of danger, he cleaves to it."

注釋　meanness: n. 卑賤；dislike: v. 不喜歡；requirement: n. 要件；contrary to: 背反；haste: n. 倉促；cleave: v. 固守於。

解說　比較以下的翻譯：The Master said: "Wealth and rank are what men desire, but unless they be obtained in the right way, they are not to be possessed. Poverty and obscurity are what men detest; but unless it can be brought about in the right way, they are not to be abandoned. If a man of honor forsakes virtue, how is he to fulfill the obligations of his name! A man of honor never disregards virtue, even for the space of a single meal. In moments of haste he cleaves to it; in seasons of peril he cleaves to it."

———— ❖ 第六章 ❖ ————

子曰：「我未見好仁者，惡不仁者。好仁者，無以尚之；惡不仁者，其為仁矣，不使不仁者加乎其身。有能一日用其力於仁矣乎？我未見力不足者。蓋有之矣，我未之見也。」

語譯　孔子說：「我沒有看過愛好仁德的人，或是厭惡不仁的人。愛好仁德的人，會覺得世間沒有比仁德更重要的事；而厭惡不仁的人，在實踐仁德的時候，至少不會心存不道德的念頭。有誰能夠花一天的功夫用心在仁德上呢？我沒有見過能力不夠的人。大概有吧，但是我還沒有看到過。」

注釋　①尚　超過。②蓋　大概。

解說　行仁真的有這麼困難嗎？孔子固然感慨仁道之不行，但是他也說每個人其實都是有能力的。

———— ❖ 第七章 ❖ ————

子曰：「人之過也，各於其黨。觀過，斯知仁矣。」

語譯　孔子說：「什麼樣的錯誤總是由什麼樣的人犯的。只要觀察他的過失，就可以知道他是否有仁心。」

注釋　①黨　類也。

解說　人都會犯錯，從每個人所犯的錯誤裡，其實也可以看出他們的人格特質。

———— ❖ 第八章 ❖ ————

子曰：「朝聞道，夕死可矣。」

語譯　孔子說：「早上明白了真理，就算那天晚上死去也可以（沒有遺憾）。」

注釋　①道　朱注：「事物當然之理。」

———— ❖ 第九章 ❖ ————

子曰：「士志於道，而恥惡衣惡食者，未足與議也。」

———※ **Chapter 6** ※———

6.1. The Master said, "I have not seen a person who loved virtue, or one who hated what was not virtuous. He who loved virtue, would esteem nothing above it. He who hated what is not virtuous, would practice virtue in such a way that he would not allow anything that is not virtuous to approach his person.

6.2. "Is any one able for one day to apply his strength to virtue? I have not seen the case in which his strength would be insufficient.

6.3. "Should there possibly be any such case, I have not seen it."

注釋　esteem: v. 尊敬；approach: v. 接近。

———※ **Chapter 7** ※———

The Master said, "The faults of men are characteristic of the class to which they belong. By observing a man's faults, it may be known that he is virtuous."

注釋　be characteristic of: 特有的、有某種特徵；class: n. 類型。

———※ **Chapter 8** ※———

The Master said, "If a man in the morning hear the right way, he may die in the evening without regret."

注釋　regret: n. 後悔。

———※ **Chapter 9** ※———

The Master said, "A scholar, whose mind is set on truth, and who is ashamed of bad clothes and bad food, is not fit to be discoursed with."

語譯　孔子說：「讀書人專心追求眞理，卻又以穿不好吃不好爲恥，那麼就不必和他談什麼了。」

注釋　①士　《正義》：「《白虎通》〈爵篇〉：『士者事也。任事之稱也。』……習於學有德行道藝者始出仕。」

———— ❀ 第十章 ❀ ————

子曰：「君子之於天下也，無適也，無莫也，義之與比。」

語譯　孔子說：「君子對於天下事，沒有必須怎麼樣或不能怎麼樣的成見，只要是合理的，他就會遵行。」

注釋　①適　朱注：「專主也。」適音迪。②莫　朱注：「不肯也。」③義之與比　比音必。朱注：「從也。」唯義是從的意思。

———— ❀ 第十一章 ❀ ————

子曰：「君子懷德，小人懷土；君子懷刑，小人懷惠。」

語譯　孔子說：「君子在意的是美德，小人在意的是地產；君子在意的是法度，小人在意的是恩惠。」

注釋　①懷　朱注：「思念也。」關心的意思。②土　田產。③刑　指禮法。④惠　恩惠。

解說　朱注：「懷德，謂存其固有之善。懷土，謂溺其所處之安。懷刑，謂畏法。懷惠，謂貪利。」

———— ❀ 第十二章 ❀ ————

子曰：「放於利而行，多怨。」

語譯　孔子說：「做事都只想到個人的權益，會招致許多抱怨。」

注釋　①放　音仿，依據或放縱的意思。

解說　朱注：「程子曰：欲利於己，必害於人，故多怨。」

注釋　scholar: n. 學者；be ashamed of: 恥於；discourse: v. 談論。

Chapter 10

The Master said, "The superior man, in the world, does not set his mind either for anything, or against anything; what is right he will follow."

注釋　set one's mind for (against): 偏好（有歧視）。

解說　比較以下的翻譯：The Master said: "The wise man in his attitude towards the world has neither predilections nor prejudices. He is on the side of what is righteous."

Chapter 11

The Master said, "The superior man thinks of virtue; the small man thinks of comfort. The superior man thinks of the sanctions of law; the small man thinks of favors which he may receive."

注釋　comfort: n. 舒適；sanction: n. 制裁；favor: n. 好處。

解說　thinks of comfort（想到的是生活的舒適），是以朱注為根據的翻譯。

Chapter 12

The Master said: "He who acts with a constant view to his own advantage will be much murmured against."

注釋　constant: adj. 時常；murmur: v. 抱怨，發牢騷 [against]。

———————————— ✦ 第十三章 ✦ ————————————

子曰：「能以禮讓為國乎？何有？不能以禮讓為國，如禮何？」

語譯　孔子說：「能夠以禮讓來治國嗎？這有什麼困難呢？如果不能以禮讓來治理國家，那麼只是有禮法，又能怎麼樣呢？」

注釋　①為國　治理國家。②何有　何難之有。

解說　禮的本質就是謙讓，如果不能以謙讓治國，那麼禮制就是徒具虛文而已。

———————————— ✦ 第十四章 ✦ ————————————

子曰：「不患無位，患所以立；不患莫己知，求為可知也。」

語譯　孔子說：「不擔心沒有職位，只擔心自己是否勝任；不擔心別人不知道我，而要在意自己有什麼才德可以讓別人知道的。」

注釋　①所以立　朱注：「謂所以立乎其位者。」擔任該職位必備的才德。

解說　程子說：「君子求其在我者而已矣。」

———————————— ✦ 第十五章 ✦ ————————————

子曰：「參乎！吾道一以貫之。」曾子曰：「唯。」子出。門人問曰：「何謂也？」曾子曰：「夫子之道，忠恕而已矣。」

語譯　孔子說：「參啊，我的學說可以用一個道理貫穿。」曾子說：「是的。」孔子出去後。其他學生便問他：「那是什麼意思啊？」曾子說：「夫子的學說，就是忠恕兩個字罷了。」

注釋　①參　曾子之名，孔子弟子。②貫　通也、行也。③忠恕　朱注：「盡己之謂忠，推己之謂恕。」④而已矣　如此罷了。

解說　孔子的學說是否真能以忠恕兩字貫通之，其實是頗多爭議。

❊ **Chapter 13** ❊

The Master said, "If a prince is able to govern his kingdom with the complaisance proper to the rules of propriety, what difficulty will he have? If he cannot govern it with that complaisance, what has he to do with the rules of propriety?"

注釋　complaisance: n. 和藹、親切。

❊ **Chapter 14** ❊

The Master said, "A man should say, I am not concerned that I have no place, I am concerned how I may fit myself for one. I am not concerned that I am not known, I seek to be worthy to be known."

注釋　to fit oneself for: 適任。

❊ **Chapter 15** ❊

15.1. The Master said, "Shan, my doctrine is that of an all-pervading unity." The disciple Tsang replied, "Yes."

15.2. The Master went out, and the other disciples asked, saying, "What do his words mean?" Tsang said, "The doctrine of our master is to be true to the principles of our nature and the benevolent exercise of them to others, -- this and nothing more."

注釋　doctrine: n. 學說、教義；pervade: v. 遍及、充滿；unity: n. 單一體；disciple: n. 門徒；be true to: 忠實於；principle: n. 原理；benevolent: adj. 仁慈的、善意的；exercise: n. 運用。

解說　忠恕譯為 to be true to the principles of our nature and the benevolent exercise of them to others（忠實於我們本性的原理，而以慈愛的心把這些原理推及別人），就是朱子「盡己之謂忠，推己之謂恕」的意思。

※ 第十六章 ※

子曰：「君子喻於義，小人喻於利。」

語譯　孔子說：「君子所了解的是義，小人所了解的是利。」

注釋　①喻　理解。

解說　「義利之辨」到了孟子以及後來的宋明理學成為重要的論題。朱注：「義者，天理之所宜。利者，人情之所欲。程子曰：『君子之於義，猶小人之於利也。唯其深喻，是以篤好。』楊氏曰：『君子有捨而取義者，以利言之，則人之所欲無甚於生，所惡無甚於死，孰肯捨生而取義哉？其所喻者義而已，不知利之為利故也，小人反是。』」

※ 第十七章 ※

子曰：「見賢思齊焉，見不賢而內自省也。」

語譯　孔子說：「看到賢德的人，想和他一樣，看到不賢的人，要自我反省，有沒有像他那樣的過失。」

注釋　①思齊　想和他一樣。

※ 第十八章 ※

子曰：「事父母幾諫。見志不從，又敬不違，勞而不怨。」

語譯　孔子說：「侍奉父母，如果他們有過錯，要委婉勸告。如果他們不聽從，也要態度恭敬，但不要放棄，雖然心裡擔憂，也不抱怨。」

注釋　①幾　音基，微也。輕微、婉轉。②志　父母之志。③違　違去也。④勞　憂心。

解說　父母有過錯，做子女的應該勸告他們。不過態度要恭敬。如果還不聽呢？「又敬不違」，這不是說恭敬而不敢違逆父母心意，而是要態度恭敬但不放棄勸告。勞者憂也，《禮記·曲禮》：「三諫而不聽，則號泣而隨之，可謂憂矣。」勞也可以解釋為責罰，《禮記·內則》：「父母有過，下氣怡色柔聲以諫，諫若不入，起敬起孝，說則復諫，不說，與其得罪於鄉黨州閭，寧孰諫。父母怒不說，而撻之流血，不敢疾怨，起敬起孝。」也就是說，即使父母因此責罰他，他也不抱怨。

✻ Chapter 16 ✻

The Master said, "The mind of the superior man is conversant with righteousness; the mind of the mean man is conversant with gain."

注釋　conversant: adj. 熟悉 [with]；gain: n. 獲利。

✻ Chapter 17 ✻

The Master said, "When we see men of worth, we should think of equaling them; when we see men of a contrary character, we should turn inwards and examine ourselves."

注釋　equal: v. 比得上；contrary: adj. 相反的；inwards: adv. 向內；examine: v. 檢視。

✻ Chapter 18 ✻

The Master said, "In serving his parents, a son may remonstrate with them, but gently; when he sees that they do not incline to follow his advice, he shows an increased degree of reverence, but does not abandon his purpose; and should they punish him, he does not allow himself to murmur."

注釋　remonstrate: v. 勸告 [with]；incline: v. 傾向；advice: n. 建議；punish: 處罰。

解說　「不違」譯為 does not abandon his purpose（不放棄目的）；「勞」譯為 should they punish him（萬一他們處罰他），這樣解釋很好。

---------------------------------- ❀ 第十九章 ❀ ----------------------------------

子曰：「父母在，不遠遊。遊必有方。」

語譯　孔子說：「父母在的時候，不出遠門。如果不得已要出遠門，也要有一定的去處。」

注釋　①**有方**　有一定的方向。鄭玄說：「方猶常也。」

解說　朱注：「遠遊，則去親遠而為日久，定省曠而音問疏；不惟己之思親不置，亦恐親之念我不忘也。遊必有方，如己告云之東，即不敢更適西，欲親必知己之所在而無憂，召己則必至而無失也。」

---------------------------------- ❀ 第二十章 ❀ ----------------------------------

子曰：「三年無改於父之道，可謂孝矣。」

解說　見〈學而〉篇。

---------------------------------- ❀ 第二十一章 ❀ ----------------------------------

子曰：「父母之年，不可不知也。一則以喜，一則以懼。」

語譯　孔子說：「父母的年紀，不可以不記在心裡，一方面欣喜父母親高壽，一方面擔憂父母衰老。」

解說　朱注：「常知父母之年，則既喜其壽，又懼其衰，而於愛日之誠，自有不能已者。」

---------------------------------- ❀ 第二十二章 ❀ ----------------------------------

子曰：「古者言之不出，恥躬之不逮也。」

語譯　孔子說：「古人不隨便說話，是害怕自己的行為跟不上而以為可恥。」

注釋　①**不出**　皇侃本作「不妄出」。②**恥**　動詞，以為可恥。③**逮**　音代，趕上。

解說　《禮記・緇衣》說：「子曰：言從而行之，則言不可飾也；行從而言之，則行不可飾也。故君子寡言而行以成其信，則民不得大其美而小其惡。」

❈ **Chapter 19** ❈

The Master said, "While his parents are alive, the son may not go abroad to a distance. If he does go abroad, he must have a fixed place to which he goes."

注釋　abroad: adv. 國外、戶外。

❈ **Chapter 20** ❈

The Master said, "If the son for three years does not alter from the way of his father, he may be called filial."

❈ **Chapter 21** ❈

The Master said, "The years of parents may by no means not be kept in the memory, as an occasion at once for joy and for fear."

注釋　years: pl. n. 年紀（特別是指老年）；occasion: 原因、理由。

❈ **Chapter 22** ❈

The Master said, "The reason why the ancients did not readily give utterance to their words, was that they feared lest their actions should not come up to them."

注釋　readily: adv. 輕易、隨便；utterance: n. 發表、吐露；lest: conj. 以免、唯恐；
　　　come up to: 達到、合乎。

———————————— ✤ 第二十三章 ✤ ————————————

子曰：「以約失之者，鮮矣。」

語譯　孔子說：「因為節制而有過失的，這種事很少吧。」

注釋　①**約**　不奢放逸。②**鮮**　音險，很少的意思。

解說　《集解》：「孔曰：俱不得中，奢則驕佚招禍，儉約無憂患。」太過節
　　　制或是太過驕奢都不好，不過節制的過失比較少吧。約可以解釋為儉約
　　　或謹慎。

———————————— ✤ 第二十四章 ✤ ————————————

子曰：「君子欲訥於言，而敏於行。」

語譯　孔子說：「君子說話總想要謹慎，而做事想要認真。」

注釋　①**訥**　音ㄋㄜˋ。遲鈍。②**敏**　敏捷、認真。③**行**　音性。

———————————— ✤ 第二十五章 ✤ ————————————

子曰：「德不孤，必有鄰。」

語譯　孔子說：「有道德的人必不會孤單，總會有人來親近他。」

注釋　①**鄰**　親近的意思。

解說　「德不孤」有兩種解釋，或者是指道德實踐，或者是指有德者。

———————————— ✤ 第二十六章 ✤ ————————————

子游曰：「事君數，斯辱矣，朋友數，斯疏矣。」

語譯　子游說：「對待君主時太過囉唆，就會招致侮辱；對待朋友太過囉唆，就
　　　會疏遠。」

注釋　①**數**　音朔。煩數也。②**疏**　疏遠。

解說　「君子之交淡如水，小人之交甘如醴。」狎近容易生侮，該說的都說了就
　　　好。「數」也可以解釋為太親近。

❊ **Chapter 23** ❊

The Master said, "The cautious seldom err.

注釋　cautious: adj. 小心謹慎；err: v. 犯錯。

❊ **Chapter 24** ❊

The Master said, "The superior man wishes to be slow in his speech and earnest in his conduct."

注釋　earnest: adj. 認真的。

❊ **Chapter 25** ❊

The Master said, "Virtue is not left to stand alone. He who practices it will have neighbors."

❊ **Chapter 26** ❊

Tsze-yu said, "In serving a prince, frequent remonstrations lead to disgrace. Between friends, frequent reproofs make the friendship distant."

注釋　remonstration: n. 勸阻；disgrace: n. 恥辱；reproof: n. 責難、勸誡；friendship: n. 友誼。

公冶長第五

------------------------ ❋ 第一章 ❋ ------------------------

子謂公冶長：「可妻也。雖在縲絏之中，非其罪也。」以其子妻之。

語譯　孔子談到公冶長說：「可以把女兒嫁給他，雖然他曾經坐過牢，但不是他的過錯。」於是孔子把自己的女兒嫁給他。

注釋　**①公冶長**　姓公冶名長，字子長，齊國人，孔子弟子。**②妻**　音企，動詞，嫁女兒的意思。**③縲絏**　音纍泄，繫縛罪人的繩索。《集解》：「孔曰：縲，黑索也；絏，攣也，所以拘罪人。」**④子**　指女兒。

解說　絏原作紲，唐朝時的人避諱作紲，也是繩索的意思，或解釋為攣，拴繫的意思。

------------------------ ❋ 第二章 ❋ ------------------------

子謂南容：「邦有道，不廢；邦無道，免於刑戮。」以其兄之子妻之。

語譯　孔子談到南容說：「國家政治清明，不會被棄置不用；國家政治黑暗，也不致遭到迫害。」於是把他哥哥的女兒嫁給南容。

注釋　**①南容**　朱注：「南容，孔子弟子，居南宮。名縚，又名适。字子容，諡敬叔。孟懿子之兄也。」**②其兄之子**　孔子的哥哥叫孟皮。

解說　《孔子家語》：「叔梁紇娶魯之施氏，生九女。其妾生孟皮，病足。乃求婚於顏氏徵在。」那時候孟皮已經過世，所以孔子為他哥哥的女兒主婚。

------------------------ ❋ 第三章 ❋ ------------------------

子謂：「子賤，君子哉若人！魯無君子者，斯焉取斯？」

語譯　孔子說：「子賤這個人真是君子啊！如果不是魯國有許多君子，他到哪裡學到如此的德性呢？」

注釋　**①子賤**　宓不齊，字子賤，孔子學生。**②斯焉取斯**　第一個斯指子賤，第二個斯指德性。取，取法。

Chapter 1

The Master said of Kung-ye Ch'ang that he might be wived; although he was put in bonds, he had not been guilty of any crime. Accordingly, he gave him his own daughter to wife.

注釋 wive: v. 娶妻；bond: n. 腳鐐、手銬；to put in bonds: 監禁；guilty: adj. 有罪的；crime: n. 罪行；be guilty of a crime: 犯了罪；accordingly: 於是。

Chapter 2

Of Nan Yung he said that if the country were well governed he would not be out of office, and if it were in governed, he would escape punishment and disgrace. He gave him the daughter of his own elder brother to wife.

注釋 escape: v. 逃避。

Chapter 3

The Master said of Tsze-chien, "Of superior virtue indeed is such a man! If there were not virtuous men in Lu, how could this man have acquired this character?"

解說 「君子」在這裡指君子之德，故譯為 superior virtue。

---※ 第四章 ※---

子貢問曰：「賜也何如？」子曰：「女器也。」曰：「何器也？」
曰：「瑚璉也。」

語譯　子貢問：「那麼我又如何呢？」孔子說：「你是個有用的器具。」子貢
　　　說：「什麼樣的器具呢？」孔子說：「像瑚璉那樣的宗廟器具。」

注釋　①女　同汝，你的意思。②器　器具、成材。③瑚璉　在宗廟裡盛黍稷的
　　　器皿，朱注：「夏日瑚，商日璉，周日簠簋，皆宗廟盛黍稷之器而飾以
　　　玉，器之貴重而華美者也。」

解說　意思是說子貢可以從政。

---※ 第五章 ※---

或曰：「雍也，仁而不佞。」子曰：「焉用佞？禦人以口給，屢憎
於人。不知其仁，焉用佞？」

語譯　有人說：「冉雍是個仁者，可惜口才不好。」孔子說：「何必要口才好
　　　呢？用伶牙利齒來對付人，時常討人厭。我不知道冉雍是否能說是個仁
　　　者，但是何必要有好口才？」

注釋　①佞　口才很好。②禦　對付。③口給　口辭敏捷。④憎　厭惡。

解說　朱注：「仲弓為人重厚簡默，而時人以佞為賢，故美其優於德，而病其短
　　　於才也。」孔子說「不知其仁」，不是否定冉雍的仁德，而是說仁者不必
　　　有好口才。

---※ 第六章 ※---

子使漆雕開仕。對曰：「吾斯之未能信。」子說。

語譯　孔子要漆雕開去做官。漆雕開回答說：「我對做官這種事還沒有信心。」
　　　孔子聽了很高興。

注釋　①仕　做官。

解說　這裡不是說漆雕開不喜歡做官，相反的，經世致用是儒家的理想。孔子是
　　　稱許他不自矜不躁進。

※ **Chapter 4** ※

Tsze-kung asked, "What do you say of me, Ts'ze! "The Master said, "You are a utensil." "What utensil?""A gemmed sacrificial utensil."

注釋　utensil: n. 用具；gem: v. 以珠寶裝飾之。

解說　瑚璉譯為 gemmed sacrificial utensil（以珠寶裝飾的祭器）。

※ **Chapter 5** ※

5.1. Some one said, "Yung is truly virtuous, but he is not ready with his tongue."
The Master said, "What is the good of being ready with the tongue?

5.2. They who encounter men with smartness of speech for the most part procure themselves hatred. I know not whether he be truly virtuous, but why should he show readiness of the tongue?"

注釋　be ready with: 敏捷、很快；encounter: 遭遇、迎戰；smartness: n. 敏捷；
procure: v. 招致。

※ **Chapter 6** ※

The Master was wishing Ch'i-tiao K'ai to enter an official employment. He replied, "I am not yet able to rest in the assurance of this."The Master was pleased.

注釋　assurance: n. 信心。

---------------- ❊ 第七章 ❊ ----------------

子曰：「道不行，乘桴浮於海。從我者其由與？」子路聞之喜。子曰：「由也，好勇過我，無所取材。」

語譯　孔子說：「我的道沒有人要採行，我想要坐小木筏到海外去。會跟我去的，大概只有由吧。」子路聽了很歡喜。孔子說：「由這個人啊，比我還勇敢，可惜不知道要到哪裡找材料編竹筏。」

注釋　①**桴**　《集解》：「馬曰：桴，編竹木，大者曰栰，小者曰桴。」②**浮**　以舟渡也。

解說　「無所取材」有不同的解釋，朱注：「材，與裁同，古字借用。」裁度的意思，就是說子路好勇而不知道要判斷事理。而古字材通哉，所以也有人解釋為「沒什麼可取的」。

---------------- ❊ 第八章 ❊ ----------------

孟武伯問：「子路仁乎？」子曰：「不知也。」又問。子曰：「由也，千乘之國，可使治其賦也，不知其仁也。」「求也何如？」子曰：「求也，千室之邑，百乘之家，可使為之宰也，不知其仁也。」「赤也何如？」子曰：「赤也，束帶立於朝，可使與賓客言也，不知其仁也。」

語譯　孟武伯問說：「子路是仁者嗎？」孔子說：「不知道。」接著又問。孔子說：「由啊，如果有千輛兵車的國家，可以派他去治理軍事，但是我不知道他是不是仁者。」「那麼冉求如何呢？」孔子說：「求啊，千戶人口的大縣，有百輛兵車的大夫封地，可以叫他去當總管，但是我不知道他是不是仁者。」「那麼公西赤如何呢？」孔子說：「赤啊，穿著禮服站在朝廷裡，可以派他接待外賓，但是我不知道他是不是仁者。」

注釋　①**賦**　兵賦也。指治軍。②**千戶之邑**　有一千家的縣邑。③**百乘之家**　諸侯稱國，卿大夫稱家；諸侯千乘，卿大夫百乘。④**宰**　家臣。⑤**赤**　公西赤，字子華，孔子弟子。⑥**束帶**　加帶於胸，以整束其衣。

解說　《集解》：「孔曰：仁道至大，不可全名也。」仁者是道德學問的最高理想，所以孔子不輕易稱許人為仁者。

Chapter 7

The Master said, "My doctrines make no way. I will get upon a raft, and float about on the sea. He that will accompany me will be Yu, I dare say." Tsze-lu hearing this was glad, upon which the Master said, "Yu is fonder of daring than I am. He does not exercise his judgment upon matters."

注釋　raft: n. 筏；float: v. 漂浮；float about: 到處漂流；I dare say: 我想、或許；daring: n. 冒險的勇氣；judgment: n. 判斷。

Chapter 8

8.1.　Mang Wu asked about Tsze-lu, whether he was perfectly virtuous. The Master said, "I do not know."

8.2.　He asked again, when the Master replied, "In a kingdom of a thousand chariots, Yu might be employed to manage the military levies, but I do not know whether he be perfectly virtuous."

8.3.　"And what do you say of Ch'iu?" The Master replied, "In a city of a thousand families, or a clan of a hundred chariots, Ch'iu might be employed as governor, but I do not know whether he is perfectly virtuous."

8.4.　"What do you say of Ch'ih?" The Master replied, "With his sash girt and standing in a court, Ch'ih might be employed to converse with the visitors and guests, but I do not know whether he is perfectly virtuous."

注釋　military: adj. 軍事的；levy: n. 徵召；clan: n. 氏族；governor: n. 主管；sash n. 飾帶；girt: adj. 圍著；converse: v. 交談。

解說　這裡的「仁」譯為 perfectly virtuous。

———❊ 第九章 ❊———

子謂子貢曰:「女與回也孰愈?」對曰:「賜也何敢望回。回也聞一以知十,賜也聞一以知二。」子曰:「弗如也!吾與女弗如也。」

語譯　孔子對子貢說:「你跟顏回哪個比較好?」子貢回答說:「我哪裡敢和顏回比呢?他啊,聽到一分道理,就可以推知十分。而我聽到一分,只能推知兩分。」孔子說:「你的確不如他,我和你都不如他。」

注釋　①愈　勝也。②望　視比也。

解說　「知十」、「知二」,只是以數字比喻其優劣。朱注:「一,數之始。十,數之終。二者,一之對也。顏子明睿所照,即始而見終;子貢推測而知,因此而識彼。」這是說,顏回能從個殊的事理推演出全體的真理,而子貢則是由某個事理推知另一個事理。「吾與女弗如也」也可以解釋為:「我同意你的話,你確實不如他。」

———❊ 第十章 ❊———

宰予晝寢。子曰:「朽木不可雕也,糞土之牆不可杇也,於予與何誅。」子曰:「始吾於人也,聽其言而信其行;今吾於人也,聽其言而觀其行。於予與改是。」

語譯　宰予大白天睡覺。孔子說:「腐朽的木頭沒辦法拿來雕刻,骯髒的土牆沒辦法再粉刷。我對宰予沒什麼可以苛責的!」孔子說:「起初我對人的看法是,聽他說的話就相信他做得到。現在我對人看法是,聽他的話以後,還要再看他的作為。是因為宰予,我才改變想法的。」

注釋　①宰予　姓宰名予,字子我,孔子弟子。②晝寢　白天睡覺。③糞土　穢土。④杇　塗牆的泥刀。這裡做動詞用,塗抹的意思。⑤與　語助詞,同以下「於予與改是」。⑥誅　責備。

解說　本章中孔子對宰予的批評非常嚴厲,錢穆認為可能不是當時實錄。

Chapter 9

9.1. The Master said to Tsze-kung, "Which do you consider superior, yourself or Hui?"

9.2. Tsze-kung replied, "How dare I compare myself with Hui? Hui hears one point and knows all about a subject; I hear one point, and know a second."

9.3. The Master said, "You are not equal to him. I grant you, you are not equal to him."

注釋　grant: v. 承認某人所說的話。

Chapter 10

10.1. Tsai Yu being asleep during the daytime, the Master said, "Rotten wood cannot be carved; a wall of dirty earth will not receive the trowel. This Yu, -- what is the use of my reproving him?"

10.2. The Master said, "At first, my way with men was to hear their words, and give them credit for their conduct. Now my way is to hear their words, and look at their conduct. It is from Yu that I have learned to make this change."

注釋　rotten: adj. 腐朽的；carve: v. 雕刻；receive: 承受；trowel: n. 泥刀；reprove: v. 責罵；give credit to: 相信。

———— ❋ 第十一章 ❋ ————

子曰：「吾未見剛者。」或對曰：「申棖。」子曰：「棖也慾，焉得剛？」

語譯　孔子說：「我沒見過剛毅的人。」有人回答說：「申棖就是啊。」孔子說：「棖啊，他嗜欲太深了，怎麼談得上剛毅呢？」

注釋　①剛　志不屈撓。②申棖　《史記》作申黨，字周，孔子弟子。

解說　剛毅不屈的人格在於不為任何境遇所動，欲望多了，意志就很容易動搖，因此談不上剛毅。

———— ❋ 第十二章 ❋ ————

子貢曰：「我不欲人之加諸我也，吾亦欲無加諸人。」子曰：「賜也，非爾所及也。」

語譯　子貢說：「我不願別人把不義加在我身上，我也不願把不義加在別人身上。」孔子說：「賜啊，這不是你做得到的。」

注釋　①加　強加。②賜也，非爾所及也　孔安國說：「言不能止人使不加非義於己。」

解說　戴震《孟子字義疏證》說：「『夫物之感人無窮。而人之好惡無節，則是物至而人化物也。人化物也者，滅天理而窮人欲者也；於是有悖逆詐偽之心，有淫佚作亂之事；是故強者脅弱，眾者暴寡，知者詐愚，勇者苦怯，疾病不養，老幼孤獨不得其所。此大亂之道也。』誠以弱、寡、愚、怯與夫疾病、老幼、孤獨，反躬而思其情。人豈異於我！蓋方其靜也，未感於物，其血氣心知，湛然無有失，故曰『天之性』；及其感而動，則欲出於性。一人之欲，天下人之所同欲也，故曰『性之欲』。好惡既形，遂己之好惡，忘人之好惡，往往賊人以逞欲；反躬者，以人之逞其欲，思身受之情也。情得其平，是為好惡之節，是為依乎天理。」人間的許多不義，不就是因為把自己的好惡強加在別人身上嗎？戴震的這段話很值得我們深思。

❋ Chapter 11 ❋

The Master said, "I have not seen a firm and unbending man."Some one replied, "There is Shan Ch'ang.""Ch'ang,"said the Master, "is under the influence of his passions; how can he be pronounced firm and unbending?"

注釋　unbending: adj. 不屈不撓的；under the influence of: 受影響；passion: n. 激情、愛好。

❋ Chapter 12 ❋

Tsze-kung said, "What I do not wish men to do to me, I also wish not to do to men." The Master said, "Ts'ze, you have not attained to that."

注釋　attain: 到達。

---※ 第十三章 ※---

子貢曰：「夫子之文章，可得而聞也；夫子之言性與天道，不可得
而聞也。」

語譯　子貢說：「夫子的詩書禮樂，是可以聽得到的；夫子談論性和天道，就很
　　　難得聽到了。」

注釋　①**文章**　指詩書禮樂。朱注：「文章，德之見乎外者，威儀文辭皆是也。」
　　　②**性**　朱注：「人所受之天理。」③**天道**　朱注：「天理，自然之本體。」

解說　心性與天道是中國哲學的重要題目。《集解》：「性者，人之所受以生
　　　也。天道者，元亨日新之道。深微故不可得而聞也。」也就是探討人的存
　　　在本質以及宇宙現象的原理的學說。那麼為什麼不可得而聞呢？《正義》
　　　說子貢指的是《易》，因為「孔子五十而學易，惟子夏、商瞿晚年弟子得
　　　傳是學。」其實以孔子的哲學風格而言，確實是很少談及形上學的問題。

---※ 第十四章 ※---

子路有聞，未之能行，唯恐有聞。

語譯　子路聽到某個道理，還沒有能夠做到，唯恐又聽到另一個。

注釋　①**唯恐有聞**　有同又。

解說　子路的個性就是勇於實踐。

---※ 第十五章 ※---

子貢問曰：「孔文子，何以謂之文也？」子曰：「敏而好學，不恥
下問，是以謂之文也。」

語譯　子貢問說：「孔文子為什麼謚為文呢？」孔子說：「他勤勉又好學，會謙
　　　虛向屬下求教而不以為恥，因此以『文』做他的謚號。」

注釋　①**孔文子**　衛國大夫，姓孔名圉，謚為文。②**敏**　敏捷、迅速。③**下問**　俞
　　　樾說：「下問者，非必以貴下賤之謂，凡以能問於不能，以多問於寡，皆
　　　是。」

Chapter 13

Tsze-kung said, "The Master's personal displays of his principles and ordinary descriptions of them may be heard. His discourses about man's nature, and the way of Heaven, cannot be heard."

解說　「文章」譯爲 personal displays of his principles and ordinary descriptions of them，是意譯自朱注「德之見乎外者，威儀文辭」，也就是聖哲的身教以及言教。

Chapter 14

When Tsze-lu heard anything, if he had not yet succeeded in carrying it into practice, he was only afraid lest he should hear something else.

Chapter 15

15.1. Tsze-kung asked, saying, "On what ground did Kung-wan get that title of Wan?"

15.2. The Master said, "He was of an active nature and yet fond of learning, and he was not ashamed to ask and learn of his inferiors! -- On these grounds he has been styled Wan."

注釋　active: adj. 主動、積極；inferior: n.下屬、晚輩；style: v. 稱呼。

---※ 第十六章 ※---

子謂:「子產有君子之道四焉:其行己也恭,其事上也敬,其養民也惠,其使民也義。」

語譯　孔子說:「子產有四種行為是合乎君子之道的:他的行為很謙恭,對在上位的人負責認眞,教養人民有恩惠,使用民力很合理。」

注釋　①**子產**　鄭國大夫,姓公孫名僑,字子產。於簡公、定公之時執政二十二年,為春秋時代的賢相。②**恭**　謙遜。③**敬**　謹恪。④**惠**　愛利人。⑤**義**　合宜。

---※ 第十七章 ※---

子曰:「晏平仲善與人交,久而敬之。」

語譯　孔子說:「晏平仲善於和人交往,相處久了,還是非常尊敬他的朋友。」

注釋　①**晏平仲**　春秋時齊國大夫,姓晏,名嬰,字仲,謚為平。②**交**　交友。③**敬**　鄭注:「敬故,不慢舊也。」

解說　孫綽說:「交有傾蓋如舊,亦有白首如新。隆始者易,克終者難。敦厚不渝,其道可久,所以難也。」這段話告訴我們很重要的交友之道。「久而敬之」也可以解釋為:「相處久了,人們越加尊敬他。」

---※ 第十八章 ※---

子曰:「臧文仲居蔡,山節藻梲,何如其知也?」

語譯　孔子說:「臧文仲藏大龜問卜的房子,柱頭斗拱刻了山形,樑上短柱畫上水藻,這樣是聰明的嗎?」

注釋　①**臧文仲**　魯國大夫,姓臧孫,名辰,謚為文。②**居**　藏也。③**蔡**　《集解》:「包曰:蔡,國君之守龜,出蔡地,因以為名焉。長尺有二寸。居蔡,僭也。」④**山節藻梲**　朱注:「節,柱頭斗栱也。藻,水草名。梲,梁上短柱也。蓋為藏龜之室,而刻山於節、畫藻於梲也。」梲音濁。

解說　臧文仲私藏大龜,又以天子廟飾修建其家廟,這些都是僭禮的行為。

--------------------------------- ❈ **Chapter 16** ❈ ---------------------------------

The Master said of Tsze-ch'an that he had four of the characteristics of a superior man -- in his conduct of himself, he was humble; in serving his superior, he was respectful; in nourishing the people, he was kind; in ordering the people, he was just."

注釋　humble: adj. 謙卑；respectful: adj. 恭敬的；nourish: v. 養育。

--------------------------------- ❈ **Chapter 17** ❈ ---------------------------------

The Master said, "Yen P'ing knew well how to maintain friendly intercourse. The acquaintance might be long, but he showed the same respect as at first."

注釋　acquaintance: 熟識。

--------------------------------- ❈ **Chapter 18** ❈ ---------------------------------

The Master said, "Tsang Wan kept a large tortoise in a house, on the capitals of the pillars of which he had hills made, and with representations of duckweed on the small pillars above the beams supporting the rafters. -- Of what sort was his wisdom?"

注釋　tortoise: n. 龜；capital: n. 柱頭；pillar: n. 柱；hill: n. 山丘；representation: n. 描繪、表現；duckweed: n. 浮萍；beam: n. 橫樑；rafter: n. 椽。

————— ✤ 第十九章 ✤ —————

子張問曰：「令尹子文，三仕為令尹，無喜色；三已之，無慍色。舊令尹之政，必以告新令尹。何如？」子曰：「忠矣。」曰：「仁矣乎？」曰：「未知，焉得仁？」「崔子弒齊君，陳文子有馬十乘，棄而違之。至於他邦，則曰：『猶吾大夫崔子也。』違之。之一邦，則又曰：『猶吾大夫崔子也。』違之。何如？」子曰：「清矣。」曰：「仁矣乎？」曰：「未知。焉得仁？」

語譯　子張問說：「楚國的令尹子文，做了三次令尹，沒有任何喜色；被革職三次，也沒有埋怨的神情。他自己做令尹的施政，都會交接給新的令尹。這種人如何呢？」孔子說：「算是盡忠國家吧！」子張說：「那麼可以說是仁者嗎？」孔子說：「我不知道，這樣怎麼算得上仁者呢？」子張又說：「崔杼殺害齊莊公，當時的齊國大夫陳文子有四十匹馬，捨棄不要，離開齊國。到了別國，就說：『這裡的人還是和我們的崔大夫沒有兩樣。』於是又離開。這個人如何呢？」孔子說：「很清高。」子張說：「算是仁者嗎？」孔子說：「這個我不知道，怎麼算得上仁者呢？」

注釋　①令尹子文　令尹，楚國官名。子文，姓鬬，名穀於菟。②已之　罷官。③崔子弒齊君　齊國大夫崔杼殺害齊莊公。④陳文子　名須無，齊國大夫。⑤十乘　四十匹馬。⑥違　離去。⑦之一邦　之，往也。⑧清　清高。

解說　朱注：「子文……其為人也，喜怒不形，物我無間，知有其國而不知有其身，其忠盛矣，故子張疑其仁。然其所以三仕三已而告新令尹者，未知其皆出於天理而無人欲之私也，是以夫子但許其忠，而未許其仁也。……陳文子潔身去亂，可謂清矣，然未知其心果見義理之當然，而能脫然無所累乎？抑不得已於利害之私，而猶未免於怨悔也。故夫子特許其清，而不許其仁。」

————— ✤ 第二十章 ✤ —————

季文子三思而後行。子聞之，曰：「再，斯可矣。」

語譯　季文子做事都會考慮多次才行動。孔子聽到以後，就說：「考慮兩次就夠了。」

※ **Chapter 19** ※

19.1. Tsze-chang asked, saying, "The minister Tsze-wan thrice took office, and manifested no joy in his countenance. Thrice he retired from office, and manifested no displeasure. He made it a point to inform the new minister of the way in which he had conducted the government; what do you say of him?" The Master replied. "He was loyal." "Was he perfectly virtuous?" "I do not know. How can he be pronounced perfectly virtuous?"

19.2. Tsze-chang proceeded, "When the officer Ch'ui killed the prince of Ch'i, Ch'an Wan, though he was the owner of forty horses, abandoned them and left the country. Coming to another state, he said, 'They are here like our great officer, Ch'ui,' and left it. He came to a second state, and with the same observation left it also; -- what do you say of him?" The Master replied, "He was pure." "Was he perfectly virtuous?" "I do not know. How can he be pronounced perfectly virtuous?"

注釋　minister: n. 部長；thrice: adv. 三次；countenance: n. 臉色、表情；retire: v. 退職、隱退；displeasure: n. 不滿、不高興；make it a point to: 必定要；proceed: v. 繼續；pure: adj. 純潔的。

※ **Chapter 20** ※

Chi Wan thought thrice, and then acted. When the Master was informed of it, he said, "Twice may do."

注釋　twice: adv. 兩次。

注釋　①**季文子**　魯國大夫，姓季孫，名行父，諡爲文。②**三思**　三去聲，《正義》：「言思之多，能審愼也。」③**斯**　語助詞。

———— ✤ 第二十一章 ✤ ————

子曰：「甯武子，邦有道則知，邦無道則愚。其知可及也，其愚不可及也。」

語譯　孔子說：「甯武子這個人，國家安定時他就顯得很有才智，國家動亂時，他就裝得很笨拙。他的才智別人還跟得上，他裝得笨拙，別人就跟不上了。」

注釋　①**甯武子**　衛國大夫，姓甯名俞，諡爲武。甯音佞。②**知**　同智。③**愚**　程子說：「邦無道能沈晦以免患，故曰不可及也。亦有不當愚者，比干是也。」

解說　積極進取固然是很好，在局勢動亂的時候，也要知道韜光養晦。

———— ✤ 第二十二章 ✤ ————

子在陳，曰：「歸與！歸與！吾黨之小子狂簡，斐然成章，不知所以裁之。」

語譯　孔子在陳國說：「回去吧！回去吧！我們家鄉的學生們志向遠大又有能力，道德學問都很可觀，就是不知道如何裁剪。」

注釋　①**陳**　陳國。②**與**　語助詞。③**黨**　鄉黨。④**小子**　指學生們。⑤**狂簡**　朱注：「志大而略於事也。」或解釋爲進取有大志。⑥**斐然成章**　有文采。⑦**裁**　剪裁。

———— ✤ 第二十三章 ✤ ————

子曰：「伯夷、叔齊不念舊惡，怨是用希。」

語譯　孔子說：「伯夷、叔齊不計較過去的嫌隙，於是心裡就沒有什麼怨恨。」

注釋　①**伯夷、叔齊**　孤竹國王的兩個兒子，武王滅紂後，他們恥食周粟，餓死在首陽山。②**念**　記掛。③**舊惡**　夙怨。④**用**　所以。⑤**希**　很少。

※ **Chapter 21** ※

The Master said, "When good order prevailed in his country, Ning Wu acted the part of a wise man. When his country was in disorder, he acted the part of a stupid man. Others may equal his wisdom, but they cannot equal his stupidity."

注釋 act: v. 扮演、表現得像是；disorder: n. 失序、動亂；stupid: adj. 笨拙。

※ **Chapter 22** ※

When the Master was in Ch'an, he said, "Let me return! Let me return! The little children of my school are ambitious and too hasty. They are accomplished and complete so far, but they do not know how to restrict and shape themselves."

注釋 ambitious: adj. 胸懷大志；hasty: adj. 性急、草率；accomplished: adj. 有才能的；complete: adj. 完備的；restrict: v. 限制；shape: v. 塑造。

※ **Chapter 23** ※

The Master said, "Po-i and Shu-ch'i did not keep the former wickednesses of men in mind, and hence the resentments directed towards them were few."

注釋 wickedness: n. 惡意；resentment: n. 憤恨。

解說 「怨用是希」譯為 and hence the resentments directed towards them were few,

解說　〈述而〉：「求仁而得仁，又何怨？」人們猜想伯夷和叔齊如此遭遇，心裡應該會有怨恨吧，然而孔子有不同的看法。「怨是用希」也可以解釋爲「於是別人對他們沒什麼怨恨」，朱注：「孟子稱其『不立於惡人之朝，不與惡人言。與鄉人立，其冠不正，望望然去之，若將浼焉。』其介如此，宜若無所容矣，然其所惡之人，能改即止，故人亦不甚怨之也。」

━━━━━━━━ ❖ 第二十四章 ❖ ━━━━━━━━

子曰：「孰謂微生高直？或乞醯焉，乞諸其鄰而與之。」

語譯　孔子說：「誰說微生高這個人正直？有人跟他要醋，他不說自己沒有，卻到鄰家要來給他。」

注釋　①微生高　魯國人。姓微生名高。或謂尾生高。《莊子》〈盜跖〉：「尾生與女子期於梁下，女子不來，水至不去，抱梁柱而死。」②乞　求。③醯　酢、醋。

解說　朱注：「人來乞時，其家無有，故乞諸鄰家以與之。夫子言此，譏其曲意徇物，掠美市恩，不得爲直也。」這種鄉愿的人，孔子不認爲是正直的。

━━━━━━━━ ❖ 第二十五章 ❖ ━━━━━━━━

子曰：「巧言、令色、足恭，左丘明恥之，丘亦恥之。匿怨而友其人，左丘明恥之，丘亦恥之。」

語譯　孔子說：「說討人喜歡的話，裝著討人喜歡的臉色，還過度的謙卑，左丘明認爲可恥，我也認爲可恥。心裡很怨他，表面上卻裝得和他很要好，左丘明認爲可恥，我也認爲可恥。」

注釋　①足恭　足音巨，過度的意思。足恭，過度卑躬。②左丘明　魯國人，姓左丘名明。③匿怨而友其人　匿，藏也。心內相怨而外詐親。

━━━━━━━━ ❖ 第二十六章 ❖ ━━━━━━━━

顏淵、季路侍。子曰：「盍各言爾志？」子路曰：「願車馬、衣輕裘，與朋友共。敝之而無憾。」顏淵曰：「願無伐善，無施勞。」

是採用朱注解釋。

⁂ Chapter 24 ⁂

The Master said, "Who says of Weishang Kao that he is upright? One begged some vinegar of him, and he begged it of a neighbor and gave it to the man."

注釋　upright: adj. 正直；beg: v. 乞求；vinegar: n. 醋。

⁂ Chapter 25 ⁂

The Master said, "Fine words, an insinuating appearance, and excessive respect; -- Tso Ch'iu-ming was ashamed of them. I also am ashamed of them. To conceal resentment against a person, and appear friendly with him; -- Tso Ch'iu-ming was ashamed of such conduct. I also am ashamed of it."

注釋　insinuating: adj. 諂媚的；excessive: adj. 過度的；ashamed: adj. 以……爲恥 [of]。

⁂ Chapter 26 ⁂

26.1. Yen Yuan and Chi Lu being by his side, the Master said to them, "Come, let each of you tell his wishes."

子路曰：「願聞子之志。」子曰：「老者安之，朋友信之，少者懷之。」

語譯　顏淵和子路站在孔子身旁，孔子說：「你們何不說說自己的志願？」子路說：「我願把自己的車馬衣服都拿來和朋友分享，就是用壞了也不會怪朋友。」顏淵說：「我願不誇耀自己的好處，不表彰自己的功勞。」子路說：「我們也想聽聽夫子的志願。」孔子說：「我願老年人得到照顧而安樂，朋友們能夠彼此信實，小孩子也能得到教養。」

注釋　①侍　侍立一旁。②盍　何不。③衣輕裘　衣去聲，動詞。裘以輕者為美。或謂輕為衍字，而做「車馬衣裘」。④敝　壞。⑤伐善　伐，誇耀的意思。⑥施勞　施，彰顯；勞，有功。自誇有功勞。⑦老者安之，朋友信之，少者懷之　朱注：「老者養之以安，朋友與之以信，少者懷之以恩。」

解說　顏淵和子路的心願是在德性的修養。子路勇於義，而顏淵不自誇。他們心裡的人我分際還是很明顯。孔子心裡想的，則是天地萬物之化育，那是出於生命之間的內在感通，也是仁者境界的自然表現，孔子的心願，像冬天的暖陽，像春天的微風，煦煦然，徐徐然。朱熹說：「凡看論語，非但欲理會文字，須要識得聖賢氣象。」

※ 第二十七章 ※

子曰：「已矣乎！吾未見能見其過，而內自訟者也。」

語譯　孔子說：「算了吧！我還沒有見過發現自己有過錯而會在心裡自我責備的人。」

注釋　①已矣乎　算了吧。②訟　責備。

※ 第二十八章 ※

子曰：「十室之邑，必有忠信如丘者焉，不如丘之好學也。」

語譯　孔子說：「就算是只有十戶的小村子，總會有本性像我這樣忠信的人，但是沒有人像我這麼好學。」

注釋　①十室之邑　只有十戶人家的小地方。

26.2. Tsze-lu said, "I should like, having chariots and horses, and light fur clothes, to share them with my friends, and though they should spoil them, I would not be displeased."

26.3. Yen Yuan said, "I should like not to boast of my excellence, nor to make a display of my meritorious deeds."

26.4. Tsze-lu then said, "I should like, sir, to hear your wishes." The Master said, "They are, in regard to the aged, to give them rest; in regard to friends, to show them sincerity; in regard to the young, to treat them tenderly."

注釋 fur: n. 毛皮；spoil: v. 損壞；boast: v. 自誇 [of]；display: n. 展示；meritorious: adj. 有價值的。

Chapter 27

The Master said, "It is all over. I have not yet seen one who could perceive his faults, and inwardly accuse himself."

注釋 perceive: v. 覺知；inwardly: adv. 在內心裡；accuse: v. 譴責。

Chapter 28

The Master said, "In a hamlet of ten families, there may be found one honorable and sincere as I am, but not so fond of learning."

注釋 hamlet: n. 小村莊；honorable: adj. 高尚正直的。

第六章 雍也

---- ❋ 第一章 ❋ ----

子曰：「雍也，可使南面。」仲弓問子桑伯子，子曰：「可也，
簡。」仲弓曰：「居敬而行簡，以臨其民，不亦可乎？居簡而行
簡，無乃大簡乎？」子曰：「雍之言然。」

語譯　孔子說：「雍啊，可以叫他當個一國之君了。」仲弓問孔子說：「那麼子
　　　桑伯子呢？」孔子說：「還可以，他很寬略。」仲弓問：「態度認真而行
　　　事寬略，這樣來治理百姓，不就可以嗎？如果是態度隨便而做事寬略，那
　　　未免太疏略了嗎？」孔子說：「雍說得對。」

注釋　①**南面**　朱注：「南面者，人君聽治之位。」《集解》：「包曰：可使南
　　　面者，言任諸侯治。」②**子桑伯子**　魯國人。③**簡**　不擾也。《說苑》：
　　　「簡者，易野也。易野者，無禮文也。」④**敬**　認真。⑤**無乃**　未免。

解說　可使南面，也可以解釋為「有做官的才能」，朱注：「言仲弓寬洪簡重，
　　　有人君之度也。」居敬而行簡，就是與民休養生息，不擾民的意思。

---- ❋ 第二章 ❋ ----

哀公問：「弟子孰為好學？」孔子對曰：「有顏回者好學，不遷
怒，不貳過。不幸短命死矣！今也則亡，未聞好學者也。」

語譯　魯哀公問孔子說：「你的學生們哪個最好學？」孔子說：「有個叫顏回的
　　　學生，他最好學，他不拿別人發脾氣，不重複犯同樣的過錯，不幸短命死
　　　了！現在就沒有聽過好學的了。」

注釋　①**遷**　怒也。②**貳**　復也。③**亡**　同「無」。

解說　《史記》〈仲尼弟子傳〉：「顏回少孔子三十歲。年二十九，髮盡白，蚤
　　　死。」《孔子家語》〈弟子解〉：「三十一，早死。」《公羊傳》說顏回
　　　死於哀公十四年，當時孔子是七十一歲，那麼顏回應該享年四十一歲。

✦ **Chapter 1** ✦

1.1. The Master said, "There is Yung! -- He might occupy the place of a prince."

1.2. Chung-kung asked about Tsze-sang Po-tsze. The Master said, "He may pass. He does not mind small matters."

1.3. Chung-kung said, "If a man cherish in himself a reverential feeling of the necessity of attention to business, though he may be easy in small matters in his government of the people, that may be allowed. But if he cherish in himself that easy feeling, and also carry it out in his practice, is not such an easy mode of procedure excessive? "

1.4. The Master said, "Yung's words are right. "

注釋 occupy: v. 充任；pass: v. 及格；cherish: v. 心裡懷著；reverential: adj. 恭敬的；procedure: n. 程序。

解說 「簡」，not to mind small matters（不在意瑣事），或譯為 easygoing（寬大、隨遇而安）；「居敬」意譯為 cherish in himself a reverential feeling of the necessity of attention to business，太複雜了，可以譯為 abide in reverence。

✦ **Chapter 2** ✦

2.1. The Duke Ai asked which of the disciples loved to learn.

2.2. Confucius replied to him, "There was Yen Hui; he loved to learn. He did not transfer his anger; he did not repeat a fault. Unfortunately, his appointed time was short and he died; and now there is not such another. I have not yet heard of any one who loves to learn as he did."

注釋 transfer: v. 轉移；appointed: adj. 被指定的。

解說 「命」在這裡譯為 appointed time。

───────※ 第三章 ※───────

子華使於齊，冉子為其母請粟。子曰：「與之釜。」請益。曰：
「與之庾。」冉子與之粟五秉。子曰：「赤之適齊也，乘肥馬，衣
輕裘。吾聞之也，君子周急不繼富。」原思為之宰，與之粟九百，
辭。子曰：「毋！以與爾鄰里鄉黨乎！」

語譯 孔子讓子華出使到齊國，冉有為子華的母親請求米糧。孔子說：「給他六
斗四升。」冉有請求多給一些。孔子說：「再給他二斗四升。」結果冉有自
己給了她八十斛。孔子說：「赤這次去齊國，車前駕著肥馬，身上穿著輕
裘。我聽人家說，君子該濟助有急難的人，而不是使有錢的人更富裕。」原
思當孔子家的總管，孔子給他俸米九百斗，原思推辭不受。孔子說：「不要
推辭！有多的就給你鄉里的窮人吧！」

注釋 ①**子華** 公西赤，字子華，孔子弟子。②**使** 《正義》：「夫子使之也。」③
冉子 指冉有。④**粟** 這裡指米。⑤**釜** 六斗四升曰釜。⑥**益** 增加。⑦
庾 戴震說：「二斗四升曰庾。」⑧**秉** 十六斛曰秉。⑨**適** 往也。⑩**周
急** 朱注：「急，窮迫也。周者，補不足。」⑪**繼富** 朱注：「繼者，續
有餘。」⑫**原思為之宰** 《集解》：「包曰：弟子原憲，思，字也。孔子為
魯司寇，以原憲為家邑宰。」⑬**辭** 辭讓。⑭**毋** 止之詞也。

───────※ 第四章 ※───────

子謂仲弓曰：「犁牛之子，騂且角，雖欲勿用，山川其舍諸？」

語譯 孔子談到仲弓時說：「雜色的牛所生的小牛，卻有純赤色的毛和端正的
角，雖然不想拿來當作祭牛，但是山川之神會捨棄不用嗎？」

注釋 ①**犁牛** 犁，雜文，山川之祀不用不純色的牛。②**騂** 音星，赤色，周禮以
騂牛為祭牲。③**舍** 同「捨」，捨棄。

解說 孔子的意思是，拔擢賢能不必問其家世如何。

───────※ 第五章 ※───────

子曰：「回也，其心三月不違仁，其餘則日月至焉而已矣。」

語譯 孔子說：「顏回啊，他的心可以很久不離仁德，其他學生則只是偶而想到

Chapter 3

3.1. Tsze-hwa being employed on a mission to Ch'i, the disciple Zan requested grain for his mother. The Master said, "Give her a fu." Yen requested more. "Give her a yi," said the Master. Yen gave her five ping.

3.2. The Master said, "When Ch'ih was proceeding to Ch'i, he had fat horses to his carriage, and wore light furs. I have heard that a superior man helps the distressed, but does not add to the wealth of the rich."

3.3. Yuan Sze being made governor of his town by the Master, he gave him nine hundred measures of grain, but Sze declined them.

3.4. The Master said, "Do not decline them. May you not give them away in the neighborhoods, hamlets, towns, and villages?"

注釋　mission: n. 使節、任務；on a mission: 出差；request: v. 請求；grain: n. 穀物；distressed: adj. 窮困的；decline: v. 婉拒。

解說　釜、庾、秉，都是計量單位，音譯爲 fu, yi, ping。

Chapter 4

The Master, speaking of Chung-kung, said, "If the calf of a brindled cow be red and horned, although men may not wish to use it, would the spirits of the mountains and rivers put it aside?"

注釋　calf: n. 小牛；brindled: adj. 有斑紋的；cow: n. 母牛；horned: adj. 有角的。

Chapter 5

The Master said, "Such was Hui that for three months there would be nothing in his mind contrary to perfect virtue. The others may attain to this on some days or in some months, but nothing more."

而已。」

注釋 ①**三月** 言其久。《正義》：「三月爲一時，過三月竟則移時。」②**日月至焉** 朱注：「或日一至焉，或月一至焉，能造其域而不能久也。」

解說 《集解》：「餘人暫有至仁時，唯回移時而不變。」

------ ※ 第六章 ※ ------

季康子問：「仲由可使從政也與？」子曰：「由也果，於從政乎何有？」曰：「賜也可使從政也與？」曰：「賜也達，於從政乎何有？」曰：「求也可使從政也與？」曰：「求也藝，於從政乎何有？」

語譯 季康子問孔子說：「可以叫仲由處理政事嗎？」孔子說：「仲由很果斷，處理政事有什麼難的呢？」季康子又問：「那麼端木賜呢？可以叫他處理政事嗎？」孔子說：「賜通情達理，處理政事有什麼難的呢？」又問：「那麼冉求呢？可以叫他處理政事嗎？」孔子說：「冉求多才多藝，處理政事有什麼難的呢？」

注釋 ①**果** 果敢決斷。②**何有** 何難之有。③**達** 通達。④**藝** 多才藝。

------ ※ 第七章 ※ ------

季氏使閔子騫為費宰。閔子騫曰：「善為我辭焉。如有復我者，則吾必在汶上矣。」

語譯 季氏請人叫閔子騫當費邑的邑長。閔子騫說：「好好地替我推辭掉吧。如果再來找我的話，那麼我就不得不逃到汶水以北了。」

注釋 ①**閔子騫** 姓閔名損，字子騫，孔子弟子。②**費** 音必，季氏邑。③**復** 又來找我。④**汶上** 汶水在齊南魯北。

------ ※ 第八章 ※ ------

伯牛有疾，子問之，自牖執其手，曰：「亡之，命矣夫！斯人也，而有斯疾也！斯人也，而有斯疾也！」

⁂ **Chapter 6** ⁂

Chi K'ang asked about Chung-yu, whether he was fit to be employed as an officer of government. The Master said, "Yu is a man of decision; what difficulty would he find in being an officer of government?" K'ang asked, "Is Ts'ze fit to be employed as an officer of government?" and was answered, "Ts'ze is a man of intelligence; what difficulty would he find in being an officer of government?" And to the same question about Ch'iu the Master gave the same reply, saying, "Ch'iu is a man of various ability."

注釋　various: adj. 各式各樣的。

⁂ **Chapter 7** ⁂

The chief of the Chi family sent to ask Min Tsze-ch'ien to be governor of Pi. Min Tszech'ien said, "Decline the offer for me politely. If any one come again to me with a second invitation, I shall be obliged to go and live on the banks of the Wan."

注釋　offer: n. 提議；politely: adv. 有禮貌地；invitation: n. 邀請；obliged: adj. 不得不；bank: n. 河岸。

⁂ **Chapter 8** ⁂

Po-niu being ill, the Master went to ask for him. He took hold of his hand through the window, and said, "It is killing him. It is the appointment of

語譯　冉伯牛生了重病，孔子去探望他，從南窗外握他的手說：「活不成了，這是命吧！這樣的人，居然會有這種病！這樣的人，居然會有這種病！」

注釋　①伯牛　孔子弟子，姓冉名耕，字伯牛。②牖　窗戶，音「有」。朱注：「牖，南牖也。禮：病者居北牖下。君視之，則遷於南牖下，使君得以南面視己。時伯牛家以此禮尊孔子，孔子不敢當，故不入其室，而自牖執其手，蓋與之永訣也。」③亡之　《集解》：「孔曰：亡，喪也。疾甚，故執其手曰喪之。」

解說　「亡之」也可以讀爲「無之」，就是說「沒這個道理啊」。《淮南子》：「子夏失明，冉伯牛爲厲。」或謂伯牛感染類似痲瘋病的惡疾，所以孔子沒有進房間去探視。

※ 第九章 ※

子曰：「賢哉，回也！一簞食，一瓢飲，在陋巷。人不堪其憂，回也不改其樂。賢哉，回也！」

語譯　孔子說：「眞是賢者啊，顏回！一竹筐的飯，一瓜瓢的水，住在破屋子裡。別人都受不了這種苦，顏回卻不改變他的快樂。眞是賢者啊，顏回！」

注釋　①簞　音單，笥也，竹器。②瓢　瓠、勺也。③陋巷　狹小的屋子。

解說　朱注：「程子曰：昔受學於周茂叔，令尋顏子仲尼樂處，所樂何事。」孔顏所樂何事，是宋明理學的重要課題。

※ 第十章 ※

冉求曰：「非不說子之道，力不足也。」子曰：「力不足者，中道而廢。今女畫。」

語譯　冉求說：「我不是不喜歡老師的道理，而是我的能力不夠。」孔子說：「能力不夠的，會走到半途才停下來。而你卻是畫地自限不想走。」

注釋　①說　同悅。②中道而廢　《集解》：「鄭曰：廢，喻力極罷頓，不能復行則止也。」走到力氣不夠了才停下來。③畫　朱注：「畫者，能進而不欲。謂之畫者，如畫地以自限也。」

Heaven, alas! That such a man should have such a sickness! That such a man should have such a sickness!"

注釋　alas: interj. 唉。

解說　「命」譯爲 the appointment of Heaven。

─────────── ❋ **Chapter 9** ❋ ───────────

The Master said, "Admirable indeed was the virtue of Hui! With a single bamboo dish of rice, a single gourd dish of drink, and living in his mean narrow lane, while others could not have endured the distress, he did not allow his joy to be affected by it. Admirable indeed was the virtue of Hui!"

注釋　admirable: adj. 傑出的、值得讚賞的；bamboo: n. 竹；gourd: n. 葫蘆、瓜科植物；mean: adj. 簡陋的；endure: v. 忍受；affect: v.影響。

─────────── ❋ **Chapter 10** ❋ ───────────

Yen Ch'iu said, "It is not that I do not delight in your doctrines, but my strength is insufficient." The Master said, "Those whose strength is insufficient give over in the middle of the way but now you limit yourself."

注釋　delight: v. 很喜歡 [in]；insufficient: adj. 不足；give over: 停止；limit: v. 限制。

---※ 第十一章 ※---

子謂子夏曰：「女為君子儒，無為小人儒。」

語譯　孔子對子夏說：「你該做個君子儒，不要做個小人儒。」

注釋　①無　同「毋」。

解說　《正義》：「周官太宰：四曰儒以道得民。注：儒，諸侯保氏有六藝以教
　　　民者。大司徒：四曰聯師儒。注：師儒，鄉里教以道藝者。據此，則儒為
　　　教民者。子夏於時設教，有門人，故夫子告以為儒之道。君子儒，能識
　　　大而可大受，小人儒，則但務卑近而已。」關於「儒」的定義，《孔子家
　　　語・儒行解》也有精闢的闡述。

---※ 第十二章 ※---

子游為武城宰。子曰：「女得人焉爾乎？」曰：「有澹臺滅明者，
行不由徑。非公事，未嘗至於偃之室也。」

語譯　子游當武城的邑宰。孔子說：「你在那裡有沒有發掘到什麼人才？」子游
　　　說：「有個叫澹臺滅明的，從來不走小路捷徑。除了公事以外，從來不到
　　　我屋子裡來。」

注釋　①武城　魯邑。②焉爾　於此。③澹臺滅明　字子羽，孔子弟子。④徑　路
　　　之小而捷者。

解說　朱注：「不由徑，則動必以正，而無見小欲速之意可知。非公事不見邑
　　　宰，則其有以自守，而無枉己徇人之私可見矣。」

---※ 第十三章 ※---

子曰：「孟之反不伐。奔而殿，將入門，策其馬，曰：『非敢後也，
馬不進也。』」

語譯　孔子說：「孟之反從不自誇。敗戰時他殿後，要進城門時，他還故意鞭打
　　　自己的馬說：『我不是敢押後拒敵，實在是我的馬跑不快啊！』」

注釋　①孟之反　魯國大夫，《左傳》作孟之側。②不伐　不自誇。③奔而殿　朱
　　　注：「奔，敗走也。軍後曰殿。」④策　鞭打。

--- ⁕ **Chapter 11** ⁕ ---

The Master said to Tsze-hsia, "Do you be a scholar after the style of the superior man, and not after that of the mean man."

--- ⁕ **Chapter 12** ⁕ ---

Tsze-yu being governor of Wu-ch'ang, the Master said to him, "Have you got good men there?" He answered, "There is Tan-t'ai Miehming, who never in walking takes a short cut, and never comes to my office, excepting on public business."

注釋 short cut: 捷徑。

--- ⁕ **Chapter 13** ⁕ ---

The Master said, "Mang Chih-fan does not boast of his merit. Being in the rear on an occasion of flight, when they were about to enter the gate, he whipped up his horse, saying, 'It is not that I dare to be last. My horse would not advance.'"

注釋 boast: 自誇 [of]；in the rear: 在後面、後陣；whip: v. 鞭打；advance: v. 前進。

———————※ 第十四章 ※———————

子曰：「不有祝鮀之佞，而有宋朝之美，難乎免於今之世矣！」

語譯　孔子說：「如果沒有祝鮀那樣的口才，反而有宋朝那樣的美貌，在今天的社會裡，難免要招來災禍吧！」

注釋　①**祝鮀**　衛大夫，字子魚。祝，宗廟官名。②**佞**　有口才。③**宋朝**　宋公子朝，有美色。

解說　朱注：「言衰世好諛悅色，非此難免，蓋傷之也。」

———————※ 第十五章 ※———————

子曰：「誰能出不由戶？何莫由斯道也？」

語譯　孔子說：「誰能出外不經過大門的？為什麼沒有人要走正當的路呢？」

注釋　①**莫**　無也。

———————※ 第十六章 ※———————

子曰：「質勝文則野，文勝質則史。文質彬彬，然後君子。」

語譯　孔子說：「本質多過文采，就難免粗野，文采多過本質，又會太虛誇。只有文采和本質配合適當，才能成為君子。」

注釋　①**質**　《正義》：「質，本也。」②**文**　文飾。③**野**　《集解》：「包曰：野如野人，言鄙略也。」④**史**　朱注：「史，掌文書，多聞習事，而誠或不足也。」⑤**彬彬**　鄭注：「雜半貌也。」

解說　無論是社會或是個人，在原始的人性和文化的教養之間，都要取得平衡。

———————※ 第十七章 ※———————

子曰：「人之生也直，罔之生也幸而免。」

語譯　孔子說：「人的存在有其正道，但是不正直的人也可以生存，那只是他僥倖免於禍害而已。」

---------------- ❋ **Chapter 14** ❋ ----------------

The Master said, "Without the specious speech of the litanist T'o and the beauty of the prince Chao of Sung, it is difficult to escape in the present age."

注釋　litanist: n. 廟官。

解說　比較另一種譯法：Confucius said: "Without the smooth speech of Preacher T'o or the good looks of Prince Chao of Sung, it is difficult to stay out of trouble in the present age."

---------------- ❋ **Chapter 15** ❋ ----------------

The Master said, "Who can go out but by the door? How is it that men will not walk according to these ways?"

注釋　but: 而不。

---------------- ❋ **Chapter 16** ❋ ----------------

The Master said, "Where the solid qualities are in excess of accomplishments, we have rusticity; where the accomplishments are in excess of the solid qualities, we have the manners of a clerk. When the accomplishments and solid qualities are equally blended, we then have the man of virtue."

注釋　in excess of: 超過；rusticity: n. 粗魯；clerk: n. 辦事員；blend: v. 混合。

解說　「質」在這裡直譯為 solid quality，也可以譯為 nature。

---------------- ❋ **Chapter 17** ❋ ----------------

The Master said, "Man is born for uprightness. If a man lose his uprightness, and yet live, his escape from death is the effect of mere good fortune."

注釋　fortune: n. 運氣。

注釋　①**人之生也直**　《集解》：「馬曰：言人所以生於世而自終者，以其正直也。」生，存在的意思。②**罔**　不直也。

解說　《正義》：「鄭此注云：始生之性皆正直。」朱注：「上生字爲始生之生，下生字爲生存之生。雖不同而意相足。」劉宗周說：「舉人生而歸之直，此夫子之道性善也。」宋明理學認爲這句話是在談人性的問題，似乎是過度解釋。

———— ✻ 第十八章 ✻ ————

子曰：「知之者不如好之者，好之者不如樂之者。」

語譯　孔子說：「做學問的人，知道的不如喜好的，而喜好的又不如樂在其中的。」

解說　《集解》：「包曰：學問知之者，不如好之者篤。好之者，不如樂之者深。」

———— ✻ 第十九章 ✻ ————

子曰：「中人以上，可以語上也；中人以下，不可以語上也。」

語譯　孔子說：「中等資質以上的人，可以和他談高深的學問；中等資質以下的人，很難和他談高深的學問。」

注釋　①**語**　去聲。告也。②**不可**　難以。

解說　這是因材施教。

———— ✻ 第二十章 ✻ ————

樊遲問知。子曰：「務民之義，敬鬼神而遠之，可謂知矣。」問仁。曰：「仁者先難而後獲，可謂仁矣。」

語譯　樊遲問如何才是智。孔子說：「專注於人所應該做的事，尊敬鬼神但是保持距離，就可以說是智了。」又問如何是仁：「仁者比別人還勇於吃苦，而賞報的時候則退居人後，就可以說是仁了。」

解說 「人之生也直」譯爲 Man is born for uprightness，是依據朱注的解釋。

──────────────── ❋ **Chapter 18** ❋ ────────────────

The Master said, "They who know the truth are not equal to those who love it, and they who love it are not equal to those who delight in it."

──────────────── ❋ **Chapter 19** ❋ ────────────────

The Master said, "To those whose talents are above mediocrity, the highest subjects may be announced. To those who are below mediocrity, the highest subjects may not be announced."

注釋 talent: n. 才能；mediocrity: n. 平庸、中等；subject: n. 主題。

──────────────── ❋ **Chapter 20** ❋ ────────────────

Fan Ch'ih asked what constituted wisdom. The Master said, "To give one's self earnestly to the duties due to men, and, while respecting spiritual beings, to keep aloof from them, may be called wisdom." He asked about perfect virtue. The Master said, "The man of virtue makes the difficulty to be overcome his first business, and success only a subsequent consideration; -- this may be called perfect virtue."

注釋　①民　人也。

解說　《禮記‧表記》：「子曰：夏道尊命，事鬼敬神而遠之，近人而忠焉。殷人尊神，率民以事神，先鬼而後禮。周人尊禮尙施，事鬼神而遠之，近人而忠焉。」《正義》：「敬鬼神而遠之，謂以禮敬事鬼神也。」孔子推崇周朝的人文主義精神。「先難而後獲」就是范仲淹所說的「先天下之憂而憂，後天下之樂而樂」。朱注：「先其事之所難，而後其效之所得，仁者之心也。」則是說先勞苦然後才想到收穫。

———————— ❋ 第二十一章 ❋ ————————

子曰：「知者樂水，仁者樂山；知者動，仁者靜；知者樂，仁者壽。」

語譯　孔子說：「智者喜好水，仁者喜好山；智者好動而積極進取，仁者好靜而少欲知足；智者快樂，仁者活得久。」

注釋　①知者樂水　樂音要。②知者樂　樂音勒。

解說　朱注：「知者達於事理而周流無滯，有似於水，故樂水；仁者安於義理而厚重不遷，有似於山，故樂山。動靜以體言，樂壽以效言也。動而不括故樂，靜而有常故壽。」孔子以山水比喻智者和仁者的情境，也透顯出以天地萬物爲一體的生命感通。

———————— ❋ 第二十二章 ❋ ————————

子曰：「齊一變，至於魯；魯一變，至於道。」

語譯　孔子說：「齊國一次的改革，就可以媲美魯國，而魯國一次的改革，就可以合於正道。」

解說　朱注：「孔子之時，齊俗急功利，喜夸詐，乃霸政之餘習。魯則重禮教，崇信義，猶有先王之遺風焉，但人亡政息，不能無廢墜爾。道，則先王之道也。言二國之政俗有美惡，故其變而之道有難易。」

注釋　to give oneself to: 埋首於；earnestly: adv. 認眞地；due to: 應歸於；aloof: adj. 遠離 [from]；subsequent: adj. 以後的。

解說　「先難而獲」採朱注意譯。

✳ **Chapter 21** ✳

The Master said, "The wise find pleasure in water; the virtuous find pleasure in hills. The wise are active; the virtuous are tranquil. The wise are joyful; the virtuous are long-lived."

注釋　hill: n. 山丘；tranquil: adj. 平靜的；long-lived: 長命。

✳ **Chapter 22** ✳

The Master said, "Ch'i, by one change, would come to the State of Lu. Lu, by one change, would come to a State where true principles predominated."

注釋　predominate: 支配、佔優勢。

———————※ 第二十三章 ※———————

子曰：「觚不觚，觚哉！觚哉！」

語譯　孔子說：「觚不像個觚，還叫什麼觚啊！還叫什麼觚啊！」

注釋　①觚　禮器。

解說　朱注：「觚，棱也，或曰酒器，或曰木簡，皆器之有棱者也。不觚者，蓋
　　　當時失其制而不爲棱也。觚哉觚哉，言不得爲觚也。」是說觚應該是有稜
　　　角的，而當時的人破觚爲圓，仍稱爲觚，是故孔子嘆名實不符。《五經異
　　　義》：「今韓詩說，一升曰爵。爵，盡也，足也。二升曰觚，寡也，飲當
　　　寡少。」也有說是觚有飲酒寡少的含意，而時人用觚酌酒，卻沉湎無度，
　　　所以孔子嘆不知禮。

———————※ 第二十四章 ※———————

宰我問曰：「仁者，雖告之曰：『井有仁焉。』其從之也？」子曰：
「何爲其然也？君子可逝也，不可陷也；可欺也，不可罔也。」

語譯　宰我問孔子說：「有人告訴仁者說：『有人掉到井裡去。』他會跟著跳下
　　　去嗎？」孔子說：「怎麼可能呢？你可以騙君子過去看，但是不可能騙他
　　　跳下去。你可以用合理的事去欺騙他，但是沒辦法用不合理的事使他上
　　　當。」

注釋　①井有仁焉　「仁」從「人」字解。②逝　往救也。③陷　陷害。④罔　誣
　　　罔也。

解說　朱注：「欺，謂誑之以理之所有。罔，謂昧之以理之所無。蓋身在井上，
　　　乃可以救井中之人；若從之於井，則不復能救之矣。此理甚明，人所易
　　　曉，仁者雖切於救人而不私其身，然不應如此之愚也。」俞樾說：「君子
　　　殺身成仁則有之，故可得而摧折，不可以非理陷害之。」

———————※ 第二十五章 ※———————

子曰：「君子博學於文，約之以禮，亦可以弗畔矣夫！」

語譯　孔說：「君子廣泛地學習典章文獻，以禮來約束自己，也就可以不背離正

❈ **Chapter 23** ❈

The Master said, "A cornered vessel without corners -- a strange cornered vessel! A strange cornered vessel!"

注釋　cornered: adj. 有角的。

❈ **Chapter 24** ❈

Tsai Wo asked, saying, "A benevolent man, though it be told him, -- 'There is a man in the well'" will go in after him, I suppose." Confucius said, "Why should he do so?" A superior man may be made to go to the well, but he cannot be made to go down into it. He may be imposed upon, but he cannot be fooled."

注釋　to impose upon: 欺騙；fool: v. 愚弄。

❈ **Chapter 25** ❈

The Master said, "The superior man, extensively studying all learning, and keeping himself under the restraint of the rules of propriety, may thus likewise not overstep what is right."

道了。」

注釋　①文　典籍制度。②約　約束。③弗畔　畔同叛。弗畔，不違道。

※ 第二十六章 ※

子見南子，子路不說。夫子矢之曰：「予所否者，天厭之！天厭之！」

語譯　孔子去見南子，子路很不高興。孔子發誓說：「我所做所爲，如果有不義的地方，天會棄絕我！天會棄絕我！」

注釋　①南子　衛靈公夫人，有淫行。②不說　不悅。③矢　誓也。④所　如果。⑤否　謂不合於禮。⑥厭　厭棄。

解說　《史記·孔子世家》：「去即過蒲。月餘，反乎衛，主蘧伯玉家。靈公夫人有南子者，使人謂孔子曰：四方之君子不辱欲與寡君爲兄弟者，必見寡小君。寡小君願見。孔子辭謝，不得已而見之。夫人在絺帷中。孔子入門，北面稽首。夫人自帷中再拜，環珮玉聲璆然。孔子曰：吾鄉爲弗見，見之禮答焉。」

※ 第二十七章 ※

子曰：「中庸之為德也，其至矣乎！民鮮久矣。」

語譯　孔子說：「中庸這種道德，可以說是極致了！但是人們很久都沒有這個德性了。」

注釋　①中庸　《集解》：「庸，常也。中和可常行之德。」②至　極致。

解說　朱注：「程子曰：不偏之謂中，不易之謂庸；中者天下之正道，庸者天下之定理。自世教衰，民不興於行，少有此德久矣。」

※ 第二十八章 ※

子貢曰：「如有博施於民而能濟眾，何如？可謂仁乎？」子曰：「何事於仁，必也聖乎！堯舜其猶病諸！夫仁者，己欲立而立人，己欲達而達人。能近取譬，可謂仁之方也已。」

注釋　extensively: adv. 廣泛地；learning: n. 學問；overstep: v. 逾越。

Chapter 26

The Master having visited Nan-tsze, Tsze-lu was displeased, on which the Master swore, saying, "Wherein I have done improperly, may Heaven reject me, may Heaven reject me!"

注釋　swear: [swore; sworn] v. 發誓；wherein adv. 在什麼地方；reject: v. 拒絕。

Chapter 27

The Master said, "Perfect is the virtue which is according to the Constant Mean! Rare for a long time has been its practice among the people."

注釋　constant: adj. 不變的；mean: adj. 中間的。

解說　「中庸」直譯為 the Constant Mean。

Chapter 28

28.1. Tsze-kung said, "Suppose the case of a man extensively conferring benefits on the people, and able to assist all, what would you say of him? Might he be called perfectly virtuous?" The Master said, "Why

語譯　子貢說：「如果有人可以廣泛地為百姓謀福利，又能夠濟助大眾，怎麼樣，可以說是仁者嗎？」孔子說：「何止是仁者呢，那必定是聖人了！堯舜恐怕還做不到呢！所謂仁者，自己想安身立命，也要幫助別人安身立命，自己想要施展抱負，也要幫助別人施展抱負。能以自己做例子，為別人設想，就可以說是仁道的方向了。」

注釋　①**博施**　朱注：「施，去聲。博，廣也。」廣施恩惠。②**濟眾**　濟民於患難。③**何事於仁**　何止於仁。④**諸**　之乎。⑤**譬**　譬喻。⑥**方**　途徑、方法。

解說　如果能夠博施濟眾，那可以說是聖人了。那麼仁是什麼呢？孔子說是己立立人，己達達人。先從自身做起，不必好高騖遠。《正義》：「立謂身能立道也，達謂道可行諸人也。」

speak only of virtue in connection with him? Must he not have the qualities of a sage? Even Yao and Shun were still solicitous about this.

28.2. "Now the man of perfect virtue, wishing to be established himself, seeks also to establish others; wishing to be enlarged himself, he seeks also to enlarge others.

28.3. "To be able to judge of others by what is nigh in ourselves; -- this may be called the art of virtue."

注釋　confer: 授與 [on]；benefit: n. 恩惠；assist: v. 援助；sage: n. 聖哲；solicitous: adj. 擔心 [about]；establish: v. 立身；enlarge: v. 擴展；judge: v. 判斷 [of]； nigh: adj. 接近的。

述而第七

※ 第一章 ※

子曰：「述而不作，信而好古，竊比於我老彭。」

語譯　孔子說：「我只傳述古人的遺法，而不創始制作，篤信而喜好古代的典章制度，我私自效法老彭。」

注釋　①述而不作　《正義》：「說文云：述，循也。作，起也。述是循舊，作是創始。」②竊比　私自比擬。③老彭　《集解》：「包曰：老彭，殷賢大夫，好述古事。」

解說　《正義》：「禮記中庸云：非天子不議禮，不制度，不考文。議禮、制度、考文皆作者之事，然必天子乃得爲之。」孔子不在其位，不敢創制禮樂，而只是傳述之。鄭注以「老彭」爲老聃和彭祖二人，異於包咸的說法。

※ 第二章 ※

子曰：「默而識之，學而不厭，誨人不倦，何有於我哉？」

語譯　孔子說：「把所學到的知識默默記在心裡，勤學而不厭棄，教導別人而不倦怠，這些對我有什麼困難呢？」

注釋　①識　記住。②誨　教導。③何有　有何困難。

解說　「何有於我哉」，朱注：「何有於我，言何者能有於我也。」楊伯峻譯爲「這些事情我做到了哪些呢？」

※ 第三章 ※

子曰：「德之不脩，學之不講，聞義不能徙，不善不能改，是吾憂也。」

語譯　孔子說：「品德不加以修養，學問不加以講習，聽到合於義的事卻無法遵行，有了過失卻不能改正，這是我擔憂的。」

注釋　①之　語助詞，無意義。②講　習也。③徙　遷而從之。

---- ❖ **Chapter 1** ❖ ----

The Master said, "A transmitter and not a maker, believing in and loving the ancients, I venture to compare myself with our old P'ang."

注釋　transmitter: n. 傳達者；venture: v. 膽敢、冒昧。

---- ❖ **Chapter 2** ❖ ----

The Master said, "The silent treasuring up of knowledge; learning without satiety; and instructing others without being wearied: -- which one of these things belongs to me?"

注釋　silent: adj. 沉默的；treasure: v. 銘記於心 [up]；satiety: n. 饜足；wearied: adj. 厭倦的。

---- ❖ **Chapter 3** ❖ ----

The Master said, "The learning virtue without proper cultivation; the not thoroughly discussing what is learned; not being able to move towards righteousness of which a knowledge is gained; and not being able to change what is not good: -- these are the things which occasion me solicitude."

注釋　cultivation: n. 教養；thoroughly: adv. 徹底地；solicitude: n. 擔心。

解說　比較以下譯法：Confucius said: "Having virtue and not cultivating it; studying and not sifting; hearing what is just and not following; not being able to change wrongdoing: these are the things that make me uncomfortable."

———— ✦ 第四章 ✦ ————

子之燕居，申申如也，夭夭如也。

語譯　孔子閒居在家的時候，舒適而怡然自得。

注釋　①**燕居**　燕或作晏，安也。燕居，閒居的意思。②**申申如也，夭夭如也**　朱
　　　　注：「楊氏曰：申申，其容舒也。夭夭，其色愉也。」

———— ✦ 第五章 ✦ ————

子曰：「甚矣吾衰也！久矣吾不復夢見周公。」

語譯　孔子說：「我衰老得真是快啊！很久了，我已經不再夢見周公了。」

注釋　①**周公**　姓姬名旦，武王之弟，成文、武之德，致治太平，制禮作樂。

解說　朱注：「孔子盛時，志欲行周公之道，故夢寐之間，如或見之。至其老而
　　　　不能行也，則無復是心，而亦無復是夢矣，故因此而自歎其衰之甚也。」

———— ✦ 第六章 ✦ ————

子曰：「志於道，據於德，依於仁，游於藝。」

語譯　孔子說：「以淑世之道為志向，以德性為根據，以仁德為依歸，而優游於
　　　　六藝之間。」

解說　這是孔子教學的四個條目。朱注：「志者，心之所之之謂。道，則人倫日
　　　　用之間所當行者是也。如此而心必之焉，則所適者正，而無他歧之惑矣。
　　　　據者，執守之意。德則行道而有得於心者也。得之於心而守之不失，則
　　　　終始惟一，而有日新之功矣。依者，不違之謂。仁，則私欲盡去而心德
　　　　之全也。功夫至此而無終食之違，則存養之熟，無適而非天理之流行矣。
　　　　游者，玩物適情之謂。藝，則禮樂之文，射、御、書、數之法，皆至理所
　　　　寓，而日用之不可闕者也。朝夕游焉，以博其義理之趣，則應務有餘，而
　　　　心亦無所放矣。」

———— ✦ 第七章 ✦ ————

子曰：「自行束脩以上，吾未嘗無誨焉。」

—※ **Chapter 4** ※—

When the Master was unoccupied with business, his manner was easy, and he looked pleased.

注釋　unoccupied: adj. 空閒的；manner: n. 舉止、態度。

—※ **Chapter 5** ※—

The Master said, "Extreme is my decay. For a long time, I have not dreamed, as I was wont to do, that I saw the duke of Chau."

注釋　decay: n. 衰退；wont: adj. 慣於、經常。

—※ **Chapter 6** ※—

6.1.　The Master said, "Let the will be set on the path of duty.

6.2.　"Let every attainment in what is good be firmly grasped.

6.3.　"Let perfect virtue be accorded with.

6.4.　"Let relaxation and enjoyment be found in the polite arts."

注釋　set on: 朝向；firmly: adv. 牢固；grasp: v. 緊握；accord: v. 相符 [with]；relaxation: n. 消遣、娛樂；polite: adj. 高雅的、有教養的。

解說　本章意譯自朱注的解釋，語譯爲：「孔子說：『使意志朝向（心之所之）義務之路（人倫日用之間所當行者）；心裡領悟到的德性（行道而有得於心者也）牢牢把握（守之不失）；和仁德一致（不違）；在六藝裡找到快樂（玩物適情）。』」

—※ **Chapter7** ※—

The Master said, "From the man bringing his bundle of dried flesh for my

語譯　孔子說：「只要自行準備十條肉乾以上的見面禮，我沒有不予以教導的。」

注釋　①**束脩**　脩者肉乾，十脡爲束。皇侃疏：「古者相見，必執物爲贄……束脩，最輕者。」

※ 第八章 ※

子曰：「不憤不啓，不悱不發，舉一隅不以三隅反，則不復也。」

語譯　孔子說：「如果不是很想求知而不得的時候，我不會去開導他，如果不是很想表達而說不出來的時候，我不會去啓發他，告訴他桌子有一個角，而不知道還有其他三個角，我也不再教他了。」

注釋　①**憤**　朱注：「心求通而未得之意。」②**悱**　朱注：「口欲言而未能之貌。」③**隅**　角也。④**不復**　不再教了。

解說　這就是孔子啓發式教學方法，在現代的教育理論裡仍然非常重要。《集解》：「鄭曰：孔子與人言，必待其人心憤憤，口悱悱，乃後啓發爲說之。如此，則識思之深也。說則舉一隅以語之，其人不思其類，則不復重教之。」學生必須先對問題認眞思考並且試著去解說，然後老師才予以解答，有孜孜不倦的學習動機，習得的知識才會根基深厚；其次，學生也要能夠舉一反三，才不會讀死書。

※ 第九章 ※

子食於有喪者之側，未嘗飽也。子於是日哭，則不歌。

語譯　孔子在服喪的人旁邊吃飯的時候，從來沒有吃飽過。在那天弔喪哭過後，就不再唱歌。

解說　這是人類同情心的自然流露。《集解》：「喪者哀慼，飽食於其側，是無惻隱之心。一日之中，或哭或歌，是褻於禮容。」

※ 第十章 ※

子謂顏淵曰：「用之則行，舍之則藏，唯我與爾有是夫！」子路曰：「子行三軍，則誰與？」子曰：「暴虎馮河，死而無悔者，吾不與也。必也臨事而懼，好謀而成者也。」

teaching upwards, I have never refused instruction to any one."

注釋　bundle: n. 捆、把、束；upwards: adv.以上。

Chapter 8

The Master said, "I do not open up the truth to one who is not eager to get knowledge, nor help out any one who is not anxious to explain himself. When I have presented one corner of a subject to any one, and he cannot from it learn the other three, I do not repeat my lesson."

注釋　anxious: adj. 渴望的；repeat: v. 重複。

Chapter 9

9.1. When the Master was eating by the side of a mourner, he never ate to the full.

9.2. He did not sing on the same day in which he had been weeping.

注釋　mourner: n. 服喪者；weep: v. 哭泣。

Chapter 10

10.1. The Master said to Yen Yuan, "When called to office, to undertake its duties; when not so called, to lie retired; -- it is only I and you who have attained to this."

語譯　孔子對顏淵說：「有人用我的時候，就行道於世，沒有人要用我的時候，就藏道於身，只有我和你才能做得到吧：」子路說：「如果夫子指揮軍隊要打仗，要和誰一起去呢？」孔子說：「徒手打老虎，游泳渡河，死了都不後悔的人，我不會和他共事。遇事小心謹慎、計畫周詳才行動的人，我才會和他共事。」

注釋　①舍　同捨。②爾　指顏淵。③三軍　皇侃疏：「天子六軍，大國三軍，小國一軍。」④暴虎　徒手搏虎。⑤馮河　馮音平，徒身涉河。⑥成　決定。

解說　朱注：「尹氏曰：用舍無與於己，行藏安於所遇，命不足道也。顏子幾於聖人，故亦能之。」孟子說：「古之人，得志，澤加於民；不得志，脩身見於世。窮則獨善其身，達則兼善天下。」無論窮通順逆，舒卷之間，無入而不自得，這是仁者的境界吧。《集解》：「孔曰：子路見孔子獨美顏淵，以爲己勇。至於夫子爲三軍將，亦當誰與己同，故發此問。」

※ 第十一章 ※

子曰：「富而可求也，雖執鞭之士，吾亦爲之；如不可求，從吾所好。」

語譯　孔子說：「財富如果是可以求得的話，就是執鞭的工作，我也會去做。如果是不可求得的，那還是照我自己喜歡的方式去做吧。」

注釋　①執鞭　賤者之事。《周禮‧秋官》：「條狼氏掌執鞭以趨辟。王出入則八人夾道，公則六人，侯伯則四人，子男則二人。」指在天子或諸侯出入時，執皮鞭使行人讓路的侍役。②從吾所好　《集解》：「孔曰：所好者，古人之道。」

解說　朱注：「設言富若可求，則雖身爲賤役以求之，亦所不辭。然有命焉，非求之可得也，則安於義理而已矣，何必徒取辱哉？」

※ 第十二章 ※

子之所慎：齊、戰、疾。

語譯　孔子會小心謹慎的有三件事：齋戒、戰爭和疾病。

注釋　①齊　同齋。

10.2. Tsze-lu said, "If you had the conduct of the armies of a great state, whom would you have to act with you?"

10.3. The Master said, "I would not have him to act with me, who will unarmed attack a tiger, or cross a river without a boat, dying without any regret. My associate must be the man who proceeds to action full of solicitude, who is fond of adjusting his plans, and then carries them into execution."

注釋　retired: adv. 隱蔽地、偏遠地；unarmed: adv. 不帶武器、徒手；associate: n. 同伴；adjust: v. 調整；execution: n. 執行。

❋ Chapter 11 ❋

The Master said, "If the search for riches is sure to be successful, though I should become a groom with whip in hand to get them, I will do so. As the search may not be successful, I will follow after that which I love."

注釋　search: n. 追求；successful: adj. 成功的；groom: n. 馬夫；whip: n. 鞭子。

❋ Chapter 12 ❋

The things in reference to which the Master exercised the greatest caution were -- fasting, war, and sickness.

注釋　in reference to: 關於；exercise caution: 謹慎；fasting: n. 齋戒。

───────────────── ❦ 第十三章 ❦ ─────────────────

子在齊聞韶，三月不知肉味。曰：「不圖爲樂之至於斯也！」

語譯　孔子在齊國聽了韶樂，三個月來連肉味都不知道。他說：「我沒想到音樂
　　　的美竟然到了這樣的境界。」

注釋　①**韶**　舜樂名。②**不圖**　沒有預先想到。

解說　陶醉在悠揚的音樂裡，吃東西都不知道美味如何了。《史記‧孔子世家》：
　　　「孔子適齊，與齊大師語樂。聞韶音，學之三月，不知肉味。」解釋爲「學
　　　了三個月」。

───────────────── ❦ 第十四章 ❦ ─────────────────

冉有曰：「夫子爲衛君乎？」子貢曰：「諾。吾將問之。」入，曰：
「伯夷、叔齊何人也？」曰：「古之賢人也。」曰：「怨乎？」曰：
「求仁而得仁，又何怨。」出，曰：「夫子不爲也。」

語譯　冉有說：「夫子會不會爲衛君做事呢？」子貢說：「是啊，我去問問。」
　　　子貢進去見孔子，問說：「伯夷、叔齊是什麼樣的人？」孔子說：「是古
　　　代的賢人。」子貢又問：「他們心裡有怨恨嗎？」孔子說：「他們求得心
　　　安，而且心裡也眞的平安，又有什麼怨恨呢？」子貢出來說：「夫子不會
　　　爲衛君做事。」

注釋　①**爲**　助也。②**衛君**　指衛出公輒。③**諾**　應辭。

解說　朱注：「靈公逐其世子蒯聵。公薨，而國人立蒯聵之子輒。於是晉納蒯聵
　　　而輒拒。時孔子居衛，衛人以蒯聵得罪於父，而輒嫡孫當立，故冉有疑
　　　而問之。」蒯聵和輒父子爭奪王位，和伯夷、叔齊兄弟的辭讓王位正好成
　　　爲對比，所以子貢問伯夷、叔齊於孔子，以了解夫子對於衛君的看法。

───────────────── ❦ 第十五章 ❦ ─────────────────

子曰：「飯疏食，飲水，曲肱而枕之，樂亦在其中矣。不義而富且
貴，於我如浮雲。」

❈ **Chapter 13** ❈

When the Master was in Ch'i, he heard the Shao, and for three months did not know the taste of flesh. "I did not think" he said, "that music could have been made so excellent as this."

注釋 taste: n. 味道。

❈ **Chapter 14** ❈

14.1. Yen Yu said, "Is our Master for the ruler of Wei?" Tsze-kung said, "Oh! I will ask him."

14.2. He went in accordingly, and said, "What sort of men were Po-i and Shu-ch'i?" "They were ancient worthies," said the Master. "Did they have any repinings because of their course?" The Master again replied, "They sought to act virtuously, and they did so; what was there for them to repine about?" On this, Tsze-kung went out and said, "Our Master is not for him."

注釋 worthy: n. 傑出人物、名人；repining: n. 抱怨；repine: v. 抱怨。

❈ **Chapter 15** ❈

The Master said, "With coarse rice to eat, with water to drink, and my bended arm for a pillow; -- I have still joy in the midst of these things. Riches and honors acquired by unrighteousness, are to me as a floating cloud."

語譯 孔子說：「吃粗飯，喝冷水，彎著胳膊做枕頭，這裡頭自有樂趣。以不義的方式求得的富貴，對我來說，只是像天邊的浮雲。」

注釋 ①飯 動詞，吃。②疏食 指粗飯。也指稷，就是現在的高粱。③水 冷水。④肱 音公，胳膊。⑤枕 動詞，去聲。

解說 這是孔子饒富詩意的名句，清風拂體，明月照人，仁者心境，悠然自得。朱熹說：「此章見聖人之心，但覺義理之無窮，絕不知身世之可憂，歲月之有變。」

※ 第十六章 ※

子曰：「加我數年，五十以學易，可以無大過矣。」

語譯 孔子說：「再給我多活幾年，到了五十歲時去學習易理，我可以沒什麼大過失吧。」

注釋 ①加 《史記·孔子世家》作「假我數年」。②易 指《易經》。

解說 《集解》：「易，窮理盡性以至於命，年五十而知天命。以知命之年，讀至命之書，故可以無大過。」《史記·孔子世家》：「孔子晚而喜易，序象、繫、象、說卦、文言。讀易，韋編三絕。曰：『假我數年，若是，我於易則彬彬矣。』」這句話也解為「加我數年，五十以學，亦可無大過矣。」惠棟《九經古義》：「《外黃令高彪碑》：『恬虛守約，五十以學。』此從《魯論》，『亦』字連下讀也。」《經典釋文》：「學易如字，魯讀易為亦，今從古。」錢穆譯為：「再假我幾年，讓我學到五十歲，庶可不致有大過失了。」毛子水則根據龔元玠《十三經客難》的說法，譯為：「讓我多活幾年（或五或十），以從事學問，那我就不會有什麼大過失了。」

※ 第十七章 ※

子所雅言，詩、書、執禮，皆雅言也。

語譯 孔子有時候會說周朝王室的正音，例如誦詩、讀書和行禮的時候，都會用到正音。

注釋 ①雅言 《集解》：「孔曰：雅言，正言也。」②執 守也。

注釋 coarse: adj. 粗糙的；bend: v. 彎曲；pillow: 枕頭；in the midst of: 在其中；float: v. 飄浮。

※ **Chapter 16** ※

The Master said, "If some years were added to my life, I would give fifty to the study of the Yi, and then I might come to be without great faults.

注釋 fault: n. 過失。

解說 《易經》音譯爲Yi，或譯爲 The Book of Changes。

※ **Chapter17** ※

The Master's frequent themes of discourse were -- the Odes, the History, and the maintenance of the Rules of Propriety. On all these he frequently discoursed.

注釋 frequent: adj. 經常的、慣常的；theme: n. 主題；discourse: n. 談話、演說；maintenance: n. 維持。

解說　《集解》：「鄭曰：讀先王典法，必正其音，然後義全，故不可有所諱。禮不誦，故言執。」朱注：「雅，常也。執，守也。詩以理情性，書以道政事，禮以謹節文，皆切於日用之實，故常言之。禮獨言執者，以人所執守而言，非徒誦說而已也。」把「雅言」解釋爲「經常談論的主題」。

※ 第十八章 ※

葉公問孔子於子路，子路不對。子曰：「女奚不曰，其爲人也，發憤忘食，樂以忘憂，不知老之將至云爾。」

語譯　葉公向子路詢問孔子的爲人如何，子路不知如何回答。孔子說：「你爲什麼不這麼說：『他這個人，用功時會忘了吃飯，心裡快樂時會忘記所有的憂愁，甚至不知道自己就要衰老，如此而已。』」

注釋　①葉公　《集解》：「孔曰：葉公名諸梁，楚大夫。食采於葉，僭稱公。」葉音攝。②不對　不知道怎麼回答。③奚　何也。④云爾　如此而已。

解說　孔子自述其好學不倦且樂在其中的生命境界。

※ 第十九章 ※

子曰：「我非生而知之者，好古，敏以求之者也。」

語譯　孔子說：「我不是生來就知道這些道理的，而是喜好古代的典章制度，勤奮習得的。」

注釋　①敏　朱注：「速也。謂汲汲也。」

解說　孔子強調自己不是生而知之，而是從文化傳統裡努力習得道理的。

※ 第二十章 ※

子不語：怪、力、亂、神。

語譯　孔子不談怪異、勇力、作亂和鬼神的事。

解說　《集解》：「怪，怪異也。力謂若奡盪舟，烏獲舉千鈞之屬。亂謂臣弒君，子弒父。神謂鬼神之事。或無益於教化，或所不忍言。」朱注：「謝氏曰：聖人語常而不語怪，語德而不語力，語治而不語亂，語人而不語神。」

解說　雅言譯為 frequent themes of discourse，是根據朱注的翻譯。

❊ Chapter 18 ❊

18.1. The Duke of Sheh asked Tsze-lu about Confucius, and Tsze-lu did not answer him.

18.2. The Master said, "Why did you not say to him, -- He is simply a man, who in his eager pursuit of knowledge forgets his food, who in the joy of its attainment forgets his sorrows, and who does not perceive that old age is coming on?"

注釋　sorrow: n. 憂愁；perceive: v. 知覺。

❊ Chapter 19 ❊

The Master said, "I am not one who was born in the possession of knowledge; I am one who is fond of antiquity, and earnest in seeking it there."

注釋　in the possession of: 擁有； antiquity: n. 古代；earnest: adj. 認眞的。

❊ Chapter 20 ❊

The subjects on which the Master did not talk, were -- extraordinary things, feats of strength, disorder, and spiritual beings.

注釋　extraordinary: adj. 異常的；feat: n. 功績；disorder: n. 混亂、失序；spiritual: adj. 鬼神的；being: n. 存有者。

———— ❀ 第二十一章 ❀ ————

子曰：「三人行，必有我師焉。擇其善者而從之，其不善者而改之。」

語譯　孔子說：「三人同行，其中必定有可以做我老師的人。選擇他們的長處去效法，而他們的缺點則做爲自我改正的警惕。」

注釋　①三人行　《正義》：「三人者，眾辭也。行者，行於道路也。」

解說　《集解》：「尹氏曰：見賢思齊，見不善而內自省，則善惡皆我之師，進善其有窮乎？」三人只是泛稱多數，不一定是三個人。

———— ❀ 第二十二章 ❀ ————

子曰：「天生德於予，桓魋其如予何？」

語譯　孔子說：「上天既然給我這樣的德性，桓魋能拿我怎麼樣呢？」

注釋　①桓魋　宋司馬。②其如予何　對我無可奈何。

解說　《史記·孔子世家》：「孔子去曹適宋，與弟子習禮大樹下。宋司馬桓魋欲殺孔子，拔其樹。孔子去。弟子曰：可以速矣。孔子曰：天生德於予，桓魋其如予何！」

———— ❀ 第二十三章 ❀ ————

子曰：「二三子以我爲隱乎？吾無隱乎爾。吾無行而不與二三子者，是丘也。」

語譯　孔子說：「你們學生們以爲我有所隱匿而不告訴你們的嗎？我實在沒什麼好隱藏的。我沒有什麼事是你們不知道的。我就是這樣。」

注釋　①二三子　謂諸弟子。②乎爾　句末語助辭。③行　所做的事。④與　示也，教也。

解說　《集解》：「包曰：聖人知廣道深，弟子學之不能及，以爲有所隱匿，故解之我所爲無不與爾共之者，是丘之心。」

⁂ **Chapter 21** ⁂

The Master said, "When I walk along with two others, they may serve me as my teachers. I will select their good qualities and follow them, their bad qualities and avoid them."

⁂ **Chapter 22** ⁂

The Master said, "Heaven produced the virtue that is in me. Hwan T'ui -- what can he do to me?"

⁂ **Chapter 23** ⁂

The Master said, "Do you think, my disciples, that I have any concealments? I conceal nothing from you. There is nothing which I do that is not shown to you, my disciples; that is my way."

注釋　concealment: n. 隱藏；show: v. 顯示。

————— ✤ 第二十四章 ✤ —————

子以四教：文、行、忠、信。

語譯　孔子的教育有四個方面：典籍文獻、德行修養、做人誠懇，待人信實。

注釋　①**文**　詩、書、禮、樂等典籍。②**行**　去聲，德行的意思。

————— ✤ 第二十五章 ✤ —————

子曰：「聖人，吾不得而見之矣；得見君子者，斯可矣。」子曰：
「善人，吾不得而見之矣；得見有恆者，斯可矣。亡而為有，虛而
為盈，約而為泰，難乎有恆矣。」

語譯　孔子說：「聖人我是看不到了，能見到君子，也就可以了。」孔子說：
　　　「好人我是看不到了，能看到堅持到底的人，也就可以了。沒有的假裝
　　　有，空虛的矯飾爲充實，貧乏卻要充闊，這樣就很難堅持到底了。」

注釋　①**亡**　同無。

解說　朱注：「聖人，神明不測之號。君子，才德出眾之名。……張子曰：有恆
　　　者，不貳其心。善人者，志於仁而無惡。」孔子感嘆當時的社會崇尚浮
　　　誇虛飾，而難以有恆。至於聖人和君子之分，《正義》：「《大戴禮·五義
　　　篇》：『所謂聖人者，知通乎大道，應變而無窮，能測萬物之情性者也。』
　　　是言聖人無所不通，能成己成物也。《禮記·哀公問篇》：『子曰：君子
　　　者，人之成名也。』《韓詩外傳》：『言行多當，未安愉也；知慮多當，未
　　　周密也。是篤君子，未及聖人也。』」

————— ✤ 第二十六章 ✤ —————

子釣而不綱，弋不射宿。

語譯　孔子用釣竿釣魚，而不用繩網捕魚；射鳥的時候不射棲巢的鳥。

注釋　①**釣**　用釣鉤釣魚。②**綱**　用大繩連接網絕流捕魚。③**弋**　用絲繫在箭上射
　　　鳥。④**射宿**　射棲宿的鳥。

解說　朱注：「洪氏曰：孔子少貧賤，爲養與祭，或不得已而釣弋，如獵較是

⚜ Chapter 24 ⚜

There were four things which the Master taught, -- letters, ethics, devotion of soul, and truthfulness.

注釋　letters: n. 文學、知識；ethics: n. 倫理；devotion: n. 奉獻；truthfulness: n. 信實。

⚜ Chapter 25 ⚜

25.1. The Master said, "A sage it is not mine to see; could I see a man of real talent and virtue, that would satisfy me." The Master said, "A good man it is not mine to see; could I see a man possessed of constancy, that would satisfy me.

25.2. "Having not and yet affecting to have, empty and yet affecting to be full, straitened and yet affecting to be at ease: -- it is difficult with such characteristics to have constancy."

注釋　satisfy: v. 使滿足；constancy: n. 恆久、堅定不移；affect: v. 假裝；straitened: adj. 缺錢的；characteristic: n. 特質。

⚜ Chapter 26 ⚜

The Master angled, -- but did not use a net. He shot, -- but not at birds perching.

注釋　angle: v. 釣魚；perch: v. 停歇。

解說　比較以下的翻譯：The Master fished with a line but not with a net；when shooting he did not aim at a resting bird.

也。然盡物取之，出其不意，亦不爲也。此可見仁人之本心矣。待物如此，待人可知；小者如此，大者可知。」

※ 第二十七章 ※

子曰：「蓋有不知而作之者，我無是也。多聞，擇其善者而從之，多見而識之，知之次也。」

語譯　孔子說：「大概有還不明白道理就妄自創制的人吧，我是不會這麼做的。多多聽聞，選擇好的去遵從，多多觀察而記在心裡，也就很接近智慧了。」

注釋　①作　創制立說。②識　默記。③知之次　次於知。

解說　《集解》：「包曰：時人有穿鑿妄作篇籍者，故云然。孔曰：言如此者，次於天生知之。」這裡把「知」解釋爲「生而知之」的知。

※ 第二十八章 ※

互鄉難與言，童子見，門人惑。子曰：「與其進也，不與其退也，唯何甚！人潔己以進，與其潔也，不保其往也。」

語譯　孔子說：「互鄉的人很難和他們講道」，有個互鄉的小孩子得見孔子，學生們感到很奇怪。孔子說：「我才要稱許他知道上進，不樂見到他怠墮退步，又何必太嚴厲呢？人家潔身自愛又肯上進，應該稱許他的潔身自愛，何必計較他的過去呢？」

注釋　①互鄉　鄉名。②見　音現③與　稱許。④潔　脩治也，唐、宋石經作「絜」。⑤保　守也，惦記的意思。⑥往　指過往，《集解》：「鄭曰，往猶去也。」則是解釋爲往後。

※ 第二十九章 ※

子曰：「仁，遠乎哉？我欲仁，斯仁至矣。」

語譯　孔子說：「仁德會很遠嗎？我想要仁德，仁德就來了。」

❈ Chapter 27 ❈

The Master said, "There may be those who act without knowing why. I do not do so. Hearing much and selecting what is good and following it; seeing much and keeping it in memory: this is the second style of knowledge."

解說　「不知而作之者」的「作」譯爲 act（作爲），錢穆認爲把「作」解釋爲「作爲」所指太泛，應該是指創制立說而言。也有人譯爲 act creatively。

❈ Chapter 28 ❈

28.1. It was difficult to talk profitably and reputably with the people of Hu-hsiang, and a lad of that place having had an interview with the Master, the disciples doubted.

28.2. The Master said, "I admit people's approach to me without committing myself as to what they may do when they have retired. Why must one be so severe? If a man purify himself to wait upon me, I receive him so purified, without guaranteeing his past conduct."

注釋　profitably: adv. 有益地；reputably: 高尚地；lad: n. 少年；interview: n. 會見；admit: v. 許可；approach: v. 接近；to commit oneself to: 承諾；retire: v. 退去；severe: adj. 苛刻；purify: v. 潔淨；wait upon: 拜訪、請安；receive: v. 領受；guarantee: v. 保證。

❈ Chapter 29 ❈

The Master said, "Is virtue a thing remote? I wish to be virtuous, and lo! virtue is at hand."

解說　《集解》：「包曰：仁道不遠，行之即是。」朱注：「仁者，心之德，非在外也。放而不求，故有以爲遠者；反而求之，則即此而在矣，夫豈遠哉？程子曰：爲仁由己，欲之則至，何遠之有？」

───── ❀ 第三十章 ❀ ─────

陳司敗問昭公知禮乎？孔子曰：「知禮。」孔子退，揖巫馬期而進之，曰：「吾聞君子不黨，君子亦黨乎？君取於吳，爲同姓，謂之吳孟子。君而知禮，孰不知禮？」巫馬期以告。子曰：「丘也幸，苟有過，人必知之。」

語譯　陳司敗問孔子：「魯昭公懂得禮嗎？」孔子說：「懂禮。」孔子走了出來，陳司敗向巫馬期作個揖，請他進來，對他說：「我聽說君子無所偏袒，難道孔子也會偏袒人嗎？魯君娶了吳國的女子，而吳國和魯國是同姓，所以她改稱爲吳孟子。魯君如果懂得禮，那還有誰不懂呢？」巫馬期把這些話轉告孔子。孔子說：「我眞是幸運，如果有什麼過失，總有人會告訴我。」

注釋　①**陳司敗**　有人說是人名，有人則認爲司敗是官名，指陳國司寇。②**昭公**　指魯昭公。③**巫馬期**　姓巫馬名施，字子期，孔子弟子。④**黨**　偏私。⑤**取**　同娶。⑥**吳孟子**　《集解》：「孔曰：魯、吳俱姬姓。禮，同姓不婚，而君取之，當稱吳姬，諱曰孟子。」

解說　朱注：「孔子不可自謂諱君之惡，又不可以娶同姓爲知禮，故受以爲過而不辭。」

───── ❀ 第三十一章 ❀ ─────

子與人歌而善，必使反之，而後和之。

語譯　孔子和人一起唱歌，聽到別人唱得好，總會請他再唱一次遍，然後自己跟著唱和。

注釋　①**反**　反覆。

注釋 remote: adj. 遙遠的；lo: interj. 你瞧；at hand: 在手邊、即將到來。

✤ **Chapter 30** ✤

30.1. The minister of crime of Ch'an asked whether the duke Chao knew propriety, and Confucius said, "He knew propriety."

30.2. Confucius having retired, the minister bowed to Wu-ma Ch'i to come forward, and said, "I have heard that the superior man is not a partisan. May the superior man be a partisan also? The prince married a daughter of the house of Wu, of the same surname with himself, and called her, -- 'The elder Tsze of Wu.' If the prince knew propriety, who does not know it?"

30.3. Wu-ma Ch'i reported these remarks, and the Master said, "I am fortunate! If I have any errors, people are sure to know them."

注釋 bow: v. 鞠躬；partisan: n. 黨派觀念很強的人；surname: n. 姓氏。

✤ **Chapter 31** ✤

When the Master was in company with a person who was singing, if he sang well, he would make him repeat the song, while he accompanied it with his own voice.

注釋 accompany: v. 伴奏。

---- ❋ 第三十二章 ❋ ----

子曰：「文莫，吾猶人也。躬行君子，則吾未之有得。」

語譯　孔子說：「說到努力，我或許比得上別人。至於親自實踐君子之道，我還做不到呢。」

注釋　①**文莫**　努力的意思。

解說　「文莫，吾猶人也」也可以斷句為「文，莫吾猶人也」，莫，疑問詞，譯為：「說到典章文獻，可能趕得上別人。」

---- ❋ 第三十三章 ❋ ----

子曰：「若聖與仁，則吾豈敢？抑為之不厭，誨人不倦，則可謂云爾已矣。」公西華曰：「正唯弟子不能學也。」

語譯　孔子說：「說到聖人和仁者，我怎麼敢當呢？我只是努力不懈地學習，又不厭其煩地教導別人，如此罷了。」公西華說：「這正是我們學不到的啊。」

注釋　①**為之**　為學之義。②**抑**　語助詞。③**云爾已矣**　如此而已。

解說　朱注：「聖者，大而化之。仁，則心德之全而人道之備也。為之，謂為仁聖之道。誨人，亦謂以此教人也。然不厭不倦，非己有之則不能，所以弟子不能學也。」《正義》：「學不厭，教不倦，即是仁聖。」

---- ❋ 第三十四章 ❋ ----

子疾病，子路請禱。子曰：「有諸？」子路對曰：「有之。誄曰：『禱爾於上下神祇。』」子曰：「丘之禱久矣。」

語譯　孔子病重，子路請示要為老師祈禱。孔子說：「有這種事嗎？」子路回答說：「有啊。誄文說：『為你向天地神祇禱告。』」孔子（打斷子路的話）說：「我自己早就祈禱過了。」

注釋　①**禱**　請禱於鬼神。②**誄**　朱注：「哀死而述其行之辭也。」③**上下神祇**　「上下」指天地，天神曰神，地神曰祇。

❊ Chapter 32 ❊

The Master said, "In letters I am perhaps equal to other men, but the character of the superior man, carrying out in his conduct what he professes, is what I have not yet attained to."

注釋　letters: n. 文學；profess: v. 信仰；attain: v. 到達。

❊ Chapter 33 ❊

The Master said, "The sage and the man of perfect virtue; -- how dare I rank myself with them? It may simply be said of me, that I strive to become such without satiety, and teach others without weariness." Kung-hsi Hwa said, "This is just what we, the disciples, cannot imitate you in."

注釋　rank: v. 列於之間 [with]；strive: v. 努力；weariness: n. 厭倦；imitate: v. 模仿。

❊ Chapter 34 ❊

The Master being very sick, Tsze-lu asked leave to pray for him. He said, "May such a thing be done?" Tsze-lu replied, "It may. In the Eulogies it is said, 'Prayer has been made for thee to the spirits of the upper and lower worlds.' " The Master said, "My praying has been for a long time."

注釋　eulogy: n. 頌辭。

解說　《正義》：「案：夫子平時心存兢業，故恭肅於鬼神，自知可無大過，不待有疾然後禱也。言此者，所以止子路。」

※ 第三十五章 ※

子曰：「奢則不孫，儉則固。與其不孫也，寧固。」

語譯　孔子說：「奢華顯得驕矜，儉樸顯得寒傖。與其驕矜，還寧可寒傖。」

注釋　①**不孫**　孫同遜。②**固**　固陋。

※ 第三十六章 ※

子曰：「君子坦蕩蕩，小人長戚戚。」

語譯　孔子說：「君子心胸平坦寬闊，小人則時常擔心害怕。」

注釋　①**坦蕩蕩**　寬廣貌。②**長戚戚**　多憂懼。

解說　朱注：「程子曰：君子循理，故常舒泰；小人役於物，故多憂戚。」皇侃疏：「江熙曰：君子坦爾夷任，蕩然無私；小人馳競於榮利，耿介於得失，故長爲愁府也。」

※ 第三十七章 ※

子溫而厲，威而不猛，恭而安。

語譯　孔子既溫和又嚴肅，有威儀卻不凶猛，既恭敬又安詳。

注釋　①**厲**　嚴肅。②**猛**　凶猛。

解說　朱注：「人之德性本無不備，而氣質所賦，鮮有不偏，惟聖人全體渾然，陰陽合德，故其中和之氣見於容貌之間者如此。」

────────────── ❋ **Chapter 35** ❋ ──────────────

The Master said, "Extravagance leads to insubordination, and parsimony to meanness. It is better to be mean than to be insubordinate."

注釋　extravagance: v. 奢侈、放縱；insubordination: n. 不順從；parsimony: n. 吝嗇；meanness: n. 鄙陋。

────────────── ❋ **Chapter 36** ❋ ──────────────

The Master said, "The superior man is satisfied and composed; the mean man is always full of distress."

注釋　composed: adj. 沉著的；distress: n. 苦惱。

────────────── ❋ **Chapter 37** ❋ ──────────────

The Master was mild, and yet dignified; majestic, and yet not fierce; respectful, and yet easy.

注釋　dignified: adj. 有威嚴的；majestic: adj. 莊嚴的、雄偉的；fierce: adj. 凶暴的；respectful: adj. 謙恭有禮的。

泰伯第八

---※ 第一章 ※---

子曰：「泰伯，其可謂至德也已矣！三以天下讓，民無得而稱焉。」

語譯　孔子說：「泰伯大概可以說是至德了！他三次把天下讓給弟弟，百姓卻不知道怎麼去稱頌他。」

注釋　①**泰伯**　《史記・吳太伯世家》：「吳太伯，太伯弟仲雍，皆周太王之子，而王季歷之兄也。季歷賢，而有聖子昌，太王欲立季歷以及昌，於是太伯、仲雍二人乃奔荊蠻，文身斷髮，示不可用，以避季歷。季歷果立，是爲王季，而昌爲文王。太伯之奔荊蠻，自號句吳。荊蠻義之，從而歸之千餘家，立爲吳太伯。」②**三讓**　朱注：「謂固遜也。」《集解》：「鄭曰：太王疾，太伯因適吳、越採藥，太王歿而不返，季歷爲喪主，一讓也。季歷赴之，不來奔喪，二讓也。免喪之後，遂斷髮文身，三讓也。」③**民無得而稱焉**　《集解》：「王曰：其讓隱，故無得而稱言之者，所以爲至德也。」

解說　朱注：「夫以泰伯之德，當商周之際，固足以朝諸侯有天下矣，乃棄不取而又泯其跡焉，則其德之至極爲何如哉！蓋其心即夷齊扣馬之心，而事之難處有甚焉者，宜夫子之歎息而贊美之也。」

---※ 第二章 ※---

子曰：「恭而無禮則勞。慎而無禮則葸。勇而無禮則亂。直而無禮則絞。君子篤於親，則民興於仁；故舊不遺，則民不偷。」

語譯　孔子說：「恭敬而不知禮，會勞擾不安。謹慎而不知禮，會畏怯多懼。好勇而不知禮，會犯上作亂。直率而不知禮，會尖刻刺人。在上位的人若能厚待其親屬，那麼百姓也會興起仁愛的風氣。在上位的人若能不遺棄故交舊友，百姓也就不會冷淡澆薄。」

注釋　①**勞**　勞擾不安。②**葸**　音洗，畏怯。③**亂**　悖亂。④**絞**　急切。⑤**篤**　厚待。⑥**偷**　澆薄。

解說　朱注：「張子曰：人道知所先後，則恭不勞、慎不葸、勇不亂、直不絞，民化而德厚矣。」

⁂ **Chapter 1** ⁂

The Master said, "T'ai-po may be said to have reached the highest point of virtuous action. Thrice he declined the kingdom, and the people in ignorance of his motives could not express their approbation of his conduct."

注釋　thrice: adv. 三次；decline: v. 拒絕；ignorance: n. 不知道；motive: n. 動機；approbation: n. 讚美。

⁂ **Chapter 2** ⁂

2.1. The Master said, "Respectfulness, without the rules of propriety, becomes laborious bustle; carefulness, without the rules of propriety, becomes timidity; boldness, without the rules of propriety, becomes insubordination; straightforwardness, without the rules of propriety, becomes rudeness.

2.2. "When those who are in high stations perform well all their duties to their relations, the people are aroused to virtue. When old friends are not neglected by them, the people are preserved from meanness."

注釋　laborious: adj. 費力的；bustle: n. 擾攘；timidity: n. 膽怯；boldness: n. 勇敢、鹵莽；insubordination: n. 不順從；straightforwardness: n. 直率；rudeness: n. 粗野；arouse: v. 使、激勵 [to]；preserve: v. 保護而使免於 [from]；meanness: n. 卑鄙、吝嗇。

———— ❖ 第三章 ❖ ————

曾子有疾，召門弟子曰：「啓予足！啓予手！詩云：『戰戰兢兢，如臨深淵，如履薄冰。』而今而後，吾知免夫！小子！」

語譯　曾子病重，把學生們叫來，說：「看看我的腳！看看我的手！《詩經》說：『小心謹慎啊！像臨到深潭邊，像踩在薄冰上面。』從今以後，我知道可以不必這樣了，弟子們啊！」

注釋　①啓　有兩種解釋。可以解釋爲「開啓」，是說曾子要弟子掀開被子看他的手腳，也可以說是「使視之」。②戰戰　恐懼貌。③兢兢　戒謹貌。④臨　居上臨下也。⑤履　踐踏也。

解說　《集解》：「鄭曰：曾子以爲受身體於父母，不敢毀傷，故使弟子開衾而視之也。」從這裡可以看到曾子守約戒愼的個性。「戰戰兢兢，如臨深淵，如履薄冰。」出自《詩經‧小旻》。

———— ❖ 第四章 ❖ ————

曾子有疾，孟敬子問之。曾子言曰：「鳥之將死，其鳴也哀；人之將死，其言也善。君子所貴乎道者三：動容貌，斯遠暴慢矣；正顏色，斯近信矣；出辭氣，斯遠鄙倍矣。籩豆之事，則有司存。」

語譯　曾子病重，孟敬子去探望他。曾子說：「鳥將要死的時候，叫聲很悲哀；人要死的時候，所說的話是善意的。在上位的人，應該重視三個道理：重視自己的態度，便可以遠離別人的粗暴和怠慢；注意自己的臉色，就容易使人信任；留意自己的談吐，就可以避免鄙陋和背理。至於禮儀細節，則有專人在照料。」

注釋　①孟敬子　魯國大夫仲孫捷，孟武伯之子。②動容貌　容貌依禮而動。③暴慢　粗厲放肆。④辭氣　言語聲調。⑤鄙倍　倍同悖。鄙陋悖理的意思。⑥籩豆　籩音邊，籩豆是禮器，指禮儀細節。⑦有司　管事者。

解說　朱注：「鳥畏死，故鳴哀。人窮反本，故言善。此曾子之謙辭，欲敬子知其所言之善而識之也。」《正義》：「動容貌，謂以禮動之；正顏色，謂以禮正之；出辭氣，謂以禮出之。」

Chapter 3

The philosopher Tsang being ill, he called to him the disciples of his school, and said, "Uncover my feet, uncover my hands. It is said in the Book of Poetry, 'We should be apprehensive and cautious, as if on the brink of a deep gulf, as if treading on thin ice, I and so have I been.' Now and hereafter, I know my escape from all injury to my person. O ye, my little children."

注釋 uncover: v. 打開；apprehensive: adj. 憂慮的；cautious: adj. 謹慎的；on the brink of: 瀕臨於；gulf: n. 深淵；tread: v. 踩踏；escape: n. 避免；injury: n. 傷害；ye: pron. 你們。

Chapter 4

4.1. The philosopher Tsang being ill, Meng Chang went to ask how he was.

4.2. Tsang said to him, "When a bird is about to die, its notes are mournful; when a man is about to die, his words are good.

4.3. "There are three principles of conduct which the man of high rank should consider specially important: -- that in his deportment and manner he keep from violence and heedlessness; that in regulating his countenance he keep near to sincerity; and that in his words and tones he keep far from lowness and impropriety. As to such matters as attending to the sacrificial vessels, there are the proper officers for them."

注釋 note: n. 鳥叫聲；mournful: adj. 哀傷；deportment: n. 舉止、動作；heedlessness: n. 輕忽；countenance: n. 臉色；lowness: n. 卑鄙的、低級的；vessel: n. 容器。

---※ 第五章 ※---

子曰：曾子曰：「以能問於不能，以多問於寡；有若無，實若虛，犯而不校，昔者吾友嘗從事於斯矣。」

語譯 曾子說：「有能力的人去問能力差的人，見聞多的人去問見聞少的人；有學問像是沒學問一樣，雖然很充實，卻很空虛似的，被別人侵犯，也不去計較，我以前的朋友曾經努力這麼做過。」

注釋 ①校 計較。②吾友 《集解》：「馬曰：友謂顏淵。」

解說 朱注：「顏子之心，惟知義理之無窮，不見物我之有間，故能如此。」也只有顏回這樣坦蕩無私的人，才能夠如此虛懷若谷，得失不縈懷。

---※ 第六章 ※---

曾子曰：「可以託六尺之孤，可以寄百里之命，臨大節而不可奪也。君子人與？君子人也。」

語譯 曾子說：「可以把幼主託付給他，可以把國家的政事交付給他，在危急存亡的重要關頭，不會動搖意志。這樣的人可以算是君子嗎？真的可以說是君子了。」

注釋 ①六尺之孤 幼君。六尺指十五歲以下。②百里 指大國。③奪 動搖。④與 同歟，語助詞。

解說 劉宗周說：「大節不可奪，乃託孤寄命之本。古人濟大事者，皆是不從身家名位上起念。凡臨大節而可奪者，必此等念之為祟也。」

---※ 第七章 ※---

曾子曰：「士不可以不弘毅，任重而道遠。仁以為己任，不亦重乎？死而後已，不亦遠乎？」

語譯 曾子說：「讀書人的志氣不可以不弘大而剛毅，因為他責任重大而路途遙遠。把篤行仁道視為自己的責任，這還不重嗎？到死後才放下這重擔，這還不遙遠嗎？」

※ **Chapter 5** ※

The philosopher Tsang said, "Gifted with ability, and yet putting questions to those who were not so; possessed of much, and yet putting questions to those possessed of little; having, as though he had not; full, and yet counting himself as empty; offended against, and yet entering into no altercation; formerly I had a friend who pursued this style of conduct."

注釋 gifted: adj. 有才能 [with]；possessed: adj. 擁有 [of]；altercation: n. 爭吵；
formerly: adv. 從前；pursue: v. 從事、追求。

※ **Chapter 6** ※

The philosopher Tsang said, "Suppose that there is an individual who can be entrusted with the charge of a young orphan prince, and can be commissioned with authority over a state of a hundred li, and whom no emergency however great can drive from his principles: -- is such a man a superior man? He is a superior man indeed."

注釋 entrust: v. 託付；orphan: n. 孤兒；authority: n. 職權；drive: v. 驅趕 [from]。

※ **Chapter 7** ※

7.1. The philosopher Tsang said, "The officer may not be without breadth of mind and vigorous endurance. His burden is heavy and his course is long.

7.2. "Perfect virtue is the burden which he considers it is his to sustain; -- is it not heavy? Only with death does his course stop; -- is it not long? "

注釋 officer: n. 官員；breadth: n. 寬闊、雄渾；vigorous: adj. 有活力的；endurance:

注釋　①弘毅　《集解》：「包曰：弘，大也。毅，彊而能斷也。」

———————————※ 第八章 ※———————————

子曰：「興於詩，立於禮，成於樂。」

語譯　孔子說：「詩篇可以激勵人，禮制使人操守堅定，音樂使人德性完備。」

注釋　①**興**　振奮。②**立**　堅定。③**成**　完成。

解說　《集解》：「包曰：興，起也。言修身當先學詩。禮者，所以立身。樂者，所以成性。」

———————————※ 第九章 ※———————————

子曰：「民可使由之，不可使知之。」

語譯　孔子說：「役使百姓做事還容易，卻很難要求百姓明白這麼做的道理。」

注釋　①**由**　用也。

解說　這句話很有愚民政治的意味，於是各家解釋都很牽強辛苦。這裡採取毛子水的譯法，把「可」解釋爲「能夠」。

———————————※ 第十章 ※———————————

子曰：「好勇疾貧，亂也。人而不仁，疾之已甚，亂也。」

語譯　孔子說：「逞強好勇而又厭惡貧窮的人，必定會作亂。對於不仁的人，如果深惡痛絕，也會招致禍亂。」

注釋　①**疾**　厭惡。②**已甚**　太甚。

———————————※ 第十一章 ※———————————

子曰：「如有周公之才之美，使驕且吝，其餘不足觀也已。」

語譯　孔子說：「如果有像周公那麼好的才能，卻驕傲而吝嗇，那麼其餘的也不

n. 忍受力；course: n. 過程；sustain: v. 承受。

——————————— ❊ **Chapter 8** ❊ ———————————

8.1.　The Master said, "It is by the Odes that the mind is aroused.

8.2.　"It is by the Rules of Propriety that the character is established.

8.3.　"It is from Music that the finish is received."

注釋　finish: n. 完美、優雅。

解說　比較以下的翻譯：Confucius said: "Be aroused by poetry; structure yourself with propriety, refine yourself with music."

——————————— ❊ **Chapter 9** ❊ ———————————

The Master said, "The people may be made to follow a path of action, but they may not be made to understand it."

注釋　path: n. 路線、方向。

——————————— ❊ **Chapter 10** ❊ ———————————

The Master said, "The man who is fond of daring and is dissatisfied with poverty, will proceed to insubordination. So will the man who is not virtuous, when you carry your dislike of him to an extreme."

注釋　daring: n. 大膽；proceed: v. 轉移到；dislike: n. 厭惡。

——————————— ❊ **Chapter 11** ❊ ———————————

The Master said, "Though a man have abilities as admirable as those of the Duke of Chau, yet if he be proud and niggardly, those other things are really not worth being looked at."

值得一看了。」

注釋　①驕　矜誇。②吝　鄙嗇。

———————————— ✤ 第十二章 ✤ ————————————

子曰：「三年學，不至於穀，不易得也。」

語譯　孔子說：「做了三年學問而沒有功名利祿的念頭，這種人很難得見到了。」

注釋　①穀　祿也。

———————————— ✤ 第十三章 ✤ ————————————

子曰：「篤信好學，守死善道。危邦不入，亂邦不居。天下有道則
見，無道則隱。邦有道，貧且賤焉，恥也；邦無道，富且貴焉，恥
也。」

語譯　孔子說：「有堅定的信念，又能夠好學，誓死固守善道。不到危險的國家
　　　去，不住在混亂的國家。天下太平時，就有所表現，天下紛亂時，就隱居
　　　起來。國家安定時，如果貧賤而不上進，是可恥的事；國家動亂的時候，
　　　卻戀棧財富和權貴，也是可恥的事。」

注釋　①守死　守之以至於死。②見　同現，表現的意思。

解說　朱注：「世治而無可行之道，世亂而無能守之節，碌碌庸人，不足以為士
　　　矣，可恥之甚也。」有所為有所不為，這才是君子之道。

———————————— ✤ 第十四章 ✤ ————————————

子曰：「不在其位，不謀其政。」

語譯　孔子說：「不擔任某個職位，就不去參與那個職位的事。」

注釋　①謀　《正義》：「『謀』謂為之論議也。」

注釋　admirable: adj. 出色的、值得稱讚的；niggardly: adj. 吝嗇的。

※ **Chapter 12** ※

The Master said, "It is not easy to find a man who has learned for three years without coming to be good."

解說　這裡的英譯把「不至於穀」譯爲 without coming to be good，是根據孔安國的解釋，《集解》：「孔曰：穀，善也。言人三年學，不至於善，不可得。」

※ **Chapter 13** ※

13.1. The Master said, "With sincere faith he unites the love of learning; holding firm to death, he is perfecting the excellence of his course.

13.2. "Such an one will not enter a tottering state, nor dwell in a disorganized one. When right principles of government prevail in the kingdom, he will show himself; when they are prostrated, he will keep concealed.

13.3. "When a country is well governed, poverty and a mean condition are things to be ashamed of. When a country is ill governed, riches and honor are things to be ashamed of."

注釋　unite: v. 結合 [with]；perfect: v. 完成、貫徹；tottering: adj. 動搖的、瀕臨崩潰的；disorganized: adj. 混亂的；prevail: v. 盛行；prostrate: v. 屈服。

※ **Chapter 14** ※

The Master said, "He who is not in any particular office has nothing to do with plans for the administration of its duties."

注釋　administration: n. 執行。

---- ❊ 第十五章 ❊ ----

子曰：「師摯之始，關雎之亂，洋洋乎！盈耳哉。」

語譯　孔子說：「典禮時，由樂師摯作升歌開始，到關雎的合樂終結，樂聲悠揚，眞是悅耳啊！」

注釋　①**師摯**　魯國樂師，名摯。②**始**　樂之始。③**亂**　樂之終。④**洋洋**　美盛。

解說　《正義》：「先從叔丹徒君駢枝曰：凡樂之大節，有歌有笙，有閒有合，是爲一成。始於升歌，終於合樂。是故升歌謂之始，合樂謂之亂。」升歌是指由樂師登歌，合樂是指關雎、召南、葛覃、卷耳、鵲巢、采蘩、采蘋六篇。

---- ❊ 第十六章 ❊ ----

子曰：「狂而不直，侗而不愿，悾悾而不信，吾不知之矣。」

語譯　孔子說：「狂妄卻不直率，幼稚卻不忠厚，無能卻不守信，我不知道這種人還能做什麼。」

注釋　①**侗**　侗音同，無知也。②**愿**　忠厚。③**悾悾**　無能。悾音空。

---- ❊ 第十七章 ❊ ----

子曰：「學如不及，猶恐失之。」

語譯　孔子說：「做學問的態度，總好像是趕不上似的，還會怕有所遺失。」

解說　朱注：「程子曰：學如不及，猶恐失之，不得放過。纔說姑待明日，便不可也。」

---- ❊ 第十八章 ❊ ----

子曰：「巍巍乎！舜禹之有天下也，而不與焉。」

語譯　孔子說：「眞是崇高啊！雖然有了天下，卻像沒什麼似的。」

注釋　①**巍巍**　高大的樣子。②**與**　猶言不相關。

---------------------------------- ✳ **Chapter 15** ✳ ----------------------------------

The Master said, "When the music master Chih first entered on his office, the finish of the Kwan Tsu was magnificent; -- how it filled the ears!"

注釋　magnificent: adj. 壯麗、宏偉。

---------------------------------- ✳ **Chapter 16** ✳ ----------------------------------

The Master said, "Ardent and yet not upright, stupid and yet not attentive; simple and yet not sincere: -- such persons I do not understand."

注釋　ardent: adj. 熱情的；attentive: adj. 體貼的。

解說　比較以下的譯法：Confucius said: "I really don't know what to do with those who are ardent but not upright, frank but not careful, and naive but not honest."

---------------------------------- ✳ **Chapter 17** ✳ ----------------------------------

The Master said, "Learn as if you could not reach your object, and were always fearing also lest you should lose it."

---------------------------------- ✳ **Chapter 18** ✳ ----------------------------------

The Master said, "How majestic was the manner in which Shun and Yu held possession of the empire, as if it were nothing to them!"

注釋　majestic: adj. 莊嚴的、雄偉的；empire: n. 帝國。

解說　王充《論衡》：「舜承安繼治，任賢使能，恭己無為而天下治。」這是說舜禹無為而治。《集解》：「美舜禹也。言己不與求天下而得之。」這是說舜禹受禪得天下，而非求而得之。朱注：「不與，猶言不相關，言其不以位為樂也。」這是說天下得失不放在心上。

※ 第十九章 ※

子曰：「大哉，堯之為君也！巍巍乎！唯天為大，唯堯則之。蕩蕩乎！民無能名焉。巍巍乎！其有成功也；煥乎，其有文章！」

語譯　孔子說：「堯真是偉大的君王啊！天是最高的了，只有堯才能效法天。他的德澤真是廣遠，民眾都不知道如何歌頌他。他的功績太偉大了！他所創制的禮樂典章真是燦爛啊！」

注釋　①則　效法。②蕩蕩　廣遠。③名　稱說。④煥　光明貌。⑤文章　禮樂法度。

解說　《正義》：「人受天地之中以生，賦氣成形，故言人之性必本乎天。本乎天即當法天，故自天子以至於庶人，凡同在覆載之內者，崇效天，卑法地，未有能違天而能成德布治者也。」朱注：「尹氏曰：天道之大，無為而成。唯堯則之以治天下，故民無得而名焉。所可名者，其功業文章巍然煥然而已。」

※ 第二十章 ※

舜有臣五人而天下治。武王曰：「予有亂臣十人。」孔子曰：「才難，不其然乎？唐虞之際，於斯為盛。有婦人焉，九人而已。三分天下有其二，以服事殷。周之德，其可謂至德也已矣。」

語譯　舜有五個賢臣，天下就治理得很好。武王說：「我有十個能夠輔政的臣子。」孔子說：「古人說人才難得，不是嗎？唐虞的時代，乃至於周武王的時代，人才最多了，但其中還有一個婦人，此外只有九個人而已。三分天下，周朝有其二，但還是臣服於商朝。文王可以說是至德了。」

注釋　①有臣五人　《集解》：「孔曰：五人，禹、稷、契、皋陶、伯益。」②亂臣十人　《集解》：「馬曰：亂，治也。治官者十人，謂周公旦、召公奭、

✤ **Chapter 19** ✤

The Master said, "Great indeed was Yao as a sovereign! How majestic was he! It is only Heaven that is grand, and only Yao corresponded to it. How vast was his virtue! The people could find no name for it. How majestic was he in the works which he accomplished! How glorious in the elegant regulations which he instituted!"

注釋　sovereign: n. 國王；grand: adj. 雄偉的；correspond: v. 相當於；glorious: adj. 光輝燦爛；elegant: adj. 優雅的；institute: v. 制定。

解說　「則之」譯爲 corresponded to it，是根據朱注的解釋：「則，猶準也。」指與天平齊。

✤ **Chapter 20** ✤

20.1.　Shun had five ministers, and the empire was well governed.

20.2.　King Wu said, "I have ten able ministers."

20.3.　Confucius said, "Is not the saying that talents are difficult to find, true? Only when the dynasties of T'ang and Yu met, were they more abundant than in this of Chau, yet there was a woman among them. The able ministers were no more than nine men.

20.4.　"King Wan possessed two of the three parts of the empire, and with those he served the dynasty of Yin. The virtue of the house of Chau may be said to have reached the highest point indeed."

太公望、畢公、榮公、太顛、閎夭、散宜生、南宮适,其一人謂文母。」
③**才難** 人才難得。④**唐虞** 唐,堯號;虞,舜號。⑤**有婦人焉** 或謂文
母,即文王后太姒,或謂武王妻邑姜。

※ 第二十一章 ※

子曰:「禹,吾無間然矣。菲飲食,而致孝乎鬼神;惡衣服,而致
美乎黻冕;卑宮室,而盡力乎溝洫。禹,吾無間然矣。」

語譯 孔子說:「禹,我對他沒有什麼可以批評的了。他自己的飲食菲薄,而盡
心祭祀鬼神;自己的衣服粗劣,而祭服卻很講究;自己的宮室很簡陋,卻
盡力修治溝渠。禹啊,我對他真是沒有什麼可以批評的了。」

注釋 ①**間** 或作「閒」。朱注:「閒,罅隙也,謂指其罅隙而非議之也。」②
菲 菲薄。③**黻冕** 祭服和祭冠。黻音扶。④**溝洫** 田間水道。

注釋 able:adj. 能幹的；abundant: adj. 豐富的。

解說 「唐虞之際，於斯爲盛」譯爲 only when the dynasties of T'ang and Yu met, were they more abundant than in this of Chau（只有唐虞之際比周朝的人才還多），是根據朱注的解釋。

❋ **Chapter 21** ❋

The Master said, "I can find no flaw in the character of Yu. He used himself coarse food and drink, but displayed the utmost filial piety towards the spirits. His ordinary garments were poor, but he displayed the utmost elegance in his sacrificial cap and apron. He lived in a low, mean house, but expended all his strength on the ditches and water channels. I can find nothing like a flaw in Yu."

注釋 flaw: n. 缺點、瑕疵；use oneself: 習慣於；garment: n. 衣服；cap: n. 帽子；apron: n. 圍裙；ditch: n. 水溝；channel: n. 水道、運河。

子罕第九

---------------- ❊ 第一章 ❊ ----------------

子罕言利與命與仁。

語譯　孔子很少談到利、命和仁。

注釋　①**罕**　稀少。②**與**　以及。

解說　《集解》：「罕者，希也。利者，義之和也。命者，天之命也。仁者，行
　　　之盛也。寡能及之，故希言也。」《正義》：「君子明於義利，當**趨**而
　　　趨，當避而避。其趨者，利也，即義也；其避者，不利也，即不義也。」
　　　在《易經》裡可以看到以「義」來解釋「利」，直到後來才有義利之辨，
　　　那就是把「利」解釋爲私利了。利、命、仁，孔子以爲義理精微，所以很
　　　少主動談到。

---------------- ❊ 第二章 ❊ ----------------

達巷黨人曰：「大哉孔子！博學而無所成名。」子聞之，謂門弟子
曰：「吾何執？執御乎？執射乎？吾執御矣。」

語譯　達巷那個地方的人說：「孔子眞是偉大啊！學識淵博，可惜沒有足以成名
　　　的專長。」孔子聽了就對學生們說：「我要專注於哪個長才呢？專注於駕
　　　車嗎？或是專注於射箭？我想還是專注於駕車吧。」

注釋　①**達巷黨人**　《集解》：「達巷者，黨名也。五百家爲黨。」②**執**　專執也。

---------------- ❊ 第三章 ❊ ----------------

子曰：「麻冕，禮也；今也純，儉。吾從眾。拜下，禮也；今拜乎
上，泰也。雖違眾，吾從下。」

語譯　孔子說：「祭禮戴麻織的帽子，這是古禮；現在的人都用絲，是比較節
　　　儉，我同意大家的做法。臣子對國君行禮，先在堂下磕頭，這也是古禮；
　　　現在只在升堂後磕頭，未免太驕傲了些。雖然違逆大眾，我還是選擇在堂
　　　下拜。」

❋ **Chapter 1** ❋

The subjects of which the Master seldom spoke were -- profitableness, and also the appointments of Heaven, and perfect virtue.

注釋　profitability: n. 有利；appointment: n. 任命。

❋ **Chapter 2** ❋

2.1.　A man of the village of Ta-hsiang said, "Great indeed is the philosopher K'ung! His learning is extensive, and yet he does not render his name famous by any particular thing."

2.2.　The Master heard the observation, and said to his disciples, "What shall I practice? Shall I practice charioteering, or shall I practice archery? I will practice charioteering."

注釋　extensive: adj. 廣闊的；render: v. 使成為；observation: n. 看法、意見；
　　　practice: v. 以……爲業；charioteering: n. 駕車；archery: n. 射箭。

❋ **Chapter 3** ❋

3.1.　The Master said, "The linen cap is that prescribed by the rules of ceremony, but now a silk one is worn. It is economical, and I follow the common practice.

3.2.　"The rules of ceremony prescribe the bowing below the hall, but now the practice is to bow only after ascending it. That is arrogant. I continue to bow below the hall, though I oppose the common practice."

注釋　①**麻冕**　《集解》：「孔曰：冕，緇布冠也。古者績麻三十升布以爲之。」
②**純**　絲也。③**拜下**　在堂下拜的意思。《集解》：「王曰：臣之於君行禮
者，下拜然後升成禮。時臣驕泰，故於上拜。」

解說　各種典章制度，總是要因時制宜，隨俗與否，在於不失禮的精神。

※ 第四章 ※

子絕四：毋意，毋必，毋固，毋我。

語譯　孔子平時絕無四種過失：不憑空妄測、不絕對肯定、不拘泥固執、不自以
爲是。

注釋　①**絕**　絕對沒有。②**毋**　同「無」。③**意**　臆測。④**必**　必然如此。⑤**固**　固
執。⑥**我**　以自我爲中心。

解說　《集解》：「以道爲度，故不任意。用之則行，舍之則藏，故無專必。無
可無不可，故無固行。述古而不自作，處群萃而不自異，唯道是從，故不
有其身。」從日常生活的邏輯判斷，以至於道德人格的養成，這個原則都
值得我們認眞思考。

※ 第五章 ※

子畏於匡。曰：「文王既沒，文不在茲乎？天之將喪斯文也，後死
者不得與於斯文也；天之未喪斯文也，匡人其如予何？」

語譯　孔子在匡地遭到拘禁。他說：「文王死後，傳統文化不是都在我這裡了
嗎？上天如果要消滅這個傳統，那麼也不會讓我知道這些文化。如果上天
不想消滅這個傳統，那麼匡人又能把我怎麼樣呢？」

注釋　①**畏**　受危難。②**匡**　邑名。③**文**　傳統文化。④**後死者**　孔子自稱。⑤**與**　參
與。

解說　《集解》：「匡人誤圍夫子，以爲陽虎，陽虎曾暴於匡。夫子弟子顏剋，時
又與虎俱行，後剋爲夫子御，至於匡，匡人相與共識剋。又夫子容貌與虎
相似，故匡人以兵圍之。」《正義》：「夫子見圍於匡，有畏懼之意。」不
過我們看不出孔子的話語裡有任何畏懼的意思。

注釋　linen: adj. 亞麻布的；prescribe: v. 規定；economical: adj. 節約的；practice: n. 風俗、慣例；arrogant: adj. 傲慢的。

 **Chapter 4**

There were four things from which the Master was entirely free. He had no foregone conclusions, no arbitrary predeterminations, no obstinacy, and no egoism.

注釋　foregone: adj. 先前的；conclusion: n. 結論；arbitrary: adj. 獨斷的、任意的；predetermination: n. 預定；obstinacy: n. 頑固；egoism: n. 自我中心、本位主義。

Chapter 5

5.1.　The Master was put in fear in K'wang.

5.2.　He said, "After the death of King Wan, was not the cause of truth lodged here in me?

5.3.　"If Heaven had wished to let this cause of truth perish, then I, a future mortal, should not have got such a relation to that cause. While Heaven does not let the cause of truth perish, what can the people of K'wang do to me?"

注釋　cause: n. 主義、主張；lodge: v. 授與；perish: v. 毀滅；mortal: n. 會死的生命、人類。

解說　「文」譯為 the cause of truth，是根據朱注「道之顯者謂之文」。

———————————— ✤ 第六章 ✤ ————————————

大宰問於子貢曰：「夫子聖者與？何其多能也？」子貢曰：「固天
縱之將聖，又多能也。」子聞之，曰：「大宰知我乎？吾少也賤，
故多能鄙事。君子多乎哉？不多也。」牢曰：「子云：『吾不試，
故藝。』」

語譯　太宰問子貢說：「你們老師是聖人吧？不然為什麼會如此多才多藝呢？」
　　　子貢說：「這是因為上天本來就要讓他成為大聖，又讓他多才多藝。」孔
　　　子聽了就說：「太宰真的知道我嗎？我只是小時候微賤，所以會很多粗
　　　事。君子要如此多能嗎？不用多的。」琴牢說：「老師曾經說過：『我因
　　　為沒有得到重用，所以學了許多技藝。』」

注釋　①**大宰**　即太宰，官名。②**多能**　多小藝。③**縱**　朱注：「縱，猶肆也，
　　　言不為限量也。」④**將**　大也。⑤**鄙事**　鄉野之事。⑥**牢**　琴牢，字子
　　　開，孔子弟子。⑦**試**　用也。

———————————— ✤ 第七章 ✤ ————————————

子曰：「吾有知乎哉？無知也。有鄙夫問於我，空空如也，我叩其
兩端而竭焉。」

語譯　孔子說：「我很有知識嗎？我沒有的。有個鄉下人來問我，非常誠懇。我
　　　從他問題裡的正反根據來反問他，然後窮盡問題的本源。」

注釋　①**鄙夫**　郊野之人。②**空空**　誠懇。③**叩**　反問也。④**竭**　盡也。

解說　「叩其兩端而竭焉」，很類似蘇格拉底的教學法：運用適當的問題，引導
　　　對話者去思考，進而發現永恆的真理本質。

❋ **Chapter 6** ❋

6.1. A high officer asked Tsze-kung, saying, "May we not say that your Master is a sage? How various is his ability!"

6.2. Tsze-kung said, "Certainly Heaven has endowed him unlimitedly. He is about a sage. And, moreover, his ability is various."

6.3. The Master heard of the conversation and said, "Does the high officer know me? When I was young, my condition was low, and I acquired my ability in many things, but they were mean matters. Must the superior man have such variety of ability? He does not need variety of ability." Lao said, "The Master said, 'Having no official employment, I acquired many arts.'"

注釋 endow: v. 授與；unlimitedly: adv. 無限制地；about: adv. 大概；condition: n. 生活情況；mean: adj. 卑鄙的。

解說 「將聖」譯為 He is about a sage.（他大概是個聖人吧），是根據朱注的解釋：「將，殆也，謙若不敢知之辭。」「鄙事」譯為 mean matters，不很恰當，或許可以譯為 worldly skill 或 common matters。

❋ **Chapter 7** ❋

The Master said, "Am I indeed possessed of knowledge? I am not knowing. But if a mean person, who appears quite empty-like, ask anything of me, I set it forth from one end to the other, and exhaust it."

注釋 exhaust: v. 窮盡。

解說 比較以下的翻譯：The Master said: "Am I indeed a man with (innate) knowledge? I have no knowledge, but when an uncultivated person, in all simplicity, comes to me with a question, I thrash out its pros and cons until I get to the bottom of it."
innate: adj. 與生俱來的；uncultivated: adj. 沒有教養的；thrash out: 研討；pros and cons: 正反意見；get to the bottom of: 徹底了解。

━━━━━━━━━━━━ ❋ 第八章 ❋ ━━━━━━━━━━━━

子曰：「鳳鳥不至，河不出圖，吾已矣夫！」

語譯　孔子說：「鳳鳥不飛來了，黃河也沒有出現圖畫了，我的希望大概也完了吧！」

注釋　①鳳鳥不至，河不出圖　鳳鳥至，河出圖，都是聖人受命的瑞兆。

解說　《淮南子・繆稱訓》：「昔二皇鳳凰至於庭，三代至乎門，周室至乎澤。德彌麤，所至彌遠；德彌精，所至彌近。」《正義》：「《書・顧命》有河圖，與大玉、夷玉、天球並列東序，當是玉石之類自然成文。」

━━━━━━━━━━━━ ❋ 第九章 ❋ ━━━━━━━━━━━━

子見齊衰者、冕衣裳者與瞽者，見之，雖少必作；過之，必趨。

語譯　孔子看到服喪者、在高位者和視障者，相見的時候，即使他們比自己年輕，還是會從坐席站起來；從這些人身邊走過時，也必定加快腳步。

注釋　①齊衰　音茲崔，喪服。②冕衣裳　朱注：「冕，冠也。衣，上服。裳，下服。冕而衣裳，貴者之盛服也。」錢大昕認為「冕」同「絻」，是祭服的意思。③瞽　音鼓，瞎眼。④少　年輕。⑤作　站起來。⑥趨　快步走。

解說　從日常生活裡就可以看到仁者愛人之心的自然流露。

━━━━━━━━━━━━ ❋ 第十章 ❋ ━━━━━━━━━━━━

顏淵喟然歎曰：「仰之彌高，鑽之彌堅；瞻之在前，忽焉在後。夫子循循然善誘人，博我以文，約我以禮，欲罷不能。既竭吾才，如有所立卓爾。雖欲從之，末由也已。」

語譯　顏淵嘆說：「老師的道理，越抬頭看，越覺得高，越是鑽研，越覺得堅固而穿不透；似乎看到在前面，忽然又到後面去了。老師按步就班地誘導我們，以各種文獻增廣我的知識，以禮節規範我的行為，使我想停下來都沒辦法。我竭盡全力，卻看到老師的道理還是矗立在前面。雖然想要追隨，卻沒有路可以走。」

Chapter 8

The Master said, "The Fang bird does not come; the river sends forth no map: -- it is all over with me!"

注釋 「鳳」音譯爲 the Fang bird，或譯爲 phoenix。

Chapter 9

When the Master saw a person in a mourning dress, or any one with the cap and upper and lower garments of full dress, or a blind person, on observing them approaching, though they were younger than himself, he would rise up, and if he had to pass by them, he would do so hastily.

注釋 hastily: adv. 急忙地。

Chapter 10

10.1. Yen Yuan, in admiration of the Master's doctrines, sighed and said, "I looked up to them, and they seemed to become more high; I tried to penetrate them, and they seemed to become more firm; I looked at them before me, and suddenly they seemed to be behind.

10.2. "The Master, by orderly method, skillfully leads men on. He enlarged my mind with learning, and taught me the restraints of propriety.

10.3. "When I wish to give over the study of his doctrines, I cannot do so, and having exerted all my ability, there seems something to stand right up before me; but though I wish to follow and lay hold of it, I really find

注釋　①喟然　嘆息聲。②彌　更加的。③循循　循序漸進。④誘　引導。⑤卓爾　高聳的樣子。⑥末由也己　無路可循。

解說　錢穆說：「唯孔子之道，雖極高深，若為不可幾，亦不過在人性情之間，動容之際，飲食起居交接應酬之務，君臣父子夫婦兄弟之常，出處去就辭受取舍，以至政事之設施，禮樂文章之講貫。細讀論語，孔子之道，盡在其中，所謂無行而不與二三子者是丘也。非捨具體可見之外，別有一種不可測想推論之道，使人無從窺尋。學者熟讀論語，可見孔子之道，實平易而近人。而細玩此章，可之即在此平易近人之中，而自有其高深不可及之處。」

※ 第十一章 ※

子疾病，子路使門人為臣。病閒，曰：「久矣哉！由之行詐也！無臣而為有臣，吾誰欺？欺天乎？且予與其死於臣之手也，無寧死於二三子之手乎？且予縱不得大葬，予死於道路乎？」

語譯　孔子病得很重，子路叫孔子的學生們以家臣的身分預備喪事。孔子病好一點，就說：「這麼久了！子路做這種欺騙人的事！我根本沒有家臣，卻要裝作有家臣的樣子，我要欺騙誰呢？是要欺騙天嗎？而且與其有家臣為我送終，讓學生們陪伴我不是更好嗎？就算我沒有大官的葬禮，難道我就會死在路邊，沒有人來葬我嗎？」

注釋　①臣　家臣。②病閒　病稍微減輕。③久矣哉　指孔子生病時不知道這件事。④無寧　寧可。⑤大葬　以君臣之禮葬之。

解說　《正義》：「《王制》云：『大夫廢其事，終身不仕，死以士禮葬之。』是也。夫子去魯是退，當以士禮葬。今子路以大夫之禮，故夫子責之。」

※ 第十二章 ※

子貢曰：「有美玉於斯，韞匵而藏諸？求善賈而沽諸？」子曰：「沽之哉！沽之哉！我待賈者也。」

語譯　子貢說：「這裡有一塊美玉，我們要放到箱子裡藏起來呢？還是等個好價錢賣出去呢？」孔子說：「賣啊！賣啊！我在等出價的人呢。」

no way to do so."

注釋　admiration: n. 讚嘆；sigh: v. 嘆息；penetrate: v. 穿透；firm: adj. 堅實；orderly: adj. 有秩序的；skillfully: adv. 熟練地；lead on: 引導；enlarge: v. 擴大；restraint: n. 約束；give over: 放棄；exert: v. 發揮、運用；lay hold of: 抓住、發現。

⁕ **Chapter 11** ⁕

11.1. The Master being very ill, Tsze-lu wished the disciples to act as ministers to him.

11.2. During a remission of his illness, he said, "Long has the conduct of Yu been deceitful! By pretending to have ministers when I have them not, whom should I impose upon? Should I impose upon Heaven?

11.3. "Moreover, than that I should die in the hands of ministers, is it not better that I should die in the hands of you, my disciples? And though I may not get a great burial, shall I die upon the road?"

注釋　remission: n. 減輕；deceitful: adj. 欺騙的；impose upon: 欺騙；burial: n. 葬禮。

⁕ **Chapter 12** ⁕

Tsze-kung said, "There is a beautiful gem here. Should I lay it up in a case and keep it? Or should I seek for a good price and sell it?" The Master said, "Sell it! Sell it! But I would wait for one to offer the price."

注釋　gem: n. 珠寶；case: n. 箱子。

注釋　①韞　藏也。②匵　音讀，箱子。③善賈　賈同價，好價錢。④沽　賣。

解說　朱注：「范氏曰：君子未嘗不欲仕也，又惡不由其道。士之待禮，猶玉之待賈也。若伊尹之耕於野，伯夷、太公之居於海濱，世無成湯文王，則終焉而已，必不枉道以從人，衒玉而求售也。」

———————————— ❊ 第十三章 ❊ ————————————

子欲居九夷。或曰：「陋，如之何！」子曰：「君子居之，何陋之有？」

語譯　孔子想住到九夷去。有人說：「那個地方很簡陋，怎麼能住呢？」孔子說：「有君子去住，哪裡會簡陋呢？」

注釋　①九夷　《集解》：「馬曰：九夷，東方之夷，有九種。」可能是指朝鮮。②陋　指地處偏僻，人不知禮儀。③君子　《論語正義》認為是指箕子。《後漢書·東夷列傳》：「昔箕子違衰殷之運，避地朝鮮。」

———————————— ❊ 第十四章 ❊ ————————————

子曰：「吾自衛反魯，然後樂正，雅、頌各得其所。」

語譯　孔子說：「我從衛國回到魯國，然後才釐正了音樂，使雅、頌各有適當的位置。」

注釋　①反　同返。②樂正　正樂音或樂章。③各得其所　指適當的演奏時機，或指正確的音律。

解說　朱注：「魯哀公十一年冬，孔子自衛反魯。是時周禮在魯，然詩樂亦頗殘闕失次。孔子周流四方，參互考訂，以知其說。晚知道終不行，故歸而正之。」

———————————— ❊ 第十五章 ❊ ————————————

子曰：「出則事公卿，入則事父兄，喪事不敢不勉，不為酒困，何有於我哉？」

✳ Chapter 13 ✳

13.1. The Master was wishing to go and live among the nine wild tribes of the east.

13.2. Someone said, "They are rude. How can you do such a thing?" The Master said, "If a superior man dwelt among them, what rudeness would there be?"

注釋　tribe: n. 部落

✳ Chapter 14 ✳

The Master said, "I returned from Wei to Lu, and then the music was reformed, and the pieces in the Royal songs and Praise songs all found their proper places."

注釋　reform: v. 改正。

✳ Chapter 15 ✳

The Master said, "Abroad, to serve the high ministers and nobles; at home, to serve one's father and elder brothers; in all duties to the dead, not to dare not to exert one's self; and not to be overcome of wine: -- which one of these things do I attain to?"

語譯　孔子說：「出外爲公卿做事，在家服事父兄，服喪時不敢不盡力去做，不被酒所困擾，這些事我做到了哪些呢？」」

注釋　①困　困擾。

───────── ✻ 第十六章 ✻ ─────────

子在川上，曰：「逝者如斯夫！不舍晝夜。」

語譯　孔子在河邊說：「逝去的光陰就像河水一樣啊！日夜不停地向前流。」

注釋　①舍　同捨，止息。

解說　這句話可以解釋爲孔子遲暮傷逝，也可以說是勸勉進學，效法自然的周行不息。

───────── ✻ 第十七章 ✻ ─────────

子曰：「吾未見好德如好色者也。」

語譯　孔子說：「我沒見過喜歡道德像喜歡美色一樣的人啊。」

───────── ✻ 第十八章 ✻ ─────────

子曰：「譬如為山，未成一簣，止，吾止也；譬如平地，雖覆一簣，進，吾往也。」

語譯　孔子說：「就像堆土成山一樣，只要再堆一籠土就完成了，而這時候停下來，這是我自己停止的；譬如在平地上，即使剛堆好一籠土，想要繼續努力，也要我堅持下去才行啊。」

注釋　①簣　音匱，土籠。

解說　朱注：「蓋學者自彊不息，則積少成多；中道而止，則前功盡棄。其止其往，皆在我而不在人也。」《荀子‧勸學》：「積土成山，風雨興焉；積水成淵，蛟龍生焉；積善成德，而神明自得，聖心備焉。故不積蹞步，無以致千里；不積小流，無以成江海。騏驥一躍，不能十步；駑馬十駕，功在不舍。鍥而舍之，朽木不折；鍥而不舍，金石可鏤。」學者共勉之。

注釋　overcome:v. 打倒。

──────────── ✤ **Chapter 16** ✤ ────────────

The Master standing by a stream, said, "It passes on just like this, not ceasing day or night!"

注釋　cease: v. 停止。

──────────── ✤ **Chapter 17** ✤ ────────────

The Master said, "I have not seen one who loves virtue as he loves beauty."

──────────── ✤ **Chapter 18** ✤ ────────────

The Master said, "The prosecution of learning may be compared to what may happen in raising a mound. If there want but one basket of earth to complete the work, and I stop, the stopping is my own work. It may be compared to throwing down the earth on the level ground. Though but one basketful is thrown at a time, the advancing with it is my own going forward."

注釋　prosecution: n. 實行、經營；mound: n. 小丘、土堆；basket: n. 籃子；level: adj. 平坦的。

＊ 第十九章 ＊

子曰：「語之而不惰者，其回也與！」

語譯　孔子說：「告訴他去做，而能夠努力不懈怠的，大概只有顏回吧！」

注釋　①語　音預，告訴。②與　同歟，感嘆詞。

＊ 第二十章 ＊

子謂顏淵，曰：「惜乎！吾見其進也，未見其止也。」

語譯　孔子談到顏淵時說：「（顏回過世了）真可惜啊！我只看見他不斷進步，從沒看到他停滯不前。」

＊ 第二十一章 ＊

子曰：「苗而不秀者有矣夫！秀而不實者有矣夫！」

語譯　孔子說：「有長了苗卻不抽穗的！也有結了穗卻沒有長成穀子的！」

注釋　①苗　禾苗。②秀　抽穗、開花。③實　成穀。

解說　或謂本章是孔子痛惜顏回早逝。

＊ 第二十二章 ＊

子曰：「後生可畏，焉知來者之不如今也？四十、五十而無聞焉，斯亦不足畏也已。」

語譯　孔子說：「年輕人真是值得敬畏，怎麼知道下一代就不如這一代呢？如果到了四、五十歲還沒有什麼可以稱道的，那就不足以敬畏了。」

注釋　①無聞　無聲聞於世。王陽明《傳習錄》則說：「『四十五十而無聞』，是不聞道，非無聲聞也。孔子云：『是聞也，非達也。』安肯以此忘人？」

❋ Chapter 19 ❋

The Master said, "Never flagging when I set forth anything to him; -- ah! that is Hui."

注釋　flag: v. 衰退；set forth: 宣布。

解說　比較以下的翻譯：The Master said: "Ah! Hui was the one to whom I could tell things and who never failed to attend to them."

❋ Chapter 20 ❋

The Master said of Yen Yuan, "Alas! I saw his constant advance. I never saw him stop in his progress."

❋ Chapter 21 ❋

The Master said, "There are cases in which the blade springs, but the plant does not go on to flower! There are cases where it flowers but fruit is not subsequently produced!"

注釋　blade: n. 葉片；spring: v. 長出、萌芽；flower: v. 開花。

❋ Chapter 22 ❋

The Master said, "A youth is to be regarded with respect. How do we know that his future will not be equal to our present? If he reach the age of forty or fifty, and has not made himself heard of, then indeed he will not be worth being regarded with respect."

注釋　regard: v. 注視、看待。

━━━━━━━━━━━━━━ ❀ 第二十三章 ❀ ━━━━━━━━━━━━━━

子曰：「法語之言，能無從乎？改之為貴。巽與之言，能無說乎？
繹之為貴。說而不繹，從而不改，吾末如之何也已矣。」

語譯　孔子說：「正言告誡的話，能夠不接受嗎？但是要能改正，這才是可貴
　　　的。委婉規勸的話，能不喜悅吧？但是要能尋繹其中的意思，這才是可貴
　　　的。只知道喜悅，而不知道要尋繹，只是接受而不知道要改正，那麼我也
　　　拿他沒辦法了。」

注釋　①**法語**　以正道告之。②**巽與之言**　婉言相勸。③**說**　同悅。④**繹**　尋繹。

━━━━━━━━━━━━━━ ❀ 第二十四章 ❀ ━━━━━━━━━━━━━━

子曰：「主忠信，毋友不如己者，過則勿憚改。」

解說　見〈學而篇〉。

━━━━━━━━━━━━━━ ❀ 第二十五章 ❀ ━━━━━━━━━━━━━━

子曰：「三軍可奪帥也，匹夫不可奪志也。」

語譯　孔子說：「可以把軍隊的統帥擄去，但是匹夫的意志卻是不能夠奪走的。」
注釋　①**匹夫**　庶人也。

━━━━━━━━━━━━━━ ❀ 第二十六章 ❀ ━━━━━━━━━━━━━━

子曰：「衣敝縕袍，與衣狐貉者立，而不恥者，其由也與？『不忮
不求，何用不臧？』」子路終身誦之。子曰：「是道也，何足以
臧？」

語譯　孔子說：「穿著襤褸的棉袍，和穿著狐裘的人站在一起，而不感到羞恥
　　　的，大概只有子路吧？《詩經》說：『不妒嫉，不貪求，那還有什麼不好
　　　的呢？』」子路便經常唸這句詩。孔子說：「這只是起碼的道理，怎麼能
　　　稱得上好？」

❊ Chapter 23 ❊

The Master said, "Can men refuse to assent to the words of strict admonition? But it is reforming the conduct because of them which is valuable. Can men refuse to be pleased with words of gentle advice? But it is unfolding their aim which is valuable. If a man be pleased with these words, but does not unfold their aim, and assents to those, but does not reform his conduct, I can really do nothing with him."

注釋 assent: v. 同意；strict: adj. 嚴格的；admonition: n. 告誡；unfold: v. 開展、表現。

❊ Chapter 24 ❊

The Master said, "Hold faithfulness and sincerity as first principles. Have no friends not equal to yourself. When you have faults, do not fear to abandon them."

❊ Chapter 25 ❊

The Master said, "The commander of the forces of a large state may be carried off, but the will of even a common man cannot be taken from him."

注釋 commander: n. 司令、統帥；carry off: 劫持。

❊ Chapter 26 ❊

26.1. The Master said, "Dressed himself in a tattered robe quilted with hemp, yet standing by the side of men dressed in furs, and not ashamed; -- ah! it is Yu who is equal to this!

26.2. "He dislikes none, he covets nothing; -- what can he do but what is good!"

26.3. Tsze-lu kept continually repeating these words of the ode, when the Master said, "Those things are by no means sufficient to constitute perfect excellence."

注釋　①敝　破爛。②縕　亂絮。③狐貉　以狐貉之皮為裘。④不忮不求，何用不臧　語出《詩經‧衛風‧雄雉》。忮音至，害也。妒忌別人而有傷人之意。臧，善也。

———— ✦ 第二十七章 ✦ ————

子曰：「歲寒，然後知松柏之後彫也。」

語譯　孔子說：「到了寒冬，才知道松柏是最後才凋謝的。」

注釋　①彫　同凋，凋零。

———— ✦ 第二十八章 ✦ ————

子曰：「知者不惑，仁者不憂，勇者不懼。」

語譯　孔子說：「智者不會疑惑，仁者不會憂慮，勇者不會恐懼。」

解說　朱注：「明足以燭理，故不惑；理足以勝私，故不憂；氣足以配道義，故不懼。此學之序也。」

———— ✦ 第二十九章 ✦ ————

子曰：「可與共學，未可與適道；可與適道，未可與立；可與立，未可與權。」

語譯　孔子說：「有人可以和他一起學習，未必能夠一起向道；可以一起向道，未必可以一起堅定不移，可以一起堅定不移，未必可以一起權衡輕重。」

注釋　①適道　向道。②立　堅定不移。③權　權衡。

———— ✦ 第三十章 ✦ ————

「唐棣之華，偏其反而。豈不爾思？室是遠而。」子曰：「未之思也，夫何遠之有？」

注釋　tattered: adj. 破爛的；quilt: v. 縫合；hemp: n. 麻；fur: n. 皮衣。

✦ Chapter 27 ✦

The Master said, "When the year becomes cold, then we know how the pine and the cypress are the last to lose their leaves."

注釋　pine: n. 松樹；cypress: n. 柏樹。

✦ Chapter 28 ✦

The Master said, "The wise are free from perplexities; the virtuous from anxiety; and the bold from fear."

注釋　perplexity: n. 困惑。

✦ Chapter 29 ✦

The Master said, "There are some with whom we may study in common, but we shall find them unable to go along with us to principles. Perhaps we may go on with them to principles, but we shall find them unable to get established in those along with us. Or if we may get so established along with them, we shall find them unable to weigh occurring events along with us."

注釋　established: adj. 安頓下來的；weigh: v. 斟酌、衡量。

✦ Chapter 30 ✦

30.1. "How the flowers of the aspen-plum flutter and turn! Do I not think of you? But your house is distant."

30.2. The Master said, "It is the want of thought about it. How is it distant?"

語譯　「唐棣的花，翩然翻動。我難道不想念你嗎？只是我們住得太遠了。」孔子說：「只怕是沒有想念吧，如果眞的想念，又哪裡會遠呢？」

注釋　①**唐棣**　樹名。有人說是郁李，或以爲是枎栘。②**偏其反而**　偏同翩，反同翻。翩翩，搖曳生姿的意思。③**而**　語助詞。

解說　孔子引述這首逸詩，說明「我欲仁，斯仁至矣」的道理。

注釋　aspen-plum: 白楊李樹；flutter: v. 飄動；want: n. 缺少。

鄉黨第十

———————— ❖ 第一章 ❖ ————————

孔子於鄉黨，恂恂如也，似不能言者。其在宗廟朝廷，便便言，唯
謹爾。

語譯　孔子在自己的鄉里時，態度謙恭信實，好像不太會講話似的。他在宗廟和
　　　朝廷時，說話清楚明白，但是非常謹慎。

注釋　①鄉黨　家鄉。孔子生於鄹邑，後來遷居到闕黨。②恂恂如　恂音循，溫
　　　恭貌。③便便　辯也。說理清楚明白。

解說　〈鄉黨篇〉記述孔子的日常生活，原來不分章節，依朱注分為十七節。朱
　　　注：「似不能言者，謙卑遜順。不以賢知先人也。鄉黨，父兄宗族之所
　　　在，故孔子居之，其容貌辭氣如此。……宗廟，禮法之所在；朝廷，政事
　　　之所出：言不可以不明辨。故必詳問而極言之，但謹而不放爾。」

———————— ❖ 第二章 ❖ ————————

朝，與下大夫言，侃侃如也；與上大夫言，誾誾如也。君在，踧踖
如也。與與如也。

語譯　孔子在朝廷和下大夫說話時，態度溫和又快樂；和上大夫談話時，態度中
　　　正適度。國君視朝時，孔子的態度恭敬而自在。

注釋　①朝　指國君尚未視朝時。②侃侃如　和樂的樣子。③誾誾如　誾音因，
　　　《集解》：「孔曰：誾誾，中正之貌。」④踧踖　音促即，恭敬的樣子。⑤
　　　與與　皇侃疏：「與與猶徐徐也，所以恭而安也。」

解說　朱注：「王制，諸侯上大夫卿，下大夫五人。」諸侯有上大夫為三卿，即
　　　司徒、司馬、司空，三卿以下的大夫都稱為下大夫，孔子時仕魯為司寇，
　　　在司空之下，是下大夫。

———————— ❖ 第三章 ❖ ————————

君召使擯，色勃如也，足躩如也。揖所與立，左右手。衣前後，襜
如也。趨進，翼如也。賓退，必復命曰：「賓不顧矣。」

❖ Chapter 1 ❖

1.1. Confucius, in his village, looked simple and sincere, and as if he were not able to speak.

1.2. When he was in the prince's ancestral temple, or in the court, he spoke minutely on every point, but cautiously.

注釋　village: n. 村莊；ancestral: adj. 祖先的；minutely: adv. 詳細地。

❖ Chapter 2 ❖

2.1. When he was waiting at court, in speaking with the great officers of the lower grade, he spoke freely, but in a straightforward manner; in speaking with those of the higher grade, he did so blandly, but precisely.

2.2. When the ruler was present, his manner displayed respectful uneasiness; it was grave, but self-possessed.

注釋　freely: adv. 自由地、隨意地；straightforward: adj. 直率的；blandly: adv. 溫和地；precisely: adv. 準確地；uneasiness: n. 侷促不安；self-possessed: adj. 沉著的、冷靜的。

❖ Chapter 3 ❖

3.1. When the prince called him to employ him in the reception of a visitor, his countenance appeared to change, and his legs to move forward with difficulty.

語譯　魯君派孔子做接待賓客的擯相，他的神情莊重，步履謹慎。向兩旁的擯相作揖，或者向左拱手，或者向右拱手，衣服前後整齊飄動。由庭中趨進時，像鳥翼般舒展。賓客走了，一定回報說：「賓客已經離開了。」

注釋　①擯　接待國賓。②**勃如**　莊重的樣子。《集解》：「孔曰：必變色也。」③**躩**　音卻，《集解》：「包曰：盤辟貌。」走路時很謹慎的樣子。④**所與立**　同為擯相者。⑤**左右手**　朱注：「揖左人，則左其手；揖右人，則右其手。」⑥**襜**　音攙。整齊的樣子。⑦**翼如**　如鳥舒翼。⑧**不顧**　不回頭。

※ 第四章 ※

入公門，鞠躬如也，如不容。立不中門，行不履閾。過位，色勃如也，足躩如也，其言似不足者。攝齊升堂，鞠躬如也，屏氣似不息者。出降一等，逞顏色，怡怡如也。沒階，趨進，翼如也。復其位，踧踖如也。

語譯　孔子走進朝廷的門時，態度謹慎恭敬，好像沒有容身之地似的。站立的時候不站門的中央，走路的時候不踏門檻。經過國君的座位時，神情莊重，步履謹慎，說話好像沒說完似的。提起下襬升堂時，態度謹慎恭敬，屏氣像是沒有呼吸似的。出堂走下一級台階，便舒展臉色，很和悅的樣子。走完台階，便加快腳步，像鳥翼般舒展。再走過國君的座位時，又是恭敬的樣子。

注釋　①**公門**　君主之門。戴震：「諸侯之室，有庫門、有雉門、有路門。」這裡是指庫門。②**鞠躬**　恭謹的樣子。或解釋為曲身。③**閾**　門限。閾音欲。④**攝齊**　攝，收斂整飭。齊，衣下襬。⑤**逞**　舒展。⑥**沒階**　走完台階。

※ 第五章 ※

執圭，鞠躬如也，如不勝。上如揖，下如授。勃如戰色，足蹜蹜，如有循。享禮，有容色。私覿，愉愉如也。

3.2. He inclined himself to the other officers among whom he stood, moving his left or right arm, as their position required, but keeping the skirts of his robe before and behind evenly adjusted.

3.3. He hastened forward, with his arms like the wings of a bird.

3.4. When the guest had retired, he would report to the prince, "The visitor is not turning round any more."

注釋　reception: n. 接待；countenance: n. 臉色、表情；incline oneself to: 躬身；evenly:adv. 平整地；hasten: v. 疾行；turn round: 回頭。

※ Chapter 4 ※

4.1. When he entered the palace gate, he seemed to bend his body, as if it were not sufficient to admit him.

4.2. When he was standing, he did not occupy the middle of the gateway; when he passed in or out, he did not tread upon the threshold.

4.3. When he was passing the vacant place of the prince, his countenance appeared to change, and his legs to bend under him, and his words came as if he hardly had breath to utter them.

4.4. He ascended the reception hall, holding up his robe with both his hands, and his body bent; holding in his breath also, as if he dared not breathe.

4.5. When he came out from the audience, as soon as he had descended one step, he began to relax his countenance, and had a satisfied look. When he had got the bottom of the steps, he advanced rapidly to his place, with his arms like wings, and on occupying it, his manner still showed respectful uneasiness.

注釋　threshold: n. 門檻；vacant: adj. 空的；breath: n. 呼吸、氣息。

※ Chapter 5 ※

5.1. When he was carrying the scepter of his ruler, he seemed to bend his body, as if he were not able to bear its weight. He did not hold it higher than the position of the hands in making a bow, nor lower than their

語譯　孔子出使到外國，執君之圭，恭敬謹慎，好像無法勝任似的。執圭向上舉，像是在作揖，執圭向下擺，像是要交給別人。臉色凝重像在打仗，腳步很細碎，像是沿著一條線走路，獻玉以後，臉色便舒展開來。私人相見時，則是和顏悅色。

注釋　①**執圭**　《集解》：「包曰：爲君聘使鄰國，執持君之圭。」圭是玉器，上圓下方。②**上如揖，下如授**　朱注：「謂執圭平衡，手與心齊，高不過揖，卑不過授也。」③**蹜蹜如有循**　走路腳不離地，不敢放開大步，彷彿沿著軌道前進。④**享禮**　獻禮。⑤**有容色**　臉色從容。⑥**私覿**　和鄰國國君以私人身分見面。⑦**愉愉**　神情和氣。

※ 第六章 ※

君子不以紺緅飾，紅紫不以為褻服。當暑，袗絺綌，必表而出之。緇衣羔裘，素衣麑裘，黃衣狐裘。褻裘長，短右袂。必有寢衣，長一身有半。狐貉之厚以居。去喪，無所不佩。非帷裳，必殺之。羔裘玄冠不以弔。吉月，必朝服而朝。

語譯　君子不以深青色和絳色做鑲邊，不以紅色和紫色做居家便服。天熱的時候，穿葛布的單衣，出門必定再穿著上衣。黑色的衣服搭配黑羊皮裘，白色衣服搭配小鹿皮裘，黃衣搭配狐裘。在家穿的皮裘要比較長，但是右邊的袖子要短一些。睡覺要有小被，其長過身一半。冬天以狐貉的厚皮做爲坐墊。除了喪事以外，隨身佩戴玉器。除了祭祀穿的正幅帷裳以外，其餘的裙子必定斜幅裁製。不穿戴黑皮裘和黑帽子去弔喪。每年正月初一，必定穿著朝服去上朝。

注釋　①**不以紺緅飾**　紺音幹，深青色；緅音鄒，暗紅色。不以這兩種顏色做爲領口和袖口的滾邊。②**褻服**　家居時的服裝。③**袗絺綌**　袗音枕，單衣；絺綌音吃係，葛之細者爲絺，粗者爲綌。也就是穿著葛布單衣。④**表而出之**　表，上衣。出門時要穿著上衣。⑤**緇衣羔裘，素衣麑裘，黃衣狐裘**　緇衣，黑衣；羔裘，黑羊皮裘；素衣，白衣；麑裘，白色小鹿皮。是說穿在皮裘外的上衣顏色要相稱的意思。⑥**褻裘**　家居的裘衣。⑦**短右袂**　右手的袖子稍短，方便做事。⑧**寢衣**　小臥被。或謂睡衣。⑨**一身有半**　比身體長一倍半，有音又。或謂過身一半及膝。⑩**狐貉之厚以居**　以狐貉的

position in giving anything to another. His countenance seemed to change, and look apprehensive, and he dragged his feet along as if they were held by something to the ground.

5.2. In presenting the presents with which he was charged, he wore a placid appearance.

5.3. At his private audience, he looked highly pleased.

注釋　scepter: n. 權杖、王節；apprehensive: adj. 憂慮的；drag: v. 拖行；placid: adj. 平靜的；audience: n. 謁見。

───────────── ❖ **Chapter 6** ❖ ─────────────

6.1. The superior man did not use a deep purple, or a puce color, in the ornaments of his dress.

6.2. Even in his undress, he did not wear anything of a red or reddish color.

6.3. In warm weather, he had a single garment either of coarse or fine texture, but he wore it displayed over an inner garment.

6.4. Over lamb's fur he wore a garment of black; over fawn's fur one of white; and over fox's fur one of yellow.

6.5. The fur robe of his undress was long, with the right sleeve short.

6.6. He required his sleeping dress to be half as long again as his body.

6.7. When staying at home, he used thick furs of the fox or the badger.

6.8. When he put off mourning, he wore all the appendages of the girdle.

6.9. His undergarment, except when it was required to be of the curtain shape, was made of silk cut narrow above and wide below.

6.10. He did not wear lamb's fur or a black cap on a visit of condolence.

6.11. On the first day of the month he put on his court robes, and presented himself at court.

注釋　ornament: n. 裝飾；undress: n. 居家便服；reddish: adj. 略帶紅色的；fawn: n. 幼鹿；sleeve: n. 衣袖；badger: n. 獾；appendage: n. 附加物；girdle: n. 腰

厚皮做爲坐墊。⑪**去喪，無所不佩** 去喪，去除也。佩，佩戴玉飾。⑫**非帷裳，必殺之** 帷裳，朝祭之服，古制正幅如帷；殺之，殺音煞，斜幅裁製，上窄下寬。⑬**羔裘玄冠不以弔** 《集解》：「孔曰：喪主素，吉主玄，吉凶異服。」⑭**吉月** 月朔。指正月歲首。

—— ❖ 第七章 ❖ ——

齊，必有明衣，布。齊必變食，居必遷坐。

語譯 齋戒時，必定有特別的浴衣，用布縫製。齋戒時必定改變飲食習慣，遷移日常的居處。

注釋 ①**齊** 或作齋，齋戒沐浴。②**明衣** 浴衣。或謂乾淨的衣服。

—— ❖ 第八章 ❖ ——

食不厭精，膾不厭細。食饐而餲，魚餒而肉敗，不食。色惡，不食。臭惡，不食。失飪，不食。不時，不食。割不正，不食。不得其醬，不食。肉雖多，不使勝食氣。惟酒無量，不及亂。沽酒市脯不食。不撤薑食。不多食。祭於公，不宿肉。祭肉不出三日。出三日，不食之矣。食不語，寢不言。雖疏食菜羹，瓜祭，必齊如也。

語譯 米飯不嫌精緻，肉膾不嫌細切。飯悶久了變味，魚和肉腐爛，都不吃。食物變了顏色，不吃。變味了，不吃。烹煮的火候不對，不吃。時候不對，不吃。不按照正規切肉，不吃。沒有適合的調味醬，不吃。菜餚裡的肉雖然多，但是不能吃得比吃飯多。只有酒不限量，只要不喝醉就好。街上買來的酒和肉脯，不吃。薑是永遠不收起來的，但是不多吃。國家的祭祀，不把祭肉留到第二天。其他祭祀的祭肉則可以保存三天，過了三天就不吃了。吃飯時不交談，睡覺時不說話。雖然吃的是粗飯、菜湯和瓜類，也得先祭拜，而且要很恭敬。

注釋 ①**不厭** 朱注：「以是爲善，非必欲如是也。」或謂不飽食。②**食饐而餲** 饐餲音意艾，悶久了變味的意思。③**魚餒而肉敗** 魚爛曰餒，肉腐曰敗。④**失飪** 飪音任，煮得太生或太熟。⑤**不時** 正餐時間以外。⑥**不使勝食氣** 食音似，飯也。吃肉不多過飯。《正義》：「氣猶性也。」⑦**不撤**

帶：curtain: n. 窗帘；condolence: n. 弔唁。

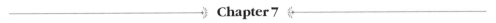

Chapter 7

7.1. When fasting, he thought it necessary to have his clothes brightly clean and made of linen cloth.

7.2. When fasting, he thought it necessary to change his food, and also to change the place where he commonly sat in the apartment.

Chapter 8

8.1. He did not dislike to have his rice finely cleaned, nor to have his mince meat cut quite small.

8.2. He did not eat rice which had been injured by heat or damp and turned sour, nor fish or flesh which was gone. He did not eat what was discolored, or what was of a bad flavor, nor anything which was ill-cooked, or was not in season.

8.3. He did not eat meat which was not cut properly, nor what was served without its proper sauce.

8.4. Though there might be a large quantity of meat, he would not allow what he took to exceed the due proportion for the rice. It was only in wine that he laid down no limit for himself, but he did not allow himself to be confused by it.

8.5. He did not partake of wine and dried meat bought in the market.

8.6. He was never without ginger when he ate. He did not eat much.

8.7. When he had been assisting at the prince's sacrifice, he did not keep the flesh which he received overnight. The flesh of his family sacrifice he did not keep over three days. If kept over three days, people could not eat it.

薑食　生薑能去腥，故不撤去。⑧**祭於公，不宿肉**　《正義》：「凡殺牲皆於祭日旦明行事，至天子諸侯祭之明日又祭，謂之繹祭，祭畢乃賜所祭之肉，及歸賓客之俎。則胙肉之來，或已三日，故不可再宿。」⑨**齊**　齊同「齋」，嚴敬貌。

※ 第九章 ※

席不正，不坐。

語譯　坐席不端正，不坐。

※ 第十章 ※

鄉人飲酒，杖者出，斯出矣。鄉人儺，朝服而立於阼階。

語譯　行鄉飲酒禮的時候，要等老年人走了，才可以走。鄉人驅逐疫鬼的時候，便穿著朝服站在家廟的東階上。

注釋　①**杖者**　老人。②**儺**　驅逐疫鬼。儺音挪。③**阼階**　阼音作。阼階，東階。

解說　皇侃疏：「孔子聞鄉人逐鬼，恐見驚動宗廟。故著朝服而立於阼階，以侍先祖，為孝之心也。朝服者，玄冠、緇布衣、素積裳，是鄉大夫之祭服也。」

※ 第十一章 ※

問人於他邦，再拜而送之。康子饋藥，拜而受之。曰：「丘未達，不敢嘗。」

語譯　請使者向外國的朋友問好，要對使者再拜送行。季康子派人送藥來問候孔子，孔子拜而接受，對使者說：「我還不清楚這藥性，還不敢試服。」

注釋　①**再拜而送之**　跪而拱手，首俯至手，頭不著地，亦即「空首」之禮。拜送使者，如拜所問候之人。②**饋**　贈送。

8.8. When eating, he did not converse. When in bed, he did not speak.

8.9. Although his food might be coarse rice and vegetable soup, he would offer a little of it in sacrifice with a grave, respectful air.

注釋　finely: adv. 美好地；mince: n. 細切的肉；damp: n. 濕氣；sour: adj. 發酸味；gone: adj. 過期的；discolored: adj. 變色的；flavor: n. 氣味；in season: 合時宜的；partake of: 吃喝；ginger: n. 薑；overnight: adv. 過夜；converse: v. 交談；coarse: adj. 粗劣的；grave: adj. 莊重的。

Chapter 9

If his mat was not straight, he did not sit on it.

注釋　mat: n. 草蓆；straight: adj. 整齊的、端正的。

Chapter 10

10.1. When the villagers were drinking together, upon those who carried staffs going out, he also went out immediately after.

10.2. When the villagers were going through their ceremonies to drive away pestilential influences, he put on his court robes and stood on the eastern steps.

注釋　staff: n. 杖、棍；pestilential: adj. 會傳染疾病的。

Chapter 11

11.1. When he was sending complimentary inquiries to any one in another state, he bowed twice as he escorted the messenger away.

11.2. Chi K'ang having sent him a present of physic, he bowed and received it, saying, "I do not know it. I dare not taste it."

注釋　complimentary: adj. 表示敬意的；inquiry: n. 詢問；escort: v. 護送；physic: n. 藥。

━━━━━━━ ✤ 第十二章 ✤ ━━━━━━━

廄焚。子退朝,曰:「傷人乎?」不問馬。

語譯　馬房失火了。孔子退朝回來知道了,便說:「有沒有人受傷?」而沒有問
　　　到馬。

注釋　①廄　馬房。

━━━━━━━ ✤ 第十三章 ✤ ━━━━━━━

君賜食,必正席先嘗之;君賜腥,必熟而薦之;君賜生,必畜之。
侍食於君,君祭,先飯。疾,君視之,東首,加朝服,拖紳。君命
召,不俟駕行矣。

語譯　國君賜熟食,必定擺正席位先吃;國君賜生食,必定煮熟後先獻祭給祖
　　　先。國君賜活的動物,必定豢養著。和國君一起吃飯,在國君獻祭時,先
　　　替國君試嘗飯。孔子生病,國君來探視,頭部朝著東邊躺著,身上披著朝
　　　服,拖著大帶。國君召喚,不待僕者駕車,立即徒步前往。

注釋　①腥　生肉。②薦之　獻祭給祖先。③生　活物。④君祭,先飯　《集解》:
　　　「於君祭,則先飯矣,若爲君嘗食然。」皇侃疏:「所以然者,亦爲君先
　　　嘗食,先知調和之是非也。」⑤東首　首音授。《正義》:「以室制尊西,
　　　君苟入室,則必在奧與屋漏之間,負西而向東,故當東首以示面君之
　　　意。」⑥紳　大帶。

━━━━━━━ ✤ 第十四章 ✤ ━━━━━━━

入太廟,每事問。

語譯　孔子進太廟,遇到每件事都要問。

❈ Chapter 12 ❈

The stable being burned down, when he was at court, on his return he said, "Has any man been hurt?" He did not ask about the horses.

注釋　stable: n. 馬廏。

❈ Chapter 13 ❈

13.1. When the prince sent him a gift of cooked meat, he would adjust his mat, first taste it, and then give it away to others. When the prince sent him a gift of undressed meat, he would have it cooked, and offer it to the spirits of his ancestors. When the prince sent him a gift of a living animal, he would keep it alive.

13.2. When he was in attendance on the prince and joining in the entertainment, the prince only sacrificed. He first tasted everything.

13.3. When he was ill and the prince came to visit him, he had his head to the east, made his court robes be spread over him, and drew his girdle across them.

13.4. When the prince's order called him, without waiting for his carriage to be yoked, he went at once.

注釋　undressed: adj. 未加調味料的；yoke: v. 套上軛。

解說　「腥」譯爲 undressed meat（未加調味料的肉），宜譯爲 fresh meat。

❈ Chapter 14 ❈

When he entered the ancestral temple of the State, he asked about everything.

---※ 第十五章 ※---

朋友死，無所歸。曰：「於我殯。」朋友之饋，雖車馬，非祭肉，不拜。

語譯 有朋友將死而沒有人為他料理後事。孔子說：「我來殯殮他。」朋友送禮，即使是車馬，只要不是祭肉，接受時都不行拜禮。

注釋 ①**無所歸** 沒有親屬為他安葬。

解說 朋友送禮，即使是車馬這麼貴重的東西，也當作平常事，所以不拜。而朋友致贈祭肉，為了尊敬其祖先，所以行拜禮。

---※ 第十六章 ※---

寢不尸，居不容。見齊衰者，雖狎，必變。見冕者與瞽者，雖褻，必以貌。凶服者式之。式負版者。有盛饌，必變色而作。迅雷風烈，必變。

語譯 睡覺時不像屍體般的挺直手腳，居家時不像有客人時的端正儀容。見到服喪的人，即使是親密的人，也要變容表示哀悼。見到大夫或盲人，即使是私下見面，也必定以禮相待。坐車時遇到穿喪服的人，要手扶車前橫木表示同情。即使是負販之賤，也要手扶車前橫木表示同情。宴會時有盛饌，必定整容起立。遇到打急雷和刮大風，也要變色表示不安。

注釋 ①**尸** 《集解》：「偃臥四體，布展手足似死人。」②**居不容** 容或作「客」。③**變** 變容表示哀悼。④**貌** 禮貌。⑤**凶服** 喪服。⑥**式之** 手扶著車前橫木。⑦**負版者** 負邦國之圖籍，賤隸人負之。或謂負販者，販夫走卒的意思。⑧**作** 起立。⑨**烈** 猛烈。

✳ Chapter 15 ✳

15.1. When any of his friends died, if he had no relations offices, he would say, "I will bury him."

15.2. When a friend sent him a present, though it might be a carriage and horses, he did not bow.

15.3. The only present for which he bowed was that of the flesh of sacrifice.

注釋　office n. 禮拜儀式。

✳ Chapter 16 ✳

16.1. In bed, he did not lie like a corpse. At home, he did not put on any formal deportment.

16.2. When he saw any one in a mourning dress, though it might be an acquaintance, he would change countenance; when he saw any one wearing the cap of full dress, or a blind person, though he might be in his undress, he would salute him in a ceremonious manner.

16.3. To any person in mourning he bowed forward to the crossbar of his carriage; he bowed in the same way to any one bearing the tables of population.

16.4. When he was at an entertainment where there was an abundance of provisions set before him, he would change countenance and rise up.

16.5. On a sudden clap of thunder, or a violent wind, he would change countenance.

注釋　corpse: n. 屍體；deportment: n. 舉止態度；acquaintance: n. 熟人；crossbar: n. 橫杆；abundance of: 很多的；provisions: n. 食物；clap: n. 隆隆聲；thunder: n. 雷。

---------------------------------- ✦ 第十七章 ✦ ----------------------------------

升車，必正立執綏。車中，不內顧，不疾言，不親指。

語譯　上車時，必定端正站著，手拉上車的繩索。在車上不回頭張望，不高聲說
　　　話，不用手指指畫畫。

注釋　①綏　挽以上車之索。②內顧　回頭張望。③疾言　高聲說話。或解釋爲
　　　說話急促。④親指　《正義》：「《曲禮》云：『車上不妄指。』『親』疑
　　　即『妄』字之誤。」

---------------------------------- ✦ 第十八章 ✦ ----------------------------------

色斯舉矣，翔而後集。曰：「山梁雌雉，時哉！時哉！」子路共
之，三嗅而作。

語譯　鳥類只要看到人們臉色不善，就會飛走，在空中迴翔很久，然後才安集。
　　　孔子說：「你們看山澗橋上的雌雉，他們也懂得時宜啊！懂得時宜啊！」
　　　子路聽了便起立拱拱手，他們回頭驚顧，便張翅飛走了。

注釋　①色　指人的臉色。或謂鳥驚飛貌。②翔　迴飛。③梁　水橋。④共　同
　　　「拱」，拱手。⑤嗅　本作「臭」，爲臭之誤，犬視貌，借作鳥之驚視。

解說　錢穆說：「此章實千古妙文，而論語編者置此於鄉黨篇末，更見深義。孔
　　　子一生，車轍馬跡環於中國，行止久速，無不得乎時中。而終老死於闕
　　　里。其處鄉黨，言行臥起，飲食衣者，一切以禮自守，可謂謹慎之至，不
　　　苟且，不鹵莽之至。學者試取莊子逍遙遊人間世與此對讀，可見聖人之學
　　　養意境，至平實，至深細，較之莊生想像，乎遠矣。」

❈ **Chapter 17** ❈

17.1. When he was about to mount his carriage, he would stand straight, holding the cord.

17.2. When he was in the carriage, he did not turn his head quite round, he did not talk hastily, he did not point with his hands.

注釋　cord: n. 繩索。

❈ **Chapter 18** ❈

18.1. Seeing the countenance, it instantly rises. It flies round, and by and by settles.

18.2. The Master said, "There is the hen-pheasant on the hill bridge. At its season! At its season!" Tsze-lu made a motion to it. Thrice it smelt him and then rose.

注釋　pheasant: 雉雞；by and by: 漸漸。

解說　「嗅」譯為 smelt，顯然有誤。

先進第十一

---------------------------※ 第一章 ※---------------------------

子曰：「先進於禮樂，野人也；後進於禮樂，君子也。如用之，則
吾從先進。」

語譯　孔子說：「在做官前先進學於禮樂的，是沒有爵祿的百姓；而做官後才進
　　　學於禮樂的，是卿大夫子弟。如果我要用人，我會選擇先學習禮樂的人。」

注釋　①**野人**　《正義》：「凡民未有爵祿之稱也。」②**君子**　《正義》：「卿大夫
　　　之稱也。」③**用之**　用人。

解說　關於「先進」和「後進」有多種解釋。或謂先進指五帝、後進三王，或謂
　　　先進指殷以前，後進指周初。朱子則說：「先進後進，猶言前輩後輩。野
　　　人，謂郊外之民。君子，謂賢士大夫也。」邢昺認為〈先進篇〉論弟子賢
　　　人之行，所以是指孔子先後輩弟子們。我們則採用劉寶楠的解釋：「是古
　　　用人之法，皆令先習禮樂而後出仕，子產所云『學而後入政』者也。其國
　　　之俊選，不嫌有卑賤……夫子以先進於禮樂為野人……春秋之時，選舉之
　　　法廢，卿大夫皆世爵祿，皆未嘗學問。及服官之後，其賢者則思為禮樂之
　　　事，故其時後進於禮樂為君子。」則所謂先進後進者，指的是弟子當中先
　　　學後仕者和先仕後學者。楊伯峻的語譯也採用這個說法。

---------------------------※ 第二章 ※---------------------------

子曰：「從我於陳、蔡者，皆不及門也。」德行：顏淵、閔子騫、
冉伯牛、仲弓。言語：宰我、子貢。政事：冉有、季路。文學：子
游、子夏。

語譯　孔子說：「以前跟我在陳國、蔡國的，現在都不在我這裡了。」德行好
　　　的，有顏淵、閔子騫、冉伯牛、仲弓。擅於使命應對的，有宰我、子貢。
　　　在政事方面，有冉有、季路。長於禮樂文章的，有子游、子夏。

注釋　①**不及門**　不在門下。或謂不及仕進之門。②**閔子騫**　姓閔名損，字子
　　　騫，孔子弟子。③**言語**　外交辭令。

解說　這就是著名的四科十哲。

⚜ Chapter 1 ⚜

1.1. The Master said, "The men of former times, in the matters of ceremonies and music were rustics, it is said, while the men of these latter times, in ceremonies and music, are accomplished gentlemen.

1.2. "If I have occasion to use those things, I follow the men of former times."

注釋　rustic: n. 鄉下人。

解說　英譯採朱注解釋。

⚜ Chapter 2 ⚜

2.1. The Master said, "Of those who were with me in Ch'an and Ts'ai, there are none to be found to enter my door."

2.2. Distinguished for their virtuous principles and practice, there were Yen Yuan, Min Tsze-ch'ien, Zan Po-niu, and Chung-kung; for their ability in speech, Tsai Wo and Tsze-kung; for their administrative talents, Zan Yu and Chi Lu; for their literary acquirements, Tsze-yu and Tsze-hsia.

注釋　distinguished: adj. 著名的、卓越的；acquirement: n. 才藝。

――――――――――― ❊ 第三章 ❊ ―――――――――――

子曰：「回也，非助我者也，於吾言無所不說。」

語譯　孔子說：「顏回啊，不是對我有助益的人啊，對我所說的話，無不欣然理解。」

注釋　①**無所不說**　說同悅，是說顏回聞言即解，心感喜悅。邢昺疏：「說，解也。」

解說　朱注：「助我，若子夏之起予，因疑問而有以相長也。顏子於聖人之言，默識心通，無所疑問。故夫子云然，其辭若有憾焉，其實乃深喜之。」

――――――――――― ❊ 第四章 ❊ ―――――――――――

子曰：「孝哉閔子騫！人不間於其父母昆弟之言。」

語譯　孔子說：「閔子騫真是孝順啊！他的父母兄弟都說他孝順，而人們聽了也沒有異議。」

注釋　①**間**　音見，非議的意思。

――――――――――― ❊ 第五章 ❊ ―――――――――――

南容三復白圭，孔子以其兄之子妻之。

語譯　南容經常複誦白圭之詩，孔子把姪女嫁給他。

注釋　①**三復**　常誦。②**白圭**　《詩經‧大雅‧抑》：「白圭之玷，尚可磨也。斯言之玷，不可為也。」勉人慎言。

――――――――――― ❊ 第六章 ❊ ―――――――――――

季康子問：「弟子孰為好學？」孔子對曰：「有顏回者好學，不幸短命死矣！今也則亡。」

語譯　季康子問孔子說：「你的弟子當中誰最好學。」孔子回答說：「有顏回好學，不幸短命死了，現在則沒有好學的。」

解說　見〈雍也篇〉。

❊ Chapter 3 ❊

The Master said, "Hui gives me no assistance. There is nothing that I say in which he does not delight."

注釋　delight: v. 高興。

❊ Chapter 4 ❊

The Master said, "Filial indeed is Min Tsze-ch'ien! Other people say nothing of him different from the report of his parents and brothers."

❊ Chapter 5 ❊

Nan Yung was frequently repeating the lines about a white scepter stone. Confucius gave him the daughter of his elder brother to wife.

注釋　line: n. 短詩。

❊ Chapter 6 ❊

Chi K'ang asked which of the disciples loved to learn. Confucius replied to him, "There was Yen Hui; he loved to learn. Unfortunately his appointed time was short, and he died. Now there is no one who loves to learn, as he did."

---※ 第七章 ※---

顏淵死，顏路請子之車以為之椁。子曰：「才不才，亦各言其子
也。鯉也死，有棺而無椁。吾不徒行以為之椁，以吾從大夫之後，
不可徒行也。」

語譯　顏淵過世後，他的父親請孔子把車子賣掉，好為顏淵做外椁。孔子說：
　　　「無論有沒有才能，總是自己的兒子。從前我兒子鯉過世的時候，也是只
　　　有棺而沒有椁。我不曾賣掉車子徒步行走來為他做椁，因為我也曾做過大
　　　夫，是不可以徒步的。」

注釋　①**顏路**　顏淵的父親，名無繇，也是孔子的弟子。②**椁**　音果，同槨，外
　　　棺。③**從大夫**　從大夫之列。

解說　《正義》：「顏路請車，禮有未合，夫子以其哀迫，不欲深責，而但婉言
　　　告知。至以鯉死為比，則亦視顏子猶子也。」

---※ 第八章 ※---

顏淵死。子曰：「噫！天喪予！天喪予！」

語譯　顏淵過世了，孔子說：「唉！天要亡我！天要亡我！」

注釋　①**噫**　感嘆詞，表示傷痛。

---※ 第九章 ※---

顏淵死，子哭之慟。從者曰：「子慟矣。」曰：「有慟乎？非夫人
之為慟而誰為！」

語譯　顏淵過世，孔子哭得很傷心。隨侍的人說：「老師過於悲傷了。」孔子
　　　說：「我悲傷過度嗎？我不為他哀慟，還為誰哀慟呢？

注釋　①**慟**　《集解》：「馬曰：哀過也。」

Chapter 7

7.1. When Yen Yuan died, Yen Lu begged the carriage of the Master to sell and get an outer shell for his son's coffin.

7.2. The Master said, "Every one calls his son his son, whether he has talents or has not talents. There was Li; when he died, he had a coffin but no outer shell. I would not walk on foot to get a shell for him, because, having followed in the rear of the great officers, it was not proper that I should walk on foot."

注釋　carriage: n. 馬車；shell: 外殼；coffin: n. 棺材；in the rear of: 在後面。

Chapter 8

When Yen Yuan died, the Master said, "Alas! Heaven is destroying me! Heaven is destroying me!"

注釋　alas: interj. 唉。

Chapter 9

9.1. When Yen Yuan died, the Master bewailed him exceedingly, and the disciples who were with him said, "Master, your grief is excessive!"

9.2. "Is it excessive?" said he. "If I am not to mourn bitterly for this man, for whom should I mourn?"

注釋　bewail: v. 哀傷；exceedingly: adv. 非常地；excessive: adj. 過度；mourn: v. 哀悼；bitterly: adv. 痛苦地。

------ ❧ 第十章 ❧ ------

顏淵死,門人欲厚葬之,子曰:「不可。」門人厚葬之。子曰:
「回也,視予猶父也,予不得視猶子也。非我也,夫二三子也。」

語譯　顏淵過世,同學們想要厚葬他。孔子說:「不可以。」結果同學們還是厚
　　　葬他。孔子說:「顏回看待我像父親一樣,但是我卻沒辦法待他如兒子一
　　　般。這不是我要如此的,都是你們這些學生幹的好事啊!」

解說　朱注:「喪具稱家之有無,貧而厚葬,不循理也。故夫子止之。門人厚葬
　　　之,蓋顏路聽之。歎不得如葬鯉之得宜,以責門人也。」

------ ❧ 第十一章 ❧ ------

季路問事鬼神。子曰:「未能事人,焉能事鬼?」「敢問死。」
曰:「未知生,焉知死?」

語譯　子路問孔子服事鬼神的方法。孔子說:「不能事奉活人,如何能事奉鬼神
　　　呢?」子路又問:「敢問死後如何?」孔子說:「生命的道理還不明白,
　　　如何知道死後的事?」

解說　《集解》:「陳曰:鬼神及死事難明,語之無益,故不答。」本章說明孔
　　　子對於鬼神和死後世界的態度。《正義》引趙佑《溫故錄》說:「禮有五
　　　經,莫重於祭。古之所為事鬼神者,嘗無不至,則子路之問,不為不切。
　　　夫先王之事鬼神,莫非由人事而推之,故生則盡養,死則盡享。唯聖人為
　　　能饗帝,唯孝子為能饗親。云『事鬼也,莫非教天下之事人也』,『吾未
　　　見孝友不敦於父兄,而愛敬能達乎宗廟者也』,則盡乎鬼神之義矣。進而
　　　問死,欲知處死之道也。人有所當死,有所不當死,死非季路所難,莫難
　　　乎其知之明,處之當。然而死非可預期之事,故為反其所自生。君子之窮
　　　理盡性,以至於命,歸於得正而斃,其不敢以父母之身行殆,不敢以匹夫
　　　之諒為名者,皆唯其知生。敬吾生,故重吾死也。否則生無以立命,死適
　　　為大愚而已,則盡乎知死之義矣。」《集解》把這句話解釋為孔子不道無
　　　益之語,實則大謬。趙佑的話可以闡明這點。

✷ **Chapter 10** ✷

10.1. When Yen Yuan died, the disciples wished to give him a great funeral, and the Master said, "You may not do so."

10.2. The disciples did bury him in great style.

10.3. The Master said, "Hui behaved towards me as his father. I have not been able to treat him as my son. The fault is not mine; it belongs to you, O disciples."

注釋　in great style: 奢華的。

✷ **Chapter 11** ✷

Chi Lu asked about serving the spirits of the dead. The Master said, "While you are not able to serve men, how can you serve their spirits?" Chi Lu added, "I venture to ask about death?" He was answered, "While you do not know life, how can you know about death?"

注釋　venture: v. 敢、冒昧。

―――――※ 第十二章 ※―――――

閔子侍側，誾誾如也；子路，行行如也；冉有、子貢，侃侃如也。
子樂。「若由也，不得其死然。」

語譯　閔子隨侍在孔子身邊，中正適度的樣子；子路則是剛強威猛；冉有、子貢
很和樂自在的樣子。孔子覺得很高興。孔子說：「像仲由這樣啊，只怕難
以善終吧。」

注釋　①**行行如**　剛強貌。

解說　朱注：「尹氏曰：子路剛強，有不得其死之理，故因以戒之。其後子路卒
死於衛孔悝之難。」

―――――※ 第十三章 ※―――――

魯人為長府。閔子騫曰：「仍舊貫，如之何？何必改作？」子曰：
「夫人不言，言必有中。」

語譯　魯國計畫要翻修長府。閔子騫說：「照著老樣子不好嗎？何必要翻修呢？」
孔子說：「這個人不說話則已，說了必定很中肯。」

注釋　①**長府**　官府名。《集解》：「鄭曰：長府，藏名也，藏財貨曰府。」②**仍
舊貫**　仍，因襲；貫，事也。仍舊貫，依照舊制的意思。③**夫人**　彼人，
指閔子騫。④**中**　合理。

解說　閻若璩《四書釋地》：「左傳昭二十五年：『公居於長府。』杜注：『長
府，官府名。』『九月戊，伐季氏，遂入其門。』長府，今不知所在，意
其與季氏家實近，公居焉，出不意而攻之。……又意公微弱，將攻權臣，
必先據藏貨財之府，庶可結士心。」魯昭公想要起兵翦除權臣，閔子騫以
微言諷之。

―――――※ 第十四章 ※―――――

子曰：「由之瑟，奚為於丘之門？」門人不敬子路。子曰：「由也
升堂矣，未入於室也。」

語譯　孔子說：「仲由鼓瑟的方式，怎麼能算是出自我的門下呢？」學生們因此

☀ **Chapter 12** ☀

12.1. The disciple Min was standing by his side, looking bland and precise; Tsze-lu, looking bold and soldierly; Zan Yu and Tsze-kung, with a free and straightforward manner. The Master was pleased.

12.2. He said, "Yu, there! -- he will not die a natural death."

注釋　bland: adj. 和藹的；soldierly: adj. 英勇的；die a natural death: 壽終正寢。

☀ **Chapter 13** ☀

13.1. Some parties in Lu were going to take down and rebuild the Long Treasury.

13.2. Min Tsze-ch'ien said, "Suppose it were to be repaired after its old style; -- why must it be altered and made anew?"

13.3. The Master said, "This man seldom speaks; when he does, he is sure to hit the point."

注釋　take down: 拆掉；treasury: 寶庫。

☀ **Chapter 14** ☀

14.1. The Master said, "What has the lute of Yu to do in my door?"

14.2. The other disciples began not to respect Tsze-lu. The Master said, "Yu has ascended to the hall, though he has not yet passed into the inner apartments."

不尊敬子路。孔子說：「仲由的學問已經不錯了，只是還不夠深入罷了。」

注釋　①**由之瑟**　《說苑·修文》：「子路鼓瑟，有北鄙之聲。」是說子路鼓瑟有殺伐之氣，不夠中正平和。瑟，樂器名。②**升堂入室**　比喻學道有深淺。

※ 第十五章 ※

子貢問：「師與商也孰賢？」子曰：「師也過，商也不及。」曰：「然則師愈與？」子曰：「過猶不及。」

語譯　子貢問道：「子張和子夏誰比較好？」孔子說：「子張太過，而子夏不及。」子貢說：「那麼是子張好一點嗎？」孔子說：「過和不及同樣不合理。」

注釋　①**愈**　勝也。

解說　朱注：「子張才高意廣，而好為苟難，故常過中。子夏篤信謹守，而規模狹隘，故常不及。」以射箭為喻，射過頭和射短了，都無法命中目標。

※ 第十六章 ※

季氏富於周公，而求也為之聚斂而附益之。子曰：「非吾徒也。小子鳴鼓而攻之可也。」

語譯　季氏比王室還要富有，而冉求為季氏宰，還為他搜括剝削百姓，增加他的財富。孔子說：「冉求不是我的學生，你們可以去聲討他。」

注釋　①**周公**　《集解》：「周公，天子之宰，卿士。」②**鳴鼓而攻之**　聲討其罪。《正義》：「凡責讓多用鼓也。」

解說　冉求怎麼可以為季孫剝削百姓呢？孔子顯然非常生氣。見《左傳·哀公十一年》：「季孫欲以田賦，使冉有訪諸仲尼。仲尼曰：『丘不識也。』三發，卒曰：『子為國老，待子而行，若之何子之不言也？』仲尼不對，而私於冉有曰：『君子之行也，度於禮，施取其厚，事舉其中，斂從其薄。如是，則以丘亦足矣。若不度於禮，而貪冒無厭，則雖以田賦，將又不足。且子季孫若欲行而法，則周公之典在。若欲苟而行，又何訪焉？』弗聽。」

注釋 lute: n. 琵琶。

解說 「丘之門」直譯爲 in my door，宜改爲 in my school。

※ **Chapter 15** ※

15.1. Tsze-kung asked which of the two, Shih or Shang, was the superior. The Master said, "Shih goes beyond the due mean, and Shang does not come up to it."

15.2. "Then," said Tsze-kung, "the superiority is with Shih, I suppose."

15.3. The Master said, "To go beyond is as wrong as to fall short."

注釋 superior: n. 優秀的人；due mean: 中庸；come up with: 趕上；fall short: 在目標前面落下。

※ **Chapter 16** ※

16.1. The head of the Chi family was richer than the duke of Chau had been, and yet Ch'iu collected his imposts for him, and increased his wealth.

16.2. The Master said, "He is no disciple of mine. My little children, beat the drum and assail him."

注釋 impost: n. 稅；assail: v. 抨擊。

————※ 第十七章 ※————

柴也愚，參也魯，師也辟，由也喭。

語譯　高柴性情愚直，曾參才質魯鈍，子張個性高傲浮誇，子路個性鹵莽。

注釋　①柴　高柴，字子羔，孔子弟子。②辟　《集解》：「馬曰：子張才過人，失在邪僻文過。」朱注：「辟，便辟也。謂習於容止，少誠實也。」③喭　音燕，剛猛的意思。朱注：「喭，粗俗也。」

解說　孔子談到學生們個性的缺失，以期自勉。

————※ 第十八章 ※————

子曰：「回也其庶乎，屢空。賜不受命，而貨殖焉，億則屢中。」

語譯　孔子說：「顏回大概是近道了，可惜經常處於貧窮當中。子貢不做官而跑去做生意，總是能夠預測物價起落。」

注釋　①庶　近也。言其近道。②屢空　經常陷於空乏。③不受命　不受祿。不做官的意思。朱注：「命，謂天命。」④貨殖　做生意。⑤億　猜測。

————※ 第十九章 ※————

子張問善人之道。子曰：「不踐迹，亦不入於室。」

語譯　子張問善人的行為。孔子說：「善人不循著前人的足迹走，但是也不會進入高深的境地。」

注釋　①善人　質美而未學者也。②踐迹　追循舊迹。

解說　《集解》：「孔曰：踐，循也。言善人不但循追舊迹而已，亦少能創業，亦不入於聖人之奧室。」《正義》則說：「踐迹者，謂學禮樂之事也。善人質美而未學，故必進於禮樂，乃可入室。」

————※ 第二十章 ※————

子曰：「論篤是與，君子者乎？色莊者乎？」

語譯　孔子說：「光是以其言論篤實便稱許他，哪裡知道他是君子呢？或者只是

⟐ Chapter 17 ⟐

Ch'ai is simple. Shan is dull. Shih is specious. Yu is coarse.

注釋　dull: adj. 遲鈍的；specious: adj. 虛有其表的；coarse: adj. 粗野的。

⟐ Chapter 18 ⟐

18.1. The Master said, "There is Hui! He has nearly attained to perfect virtue. He is often in want.

18.2. "Ts'ze does not acquiesce in the appointments of Heaven, and his goods are increased by him. Yet his judgments are often correct."

注釋　in want: 窮困；acquiesce: v. 默認、勉強同意 [in]；goods: 貨物。

⟐ Chapter 19 ⟐

Tsze-chang asked what were the characteristics of the good man. The Master said, "He does not tread in the footsteps of others, but moreover, he does not enter the chamber of the sage."

注釋　tread in a person's footsteps: 步某人的後塵、追隨某人。

⟐ Chapter 20 ⟐

The Master said, "If, because a man's discourse appears solid and sincere, we allow him to be a good man, is he really a superior man? or is his gravity only in appearance?"

外貌莊重的人呢？」

注釋　①與　稱許。②色莊　外表莊嚴。

解說　朱注：「言但以其言論篤實而與之，則未知其爲君子者乎？爲色莊者乎？言不可以言貌取人也。」

※ 第二十一章 ※

子路問：「聞斯行諸？」子曰：「有父兄在，如之何其聞斯行之？」冉有問：「聞斯行諸？」子曰：「聞斯行之。」公西華曰：「由也問聞斯行諸，子曰『有父兄在』；求也問聞斯行諸，子曰『聞斯行之』。赤也惑，敢問。」子曰：「求也退，故進之；由也兼人，故退之。」

語譯　子路問道：「聽到了道理就該立即去做嗎？」孔子說：「還有父兄在，怎麼能聽了就立即去做呢？」冉有問道：「聽到了道理就該立即去做嗎？」孔子說：「是的，該立即去做。」公西華說：「子路問：『聽到了道理就該立即去做嗎？』老師說：『有父兄在。』而冉求問：『聽到了道理就該立即去做嗎？』老師卻說：『立即去做。』我聽了很迷惑，敢再問個明白。」孔子說：「冉求總是畏縮不前，所以我得催促他前進；子路好勇過人，所以我要他退讓一些。」

注釋　①聞斯行諸　聞義即當勇爲嗎？諸，之乎，疑問詞。②兼人　勝人也。

解說　相同的問題可以有不同的答案，這是因材施教的方法，針對學生們的缺失，給他們適當的回答。

※ 第二十二章 ※

子畏於匡，顏淵後。子曰：「吾以女爲死矣。」曰：「子在，回何敢死？」

語譯　孔子被困於匡地，顏淵落在後頭。孔子說：「我以爲你死了。」顏淵說：「老師還健在，我怎麼敢輕易死去？」

解說　皇侃疏：「李充云：聖無虛慮之悔，賢無失理之患，而斯言何興乎？將以

❈ **Chapter 21** ❈

Tsze-lu asked whether he should immediately carry into practice what he heard. The Master said, "There are your father and elder brothers to be consulted; -- why should you act on that principle of immediately carrying into practice what you hear?" Zan Yu asked the same, whether he should immediately carry into practice what he heard, and the Master answered, "Immediately carry into practice what you hear." Kung-hsi Hwa said, "Yu asked whether he should carry immediately into practice what he heard, and you said, 'There are your father and elder brothers to be consulted.' Ch'iu asked whether he should immediately carry into practice what he heard, and you said, 'Carry it immediately into practice.' I, Ch'ih, am perplexed, and venture to ask you for an explanation." The Master said, "Ch'iu is retiring and slow; therefore I urged him forward. Yu has more than his own share of energy; therefore I kept him back."

注釋　perplexed: adj. 感到困惑；retiring: adj. 內向的、羞怯的。

❈ **Chapter 22** ❈

The Master was put in fear in K'wang and Yen Yuan fell behind. The Master, on his rejoining him, said, "I thought you had died." Hui replied, "While you were alive, how should I presume to die?"

注釋　rejoin: v. 重逢；presume to: 膽敢。

世道交喪，利義相蒙。或殉名以輕死，或昧利以苟生。苟生非存理，輕死
非明節。故發顏子之死對，以定死生之命也。」

───── ❀ 第二十三章 ❀ ─────

季子然問：「仲由、冉求可謂大臣與？」子曰：「吾以子為異之
問，曾由與求之問。所謂大臣者：以道事君，不可則止。今由與求
也，可謂具臣矣。」曰：「然則從之者與？」子曰：「弒父與君，
亦不從也。」

語譯　季子然問道：「仲由、冉求真可以說是大臣嗎？」孔子說：「我以為你會
　　　問別的事，哪裡知道你只問仲由和冉求而已！所謂大臣，應該是以正道為
　　　國君做事，如果不行，就辭官而去。現在仲由和冉求，只是聊備一格的臣
　　　子而已。」季子然又問：「那麼他們是聽話的臣子嗎？」孔子說：「弒父
　　　弒君的事，他們還是不會聽從的。」

注釋　①**季子然**　季氏子弟，得用仲由和冉求為臣而沾沾自喜，因而問孔子。②
　　　異之問　問別的事。③**具臣**　備位充數之臣。

解說　季氏僭竊，仲由和冉求身為家臣，卻無法以正道諫止，所以不得稱為大臣。
　　　但是兩人終究是有所不為的。孔子這句話也是在諷刺季氏的大逆之罪。

───── ❀ 第二十四章 ❀ ─────

子路使子羔為費宰。子曰：「賊夫人之子。」子路曰：「有民人焉，
有社稷焉。何必讀書，然後為學？」子曰：「是故惡夫佞者。」

語譯　子路舉薦子羔當費宰。孔子說：「害了人家的兒子。」子路說：「那裡也
　　　有百姓和社稷。何必要讀書才是做學問呢？」孔子說：「這就是為什麼我
　　　厭惡喜歡狡辯的人啊。」

注釋　①**賊**　害也。②**社稷**　社是土神，稷是穀神。這裡指的是祭祀的禮儀。③
　　　佞　朱注：「理屈辭窮，而取辦於口以禦人。」

⟡ Chapter 23 ⟡

23.1. Chi Tsze-zan asked whether Chung Yu and Zan Ch'iu could be called great ministers.

23.2. The Master said, "I thought you would ask about some extraordinary individuals, and you only ask about Yu and Ch'iu!

23.3. "What is called a great minister, is one who serves his prince according to what is right, and when he finds he cannot do so, retires.

23.4. "Now, as to Yu and Ch'iu, they may be called ordinary ministers."

23.5. Tsze-zan said, "Then they will always follow their chief; -- will they?"

23.6. The Master said, "In an act of parricide or regicide, they would not follow him."

注釋　extraordinary: adj. 非凡的；parricide: n. 弒父母之罪；regicide: n. 弒君。

⟡ Chapter 24 ⟡

24.1. Tsze-lu got Tsze-kao appointed governor of Pi.

24.2. The Master said, "You are injuring a man's son."

24.3. Tsze-lu said, "There are, there, common people and officers; there are the altars of the spirits of the land and grain. Why must one read books before he can be considered to have learned?"

24.4. The Master said, "It is on this account that I hate your glib-tongued people."

注釋　injure: v. 傷害；altar: n. 祭壇；glib-tongued: adj. 口齒伶俐的。

──────────── ✤ 第二十五章 ✤ ────────────

子路、曾皙、冉有、公西華侍坐。子曰:「以吾一日長乎爾,毋吾以也。居則曰:『不吾知也!』如或知爾,則何以哉?」子路率爾而對曰:「千乘之國,攝乎大國之間,加之以師旅,因之以饑饉;由也為之,比及三年,可使有勇,且知方也。」夫子哂之。「求!爾何如?」對曰:「方六七十,如五六十,求也為之,比及三年,可使足民。如其禮樂,以俟君子。」「赤!爾何如?」對曰:「非曰能之,願學焉。宗廟之事,如會同,端章甫,願為小相焉。」「點!爾何如?」鼓瑟希,鏗爾,舍瑟而作。對曰:「異乎三子者之撰。」子曰:「何傷乎?亦各言其志也。」曰:「莫春者,春服既成。冠者五六人,童子六七人,浴乎沂,風乎舞雩,詠而歸。」夫子喟然歎曰:「吾與點也!」三子者出,曾皙後。曾皙曰:「夫三子者之言何如?」子曰:「亦各言其志也已矣。」曰:「夫子何哂由也?」曰:「為國以禮,其言不讓,是故哂之。」「唯求則非邦也與?」「安見方六七十如五六十而非邦也者?」「唯赤則非邦也與?」「宗廟會同,非諸侯而何?赤也為之小,孰能為之大?」

語譯 子路、曾皙、冉有、公西華陪孔子坐著。孔子說:「我是比你們年紀大些,但是你們不要在意。平時你們常說:『沒有人知道我!』如果有人知道你們了,你們想做什麼?」子路立刻回答說:「假使有個千乘之國,夾在大國之間,外頭有敵軍來犯,內部又年歲饑荒;讓我來治理這個國家,只要三年,可以使百姓有勇,而且明白道義。」孔子對他笑一笑。又問:「求,那你會怎麼做呢?」冉有回答說:「假如有六、七十里的地方,或是五、六十里,要我去治理,只要三年,我可以使人民豐衣足食。至於禮樂教化,只好等待君子來設教了。」孔子又問:「赤,你會怎樣呢?」公西華回答說:「我不敢說能夠做得多麼好,只是願意學習罷了。宗廟祭祀,以及諸侯盟會,我願意穿著禮服,戴著禮帽,做個贊禮的小相。」「點,你怎麼樣?」曾皙正在鼓瑟,瑟聲稀落,鏗的一聲,推開瑟站了起來,回答說:「我沒辦法像他們三個人說得那麼好。」孔子說:「那有什麼關係呢?不過是說說各自的志願罷了。」曾皙說:「暮春三月的時候,

---
❋ **Chapter 25** ❋

25.1. Tsze-lu, Tsang Hsi, Zan Yu, and Kunghsi Hwa were sitting by the Master.

25.2. He said to them, "Though I am a day or so older than you, do not think of that.

25.3. "From day to day you are saying, 'We are not known.' If some ruler were to know you, what would you like to do?"

25.4. Tsze-lu hastily and lightly replied, "Suppose the case of a state of ten thousand chariots; let it be straitened between other large cities; let it be suffering from invading armies; and to this let there be added a famine in corn and in all vegetables: -- if I were entrusted with the government of it, in three years' time I could make the people to be bold, and to recognize the rules of righteous conduct." The Master smiled at him.

25.5. Turning to Yen Yu, he said, "Ch'iu, what are your wishes?" Ch'iu replied, "Suppose a state of sixty or seventy li square, or one of fifty or sixty, and let me have the government of it; -- in three years' time, I could make plenty to abound among the people. As to teaching them the principles of propriety, and music, I must wait for the rise of a superior man to do that."

25.6. "What are your wishes, Ch'ih," said the Master next to Kung-hsi Hwa. Ch'ih replied, "I do not say that my ability extends to these things, but I should wish to learn them. At the services of the ancestral temple, and at the audiences of the princes with the sovereign, I should like, dressed in the dark square-made robe and the black linen cap, to act as a small assistant."

25.7. Last of all, the Master asked Tsang Hsi, "Tien, what are your wishes?" Tien, pausing as he was playing on his lute, while it was yet twanging, laid the instrument aside, and "My wishes," he said, "are different from the cherished purposes of these three gentlemen." "What harm is there in that?" said the Master; "do you also, as well as they, speak out your wishes." Tien then said, "In this, the last month of spring, with the dress of the season all complete, along with five or six young men who have

穿好春天的衣服。邀青年人五、六個，小孩子六、七個，到沂水邊洗洗手臉，到舞雩那裡去乘涼，然後唱著歌回家。」孔子嘆口氣說：「我同意曾點的話啊！」子路、冉有、公西華走了，曾皙留在後頭，問孔子說：「他們三個人說得怎麼樣？」孔子說：「只不過是說說自己的志願罷了。」曾皙又說：「老師為什麼笑子路呢？」孔子說：「治國講求禮讓，他的言語卻一點也不謙虛，所以我笑他。」「然而冉求不是有志治理國家吧？」孔子說：「有地六、七十里，或是五、六十里，何以見得不算是個國家呢？」曾皙又說：「那麼赤說的不算是治國的理想了吧？」孔子說：「宗廟祭祀和諸侯盟會，不是諸侯的事是什麼？如果赤這樣的人只能做小相，那麼誰又能夠做大相呢？」

注釋　①**曾皙**　姓曾名點，曾參的父親，孔子弟子。②**毋吾以也**　不必以我年長而有所拘束。③**居**　平居之時。④**何以哉**　何以為用。⑤**率爾**　輕率。或謂急猝。⑥**攝**　促迫。⑦**師旅**　軍隊。二千五百人為師，五百人為旅。⑧**饑饉**　饑荒。穀不熟曰饑，菜不熟曰饉。⑨**比及**　比音必。將及。⑩**知方**　方，義方。道義的意思。⑪**哂**　微笑的意思。哂音審。⑫**如**　或。⑬**俟**　等待。⑭**宗廟之事**　指祭祀。⑮**會同**　盟會。⑯**端章甫**　端，玄端，衣名。章甫，冠名。古代朝祭之服。⑰**相**　相禮者。⑱**希**　稀落。⑲**撰**　《正義》：「撰，鄭本作僎，云僎讀曰詮，詮之善也。」應答得很好的意思。⑳**莫春**　暮春。近三月。㉑**春服**　單衣夾衣。㉒**浴乎沂**　到沂水洗洗手臉。沂水在曲阜縣南。㉓**舞雩**　祭天祈雨之處，有壇有樹。雩音余。㉔**風**　乘涼。㉕**與**　贊同。

解說　本章記述孔子學生們各自抒發志願。子路、冉有、公西華談的都是治國的理想，而曾點說的，則是教育的樂趣，所以孔子感嘆說：「吾與點也。」朱注：「程子曰：三子皆欲得國而治之，故夫子不取。曾點，狂者也，未必能為聖人之事，而能知夫子之志。故曰浴乎沂，風乎舞雩，詠而歸，言樂而得其所也。孔子之志，在於老者安之，朋友信之，少者懷之，使萬物莫不遂其性。曾點知之，故孔子喟然歎曰吾與點也。」經世致用是孔子的理想，學生們有此抱負，孔子應該很高興才對，未必不同意他們的想法。曾皙留在最後，想聽聽老師評論孰優孰劣，而孔子只是淡淡地說「亦各言其志也已矣」，這句話很耐人尋味。

assumed the cap, and six or seven boys, I would wash in the I, enjoy the breeze among the rain altars, and return home singing." The Master heaved a sigh and said, "I give my approval to Tien."

25.8. The three others having gone out, Tsang Hsi remained behind, and said, "What do you think of the words of these three friends?" The Master replied, "They simply told each one his wishes."

25.9. Hsi pursued, "Master, why did you smile at Yu?"

25.10. He was answered, "The management of a state demands the rules of propriety. His words were not humble; therefore I smiled at him."

25.11. Hsi again said, "But was it not a state which Ch'iu proposed for himself?" The reply was, "Yes; did you ever see a territory of sixty or seventy li or one of fifty or sixty, which was not a state?"

25.12. Once more, Hsi inquired, "And was it not a state which Ch'ih proposed for himself?" The Master again replied, "Yes; who but princes have to do with ancestral temples, and with audiences but the sovereign? If Ch'ih were to be a small assistant in these services, who could be a great one?"

注釋　straiten: v. 限制；famine: n. 饑荒；entrust: v. 交託責任；abound: v. 富足；extend to: 到達；audience: n. 謁見；twang: v. 發出弦聲；cherish: v. 懷抱；assume: v. 戴上；breeze: n. 微風；heave: v. 發出嘆息聲；pursue: v. 繼續說。

顔淵第十二

---------------------------✦ 第一章 ✦---------------------------

顏淵問仁。子曰：「克己復禮為仁。一日克己復禮，天下歸仁焉。
為仁由己，而由人乎哉？」顏淵曰：「請問其目。」子曰：「非禮
勿視，非禮勿聽，非禮勿言，非禮勿動。」顏淵曰：「回雖不敏，
請事斯語矣。」

語譯　顏淵問仁是什麼。孔子說：「約束自己，循禮而行，以實踐仁德。只要一
　　　日能夠這麼做，天下人都會稱許你是個仁者了。實踐仁德要從自己做起，
　　　難道還要靠別人嗎？」顏淵說：「請問實踐的條目。」孔子說：「不合禮
　　　的不要看，不合禮的不要聽，不合禮的不要說，不合禮的不要做。」顏淵
　　　說：「回雖然不聰敏，願意照著老師的話去做。」。

注釋　①**克己**　克，責也、勝也。克己，約束自己。②**復禮**　復，反也。也就是
　　　回歸正道的意思。③**為仁**　《正義》：「用力於仁。」④**歸仁**　歸與其仁
　　　也。把仁德歸於他的意思。⑤**目**　條目。

解說　仁是與天地萬物的生命感通，而體現在待人接物的日常生活裡，無非
　　　「視、聽、言、動」切實的反省功夫。《正義》：「《禮記‧禮器》云：『故
　　　君子有禮，則外諧而內無怨。故物無不懷仁，鬼神饗德。』鄭注以『懷
　　　仁』即『歸仁』。」

---------------------------✦ 第二章 ✦---------------------------

仲弓問仁。子曰：「出門如見大賓，使民如承大祭。己所不欲，勿
施於人。在邦無怨，在家無怨。」仲弓曰：「雍雖不敏，請事斯語
矣。」

語譯　仲弓問什麼是仁德。孔子說：「出門像是要接待貴賓，役使百姓像是舉行
　　　重大祭祀。自己不喜歡的，不要施加在別人身上。在邦國或在家族，都不
　　　使人有埋怨。」仲弓說：「雍雖然不聰敏，願意照著老師的話去做。」

注釋　①**大賓**　公侯之賓。②**承**　奉也。③**大祭**　指郊禘之祭。④**邦**　諸侯之國
　　　⑤**家**　卿大夫之家。

解說　《正義》：「左傳三十三年傳：『晉臼季曰：臣聞之，出門如賓，承事如

Chapter 1

1.1. Yen Yuan asked about perfect virtue. The Master said, "To subdue one's self and return to propriety, is perfect virtue. If a man can for one day subdue himself and return to propriety, an under heaven will ascribe perfect virtue to him. Is the practice of perfect virtue from a man himself, or is it from others?"

1.2. Yen Yuan said, "I beg to ask the steps of that process." The Master replied, "Look not at what is contrary to propriety; listen not to what is contrary to propriety; speak not what is contrary to propriety; make no movement which is contrary to propriety." Yen Yuan then said, "Though I am deficient in intelligence and vigor, I will make it my business to practice this lesson."

注釋 subdue: v. 征服、抑制；ascribe: v. 歸於；deficient: adj. 不足的 [in]；vigor: n. 活力。

解說 「天下」直譯爲 an under heaven，不如譯爲 everyone。「爲仁由已，而由人乎哉」譯爲 Is the practice of perfect virtue from a man himself, or is it from others，不合原意。

Chapter 2

Chung-kung asked about perfect virtue. The Master said, "It is, when you go abroad, to behave to every one as if you were receiving a great guest; to employ the people as if you were assisting at a great sacrifice; not to do to others as you would not wish done to yourself; to have no murmuring against you in the country, and none in the family." Chung-kung said, "Though I am deficient in intelligence and vigor, I will make it my business to practice this lesson."

注釋 murmuring: n. 埋怨 [against]。

祭，仁之則也。』亦古有此語，而臼季及夫子引之。……翟氏灝考異：
『管子小問篇引語曰：非其所欲，勿施於人，仁也。是「勿施」二句亦古
語。』」「己所不欲，勿施於人。」這句耳熟能詳的話，告訴我們在群體生
活裡要能夠互相尊重，尤其是在強調個人主義的現代社會，更能透顯其價
值。

―※ 第三章 ※―

司馬牛問仁。子曰：「仁者其言也訒。」曰：「其言也訒，斯謂之
仁已乎？」子曰：「為之難，言之得無訒乎？」

語譯　司馬牛問仁是什麼。孔子說：「仁者不輕易說話。」司馬牛說：「不輕易
　　　說話，就可以稱為仁嗎？」孔子說：「實踐的時候既然很難，說話的時候
　　　怎麼可以不慎重呢？」

注釋　①**司馬牛**　孔子弟子。《史記》：「司馬耕，字子牛，多言而躁。」②**訒**　音
　　　任。難也。鄭注：「訒，不忍言也。」或謂訒是說話遲鈍的意思。

解說　皇侃疏：「江熙曰：『禮記云：仁之為器重，其為道遠，舉者莫能勝也，
　　　行者莫能致也。勉於仁者，不亦難乎？夫易言仁者，不行者也。行仁，然
　　　後知勉仁為難，故不敢輕言也。』」

―※ 第四章 ※―

司馬牛問君子。子曰：「君子不憂不懼。」曰：「不憂不懼，斯謂
之君子已乎？」子曰：「內省不疚，夫何憂何懼？」

語譯　司馬牛問怎麼樣才算是君子。孔子說：「君子不憂不懼。」司馬牛說：
　　　「不憂不懼，就可以稱為君子嗎？」孔子說：「自我反省而沒有愧疚，有
　　　什麼好憂懼的呢？」

注釋　①**疚**　病也。

―※ 第五章 ※―

司馬牛憂曰：「人皆有兄弟，我獨亡。」子夏曰：「商聞之矣：

✳ **Chapter 3** ✳

3.1. Sze-ma Niu asked about perfect virtue.

3.2. The Master said, "The man of perfect virtue is cautious and slow in his speech."

3.3. "Cautious and slow in his speech!" said Niu; -- "is this what is meant by perfect virtue?" The Master said, "When a man feels the difficulty of doing, can he be other than cautious and slow in speaking?"

✳ **Chapter 4** ✳

4.1. Sze-ma Niu asked about the superior man. The Master said, "The superior man has neither anxiety nor fear."

4.2. "Being without anxiety or fear!" said Nui, "does this constitute what we call the superior man?" The Master said, "When internal examination discovers nothing wrong, what is there to be anxious about, what is there to fear?"

✳ **Chapter 5** ✳

5.1. Sze-ma Niu, full of anxiety, said, "Other men all have their brothers, I only have not."

『死生有命，富貴在天。』君子敬而無失，與人恭而有禮。四海之
內，皆兄弟也。君子何患乎無兄弟也？」

語譯　司馬牛憂愁地說：「人家都有兄弟，只有我沒有。」子夏說：「我聽人家
　　　說：『生死是命中註定，富貴有老天安排。』君子做事認眞而沒有過失，
　　　對人恭敬有禮，那麼天底下的人都會是你的兄弟。君子何必擔心沒有兄弟
　　　呢？」

注釋　①亡　同「無」。

解說　司馬牛的哥哥桓魋作亂，司馬牛很憂慮，孔子告訴他「君子不憂不懼」；
　　　他的其他兄長也跟著叛亂，後來四處流亡，所以司馬牛有「人皆有兄弟，
　　　我獨亡」之嘆。

※ 第六章 ※

子張問明。子曰：「浸潤之譖，膚受之愬，不行焉，可謂明也已
矣。浸潤之譖，膚受之愬，不行焉，可謂遠也已矣。」

語譯　子張問如何知人。孔子說：「像水逐漸滲透的讒言，如切膚之痛的指控，
　　　對他沒有作用，就可以說是知人。像水逐漸滲透的讒言，如切膚之痛的指
　　　控，對他沒有作用，就可以說是有遠見了。」

注釋　①明　《正義》：「明者，言任用賢人，能不疑也。《荀子・解蔽》：『傳
　　　曰：知賢之謂明。』」②浸潤之譖　《集解》：「鄭曰：譖人之言，如水之
　　　浸潤，漸以成之。」譖音ㄗㄣˋ。③膚受之愬　朱注：「膚受，謂肌膚所
　　　受，利害切身。愬，愬己之冤也。」《集解》：「馬曰：膚受之愬，皮膚外
　　　語，非其內實。」④遠　至明且遠。

解說　蘇軾說：「譖愬之言，常行於偏暗，而狹迫者。蓋有所聞而忿心應之也，
　　　明且遠者，虛以察之。則不旋踵而得其情也。」

※ 第七章 ※

子貢問政。子曰：「足食，足兵，民信之矣。」子貢曰：「必不得
已而去，於斯三者何先？」曰：「去兵。」子貢曰：「必不得已而

5.2. Tsze-hsia said to him, "There is the following saying which I have heard -- 'Death and life have their determined appointment; riches and honors depend upon Heaven.'

5.3. "Let the superior man never fail reverentially to order his own conduct, and let him be respectful to others and observant of propriety: -- then all within the four seas will be his brothers. What has the superior man to do with being distressed because he has no brothers?"

注釋　reverentially: adv. 恭敬地；distressed: adj. 苦惱的。

ᐧᔑ Chapter 6 ᔑᐧ

Tsze-chang asked what constituted intelligence. The Master said, "He with whom neither slander that gradually soaks into the mind, nor statements that startle like a wound in the flesh, are successful, may be called intelligent indeed. Yea, he with whom neither soaking slander, nor startling statements, are successful, may be called farseeing."

注釋　slander: n. 誹謗、中傷；gradually: adv. 逐漸地；soak: v. 滲透 [into]；startle: v. 使人吃驚；farseeing: adj. 有先見之明的。

ᐧᔑ Chapter 7 ᔑᐧ

7.1. Tsze-kung asked about government. The Master said, "The requisites of government are that there be sufficiency of food, sufficiency of military equipment, and the confidence of the people in their ruler."

去，於斯二者何先？」曰：「去食。自古皆有死，民無信不立。」

語譯　子貢問爲政之道。孔子說：「糧食充足，軍備充實，人民就會信任政府。」子貢說：「不得已要捨棄的時候，這三項當中，要先放棄哪一項？」孔子說：「捨棄軍備。」子貢說：「不得已要捨棄的時候，這兩者要先放棄哪一項？」孔子說：「減去糧食。自古以來，人都是要死的，但是政府失信於民，國家就無法建立了。」

注釋　①**足食，足兵，民信之矣**　朱注：「言倉廩實而武備修，然後教化行，而民信於我，不離叛也。」

解說　子貢追根究柢，問孔子這個兩難的問題。朱注：「民無食必死，然死者人之所必不免。無信則雖生而無以自立，不若死之爲安。故寧死而不失信於民，使民亦寧死而不失信於我也。」只要百姓對政府有信心，即使軍備不足，經濟窘困，也能夠風雨同舟，度過難關。《論語正義》則說「去兵、去食」是指免除兵役和賦稅，又發倉廩以振貧窮，別爲一解。皇侃疏：「李充曰：朝聞道，夕死，孔子之所貴，捨生取義，孟軻之所尚。自古有不亡之道，而無有不死之人，故有殺身非喪己，苟存非不亡己也。」

───────────────※ 第八章 ※───────────────

棘子成曰：「君子質而已矣，何以文為？」子貢曰：「惜！夫子之說君子也。駟不及舌。文猶質也，質猶文也。虎豹之鞹，猶犬羊之鞹。」

語譯　棘子成說：「君子只要本質善良就好，何必禮樂的教化呢？」子貢說：「可惜啊！先生這樣解說君子。說錯了話，就算有四匹馬的車子，也追不回來。教化如同本質，本質如同教化，是不可偏廢的。虎豹之皮去掉了花紋，和犬羊之皮就沒什麼兩樣。」

注釋　①**棘子成**　衛國大夫。②**夫子**　指棘子成。③**駟**　四馬也。古時用四馬駕一車。④**鞹**　音想廓。皮去毛者。

───────────────※ 第九章 ※───────────────

哀公問於有若曰：「年饑，用不足，如之何？」有若對曰：「盍徹

7.2. Tsze-kung said, "If it cannot be helped, and one of these must be dispensed with, which of the three should be forgone first?" "The military equipment," said the Master.

7.3. Tsze-kung again asked, "If it cannot be helped, and one of the remaining two must be dispensed with, which of them should be forgone?" The Master answered, "Part with the food. From of old, death has been the lot of all men; but if the people have no faith in their rulers, there is no standing for the state."

注釋　requisite: n. 必備條件；dispense: v. 免除 [with]；forgo: v. 放棄；part with: 割愛；lot: n. 命運；standing: n. 存續。

────────── ❊ **Chapter 8** ❊ ──────────

8.1. Chi Tsze-ch'ang said, "In a superior man it is only the substantial qualities which are wanted; -- why should we seek for ornamental accomplishments?"

8.2. Tsze-kung said, "Alas! Your words, sir, show you to be a superior man, but four horses cannot overtake the tongue.

8.3. "Ornament is as substance; substance is as ornament. The hide of a tiger or a leopard stripped of its hair, is like the hide of a dog or a goat stripped of its hair."

注釋　overtake: v. 追及；leopard: n. 花豹；strip: v. 剝去；hide: n. 獸皮。

────────── ❊ **Chapter 9** ❊ ──────────

9.1. The Duke Ai inquired of Yu Zo, saying, "The year is one of scarcity, and the returns for expenditure are not sufficient; -- what is to be done?"

乎？」曰：「二，吾猶不足，如之何其徹也？」對曰：「百姓足，
君孰與不足？百姓不足，君孰與足？」

語譯　哀公問有若說：「年歲歉收，國家財用不足，該怎麼辦？」有若回答說：
「何不實行什一稅？」哀公說：「什二稅都不夠了，怎麼可以只收什一
稅？」有若回答說：「百姓足用，國君怎麼會不足用呢？百姓不足用，國
君又怎麼會足用呢？」

注釋　①盍　何不。②徹　什一而稅謂之徹。③二　什二而稅。④孰　怎麼，疑
問詞。

解說　魯宣公十五年初稅畝，什中取二，至哀公年歲歉收，而有是問。有若則主
張回復什一稅古制以獎勵耕作，百姓足用，國庫就會充實。

———————————※ 第十章 ※———————————

子張問崇德、辨惑。子曰：「主忠信，徙義，崇德也。愛之欲其
生，惡之欲其死。既欲其生，又欲其死，是惑也。」（誠不以富，
亦祇以異。）

語譯　子張問如何增進德行、明辨疑惑。孔子說：「以忠信為主，以道義為依
歸，就可以增進德行。喜歡他的時候，要他生，不喜歡他的時候，卻要他
死。既要他生，又要他死，這就是疑惑。」（這樣對自己毫無好處，只是
使人奇怪罷了。）

注釋　①徙義　遷善也。②誠不以富，亦祇以異　出自《詩經·小雅·我行其野》。
程子認為「此錯簡，當在第十六篇。」

解說　「崇德辨惑」也是古訓，子張引以為問。

———————————※ 第十一章 ※———————————

齊景公問政於孔子。孔子對曰：「君君，臣臣，父父，子子。」公
曰：「善哉！信如君不君，臣不臣，父不父，子不子，雖有粟，吾
得而食諸？」

語譯　齊景公問孔子為政之道。孔子回答說：「國君要像個國君，臣子要像臣

9.2. Yu Zo replied to him, "Why not simply tithe the people?"

9.3. "With two tenths," said the duke, "I find it not enough; -- how could I do with that system of one tenth?"

9.4. Yu Zo answered, "If the people have plenty, their prince will not be left to want alone. If the people are in want, their prince cannot enjoy plenty alone."

注釋 scarcity: n. 不足；return: n. 收益；expenditure: n. 支出；tithe: v. 抽什一稅；want: n. 缺乏。

❈ Chapter 10 ❈

10.1. Tsze-chang having asked how virtue was to be exalted, and delusions to be discovered, the Master said, "Hold faithfulness and sincerity as first principles, and be moving continually to what is right, -- this is the way to exalt one's virtue.

10.2. "You love a man and wish him to live; you hate him and wish him to die. Having wished him to live, you also wish him to die. This is a case of delusion. 'It may not be on account of her being rich, yet you come to make a difference.'"

注釋 exalt: v. 提高；delusion: n. 迷惑、幻象。

❈ Chapter 11 ❈

11.1. The Duke Ching, of Ch'i, asked Confucius about government. Confucius replied, "There is government, when the prince is prince, and the minister is minister; when the father is father, and the son is son."

子，父親要像父親，兒子要像兒子。」景公說：「好極了，若是君不像君，臣不像臣，父不像父，子不像子，雖然有飯吃，我哪裡吃得下呢？」

注釋　①**齊景公**　朱注：「齊景公，名杵臼。魯昭公末年，孔子適齊。是時景公失政，而大夫陳氏厚施於國。景公又多內嬖，而不立太子。其君臣父子之間，皆失其道，故夫子告之以此。」②**信如**　如果。

解說　在分工的社會裡，每個人盡心扮演好自己的角色，才能維繫社會秩序於不墜。這也就是孔子所說的「正名」。《正義》引《白虎通‧三綱六紀篇》說：「君臣者，何謂也？君，群也，下之所歸心。臣者，繵堅也，屬志自堅固。父子者，何謂也？父者，矩也，以法度教子。子者，孳孳無已也。」

───────────── ✤ 第十二章 ✤ ─────────────

子曰：「片言可以折獄者，其由也與？」子路無宿諾。

語譯　孔子說：「根據片面之辭就可以做出判決，大概只有子路吧？」子路答應別人的事，絕不會拖很久。

注釋　①**片言**　即單辭。片面之辭。②**折獄**　斷獄。做出判決。③**宿諾**　宿即留也。承諾的事，不會拖很久。

解說　《集解》：「孔曰：片猶偏也。聽訟必須兩辭以定是非，偏信一言以折獄者，惟子路可。」毛奇齡《四書改錯》：「古折民獄訟，必用兩辭，故《周官‧司寇》：『以兩劑禁民獄。』先取兩劵而合之，使兩造獄詞各書其半，即今告牒與訴牒也。及聽獄後，復具一書契而兩分之，使各錄其辯，答之辭于其中，即今兩造兩口供也。是折獄之法，前劵後契，必得兩具，劵不兩具，即謂之單詞。」法官審理訴訟，必須聽取兩造當事人的陳述，怎麼可以只聽片面之詞就做出判決呢？孔子這句話使後來的學者很為難。《正義》：「人既信子路，自不敢欺，故雖片言，必是直理，即可令依此斷獄也。」錢穆亦採此說，聽起來還是很牽強。朱注：「子路忠信明決，故言出而人信服之，不待其辭之畢也。」把「片言」解釋為半句話，也就是說，三言兩語就可以斷獄，很貼近子路的個性。

───────────── ✤ 第十三章 ✤ ─────────────

子曰：「聽訟，吾猶人也，必也使無訟乎！」

11.2. "Good!" said the duke; "if, indeed, the prince be not prince, the not minister, the father not father, and the son not son, although I have my revenue, can I enjoy it?"

注釋　revenue: n. 歲入。

Chapter 12

12.1. The Master said, "Ah! it is Yu, who could with half a word settle litigations!"

12.2. Tsze-lu never slept over a promise.

注釋　settle: v. 解決；litigation: n. 訴訟；sleep over: 外宿。

解說　「子路不宿諾」或譯爲 he never delayed in giving his answer。

Chapter 13

The Master said, "In hearing litigations, I am like any other body. What is

語譯　孔子說：「審判案件，我也和別人差不多啊，最好是使人民不興訟吧！」

注釋　①聽訟　審理訴訟。

解說　朱注：「范氏曰：聽訟者，治其末，塞其流也。正其本，清其源，則無訟矣。」現在的社會濫行興訟，盲目相信訴諸法律是解決糾紛的唯一途徑，孔子的話很值得我們深思，以重新檢討法律在社會的功能。《大戴禮‧禮察》說：「凡人之知，能見已然，不能見將然。禮者，禁將然之前；而法者，禁於已然之後。是故法之用易見，而禮之所爲生難知也。若夫慶賞以勸善，刑罰以懲惡，先王執此之正，堅如金石；行此之信，順如四時；處此之功，無私如天地。爾豈顧不用哉？然如曰禮云禮云，貴絕惡於未萌，而起敬於微眇，使人日徙善遠罪而不自知也。……以禮義治之者，積禮義；以刑罰治之者，積刑罰。刑罰積而民怨倍，禮義積而民和親。」現在人們喜歡說「治亂世用重典」，卻不問問社會秩序爲什麼會崩壞。如果我們的社會講信修睦，需要用重罰嗎？

———————— ❋ 第十四章 ❋ ————————

子張問政。子曰：「居之無倦，行之以忠。」

語譯　子張問爲政之道。孔子說：「在位不要懈怠，做事要信實。」

注釋　①居之　居位。朱注：「居，謂存諸心。」

———————— ❋ 第十五章 ❋ ————————

子曰：「博學於文，約之以禮，亦可以弗畔矣夫！」

解說　見〈雍也篇〉。

———————— ❋ 第十六章 ❋ ————————

子曰：「君子成人之美，不成人之惡。小人反是。」

語譯　孔子說：「君子成全別人的好事，不成全別人的壞事。小人恰好相反。」

注釋　①成　成全也。

necessary, however, is to cause the people to have no litigations."

❈ Chapter 14 ❈

Tsze-chang asked about government. The Master said, "The art of governing is to keep its affairs before the mind without weariness, and to practice them with undeviating consistency."

注釋　weariness: n. 厭倦；undeviating: adj. 不偏不倚；consistency: n. 言行一致。

❈ Chapter 15 ❈

The Master said, "By extensively studying all learning, and keeping himself under the restraint of the rules of propriety, one may thus likewise not err from what is right."

❈ Chapter 16 ❈

The Master said, "The superior man seeks to perfect the admirable qualities of men, and does not seek to perfect their bad qualities. The mean man does the opposite of this.

注釋　perfect: v. 使其完美、貫徹。

———————— ❋ 第十七章 ❋ ————————

季康子問政於孔子。孔子對曰：「政者，正也。子帥以正，孰敢不正？」

語譯　季康子問孔子爲政之道。孔子回答說：「政就是正的意思。你以正道去帶領人民，誰敢不行正道呢？」

注釋　①帥　同率，領導。

解說　捷克文學家總統哈維爾（Vaclav Havel）說：「我贊同政治是實踐的道德，對眞理的服務，站在人類立場上對同胞愼重的關懷。」爲政者要好好反省「政者正也」這句話。

———————— ❋ 第十八章 ❋ ————————

季康子患盜，問於孔子。孔子對曰：「苟子之不欲，雖賞之不竊。」

語譯　季康子憂心魯國多盜匪。孔子回答說：「如果你自己不貪欲，就算是懸賞人民去偷盜，他們也不願意。」

注釋　①患　憂心。②欲　貪欲。③賞之不竊　朱注：「雖賞民使之爲盜，民亦知恥而不竊。」

解說　朱注：「胡氏曰：季氏竊柄，康子奪嫡，民之爲盜，固其所也。盍亦反其本耶？孔子以不欲啓之，其旨深矣。」

———————— ❋ 第十九章 ❋ ————————

季康子問政於孔子曰：「如殺無道，以就有道，何如？」孔子對曰：「子爲政，焉用殺？子欲善，而民善矣。君子之德風，小人之德草。草上之風，必偃。」

語譯　季康子問孔子爲政之道時說：「如果殺壞人以成就好人，你看怎麼樣？」孔子回答說：「你是主政者，何必用殺人的手段呢？你自己想行善，百姓也就會行善了。在上位的人好像風，老百姓像是草，風往哪邊吹，草就向哪邊倒。」

❀ **Chapter 17** ❀

Chi K'ang asked Confucius about government. Confucius replied, "To govern means to rectify. If you lead on the people with correctness, who will dare not to be correct?"

注釋　rectify: v. 改正；correctness: n. 端正。

❀ **Chapter 18** ❀

Chi K'ang, distressed about the number of thieves in the state, inquired of Confucius how to do away with them. Confucius said, "If you, sir, were not covetous, although you should reward them to do it, they would not steal."

注釋　thief: n. 小偷；do away with: 消除；covetous: adj. 貪婪的；reward: v. 獎勵；
　　　steal: v. 偷竊。

❀ **Chapter 19** ❀

Chi K'ang asked Confucius about government, saying, "What do you say to killing the unprincipled for the good of the principled?" Confucius replied, "Sir, in carrying on your government, why should you use killing at all? Let your evinced desires be for what is good, and the people will be good. The relation between superiors and inferiors is like that between the wind and the grass. The grass must bend, when the wind blows across it."

注釋　unprincipled: adj. 無道義的；evince: v. 表現。

注釋　①**就**　成就。②**偃**　仆倒。

解說　爲政者無道，只好以嚴刑重罰整飭社會，孔子則提出爲民表率之道。《集解》：「孔曰：就，成也。欲多殺以止姦。孔子欲令康子先自正。偃，仆也。加草以風，無不仆者，猶民之化於上。」《鹽鐵論・疾貧篇》說：「駻馬不馴，御者之過也。百姓不治，有司之罪也。春秋刺譏不及庶人，責其率也。故古者大夫將臨刑，聲色不御，刑以當矣，猶三巡而嗟嘆之。其恥不能以化而傷其不全也。政教闇而不著，百姓顛蹶而不扶，猶赤子臨井焉，聽其入也。若此，則何以爲民父母？故君子急於教，緩於刑。」

———————— ✵ 第二十章 ✵ ————————

子張問：「士何如斯可謂之達矣？」子曰：「何哉，爾所謂達者？」子張對曰：「在邦必聞，在家必聞。」子曰：「是聞也，非達也。夫達也者，質直而好義，察言而觀色，慮以下人。在邦必達，在家必達。夫聞也者，色取仁而行違，居之不疑。在邦必聞，在家必聞。」

語譯　子張問：「讀書人怎麼樣才是通達。」孔子說：「你所謂的通達是什麼意思呢？」子張回答說：「在國家要有名望，在卿大夫家也要有名望。」孔子說：「那是名聞，不是通達。通達的人啊，本性耿直而講道理，知道要觀察別人的言語和態度，總是想到謙退而處於別人之下。這樣的人，在國家或在卿大夫家都會通達。而有名聞的人，只是表面上愛好仁德，而行爲違背仁德，他卻心安理得，不會懷疑他自己是否有過，這樣的人，在國家或在卿大夫家，也會有名聞吧。」

注釋　①**達**　朱注：「達者，德孚於人而行無不得之謂。」《正義》：「達者通也。通於處人處己之道，故行之無所違阻。」②**聞**　名聲。③**慮以下人**　朱注：「卑以自牧。」④**色取仁而行違**　朱注：「善其顏色以取於仁，而行實背之。」⑤**居之不疑**　自以爲是，更不自疑。

Chapter 20

20.1. Tsze-chang asked, "What must the officer be, who may be said to be distinguished?"

20.2. The Master said, "What is it you call being distinguished?"

20.3. Tsze-chang replied, "It is to be heard of through the state, to be heard of throughout his clan."

20.4. The Master said, "That is notoriety, not distinction.

20.5. "Now the man of distinction is solid and straightforward, and loves righteousness. He examines people's words, and looks at their countenances. He is anxious to humble himself to others. Such a man will be distinguished in the country; he will be distinguished in his clan.

20.6. "As to the man of notoriety, he assumes the appearance of virtue, but his actions are opposed to it, and he rests in this character without any doubts about himself. Such a man will be heard of in the country; he will be heard of in the clan."

注釋　distinguished: adj. 卓越的、顯著的；clan: n. 氏族；notoriety: n. 惡名、聲名狼藉；humble: v. 謙遜；assume: v. 佯裝；rest in: 安於。

解說　「聞」未必是 notoriety（惡名），宜譯爲 fame（名聲）。

———— ✦ 第二十一章 ✦ ————

樊遲從遊於舞雩之下，曰：「敢問崇德、脩慝、辨惑？」子曰：「善哉問！先事後得，非崇德與？攻其惡，無攻人之惡，非脩慝與？一朝之忿，忘其身，以及其親，非惑與？」

語譯　樊遲跟隨孔子在舞雩臺下遊玩，他說：「敢問如何增進德行、排除惡念、明辨迷惑？」孔子說：「問得好！先做該做的事，然後得報，不就可以增進德行嗎？勇於自我反省而不去批評別人，不就可以消除惡念嗎？按捺不住一時的脾氣，忘了自己的生命安危，甚至忘記了父母親，這不就是迷惑嗎？」

注釋　①**舞雩之下**　《集解》：「包曰：舞雩之處，有壇墠樹木，故可遊焉。」
　　　②**脩慝**　《集解》：「孔曰：慝，惡也。脩，治也。治惡為善。」慝音特。

解說　魯昭公欲逐季氏，反被季氏逐，逐季氏那年適有雩禱，因此樊遲有感而問。崇德、脩慝、辨惑，都是雩禱之辭。孔子則以修身之事暗諷昭公之失，《正義》：「昭公不用子家羈，失政失民，是不能崇德。子家駒曰：『諸侯僭於天子，大夫僭於諸侯。』公曰：『吾何僭乎哉？』是攻人之惡，不知攻其惡也。『昭公不從其言，終弑之而敗焉，走之齊。』是不忍一朝之忿，忘身以及宗廟，惑之甚也。」

———— ✦ 第二十二章 ✦ ————

樊遲問仁。子曰：「愛人。」問知。子曰：「知人。」樊遲未達。子曰：「舉直錯諸枉，能使枉者直。」樊遲退，見子夏。曰：「鄉也吾見於夫子而問知，子曰：『舉直錯諸枉，能使枉者直。』何謂也？」子夏曰：「富哉言乎！舜有天下，選於眾，舉皋陶，不仁者遠矣。湯有天下，選於眾，舉伊尹，不仁者遠矣。」

語譯　樊遲問什麼是仁。孔子說：「愛人。」又問什麼是智。孔子說：「知人。」樊遲還不完全明白。孔子說：「舉用正直的人在邪曲的人之上，可以使邪曲的人正直。」樊遲離開，去見子夏。樊遲說：「剛才我去見老師，問他什麼是智，老師說：『舉用正直的人在邪曲的人之上，可以使邪曲的人正直。』這是什麼意思啊？」子夏說：「這句話的蘊義真是深遠啊！舜有了

Chapter 21

21.1. Fan Ch'ih rambling with the Master under the trees about the rain altars, said, "I venture to ask how to exalt virtue, to correct cherished evil, and to discover delusions."

21.2. The Master said, "Truly a good question!

21.3. "If doing what is to be done be made the first business, and success a secondary consideration: -- is not this the way to exalt virtue? To assail one's own wickedness and not assail that of others; -- is not this the way to correct cherished evil? For a morning's anger to disregard one's own life, and involve that of his parents; -- is not this a case of delusion?"

注釋　ramble: v. 漫步；disregard: v. 不顧；involve: v. 連累、牽扯。

Chapter 22

22.1. Fan Ch'ih asked about benevolence. The Master said, "It is to love all men." He asked about knowledge. The Master said, "It is to know all men."

22.2. Fan Ch'ih did not immediately understand these answers.

22.3. The Master said, "Employ the upright and put aside all the crooked; in this way the crooked can be made to be upright."

22.4. Fan Ch'ih retired, and, seeing Tsze-hsia, he said to him, "A little while ago, I had an interview with our Master, and asked him about knowledge. He said, 'Employ the upright, and put aside all the crooked; -- in this way, the crooked will be made to be upright.' What did he mean?"

天下，在眾人之中選出皋陶而舉用他，那些不仁的人也就遠離了。湯有了
天下，在眾人之中選出伊尹來舉用他，那些不仁的人也就遠離了。」

注釋　①未達　不明白。②鄉　又作嚮。前些時候。③皋陶　陶音姚，舜之賢
相。《書經·舜典》：「命皋陶曰：汝作士。」④伊尹　湯之賢相。

解說　《大戴禮·主言篇》：「仁者莫大於愛人，知者莫大於知人。」關於仁是
什麼，孔子有不同的回答。不過學者多以「仁者愛人」去闡述孔子的仁道
思想。徐復觀認為這個定義尚不足以窮究仁的本源，他在《中國人性論
史》說：「就仁的自身而言，它只是一個人的自覺地精神狀態……。一方
面是對自己人格的建立及知識的追求，發出無限的要求。另一方面，是對
他人毫無條件地感到有應盡的無限地責任。」勞思光也強調「仁」是道德
主體自覺的主宰性。其實「愛人」也可以是自覺的道德表現。唐君毅從個
人與自身、他人、乃至天地萬物的內在生命感通去解釋「仁」，最能發揮
孔子的聖者境界（見《中國哲學原論·原道篇·卷一》）。

———————— ✤ 第二十三章 ✤ ————————

子貢問友。子曰：「忠告而善道之，不可則止，無自辱焉。」

語譯　子貢問交友之道。孔子說：「朋友有過，要盡心地勸導他，如果不接受，
也就罷了，不要自討沒趣。」

注釋　①道　同導，導之以義。

解說　朱注：「友所以輔仁，故盡其心以告之，善其說以道之。然以義合者也，
故不可則止。若以數而見疏，則自辱矣。」

———————— ✤ 第二十四章 ✤ ————————

曾子曰：「君子以文會友，以友輔仁。」

語譯　曾子說：「君子以禮樂文章來交朋友，以朋友輔助自己增進德行。」

注釋　①文　詩書禮樂。

解說　《易經·兌卦》：「君子以朋友講習。」

22.5. Tsze-hsia said, "Truly rich is his saying!

22.6. "Shun, being in possession of the kingdom, selected from among all the people, and employed Kai-yao, on which all who were devoid of virtue disappeared. T'ang, being in possession of the kingdom, selected from among all the people, and employed I Yin -- and all who were devoid of virtue disappeared."

注釋　benevolence: n. 仁心、慈悲；interview: n. 面談；devoid of: 缺少。

※ **Chapter 23** ※

Tsze-kung asked about friendship. The Master said, "Faithfully admonish your friend, and skillfully lead him on. If you find him impracticable, stop. Do not disgrace yourself."

注釋　friendship: n. 友誼；admonish: v. 勸告；lead on: 引導；impracticable: adj. 不能實行的；disgrace oneself: 出醜、丟臉。

※ **Chapter 24** ※

The philosopher Tsang said, "The superior man on grounds of culture meets with his friends, and by friendship helps his virtue."

子路第十三

───────────── ❀ 第一章 ❀ ─────────────

子路問政。子曰：「先之，勞之。」請益。曰：「無倦。」

語譯　子路問爲政之道。孔子說：「凡事以身作則，而且不辭勞苦。」子路請孔
　　　子多說一點。孔子說：「永遠不要懈怠。」

注釋　①**先之勞之**　《集解》：「孔曰：先導之以德，使民信之，然後勞之。」朱
　　　注：「蘇氏曰：凡民之行，以身先之，則不令而行。凡民之事，以身勞之，
　　　則雖勤不怨。」這裡採朱注的解釋。身先其民而勞，則民勞而無怨。②**請
　　　益**　益，增也。請說得仔細一些。

───────────── ❀ 第二章 ❀ ─────────────

仲弓為季氏宰，問政。子曰：「先有司，赦小過，舉賢才。」曰：
「焉知賢才而舉之？」曰：「舉爾所知。爾所不知，人其舍諸？」

語譯　仲弓做了季氏的家宰，來問爲政之道。孔子說：「爲下屬做表率，不計較
　　　小過失，拔擢優秀人才。」仲弓問：「如何知道誰有才能而提拔他們呢？」
　　　孔子說：「拔擢你所知道的。那些你不知道的，別人會捨棄不用嗎？」

注釋　①**先**　以身率之。②**有司**　百官。

解說　本章的「先有司」和前章的「先之」，都是強調爲政者要以身作則。而
　　　爲政以寬，不斤斤計較下屬的小過失，有才能的人才能夠勇於任事。《集
　　　解》：「王曰：言爲政者當先任有司，而後責其事。」這裡不採此說。

───────────── ❀ 第三章 ❀ ─────────────

子路曰：「衛君待子而為政，子將奚先？」子曰：「必也正名乎！」
子路曰：「有是哉，子之迂也！奚其正？」子曰：「野哉，由也！
君子於其所不知，蓋闕如也。名不正，則言不順；言不順，則事
不成；事不成，則禮樂不興；禮樂不興，則刑罰不中；刑罰不中，
則民無所措手足。故君子名之必可言也，言之必可行也。君子於其
言，無所苟而已矣。」

Chapter 1

1.1. Tsze-lu asked about government. The Master said, "Go before the people with your example, and be laborious in their affairs."

1.2. He requested further instruction, and was answered, "Be not weary in these things."

注釋 laborious: adj. 勤勉的；weary: adj. 厭倦的。

Chapter 2

2.1. Chung-kung, being chief minister to the head of the Chi family, asked about government. The Master said, "Employ first the services of your various officers, pardon small faults, and raise to office men of virtue and talents."

2.2. Chung-kung said, "How shall I know the men of virtue and talent, so that I may raise them to office?" He was answered, "Raise to office those whom you know. As to those whom you do not know, will others neglect them?"

注釋 pardon: v. 原諒；raise: v. 擢升。

Chapter 3

3.1. Tsze-lu said, "The ruler of Wei has been waiting for you, in order with you to administer the government. What will you consider the first thing to be done?"

3.2. The Master replied, "What is necessary is to rectify names."

3.3. "So! indeed!" said Tsze-lu. "You are wide of the mark! Why must there be such rectification?"

3.4. The Master said, "How uncultivated you are, Yu! A superior man, in

語譯　子路說：「如果衛國國君要老師去執政，老師要先從哪裡下手？」孔子說：「那必定要先正名分吧！」子路：「老師迂腐到這種程度！何必要正名分呢？」孔子說：「你眞是粗鄙啊！君子對於自己不知道的事，是不會亂說話的。名分不正，言詞就不會合理，言詞不合理，政務就無法推行，政務無法推行，禮樂制度就無法建立，沒有禮樂制度，刑罰就不會得當，刑罰不得當，百姓就不知道怎麼做才好。因此君子定名分，必定是要能夠說得出口，說出來的，必定要做得到。君子對於他所說的話，絕不隨便苟且。」

注釋　①**衛君**　朱注：「衛君，謂出公輒也。是時魯哀公之十年，孔子自楚反乎衛。」②**正名**　正名分。③**迂**　迂遠不切實務。④**野**　粗鄙。⑤**不順**　不合理。⑥**中**　中於理。⑦**苟**　輕率苟且。

解說　朱注：「胡氏曰：衛世子蒯聵恥其母南子之淫亂，欲殺之不果而出奔。靈公欲立公子郢，郢辭。公卒，夫人立之，又辭。乃立蒯聵之子輒，以拒蒯聵。夫蒯聵欲殺母，得罪於父，而輒據國以拒父，皆無父之人也，其不可有國也明矣。夫子爲政，而以正名爲先。必將具其事之本末，告諸天王，請于方伯，命公子郢而立之。則人倫正，天理得，名正言順而事成矣。夫子告之之詳如此，而子路終不喻也。故事輒不去，卒死其難。徒知食爲不避其難之爲義，而不知食輒之食爲非義也。」衛君輒是靈公世子蒯聵的兒子。蒯聵得罪母親南子而出奔，靈公死後，衛人立輒爲王，晉國的趙鞅助蒯聵返衛得國，輒出奔。蒯聵與輒父子爭國，父不父，子不子，孔子所謂「正名」，其意在此。以現代社會來看，「正名」即是權利義務的畫分，這是建立社會秩序的基本條件。

※　第四章　※

樊遲請學稼，子曰：「吾不如老農。」請學爲圃。曰：「吾不如老圃。」樊遲出。子曰：「小人哉，樊須也！上好禮，則民莫敢不敬；上好義，則民莫敢不服；上好信，則民莫敢不用情。夫如是，則四方之民襁負其子而至矣，焉用稼？」

語譯　樊遲想學種五穀。孔子說：「我不如老農夫。」樊遲又想學種菜。孔子說：「我不如老菜農。」樊遲離開後，孔子說：「樊遲眞是鄙陋啊！在上位者講求禮節，百姓便不敢不謙讓；在上位者行爲正當，百姓便不敢不循

regard to what he does not know, shows a cautious reserve.

3.5. "If names be not correct, language is not in accordance with the truth of things. If language be not in accordance with the truth of things, affairs cannot be carried on to success.

3.6. "When affairs cannot be carried on to success, proprieties and music do not flourish. When proprieties and music do not flourish, punishments will not be properly awarded. When punishments are not properly awarded, the people do not know how to move hand or foot.

3.7. "Therefore a superior man considers it necessary that the names he uses may be spoken appropriately, and also that what he speaks may be carried out appropriately. What the superior man requires is just that in his words there may be nothing incorrect."

注釋　wide of the mark: 不得要領；rectification: n. 糾正；flourish: v. 興盛；award: v. 判處；appropriately: adv. 適當地。

───────────── ❈ **Chapter 4** ❈ ─────────────

4.1. Fan Ch'ih requested to be taught husbandry. The Master said, "I am not so good for that as an old husbandman." He requested also to be taught gardening, and was answered, "I am not so good for that as an old gardener."

4.2. Fan Ch'ih having gone out, the Master said, "A small man, indeed, is Fan Hsu! If a superior man love propriety, the people will not dare not to be reverent. If he love righteousness, the people will not dare not to submit to his example. If he love good faith, the people will not dare

義。在上位者說話信實，百姓便不敢不忠誠。能做到這個地步，各地的民眾都會揹著小孩來投奔，為什麼要自己種莊稼呢？」

注釋　①**稼**　種五穀。②**圃**　種蔬菜。③**小人**　朱注：「謂細民。」指老百姓。④**用情**　誠實以對。⑤**襁負**　朱注：「襁，織縷爲之，以約小兒於背者。」

解說　《集解》：「包曰：禮義與信，足以成德，何用學稼以教民乎？」孟子說：「有大人之事，有小人之事。」又說：「或勞心，或勞力；勞心者治人，勞力者治於人；治於人者食人，治人者食於人；天下之通義也。」以現代的分工觀點來看，政治也是一種專業，爲政者不必習百工技藝才能夠領導國家。

※ 第五章 ※

子曰：「誦詩三百，授之以政，不達；使於四方，不能專對；雖多，亦奚以爲？」

語譯　孔子說：「熟讀詩經三百篇，授他以政事，卻做不好；派他出使外國，卻無法獨力應對；那麼儘管讀得多，又有什麼用處呢？」

注釋　①**不達**　不能通上下之情。②**專對**　以己意應對。

解說　朱注：「程子曰：窮經將以致用也。世之誦詩者，果能從政而專對乎？然則其所學者，章句之末耳，此學者之大患也。」如果只是讀死書而無法致用，那麼讀得再多都沒有用。

※ 第六章 ※

子曰：「其身正，不令而行；其不正，雖令不從。」

語譯　孔子說：「爲政者自己行爲正當，那麼不等他下命令，百姓便會照著去做；自己行爲不正當，即使是三令五申，百姓也不會聽從。」

※ 第七章 ※

子曰：「魯衛之政，兄弟也。」

not to be sincere. Now, when these things obtain, the people from all quarters will come to him, bearing their children on their backs; what need has he of a knowledge of husbandry?"

注釋　husbandry: n. 耕作；husbandman: n. 農夫；gardening: n. 園藝；gardener: n. 園丁；submit to: 服從；good faith: 誠實；bear: 揹負。

※ **Chapter 5** ※

The Master said, "Though a man may be able to recite the three hundred odes, yet if, when entrusted with a governmental charge, he knows not how to act, or if, when sent to any quarter on a mission, he cannot give his replies unassisted, notwithstanding the extent of his learning, of what practical use is it?"

注釋　recite: v. 背誦；unassisted: adv. 獨力地；notwithstanding: prep. 儘管；practical: adj. 實際的。

※ **Chapter 6** ※

The Master said, "When a prince's personal conduct is correct, his government is effective without the issuing of orders. If his personal conduct is not correct, he may issue orders, but they will not be followed."

注釋　issue: v. 頒布。

※ **Chapter 7** ※

The Master said, "The governments of Lu and Wei are brothers."

語譯　孔子說：「魯國和衛國的政治，真像是兄弟啊！」

解說　《集解》：「包曰：魯，周公之封，衛，康叔之封。周公、康叔，既為兄弟，康叔睦於周公，其國之政，亦如兄弟。」這兩國政治到底是一樣好還是一樣糟糕，各家解釋不同。

※ 第八章 ※

子謂：「衛公子荊善居室。始有，曰：『苟合矣。』少有，曰：『苟完矣。』富有，曰：『苟美矣。』」

語譯　孔子說：「衛公子荊很會治理家室。剛有財貨時，他說：『差不多夠了。』稍多時，他說：『差不多完備了。』到了更多的時候，他說：『差不多完美了。』」

注釋　①**公子荊**　衛國大夫。②**善居室**　很會治理家室。皇侃疏：「居其家能治，不為奢侈，故曰善也。」③**苟**　差不多的意思。④**合**　足夠。⑤**少有**　稍有。

解說　《正義》：「『苟』者，誠也，信也。『合』者，言已合禮，不以儉為嫌也。『完』者，器用完備也。『美』者，盡飾也。」亦通。

※ 第九章 ※

子適衛，冉有僕。子曰：「庶矣哉！」冉有曰：「既庶矣，又何加焉？」曰：「富之。」曰：「既富矣，又何加焉？」曰：「教之。」

語譯　孔子到衛國去，冉有為孔子趕車。孔子說：「衛國的人口真多啊！」冉有說：「人口多了，接下來該怎麼辦？」孔子說：「使他們富足。」冉有又說：「富足以後，接下來該怎麼辦？」孔子說：「教育他們。」

注釋　①**庶**　眾多。

解說　孔子談到為政當先富民。《孟子・梁惠王》：「是故明君制民之產，必使仰足以事父母，俯足以畜妻子，樂歲終身飽，凶年免於死亡。然後驅而之善，故民之從之也輕。今也制民之產，仰不足以事父母，俯不足以畜妻子，樂歲終身苦，凶年不免於死亡。此惟救死而恐不贍，奚暇治禮義哉？」

✤ **Chapter 8** ✤

The Master said of Ching, a scion of the ducal family of Wei, that he knew the economy of a family well. When he began to have means, he said, "Ha! here is a collection!" When they were a little increased, he said, "Ha! this is complete!" When he had become rich, he said, "Ha! this is admirable!"

注釋　scion: n. 子孫、後裔；ducal: adj. 公爵的；admirable: adj. 極佳、很好。

✤ **Chapter 9** ✤

9.1.　When the Master went to Wei, Zan Yu acted as driver of his carriage.

9.2.　The Master observed, "How numerous are the people!"

9.3.　Yu said, "Since they are thus numerous, what more shall be done for them?" "Enrich them, " was the reply.

9.4.　"And when they have been enriched, what more shall be done?" The Master said, "Teach them."

注釋　observe: v. 評論；numerous: adj. 眾多的；enrich: v. 使富足。

《荀子‧大略》：「不富無以養民情，不教無以理民性。故家五畝宅，百畝田，務其業，而勿奪其時，所以富之也。立大學，設庠序，修六禮，明七教，所以道之也。詩曰：『飲之食之，教之誨之。』王事具矣。」誰說儒家不重視經濟問題呢？

———————— ❀ 第十章 ❀ ————————

子曰：「苟有用我者，期月而已可也，三年有成。」

語譯　孔子說：「如果有人用我，一年就差不多好了，三年便可以成功。」

注釋　①**期月**　期音基，期月，一周年。

———————— ❀ 第十一章 ❀ ————————

子曰：「『善人為邦百年，亦可以勝殘去殺矣。』誠哉是言也！」

語譯　孔子說：「古人說過：『善人相繼執政百年，也可以感化殘暴的人而免除刑罰。』這句話說得真有道理啊！」

注釋　①**勝殘去殺**　《集解》：「王曰：勝殘，勝殘暴之人，使不為惡也。去殺，不用刑殺也。」

———————— ❀ 第十二章 ❀ ————————

子曰：「如有王者，必世而後仁。」

語譯　孔子說：「如果有行王道者為政，也得要三十年才能行仁政。」

注釋　①**世**　三十年為一世。

———————— ❀ 第十三章 ❀ ————————

子曰：「苟正其身矣，於從政乎何有？不能正其身，如正人何？」

語譯　孔子說：「假如能夠持身以正，那麼從政有什麼困難呢？如果不能持身以正，又怎麼能匡正別人呢？」

❧ **Chapter 10** ❧

The Master said, "If there were any of the princes who would employ me, in the course of twelve months, I should have done something considerable. In three years, the government would be perfected."

注釋　considerable: adj. 重要的，不可忽視的；perfect: v. 使其完美。

❧ **Chapter 11** ❧

The Master said, "'If good men were to govern a country in succession for a hundred years, they would be able to transform the violently bad, and dispense with capital punishments.' True indeed is this saying!"

注釋　in succession: 連續；transform: v. 轉變；violently: adv. 粗暴地；dispense with: 免除；capital punishment: 死刑。

❧ **Chapter 12** ❧

The Master said, "If a truly royal ruler were to arise, it would still require a generation, and then virtue would prevail."

注釋　prevail: v. 盛行。

❧ **Chapter 13** ❧

The Master said, "If a minister make his own conduct correct, what difficulty will he have in assisting in government? If he cannot rectify himself, what has he to do with rectifying others?"

注釋　assist in: 幫助。

---------------- ❖ 第十四章 ❖ ----------------

冉子退朝。子曰：「何晏也？」對曰：「有政。」子曰：「其事也。如有政，雖不吾以，吾其與聞之。」

語譯　冉有從季氏的私朝回來。孔子說：「怎麼這麼晚才回來？」冉有回答說：「有國政要討論。」孔子說：「恐怕是季氏的家事吧！如果真的有國政，雖然沒有人用我，人家也會徵詢我的意見。」

注釋　①晏　很晚。②有政　有國政要討論。③事　指季氏的家事。④以　用。

---------------- ❖ 第十五章 ❖ ----------------

定公問：「一言而可以興邦，有諸？」孔子對曰：「言不可以若是，其幾也。人之言曰：『為君難，為臣不易。』如知為君之難也，不幾乎一言而興邦乎？」曰：「一言而喪邦，有諸？」孔子對曰：「言不可以若是，其幾也。人之言曰：『予無樂乎為君，唯其言而莫予違也。』如其善而莫之違也，不亦善乎？如不善而莫之違也，不幾乎一言而喪邦乎？」

語譯　定公問道：「只要一句話就可以振興國家，有這種事嗎？」孔子回答說：「一句話恐怕不會到這種地步，只能說幾乎吧。人家說：『做國君很難，當臣子也不容易。』如果能知道做國君的困難，不是幾乎可以一句話就使國家興盛了嗎？」定公又問：「一句話就可以使國家滅亡，有這種事嗎？」孔子回答說：「一句話恐怕不會到這種地步，只能說幾乎吧。人家說：『我覺得做國君沒什麼好快樂的，除了我說的話沒有人敢違逆以外。』如果他說的話是對的，而沒有人敢違逆，那不是很好嗎？如果他說的話是錯的，而沒有人敢違逆，那麼不是幾乎一句話就可以使國家滅亡了嗎？」

注釋　①言不可以若是，其幾也　《集解》：「王曰：以其大要一言，不能正興國。幾，近也。有近一言而可以興國。」

⁂ **Chapter 14** ⁂

The disciple Zan returning from the court, the Master said to him, "How are you so late?" He replied, "We had government business." The Master said, "It must have been family affairs. If there had been government business, though I am not now in office, I should have been consulted about it."

注釋 consult: v. 詢問。

⁂ **Chapter 15** ⁂

15.1. The Duke Ting asked whether there was a single sentence which could make a country prosperous. Confucius replied, "Such an effect cannot be expected from one sentence.

15.2. "There is a saying, however, which people have -- 'To be a prince is difficult; to be a minister is not easy.'

15.3. "If a ruler knows this, -- the difficulty of being a prince, -- may there not be expected from this one sentence the prosperity of his country?"

15.4. The duke then said, "Is there a single sentence which can ruin a country?" Confucius replied, "Such an effect as that cannot be expected from one sentence. There is, however, the saying which people have -- 'I have no pleasure in being a prince, but only in that no one can offer any opposition to what I say!'

15.5. "If a ruler's words be good, is it not also good that no one oppose them? But if they are not good, and no one opposes them, may there not be expected from this one sentence the ruin of his country?"

注釋 prosperous: adj. 繁榮的；ruin: v. 毀滅。

解說 「言不可以若是，其幾也」，英譯爲 Such an effect cannot be expected from one sentence（不能期望一句話就有這種效果）是採用朱注的解釋；朱注：「幾，期望義。」

---※ 第十六章 ※---

葉公問政。子曰：「近者說，遠者來。」

語譯　葉公問爲政之道。孔子說：「使自己國家的人民快樂，使遠方的人民來歸。」

注釋　①**說**　同悅。②**來**　歸附。

---※ 第十七章 ※---

子夏爲莒父宰，問政。子曰：「無欲速，無見小利。欲速，則不達；見小利，則大事不成。」

語譯　子夏做了莒父的邑宰，請問孔子爲政之道。孔子說：「不要求速成，不要只見到小利。想要求快，反而不能達到目的；貪小利就不能成大事。」

注釋　①**莒父**　魯國邑名。於今山東高密縣。②**無**　同毋。

---※ 第十八章 ※---

葉公語孔子曰：「吾黨有直躬者，其父攘羊，而子證之。」孔子曰：「吾黨之直者異於是。父爲子隱，子爲父隱，直在其中矣。」

語譯　葉公對孔子說：「我們那裡有個正直的人，他父親偷了羊，兒子便出來作證。」孔子說：「在我們那裡，正直的人不會這麼做。父親會爲兒子隱瞞，兒子會爲父親隱瞞。直道就在這裡頭。」

注釋　①**直躬**　《集解》：「孔曰：直身而行。」②**攘**　偷盜。③**隱**　掩藏。

解說　朱注：「父子相隱，天理人情之至也。故不求爲直，而直在其中。謝氏曰：『順理爲直。父不爲子隱，子不爲父隱，於理順邪？瞽瞍殺人，舜竊負而逃，遵海濱而處。當是時，愛親之心勝，其於直不直，何暇計哉？』」這是社會正義和倫理親情之間的兩難問題。不過，親情是人類最自然直接的情感，有時候的確是「其於直不直，何暇計哉」。

❋ Chapter 16 ❋

16.1. The Duke of Sheh asked about government.

16.2. The Master said, "Good government obtains when those who are near are made happy, and those who are far off are attracted."

注釋　far off: 遙遠的。

❋ Chapter 17 ❋

Tsze-hsia, being governor of Chu-fu, asked about government. The Master said, "Do not be desirous to have things done quickly; do not look at small advantages. Desire to have things done quickly prevents their being done thoroughly. Looking at small advantages prevents great affairs from being accomplished."

注釋　desirous: adj. 渴望；thoroughly: adv. 完全地、徹底地。

❋ Chapter 18 ❋

18.1. The Duke of Sheh informed Confucius, saying, "Among us here there are those who may be styled upright in their conduct. If their father have stolen a sheep, they will bear witness to the fact."

18.2. Confucius said, "Among us, in our part of the country, those who are upright are different from this. The father conceals the misconduct of the son, and the son conceals the misconduct of the father. Uprightness is to be found in this."

注釋　style: v. 稱爲；upright: adj. 正直；misconduct: n. 違法行爲。

—————— ❋ 第十九章 ❋ ——————

樊遲問仁。子曰:「居處恭,執事敬,與人忠。雖之夷狄,不可棄也。」

語譯 樊遲問仁。孔子說:「日常起居要恭敬,做事要認真,對待人要誠懇。即使是到了夷狄之邦,也不可以捨棄。」

注釋 ①**居處** 日常起居。或謂獨處。②**之** 到。

—————— ❋ 第二十章 ❋ ——————

子貢問曰:「何如斯可謂之士矣?」子曰:「行己有恥,使於四方,不辱君命,可謂士矣。」曰:「敢問其次。」曰:「宗族稱孝焉,鄉黨稱弟焉。」曰:「敢問其次。」曰:「言必信,行必果,硜硜然小人哉!抑亦可以為次矣。」曰:「今之從政者何如?」子曰:「噫!斗筲之人,何足算也。」

語譯 子貢問孔子說:「怎麼樣才可以叫作士?」孔子說:「自己行為有羞恥心,出使到其他國家,不辱沒君王的命令,就可以說是士了。」子貢又問:「請問次一等的如何?」孔子說:「宗族稱讚他孝順父母,鄉里稱讚他尊敬兄長。」子貢又問:「請問次一等的如何?」孔子說:「說話算話,做事做到底,這種人冥頑不化,只是像小人一樣啊!但也可以說是次一等的了。」子貢問說:「那麼現在從政的人如何?」孔子說:「那些器識狹隘的人算得什麼呢?」

注釋 ①**行己有恥** 《集解》:「孔曰:有恥者,有所不為。」②**言必信,行必果** 《孟子·離婁下》:「大人者,言不必信,行不必果,惟義所在。」③**硜硜** 《朱注》:「硜,小石之堅確者。」《正義》:「小人賦性愚魯,故有此貌。」④**小人** 識量淺狹之人。⑤**斗筲之人** 筲音稍,竹器。比喻人識量之小。《正義》:「言今之從政,但事聚斂也。」⑥**算** 數、計。

—————— ❋ 第二十一章 ❋ ——————

子曰:「不得中行而與之,必也狂狷乎!狂者進取,狷者有所不為也。」

❋ **Chapter 19** ❋

Fan Ch'ih asked about perfect virtue. The Master said, "It is, in retirement, to be sedately grave; in the management of business, to be reverently attentive; in intercourse with others, to be strictly sincere. Though a man go among rude, uncultivated tribes, these qualities may not be neglected."

注釋　retirement: n. 隱居；sedately: adv. 沉著地；attentive: adj. 專注的；intercourse: n. 交往；tribe: n. 部落。

❋ **Chapter 20** ❋

20.1. Tsze-kung asked, saying, "What qualities must a man possess to entitle him to be called an officer? The Master said, "He who in his conduct of himself maintains a sense of shame, and when sent to any quarter will not disgrace his prince's commission, deserves to be called an officer."

20.2. Tsze-kung pursued, "I venture to ask who may be placed in the next lower rank?" And he was told, "He whom the circle of his relatives pronounce to be filial, whom his fellow villagers and neighbors pronounce to be fraternal."

20.3. Again the disciple asked, "I venture to ask about the class still next in order." The Master said, "They are determined to be sincere in what they say, and to carry out what they do. They are obstinate little men. Yet perhaps they may make the next class."

20.4. Tsze-kung finally inquired, "Of what sort are those of the present day, who engage in government?" The Master said "Pooh! they are so many pecks and hampers, not worth being taken into account."

注釋　shame: n. 羞恥；commission: n. 委託；pronounce: v. 宣稱；obstinate: adj. 頑固的；pooh: interj. 哼；peck: n. 單位名，約九公升；hamper: n. 有蓋的籃子。

❋ **Chapter 21** ❋

The Master said, "Since I cannot get men pursuing the due medium, to whom I might communicate my instructions, I must find the ardent and

語譯　孔子說：「如果沒辦法和中道而行的人在一起，也得和狂狷的人爲伍吧！狂者能進取，狷者能有所不爲。」

注釋　①**中行**　《集解》：「包曰：行能得其中者。」依中庸之道而行。②**與之**　與之爲伍。③**狂狷**　《集解》：「包曰：狂者，進取於善道；狷者，守節無爲。」狷音倦。

解說　《孟子‧盡心下》：「孟子曰：『孔子「不得中道而與之，必也狂獧乎！狂者進取，獧者有所不爲也」。孔子豈不欲中道哉？不可必得，故思其次也。』『敢問何如斯可謂狂矣？』曰：『如琴張、曾皙、牧皮者，孔子之所謂狂矣。』『何以謂之狂也？』曰：『其志嘐嘐然，曰「古之人，古之人」。夷考其行而不掩焉者也。狂者又不可得，欲得不屑不潔之士而與之，是獧也，是又其次也。』」獧同狷。朱注：「狂者，志極高而行不掩。狷者，知未及而守有餘。」

※ 第二十二章 ※

子曰：「南人有言曰：『人而無恆，不可以作巫醫。』善夫！『不恆其德，或承之羞。』」子曰：「不占而已矣。」

語譯　孔子說：「南方人有句話說：『如果人沒有恆心，不可以做巫醫。』這句話說得眞好！易卦說：『德行不能持恆，常會有羞辱接踵而至。』」孔子說：「沒有恆心的人，也不必占卦了。」

注釋　①**巫醫**　巫師和醫師。巫，祈禱鬼神爲人治病請福者。②**不恆其德，或承之羞**　語出《易經‧恆卦》。或，經常。承，接續。③**不占而已矣**　《集解》：「鄭曰：易所以占吉凶，無恆之人，易所不占。」

※ 第二十三章 ※

子曰：「君子和而不同，小人同而不和。」

語譯　孔子說：「君子與人和諧相處，卻不阿諛盲從。小人阿諛盲從而不能與人和諧相處。」

注釋　①**和而不同**　《集解》：「君子心和，然其所見各異，故曰不同。」②**同而**

the cautiously-decided. The ardent will advance and lay hold of truth; the cautiously-decided will keep themselves from what is wrong."

注釋　medium: n. 中庸；ardent: adj. 熱情的。

❖ **Chapter 22** *❖*

22.1. The Master said, "The people of the south have a saying -- 'A man without constancy cannot be either a wizard or a doctor.' Good!

22.2. "Inconstant in his virtue, he will be visited with disgrace."

22.3. The Master said, "This arises simply from not attending to the prognostication."

注釋　constancy: n. 恆久、堅定；wizard: n. 巫師；prognostication: n. 預兆。

解說　不占而已矣，英譯 This arises simply from not attending to the prognostication（只是起因於不注意前兆），不符原意。或譯爲 You will not even be able to give a diagnosis。

❖ **Chapter 23** *❖*

The Master said, "The superior man is affable, but not adulatory; the mean man is adulatory, but not affable."

注釋　affable: adj. 親切、友善；adulatory: adj. 諂媚、逢迎。

不和 《集解》：「小人所嗜好者則同，然各爭利，故曰不和。」

※ 第二十四章 ※

子貢問曰：「鄉人皆好之，何如？」子曰：「未可也。」「鄉人皆惡之，何如？」子曰：「未可也。不如鄉人之善者好之，其不善者惡之。」

語譯　子貢問孔子說：「鄉里的人們都喜歡他，這樣的人如何呢？」孔子說：「還不能說他是好人。」「鄉里的人們都討厭他，這樣的人如何呢？」孔子說：「還不能說他是好人。不如說，鄉里的好人都喜歡他，壞人都討厭他。」

注釋　①**好之**　喜歡他。

※ 第二十五章 ※

子曰：「君子易事而難說也。說之不以道，不說也。及其使人也，器之。小人難事而易說也。說之雖不以道，說也。及其使人也，求備焉。」

語譯　孔子說：「君子很容易和他共事，但是很難以取悅他：不以正當的方法去取悅他，他是不會高興的。等到他用人的時候，則會衡量各人的才識來分配任務。小人很難和他共事，卻很容易取悅他。以不正當的方法去取悅他，他會高興。等到他用人的時候，卻處處苛責求全。」

注釋　①**說**　同悅。②**器之**　因材用人。③**求備**　苛刻求全。

解說　工作時有這種主管，會很累人。

※ 第二十六章 ※

子曰：「君子泰而不驕，小人驕而不泰。」

語譯　孔子說：「君子安詳舒泰但不驕傲。小人驕傲而不安詳舒泰。」

注釋　①**泰**　舒泰。君子心胸坦然，故常舒泰。

※ Chapter 24 ※

Tsze-kung asked, saying, "What do you say of a man who is loved by all the people of his neighborhood?" The Master replied, "We may not for that accord our approval of him." "And what do you say of him who is hated by all the people of his neighborhood?" The Master said, "We may not for that conclude that he is bad. It is better than either of these cases that the good in the neighborhood love him, and the bad hate him."

注釋　accord: v. 給與。

※ Chapter 25 ※

The Master said, "The superior man is easy to serve and difficult to please. If you try to please him in any way which is not accordant with right, he will not be pleased. But in his employment of men, he uses them according to their capacity. The mean man is difficult to serve, and easy to please. If you try to please him, though it be in a way which is not accordant with right, he may be pleased. But in his employment of men, he wishes them to be equal to everything."

注釋　equal to: 勝任。

※ Chapter 26 ※

The Master said, "The superior man has a dignified ease without pride. The mean man has pride without a dignified ease."

注釋　dignified: adj. 高貴的；ease: n. 輕鬆自在。

———————————— ✤ 第二十七章 ✤ ————————————

子曰：「剛、毅、木、訥，近仁。」

語譯　孔子說：「堅強、果決、質樸、少說話的人，近於仁德。」

注釋　①**剛毅木訥**　《集解》：「王曰：剛，無欲；毅，果敢；木，質樸；訥，遲鈍。」

———————————— ✤ 第二十八章 ✤ ————————————

子路問曰：「何如斯可謂之士矣？」子曰：「切切偲偲，怡怡如也，可謂士矣。朋友切切偲偲，兄弟怡怡。」

語譯　子路問說：「怎麼樣才能叫作士？」孔子說：「要是能互相切磋，而又和樂相處，就可以稱為士了。朋友之間要能夠互相切磋，兄弟之間要和樂相處。」

注釋　①**切切偲偲**　責勉的意思。偲音思。②**怡怡**　和樂。

———————————— ✤ 第二十九章 ✤ ————————————

子曰：「善人教民七年，亦可以即戎矣。」

語譯　孔子說：「善人執政教化百姓七年，也可以要他們上戰場打仗了。」

注釋　①**教民**　朱注：「教之孝悌忠信之行，務農講武之法。」②**即戎**　就戰。

———————————— ✤ 第三十章 ✤ ————————————

子曰：「以不教民戰，是謂棄之。」

語譯　孔子說：「以未曾受訓練的百姓去打仗，那可以說是拋棄他們。」

---- ⋇ **Chapter 27** ⋇ ----

The Master said, "The firm, the enduring, the simple, and the modest are near to virtue."

注釋　firm: adj. 堅定的；enduring: adj. 持久的；modest: adj. 謹愼的、內向的。

---- ⋇ **Chapter 28** ⋇ ----

Tsze-lu asked, saying, "What qualities must a man possess to entitle him to be called a scholar?" The Master said, "He must be thus, -- earnest, urgent, and bland: -- among his friends, earnest and urgent; among his brethren, bland."

注釋　earnest: adj. 認眞的；urgent: adj. 迫切的；bland: adj. 和藹的；brethren: pl. 兄弟。

---- ⋇ **Chapter 29** ⋇ ----

The Master said, "Let a good man teach the people seven years, and they may then likewise be employed in war."

注釋　likewise: adv. 同樣地。

---- ⋇ **Chapter 30** ⋇ ----

The Master said, "To lead an uninstructed people to war, is to throw them away."

注釋　throw away: 丟棄。

憲問第十四

━━━━━━━━━━━━━ ❖ 第一章 ❖ ━━━━━━━━━━━━━

憲問恥。子曰：「邦有道，穀；邦無道，穀，恥也。」

語譯　原憲問什麼是可恥的。孔子說：「國家政治清明時不能有所作為，只知道食祿，國家政治混亂時仍然戀棧官位，那就是可恥的。」

注釋　①憲　原思的名。②穀　俸祿。

解說　朱注：「邦有道不能有為，邦無道不能獨善，而但知食祿，皆可恥也。」只知道做官而不知道做事的政客們，或許也不知道羞恥吧。

━━━━━━━━━━━━━ ❖ 第二章 ❖ ━━━━━━━━━━━━━

「克、伐、怨、欲，不行焉，可以為仁矣？」子曰：「可以為難矣，仁則吾不知也。」

語譯　原憲又問：「好勝、自誇、怨恨和貪欲，如果能夠克制這些缺點的話，可以說是仁者嗎？」孔子說：「這可以說是很難的，至於如此是否可以稱為仁者，我就不知道了。」

注釋　①克伐怨欲　朱注：「克，好勝。伐，自矜。怨，忿恨。欲，貪欲。」②不行　克制。

解說　能夠遏制這些負面的情緒，只是消極地不去傷害別人，雖然難能可貴，但還不是仁的全德。

━━━━━━━━━━━━━ ❖ 第三章 ❖ ━━━━━━━━━━━━━

子曰：「士而懷居，不足以為士矣。」

語譯　孔子說：「讀書人如果貪圖生活舒適，那就不配稱為讀書人。」

注釋　①懷居　皇侃疏：「懷居猶求安也。」

━━━━━━━━━━━━━ ❖ 第四章 ❖ ━━━━━━━━━━━━━

子曰：「邦有道，危言危行；邦無道，危行言孫。」

❈ Chapter 1 ❈

Hsien asked what was shameful. The Master said, "When good government prevails in a state, to be thinking only of salary; and, when bad government prevails, to be thinking, in the same way, only of salary; -- this is shameful."

注釋　shameful: adj. 可恥的；salary: n. 薪俸。

❈ Chapter 2 ❈

2.1.　"When the love of superiority, boasting, resentments, and covetousness are repressed, this may be deemed perfect virtue."

2.2.　The Master said, "This may be regarded as the achievement of what is difficult. But I do not know that it is to be deemed perfect virtue. "

注釋　superiority: n. 優勢；boast: v. 自誇；resentment: n. 忿怒；covetousness: n. 貪婪；deem: v.認為是。

❈ Chapter 3 ❈

The Master said, "The scholar who cherishes the love of comfort is not fit to be deemed a scholar."

注釋　cherish: v. 懷著（想法）。

❈ Chapter 4 ❈

The Master said, "When good government prevails in a state, language may be lofty and bold, and actions the same. When bad government prevails, the

語譯　孔子說：「國家政治清明，應該正言正行；國家政治混亂，行為仍然要正直，但是言語要委婉。」

注釋　①危　《集解》：「危猶高也。」《廣雅》：「危，正也。」②孫　謙順。

解說　朱注：「尹氏曰：君子之持身不可變也，至於言則有時而不敢盡，以避禍也。然則為國者使士言孫，豈不殆哉？」在極權國家或是白色恐怖時代，說話是得小心點；反過來說，因為獨裁或意識形態的言論箝制而造成寒蟬效應，不是國家的悲哀嗎？

※ 第五章 ※

子曰：「有德者，必有言。有言者，不必有德。仁者，必有勇。勇者，不必有仁。」

語譯　孔子說：「有道德的人必定會說話，會說話的人不一定有道德。仁者必定是勇敢的，勇敢的人不一定是仁者。」

解說　「有言」指的是說出很有道理的話。

※ 第六章 ※

南宮适問於孔子曰：「羿善射，奡盪舟，俱不得其死然；禹稷躬稼，而有天下。」夫子不答，南宮适出。子曰：「君子哉若人！尚德哉若人！」

語譯　南宮适問孔子說：「羿箭術很好，奡能陸上行舟，但是都不得好死；夏禹和后稷勤勞耕作，卻得到天下。」孔子沒有回答，南宮适離開後，孔子說：「他真是個君子啊！他真是個崇德的人啊！」

注釋　①南宮适　就是南容，适音廓。②羿善射　朱注：「有窮之君，善射，滅夏后相而篡其位。其臣寒浞又殺羿而代之。」③奡盪舟　朱注：「奡，春秋傳作『澆』，浞之子也，力能陸地行舟，後為夏后少康所誅。」奡音傲。④夫子不答　《集解》：「馬曰：适欲以禹稷比孔子，孔子謙，故不答。」

解說　「盪舟」解釋為「陸上行舟」，很奇怪。或謂盪舟是「覆其舟而滅之」。

actions may be lofty and bold, but the language may be with some reserve."

注釋　lofty: adj. 崇高的；bold: adj. 勇敢的。

✲ **Chapter 5** ✲

The Master said, "The virtuous will be sure to speak correctly, but those whose speech is good may not always be virtuous. Men of principle are sure to be bold, but those who are bold may not always be men of principle."

✲ **Chapter 6** ✲

Nan-kung Kwo, submitting an inquiry to Confucius, said, "I was skillful at archery, and Ao could move a boat along upon the land, but neither of them died a natural death. Yu and Chi personally wrought at the toils of husbandry, and they became possessors of the kingdom." The Master made no reply; but when Nan-kung Kwo went out, he said, "A superior man indeed is this! An esteemer of virtue indeed is this!"

注釋　submit: v. 提問；inquiry: n. 詢問；wrought: work 的過去式；toil: n. 苦工；
　　　husbandry: 耕種；possessor: n. 所有者；esteemer: n. 尊崇者。

———— ❦ 第七章 ❦ ————

子曰:「君子而不仁者有矣夫,未有小人而仁者也。」

語譯　孔子說:「君子或許有時候也會違仁,但是從來沒有哪個小人會行仁的。」

———— ❦ 第八章 ❦ ————

子曰:「愛之,能勿勞乎?忠焉,能勿誨乎?」

語譯　孔子說:「愛一個人,能不教他勤勞嗎?忠於一個人,能不以正道去規勸他嗎?」

注釋　①勞　勉其勤勞。《正義》訓為「憂」,擔憂的意思。

———— ❦ 第九章 ❦ ————

子曰:「為命:裨諶草創之,世叔討論之,行人子羽脩飾之,東里子產潤色之。」

語譯　孔子說:「鄭國要發布外交辭命,會由裨諶草擬,經過世叔討論內容,由行人子羽修飾字句,由東里子產潤色。」

注釋　①為命　擬作外交辭命。②裨諶、世叔、子羽、子產　都是鄭國大夫。「裨諶」音「皮陳」。③行人　掌出使之官。④東里　子產住的地方。

———— ❦ 第十章 ❦ ————

或問子產。子曰:「惠人也。」問子西。曰:「彼哉!彼哉!」問管仲。曰:「人也,奪伯氏駢邑三百,飯疏食,沒齒無怨言。」

語譯　有人向孔子問子產是怎麼樣的人。孔子說:「他是施惠於民的人。」又問到子西這個人。孔子說:「他呀!他呀!」又問到管仲。孔子說:「這個人啊!齊桓公削奪伯氏的駢邑三百家給管仲,使他終身吃粗米飯,伯氏至死都沒有怨言。」

注釋　①子西　公孫夏,鄭國公子騑之子。②伯氏　齊國大夫,朱注:「伯氏自知己罪,而心服管仲之功,故窮約以終身而無怨言。」③駢邑　地名。④沒齒　終身。

---------------------------------- ❊ **Chapter 7** ❊ ----------------------------------

The Master said, "Superior men, and yet not always virtuous, there have been, alas! But there never has been a mean man, and, at the same time, virtuous."

---------------------------------- ❊ **Chapter 8** ❊ ----------------------------------

The Master said, "Can there be love which does not lead to strictness with its object? Can there be loyalty which does not lead to the instruction of its object?"

注釋　strict with：對人嚴格；object: n. 對象。

---------------------------------- ❊ **Chapter 9** ❊ ----------------------------------

The Master said, "In preparing the governmental notifications, P'i Shan first made the rough draft; Shi-shu examined and discussed its contents; Tsze-yu, the manager of foreign intercourse, then polished the style; and, finally, Tsze-ch'an of Tung-li gave it the proper elegance and finish."

注釋　notification: n. 公告；rough: adj. 粗略的、未完成的；draft: n. 草稿；polish: v. 潤飾、推敲；elegance: n. 優雅；finish: n. 完美、最後的工作。

---------------------------------- ❊ **Chapter 10** ❊ ----------------------------------

10.1. Some one asked about Tsze-ch'an. The Master said, "He was a kind man."

10.2. He asked about Tsze-hsi. The Master said, "That man! That man!"

10.3. He asked about Kwan Chung. "For him," said the Master, "the city of Pien, with three hundred families, was taken from the chief of the Po family, who did not utter a murmuring word, though, to the end of his life, he had only coarse rice to eat."

注釋　kind: adj. 慈愛的。

———— ❖ 第十一章 ❖ ————

子曰:「貧而無怨,難;富而無驕,易。」

語譯　孔子說:「貧困而沒有怨言,很難;富貴而不驕傲,比較容易。」

———— ❖ 第十二章 ❖ ————

子曰:「孟公綽,為趙、魏老則優,不可以為滕、薛大夫。」

語譯　孔子說:「孟公綽做趙、魏的家臣,是綽綽有餘,但是不可以做滕、薛的大夫。」

注釋　①**孟公綽**　魯國大夫。②**趙魏**　晉國卿大夫。③**老**　家臣。④**優**　寬綽有餘。⑤**滕薛**　當時的小國。

解說　《集解》:「公綽性寡欲,趙魏貪賢,家老無職,故優。滕薛小國,大夫職煩,故不可為。」

———— ❖ 第十三章 ❖ ————

子路問成人。子曰:「若臧武仲之知,公綽之不欲,卞莊子之勇,冉求之藝,文之以禮樂,亦可以為成人矣。」曰:「今之成人者何必然?見利思義,見危授命,久要不忘平生之言,亦可以為成人矣。」

語譯　子路問如何才是人格完備的人。孔子說:「如果有像臧武仲的智慧,有孟公綽的恬淡寡欲,有卞莊子的勇敢,有冉求的才藝,再加上禮樂的修養,也可以算是人格完備了。」孔子又說:「現在講人格完備又何必如此?看到利益時能想起道義,別人有危難時能夠捨命相救,答應別人的事,再久都不會忘記,如此也可以說是人格完備了吧。」

注釋　①**成人**　成德之人。人格完備的意思。②**臧武仲**　魯國大夫臧孫紇。③**卞莊子**　魯國卞邑大夫。④**久要**　要,約定。⑤**平生**　平日。

解說　《說苑·辨物》:「顏淵問於仲尼曰:『成人之行何若?』子曰:『成人之行,達乎情性之理,通乎物類之變,知幽明之故,睹遊氣之源,若此而

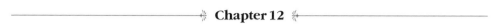
❊ **Chapter 11** ❊

The Master said, "To be poor without murmuring is difficult. To be rich without being proud is easy."

❊ **Chapter 12** ❊

The Master said, "Mang Kung-ch'o is more than fit to be chief officer in the families of Chao and Wei, but he is not fit to be great officer to either of the states Tang or Hsieh."

❊ **Chapter 13** ❊

13.1. Tsze-lu asked what constituted a COMPLETE man. The Master said, "Suppose a man with the knowledge of Tsang Wu-chung, the freedom from covetousness of Kung-ch'o, the bravery of Chwang of Pien, and the varied talents of Zan Ch'iu; add to these the accomplishments of the rules of propriety and music; -- such a one might be reckoned a COMPLETE man."

13.2. He then added, "But what is the necessity for a complete man of the present day to have all these things? The man, who in the view of gain, thinks of righteousness; who in the view of danger is prepared to give up his life; and who does not forget an old agreement however far back it extends: -- such a man may be reckoned a COMPLETE man."

注釋　varied: adj. 各行各業的；reckon: v. 認爲是；prepared to: 有心理準備；extend: v. 持續。

可謂成人。既知天道，行躬以仁義，飭身以禮樂。夫仁義禮樂，成人之行也，窮神知化德之盛也。』」這差不多是聖人的境界了吧？還是「見利思義，見危授命，久要不忘平生之言」比較容易些。

⁂ 第十四章 ⁂

子問公叔文子於公明賈曰：「信乎，夫子不言、不笑、不取乎？」公明賈對曰：「以告者過也。夫子時然後言，人不厭其言；樂然後笑，人不厭其笑；義然後取，人不厭其取。」子曰：「其然？豈其然乎？」

語譯　孔子向公明賈問起公叔文子這個人，說：「他真的不苟言笑，不貪取嗎？」公明賈回答說：「說這句話的人太誇張了。他在該說的時候才會說，人家就不會討厭他說的話；快樂的時候才會笑，人家就不會討厭他的笑；合於道義的時候才取財，人家就不會討厭他的取財。」孔子說：「是這樣嗎？難道他真是這樣嗎？」

注釋　①**公叔文子**　衛國大夫公孫拔，衛獻公之孫，諡爲文。②**公明賈**　衛國人。

解說　「其然，豈其然乎？」諸家解釋都說孔子不信其言。朱注：「文子雖賢，疑未及此，但君子與人爲善，不欲正言其非也。」孔子胸襟難道只有這麼大，而捨不得讚美別人嗎？

⁂ 第十五章 ⁂

子曰：「臧武仲，以防求爲後於魯，雖曰不要君，吾不信也。」

語譯　孔子說：「臧武仲以他的防邑，請求立其子嗣爲魯國大夫，雖然人家說他不是要挾魯君，我可是不相信。」

注釋　①**防**　武仲的食邑。②**爲後**　立後人。③**要**　音夭。勒索要挾。

解說　朱注：「武仲得罪奔邾，自邾如防，使請立後而避邑。以示若不得請，則將據邑以叛，是要君也。」

※ **Chapter 14** ※

14.1. The Master asked Kung-ming Chia about Kung-shu Wan, saying, "Is it true that your master speaks not, laughs not, and takes not?"

14.2. Kung-ming Chia replied, "This has arisen from the reporters going beyond the truth. -- My master speaks when it is the time to speak, and so men do not get tired of his speaking. He laughs when there is occasion to be joyful, and so men do not get tired of his laughing. He takes when it is consistent with righteousness to do so, and so men do not get tired of his taking." The Master said, "So! But is it so with him?"

注釋　consistent with: 符合。

※ **Chapter 15** ※

The Master said, "Tsang Wu-chung, keeping possession of Fang, asked of the duke of Lu to appoint a successor to him in his family. Although it may be said that he was not using force with his sovereign, I believe he was."

———— ❀ 第十六章 ❀ ————

子曰：「晉文公譎而不正，齊桓公正而不譎。」

語譯　孔子說：「晉文公能權謀而不正直，齊桓公正直而少權謀。」

注釋　①譎　權詐。譎音絕。

解說　齊桓公和晉文公都曾經尊王攘夷以霸諸侯，孔子在這裡評論其高下。《正義》說：「譎，權也。正，經也。言晉文能行權而不能守經，齊桓能守經而不能行權，各有所長，亦各有所短也。」

———— ❀ 第十七章 ❀ ————

子路曰：「桓公殺公子糾，召忽死之，管仲不死。曰：未仁乎？」
子曰：「桓公九合諸侯，不以兵車，管仲之力也。如其仁！如其仁！」

語譯　子路說：「桓公殺了他的哥哥公子糾，召忽自殺而死，管仲卻活著。管仲不算是個仁者吧？」孔子說：「齊桓公九次合會諸侯，而能夠不用兵力，這都是管仲的功勞。這就是管仲的仁德！這就是管仲的仁德！」

注釋　①九會　《正義》說共是十一會。朱注：「九，春秋傳作『糾』。」意即糾合。②如其仁　如，乃。這就是他的仁德。朱注：「如其仁，言誰如其仁者。」

解說　召音紹。朱注：「齊襄公無道，鮑叔牙奉公子小白奔莒。及無知弒襄公，管夷吾召忽奉公子糾奔魯。魯人納之，未克，而小白入，是爲桓公。使魯殺子糾而請管召，召忽死之，管仲請囚。鮑叔牙言於桓公以爲相。」

———— ❀ 第十八章 ❀ ————

子貢曰：「管仲非仁者與？桓公殺公子糾，不能死，又相之。」子曰：「管仲相桓公，霸諸侯，一匡天下，民到于今受其賜。微管仲，吾其被髮左衽矣。豈若匹夫匹婦之爲諒也，自經於溝瀆，而莫之知也！」

✦ Chapter 16 ✦

The Master said, "The duke Wan of Tsin was crafty and not upright. The duke Hwan of Ch'i was upright and not crafty."

注釋　crafty: adj. 詭詐的。

✦ Chapter 17 ✦

17.1. Tsze-lu said, "The Duke Hwan caused his brother Chiu to be killed, when Shao Hu died, with his master, but Kwan Chung did not die. May not I say that he was wanting in virtue?"

17.2. The Master said, "The Duke Hwan assembled all the princes together, and that not with weapons of war and chariots: -- it was all through the influence of Kwan Chung. Whose beneficence was like his? Whose beneficence was like his?"

注釋　wanting in: 缺乏；assemble: v. 召集。

✦ Chapter 18 ✦

18.1. Tsze-kung said, "Kwan Chung, I apprehend, was wanting in virtue. When the Duke Hwan caused his brother Chiu to be killed, Kwan Chung was not able to die with him. Moreover, he became prime minister to Hwan."

18.2. The Master said, "Kwan Chung acted as prime minister to the Duke

語譯　子貢說：「管仲不是仁者吧？桓公殺了公子糾，他不但不能以死殉節，還去輔佐他。」孔子說：「管仲輔佐桓公，稱霸諸侯，使天下恢復秩序，百姓到現在都還受到他的恩惠。如果沒有管仲，我大概要披頭散髮，衣襟開左邊了。難道要像老百姓一樣守著小節，自殺死在溝渠裡，而沒有人知道嗎？」

注釋　①**相**　去聲，輔佐。②**匡**　匡正。③**微**　無。④**被髮**　被同披，戎狄編髮為辮，披在身後。⑤**左衽**　衽，衣襟。中國禮服都是衣襟右鈕，戎狄無禮服，而且是衣襟左鈕。⑥**諒**　小信。⑦**自經**　自縊。⑧**溝瀆**　田間水溝。

※ 第十九章 ※

公叔文子之臣大夫僎，與文子同升諸公。子聞之曰：「可以為文矣。」

語譯　公叔文子的家臣大夫僎，和文子一起升為公朝的臣子。孔子聽到這事以後說：「公叔文子真是可以諡為『文』了。」

注釋　①**臣大夫**　家大夫。②**同升諸公**　公，公朝。公叔文子推薦他的家臣，和自己同列於公朝。③**文**　諡法有所謂錫民爵位曰文者。

※ 第二十章 ※

子言衛靈公之無道也，康子曰：「夫如是，奚而不喪？」孔子曰：「仲叔圉治賓客，祝鮀治宗廟，王孫賈治軍旅。夫如是，奚其喪？」

語譯　孔子說到衛靈公的昏亂。康子說：「既然這樣，他為什麼還不敗亡？」孔子說：「他有仲叔圉接待賓客，有祝鮀管理宗廟的事，有王孫賈統率軍隊。像這樣，怎麼會敗亡呢？」

注釋　①**奚而不喪**　何以不敗亡。②**仲叔圉**　即孔文子。圉音與。

Hwan made him leader of all the princes, and united and rectified the whole kingdom. Down to the present day, the people enjoy the gifts which he conferred. But for Kwan Chung, we should now be wearing our hair unbound, and the lappets of our coats buttoning on the left side.

18.3. "Will you require from him the small fidelity of common men and common women, who would commit suicide in a stream or ditch, no one knowing anything about them?"

注釋　prime minister: 首相；confer: v. 授與；unbound: adj. 解開繩子的；lappet: n. 衣襟；button: v. 扣上鈕鈕。

❊ **Chapter 19** ❊

19.1. The great officer, Hsien, who had been family minister to Kung-shu Wan, ascended to the prince's court in company with Wan.

19.2. The Master, having heard of it, said, "He deserved to be considered WAN (the accomplished)."

注釋　ascend: v. 登上。

❊ **Chapter 20** ❊

20.1. The Master was speaking about the unprincipled course of the duke Ling of Weil when Ch'i K'ang said, "Since he is of such a character, how is it he does not lose his state?"

20.2. Confucius said, "The Chung-shu Yu has the superintendence of his guests and of strangers; the litanist, T'o, has the management of his ancestral temple; and Wang-sun Chia has the direction of the army and forces: -- with such officers as these, how should he lose his state?"

注釋　unprincipled: adj. 沒有原則的、無道義的；course: n. 行徑；superintendence: n. 監督；litanist: n. 廟官。

———————— ❋ 第二十一章 ❋ ————————

子曰：「其言之不怍，則為之也難。」

語譯　孔子說：「說大話而不慚愧的人，要他實踐就很難了。」

注釋　①**怍**　慚愧。

———————— ❋ 第二十二章 ❋ ————————

陳成子弒簡公。孔子沐浴而朝，告於哀公曰：「陳恆弒其君，請討之。」公曰：「告夫三子！」孔子曰：「以吾從大夫之後，不敢不告也。君曰『告夫三子』者。」之三子告，不可。孔子曰：「以吾從大夫之後，不敢不告也。」

語譯　陳恆殺了齊簡公。孔子齋戒沐浴後朝見魯哀公，對哀公說：「陳恆殺了他的國君，請發兵討伐他。」哀公說：「你去告訴他們三位吧！」孔子離開後說：「因為我也忝為大夫，而不敢不告訴國君，而國君卻說『去告訴他們三位吧』。」孔子到三家告訴他們這事，他們都不同意。孔子說：「因為我也忝為大夫，不敢不來報告啊！」

注釋　①**陳成子**　齊國大夫陳恆。②**簡公**　齊簡公，名壬。《左傳‧哀公十四年》：「齊陳恆弒其君壬於舒州。孔丘三日齋，而請伐齊。」③**討**　討伐。④**三子**　即孟孫、叔孫、季孫三家。朱注：「時政在三家，哀公不得自專，故使孔子告之。」

解說　《白虎通義‧誅伐》：「王者諸侯之子，篡弒其君而立，臣下得誅之者，廣討賊之義也。春秋傳曰：『臣弒君，臣不討賊，非臣也。』」孔子做為魯國大夫，盱衡情勢以後，認為有義務告訴哀公這件事。哀公不敢作主，而三家佞臣和陳恆是一丘之貉，當然不會同意。

———————— ❋ 第二十三章 ❋ ————————

子路問事君。子曰：「勿欺也，而犯之。」

語譯　子路問如何為國君做事。孔子說：「不要欺騙他，倒是可以犯顏進諫。」

注釋　①**犯**　朱注：「謂犯顏諫爭。」

❈ **Chapter 21** ❈

The Master said, "He who speaks without modesty will find it difficult to make his words good."

注釋　modesty: n. 謙虛；make good: 實現。

❈ **Chapter 22** ❈

22.1. Chan Ch'ang murdered the Duke Chien of Ch'i.

22.2. Confucius bathed, went to court and informed the Duke Ai, saying, "Chan Hang has slain his sovereign. I beg that you will undertake to punish him."

22.3. The duke said, "Inform the chiefs of the three families of it."

22.4. Confucius retired, and said, "Following in the rear of the great officers, I did not dare not to represent such a matter, and my prince says, 'Inform the chiefs of the three families of it.'"

22.5. He went to the chiefs, and informed them, but they would not act. Confucius then said, "Following in the rear of the great officers, I did not dare not to represent such a matter."

注釋　slay: v. [-slew; slain] 殺害；undertake: v. 著手；inform: v. 告訴 [of]；represent: v. 說明。

❈ **Chapter 23** ❈

Tsze-lu asked how a ruler should be served. The Master said, "Do not impose on him, and, moreover, withstand him to his face."

注釋　impose on: 欺騙；withstand: v. 反抗；to a person's face: 當著某人的面。

———————— ❋ 第二十四章 ❋ ————————

子曰：「君子上達，小人下達。」

語譯　孔子說：「君子求上進，小人則不斷沉淪。」

解說　皇侃疏：「上達者，達於仁義也。下達謂達於財利，所以與君子反也。」

———————— ❋ 第二十五章 ❋ ————————

子曰：「古之學者為己，今之學者為人。」

語譯　孔子說：「古代的學者是為了修養自己的道德學問，現在的學者卻是為了給別人知道。」

解說　朱注：「程子曰：『為己，欲得之於己也。為人，欲見知於人也。』程子曰：『古之學者為己，其終至於成物。今之學者為人，其終至於喪己。』」

———————— ❋ 第二十六章 ❋ ————————

蘧伯玉使人於孔子。孔子與之坐而問焉，曰：「夫子何為？」對曰：「夫子欲寡其過而未能也。」使者出。子曰：「使乎！使乎！」

語譯　蘧伯玉派使者到孔子家。孔子和使者坐下，問使者說：「近來先生做些什麼？」使者說：「我們先生努力想要減少過失，但總覺得還沒做到。」使者離開後，孔子說：「好一位使者！好一位使者！」

注釋　①**蘧伯玉**　衛國大夫，名瑗。②**使乎！使乎**　指使者的回答不卑不亢，深得君子之心。

解說　孔子在衛國時曾到蘧伯玉家作客，孔子回到魯國後，伯玉派使者來問候孔子。

———————— ❋ 第二十七章 ❋ ————————

子曰：「不在其位，不謀其政。」

解說　見〈泰伯篇〉。

✳ **Chapter 24** ✳

The Master said, "The progress of the superior man is upwards; the progress of the mean man is downwards."

✳ **Chapter 25** ✳

The Master said, "In ancient times, men learned with a view to their own improvement. Nowadays, men learn with a view to the approbation of others."

注釋　improvement: n. 進步；approbation: n. 稱讚。

✳ **Chapter 26** ✳

26.1. Chu Po-yu sent a messenger with friendly inquiries to Confucius.

26.2. Confucius sat with him, and questioned him. "What," said he! "is your master engaged in?" The messenger replied, "My master is anxious to make his faults few, but he has not yet succeeded." He then went out, and the Master said, "A messenger indeed! A messenger indeed!"

注釋　engaged in: 從事於、忙於。

✳ **Chapter 27** ✳

The Master said, "He who is not in any particular office has nothing to do with plans for the administration of its duties."

---------------------------- ❋ 第二十八章 ❋ ----------------------------

曾子曰：「君子思不出其位。」

語譯　曾子說：「君子思慮的，不超出他的工作範圍。」

解說　「君子思不出其位。」是《易經・艮卦》之象辭。

---------------------------- ❋ 第二十九章 ❋ ----------------------------

子曰：「君子恥其言而過其行。」

語譯　孔子說：「君子恥於多說少做。」

解說　朱注：「恥者，不敢盡之意。過者，欲有餘之辭。」把「恥其言」和「過其行」分為兩項解釋，於文義不通。

---------------------------- ❋ 第三十章 ❋ ----------------------------

子曰：「君子道者三，我無能焉：仁者不憂，知者不惑，勇者不懼。」子貢曰：「夫子自道也。」

語譯　孔子說：「君子有三種美德，我一樣也沒能做到：仁者不憂慮，智者不迷惑，勇者不畏懼。」子貢說：「這正是老師在說自己吧！」

注釋　①**自道**　自述。

---------------------------- ❋ 第三十一章 ❋ ----------------------------

子貢方人。子曰：「賜也賢乎哉？夫我則不暇。」

語譯　子貢批評別人。孔子說：「賜啊真的夠好了嗎？像我就沒空去批評別人。」

注釋　①**方人**　朱注：「比也。」鄭玄注解釋為「言人之過惡」。

---------------------------- ❋ 第三十二章 ❋ ----------------------------

子曰：「不患人之不己知，患其不能也。」

語譯　孔子說：「不愁別人不知道我，只擔心自己能力不夠吧。」

❖ **Chapter 28** ❖

The philosopher Tsang said, "The superior man, in his thoughts, does not go out of his place."

❖ **Chapter 29** ❖

The Master said, "The superior man is modest in his speech, but exceeds in his actions."

解說　英譯採朱注解釋。

❖ **Chapter 30** ❖

30.1. The Master said, "The way of the superior man is threefold, but I am not equal to it. Virtuous, he is free from anxieties; wise, he is free from perplexities; bold, he is free from fear."

30.2. Tsze-kung said, "Master, that is what you yourself say."

❖ **Chapter 31** ❖

Tsze-kung was in the habit of comparing men together. The Master said, "Tsze must have reached a high pitch of excellence! Now, I have not leisure for this."

注釋　pitch: n. 程度；leisure: n. 閒暇。

❖ **Chapter 32** ❖

The Master said, "I will not be concerned at men's not knowing me; I will be concerned at my own want of ability."

—— ✦ 第三十三章 ✦ ——

子曰：「不逆詐，不億不信。抑亦先覺者，是賢乎？」

語譯　孔子說：「不在事前猜測別人會欺騙我，不預先揣度別人會失信於我。反過來說，能夠預先知道欺詐或失信，這就是賢者嗎？」

注釋　①**逆詐**　朱注：「逆，未至而先迎之也。」預先猜測別人可能會欺騙我。②**億**　臆測。③**抑亦先覺者，是賢乎**　抑，反語詞。朱注：「言雖不逆不億，而於人之情偽，自然先覺，乃爲賢也。」本書不從此解。

解說　《大戴禮・曾子立事篇》：「君子不先人以惡，不疑人以不信。」皇侃疏：「李充曰：人而無信，不知其可也。然閑邪存誠，不在善察。若見失信於前，必億其無信於後，則容長之風虧而改過之路塞矣。」有些人很聰明，經常懷疑別人會欺騙他，即使結果證明他是對的，他失去的其實更多。

—— ✦ 第三十四章 ✦ ——

微生畝謂孔子曰：「丘何爲是栖栖者與？無乃爲佞乎？」孔子曰：「非敢爲佞也，疾固也。」

語譯　微生畝對孔子說：「丘啊，你爲什麼總是如此忙忙碌碌呢？莫非是要逞口才之能去討好人家？」孔子說：「我不敢逞口舌之能，只是看不慣世人的固陋罷了。」

注釋　①**微生畝**　微生氏，名畝。《正義》：「微生稱夫子名，當以齒長故也。」②**栖栖**　栖音妻。不安居之意。③**爲佞**　朱注：「務爲口給以悅人也。」④**疾固**　厭惡世人的固陋。

—— ✦ 第三十五章 ✦ ——

子曰：「驥不稱其力，稱其德也。」

語譯　孔子說：「驥並不是以力氣著稱，而是以其馴良。」

注釋　①**驥**　千里馬。②**德**　指馴良。

─────────── ✣ **Chapter 33** ✣ ───────────

The Master said, "He who does not anticipate attempts to deceive him, nor think beforehand of his not being believed, and yet apprehends these things readily when they occur; -- is he not a man of superior worth?"

注釋　anticipate: v. 預料；readily: adv. 迅速地。

解說　英譯採朱注解釋。

─────────── ✣ **Chapter 34** ✣ ───────────

34.1. Wei-shang Mau said to Confucius, "Ch'iu, how is it that you keep roosting about? Is it not that you are an insinuating talker?

34.2. Confucius said, "I do not dare to play the part of such a talker, but I hate obstinacy."

注釋　roost: v. 棲息；about: adv. 四處；insinuating: adj. *巧妙奉承的*；obstinacy: n. *頑固*。

─────────── ✣ **Chapter 35** ✣ ───────────

The Master said, "A horse is called a ch'i, not because of its strength, but because of its other good qualities."

———— ✦ 第三十六章 ✦ ————

或曰：「以德報怨，何如？」子曰：「何以報德？以直報怨，以德報德。」

語譯 有人問：「人家有仇怨於我，而我以恩惠回報他，這樣如何？」孔子說：「那麼又如何報答對你有恩惠的人呢？應該以直道回報仇怨，以恩惠回報恩惠。」

注釋 ①**德** 恩惠之德。②**直** 直道。

解說 那麼直道是什麼呢？朱注：「愛憎取舍，一以至公無私。」這還不夠清楚。《正義》：「吳氏嘉賓說：『以直者不匿怨而已。……以直報怨，凡直之道非一，視吾心如何耳。吾心不能忘怨，報之直也，既報則可以忘矣。苟能忘怨而不報之，亦直也，雖不報固非有所匿矣。怨期於忘之，德期於不忘，故報怨者曰以直，欲其心之無餘怨也。報德者曰以德，欲其心之有餘德也。其心不能忘怨，而以理勝之者，亦直以其心能自勝也。直之反為偽，必若教人以德報怨，是教人使為偽也。烏乎可？』」「欲其心之無餘怨也」，說得非常好。勉強要以德報怨，心裡卻始終有怨恨，則只是顯得虛偽而已。

———— ✦ 第三十七章 ✦ ————

子曰：「莫我知也夫！」子貢曰：「何為其莫知子也？」子曰：「不怨天，不尤人；下學而上達。知我者，其天乎！」

語譯 孔子說：「沒有人知道我啊！」子貢說：「為什麼沒有人知道老師呢？」孔子說：「不怨恨天，不責怪人。學習人事而通達天命。知道我的，大概只有天吧！」

注釋 ①**尤** 非難。②**下學而上達** 《集解》：「孔曰：下學人事，上達天命。」

解說 孔子不見用於世，到底有沒有怨呢？「不怨天，不尤人，下學而上達。」孔子自述做學問的體驗，在平凡裡看到他的偉大。

---- ※ **Chapter 36** ※ ----

36.1. Some one said, "What do you say concerning the principle that injury should be recompensed with kindness?"

36.2. The Master said, "With what then will you recompense kindness?

36.3. "Recompense injury with justice, and recompense kindness with kindness."

注釋　recompense: v. 回報 [with]；justice: n. 正義。

---- ※ **Chapter 37** ※ ----

37.1. The Master said, "Alas! there is no one that knows me."

37.2. Tsze-kung said, "What do you mean by thus saying -- that no one knows you?" The Master replied, "I do not murmur against Heaven. I do not grumble against men. My studies lie low, and my penetration rises high. But there is Heaven; -- that knows me!"

注釋　grumble: v. 訴苦、抱怨。

解說　「下學而上達」英譯為 My studies lie low, and my penetration rises high，無法理解是什麼意思。

———— ✤ 第三十八章 ✤ ————

公伯寮愬子路於季孫。子服景伯以告，曰：「夫子固有惑志於公伯
寮，吾力猶能肆諸市朝。」子曰：「道之將行也與，命也。道之將
廢也與，命也。公伯寮其如命何！」

語譯　公伯寮在季孫面前誹謗子路。子服景伯告訴孔子說：「季孫已經被公伯寮
　　　給迷惑了，但是我還有能力使他陳屍於市。」孔子說：「道如果能夠行於
　　　世，那是天命。道如果要廢棄，那也是天命。公伯寮又能對天命怎麼樣
　　　呢？」

注釋　①**公伯寮**　魯國人。②**愬**　音訴，進讒言。③**子服景伯**　朱注：「子服
　　　氏，景諡，伯字，魯大夫子服何也。」④**夫子**　指季孫。⑤**肆**　殺之而陳
　　　其尸。大夫尸於朝，士尸於市。

解說　《正義》引張爾岐《蒿庵閒話》說：「人道之當然而不可違者，義也。天
　　　道之本然而不可爭者，命也。貧富、貴賤、得失，死生之有所制而不可彊
　　　也，君子與小人一也。命不可知，君子當以義知命矣。凡義所不可，即以
　　　為命所不有也。……君子以義安命，故心常泰，小人以智力爭命，故其
　　　心多怨。眾人之於命，亦有安之矣，大約皆知其無可奈何，而後安之者
　　　也。」

———— ✤ 第三十九章 ✤ ————

子曰：「賢者辟世，其次辟地，其次辟色，其次辟言。」

語譯　孔子說：「有些賢者避世隱居，其次的擇地而處，再其次的看到人家臉色
　　　不好才走，又其次的聽到人家惡言惡語才離開。」

注釋　①**辟世**　辟，避也。避世，謂天下無道而隱。②**辟地**　即亂邦不入。③**辟
　　　色**　禮貌衰而去。④**辟言**　有違言而後去。

———— ✤ 第四十章 ✤ ————

子曰：「作者七人矣。」

語譯　孔子說：「起而避世的已經有七位了。」

❄ **Chapter 38** ❄

38.1. The Kung-po Liao, having slandered Tsze-lu to Chi-sun, Tsze-fu Ching-po informed Confucius of it, saying, "Our master is certainly being led astray by the Kung-po Liao, but I have still power enough left to cut Liao off, and expose his corpse in the market and in the court."

38.2. The Master said, "If my principles are to advance, it is so ordered. If they are to fall to the ground, it is so ordered. What can the Kung-po Liao do where such ordering is concerned?"

注釋　slander: v. 誹謗；lead astray: 引入歧途；corpse: n. 屍體；advance: v. 前進。

❄ **Chapter 39** ❄

The Master said, "Some men of worth retire from the world. Some retire from particular states. Some retire because of disrespectful looks. Some retire because of contradictory language."

注釋　disrespectful: adj. 無禮的；contradictory: adj. 對立的。

❄ **Chapter 40** ❄

The Master said, "Those who have done this are seven men."

解說　《集解》：「包曰：作，爲也。爲之者凡七人，謂長沮、桀溺、丈人、石門、荷蕢、儀封人、楚狂接輿。」

———— ❊ 第四十一章 ❊ ————

子路宿於石門。晨門曰：「奚自？」子路曰：「自孔氏。」曰：「是知其不可而為之者與？」

語譯　子路在石門過夜。第二天清早進城，守門人問：「你從哪裡來的？」子路說：「從孔家來。」守門人說：「就是那個明知做不到卻還是去做的人嗎？」

注釋　①石門　魯城外門。②晨門　守門人。③奚自　來自何方。

解說　孔子知道「知其不可而爲之」正是他的天命吧。

———— ❊ 第四十二章 ❊ ————

子擊磬於衛。有荷蕢而過孔氏之門者，曰：「有心哉！擊磬乎！」既而曰：「鄙哉！硜硜乎！莫己知也，斯已而已矣。『深則厲，淺則揭。』」子曰：「果哉！末之難矣。」

語譯　孔子在衛國，有一天正在擊磬。有個挑著草器的人經過孔子門口，說：「這磬聲真是有深意啊！」聽了一會又說：「真是鄙陋啊！心志如此固執！如果沒有人知道你，那麼自顧自就罷了。『水深濕衣渡，水淺拉起衣。』」孔子說：「真是堅決啊！我沒有什麼可以反駁他的。」

注釋　①荷蕢　擔草器。②硜硜　石聲。比喻頑固。③深則厲，淺則揭　語出《詩經‧衛風‧匏有苦葉》。朱注：「以衣涉水曰厲，攝衣涉水曰揭。」④果　果決。指荷蕢者果於忘世。⑤末之難矣　無所非難。或解釋爲「沒什麼困難的」。

———— ❊ 第四十三章 ❊ ————

子張曰：「書云：『高宗諒陰，三年不言。』何謂也？」子曰：「何必高宗，古之人皆然。君薨，百官總己以聽於冢宰，三年。」

⁂ **Chapter 41** ⁂

Tsze-lu happening to pass the night in Shih-man, the gatekeeper said to him, "Whom do you come from?" Tsze-lu said, "From Mr. K'ung." "It is he, is it not?" said the other, "who knows the impracticable nature of the times and yet will be doing in them."

注釋　gatekeeper: n. 守門人；impracticable: adj. 不能實行的。

⁂ **Chapter 42** ⁂

42.1. The Master was playing, one day, on a musical stone in Weil when a man carrying a straw basket passed door of the house where Confucius was, and said, "His heart is full who so beats the musical stone."

42.2. A little while after, he added, "How contemptible is the one-ideaed obstinacy those sounds display! When one is taken no notice of, he has simply at once to give over his wish for public employment. 'Deep water must be crossed with the clothes on; shallow water may be crossed with the clothes held up.'"

42.3. The Master said, "How determined is he in his purpose! But this is not difficult!"

注釋　straw: n. 稻草；basket: n. 籃子；contemptible: adj. 鄙陋；display: v. 表露；shallow: adj. 淺。

⁂ **Chapter 43** ⁂

43.1. Tsze-chang said, "What is meant when the Shu says that Kao-tsung, while observing the usual imperial mourning, was for three years without speaking?"

語譯　子張說：「《書經》說：『殷高宗守孝，三年都不發布政令。』這是什麼意思？」孔子說：「何必要是高宗呢？古人都是這樣的。國君死了，繼任的國君三年不問政事，百官都總攝自己的職務，聽從太宰的命令。」

注釋　①**高宗諒陰，三年不言**　出自《尚書‧無逸篇》。高宗，商王武丁。諒陰，君王居喪。不言，不言及政事。②**薨**　公侯卒。③**總己**　總攝已職。④**冢宰**　太宰。《集解》：「冢宰，天官卿，佐王治者。三年喪畢，然後王自聽政。」

解說　孔子慨嘆其時已不行三年之喪。

⁂ 第四十四章 ⁂

子曰：「上好禮，則民易使也。」

語譯　孔子說：「在上位的人好禮，那麼民眾就容易役使了。」

⁂ 第四十五章 ⁂

子路問君子。子曰：「脩己以敬。」曰：「如斯而已乎？」曰：「脩己以安人。」曰：「如斯而已乎？」曰：「脩己以安百姓。脩己以安百姓，堯舜其猶病諸！」

語譯　子路問如何才是君子。孔子說：「以敬修養自己。」子路說：「這樣就夠了嗎？」孔子說：「自己修養好了，可以使別人安樂。」子路說：「這樣就夠了嗎？」孔子說：「自己修養好了，可以使百姓安樂。修養自己而使百姓安樂，恐怕連堯舜都做不到呢！」

注釋　①**脩己以敬**　即脩己以禮。②**病**　擔心做不到。③**諸**　語助詞。

⁂ 第四十六章 ⁂

原壤夷俟。子曰：「幼而不孫弟，長而無述焉，老而不死，是為賊！」以杖叩其脛。

語譯　原壤蹲著等候孔子。孔子說：「年輕的時候不曉得謙讓長輩，長大後又沒有什麼可稱道的，活了大把年紀了還不死，只是個苟且偷生的賊罷了！」

43.2. The Master said, "Why must Kao-tsung be referred to as an example of this? The ancients all did so. When the sovereign died, the officers all attended to their several duties, taking instructions from the prime minister for three years."

注釋　observe: v. 行禮；mourning: n. 服喪期間；attend to: 照料。

解說　「不言」是指不言政事，不宜譯爲 without speaking。

☀ **Chapter 44** ☀

The Master said, " When rulers love to observe the rules of propriety, the people respond readily to the calls on them for service."

☀ **Chapter 45** ☀

45.1. Tsze-lu asked what constituted the superior man. The Master said, "The cultivation of himself in reverential carefulness." "And is this all?" said Tsze-lu. "He cultivates himself so as to give rest to others," was the reply. "And is this all?" again asked Tsze-lu. The Master said, "He cultivates himself so as to give rest to all the people. He cultivates himself so as to give rest to all the people: -- even Yao and Shun were still solicitous about this."

注釋　solicitous: adj. 擔心 [about]。

☀ **Chapter 46** ☀

Yuan Zang was squatting on his heels, and so waited the approach of the Master, who said to him, "In youth not humble as befits a junior; in manhood, doing nothing worthy of being handed down; and living on to old age: -- this is to be a pest." With this he hit him on the shank with his staff.

孔子說著就用拐杖打他的腳脛。

注釋　①**原壤**　魯國人，孔子的老朋友。②**夷俟**　蹲著等候。③**不孫弟**　對長輩不恭敬。④**述**　稱述。⑤**叩**　擊。⑥**脛**　腳脛。

———————— ❈ 第四十七章 ❈ ————————

闕黨童子將命。或問之曰：「益者與？」子曰：「吾見其居於位也，見其與先生並行也。非求益者也，欲速成者也。」

語譯　孔子叫闕黨的孩子去傳話。有人問孔子說：「那個孩子是肯上進的人嗎？」孔子說：「我看到他坐在成年人的席位，又看到他和長輩並肩而行。那孩子不是求上進，而只是想快點變成大人罷了。」

注釋　①**闕黨**　孔子的故里。②**將命**　傳達賓主之言。③**益**　長進。④**居於位**　朱注：「禮，童子當隅坐隨行。」⑤**先生**　成人。⑥**並行**　《集解》：「不差在後，違禮。」

注釋 squat: v. 蹲；heel: n. 腳跟；as befits: 符合；hand down: 傳給後代；pest: n. 害蟲、討厭鬼；shank: n. 腳脛。

❖ **Chapter 47** ❖

47.1. A youth of the village of Ch'ueh was employed by Confucius to carry the messages between him and his visitors. Some one asked about him, saying, "I suppose he has made great progress."

47.2. The Master said, "I observe that he is fond of occupying the seat of a full-grown man; I observe that he walks shoulder to shoulder with his elders. He is not one who is seeking to make progress in learning. He wishes quickly to become a man."

注釋 full-grown: 成熟的。

衛靈公第十五

———— ❀ 第一章 ❀ ————

衛靈公問陳於孔子。孔子對曰：「俎豆之事，則嘗聞之矣；軍旅之事，未之學也。」明日遂行。在陳絕糧，從者病，莫能興。子路慍見曰：「君子亦有窮乎？」子曰：「君子固窮，小人窮斯濫矣。」

語譯　衛靈公問孔子兵陣之事。孔子回答說：「祭祀禮制的事，我倒聽過；軍隊的事，我從來沒有學過。」第二天便離開衛國。在陳國斷了糧，隨行的弟子都生病了，起不來。子路臉色很不高興地說：「君子也有這麼窮的時候嗎？」孔子說：「君子雖然窮，還是會堅持原則，小人窮困的時候，就會放濫橫行。」

注釋　①陳　同陣，軍陣行列之法。②俎豆　禮器。③興　起床。④慍見　帶著怨恨的臉色。⑤固窮　窮當固守。或解釋為「固然亦有窮困之時」。⑥濫　溢也。濫溢為非。

———— ❀ 第二章 ❀ ————

子曰：「賜也，女以予為多學而識之者與？」對曰：「然，非與？」曰：「非也，予一以貫之。」

語譯　孔子說：「賜啊，你以為我是博學而強記的人嗎？」子貢回答說：「是啊，難道不是嗎？」孔子說：「不是的，我有個貫通這些道理的基本觀念。」

注釋　①識　記識。②與　同歟。疑問語助詞。③貫　貫穿。

解說　在做學問的時候，如果沒有了解基礎原理，那麼死記再多的知識片段，也是沒有用的。〈里仁篇〉說過：「吾道一以貫之。」學者認為這裡所指的也是忠恕之道。而阮元認為「貫」指的是行動，劉寶楠也說：「學問思辨，多學而識之也；篤行，一以貫之也。」則是強調道德實踐的重要性。

———— ❀ 第三章 ❀ ————

子曰：「由！知德者鮮矣。」

語譯　孔子說：「由啊！知道道德的人太少了。」

❧ **Chapter 1** ❧

1.1. The Duke Ling of Wei asked Confucius about tactics. Confucius replied, "I have heard all about sacrificial vessels, but I have not learned military matters." On this, he took his departure the next day.

1.2. When he was in Chan, their provisions were exhausted, and his followers became so in that they were unable to rise.

1.3. Tsze-lu, with evident dissatisfaction, said, "Has the superior man likewise to endure in this way?" The Master said, "The superior man may indeed have to endure want, but the mean man, when he is in want, gives way to unbridled license."

注釋 tactic: n. 戰術；take one's departure: 動身、起程；provisions: 糧食；exhausted: adj. 耗盡的；evident: adj. 明顯的；dissatisfaction: n. 不滿；unbridle: adj. 不受約束的、放縱的；license: n. 行動的自由。

❧ **Chapter 2** ❧

2.1. The Master said, "Ts'ze, you think, I suppose, that I am one who learns many things and keeps them in memory?"

2.2. Tsze-kung replied, "Yes, -- but perhaps it is not so?"

2.3. "No," was the answer; "I seek a unity all pervading."

注釋 pervade: v. 遍及。

❧ **Chapter 3** ❧

The Master said, "Yu, those who know virtue are few."

———— ❈ 第四章 ❈ ————

子曰：「無為而治者，其舜也與？夫何為哉，恭己正南面而已矣。」

語譯　孔子說：「能無爲而治的，大概只有舜吧？他做些什麼呢？只不過恭敬自守，端坐君位而已。」

解說　這裡的「無爲」是指任用有才能的人，所以不用事必躬親。《漢書‧董仲舒傳》：「堯在位七十載，乃遜于位以禪虞舜。堯崩，天下不歸堯子丹朱而歸舜。舜知不可辟，迺即天子之位，以禹爲相，因堯之輔佐，繼其統業，是以垂拱無爲而天下治。」

———— ❈ 第五章 ❈ ————

子張問行。子曰：「言忠信，行篤敬，雖蠻貊之邦行矣；言不忠信，行不篤敬，雖州里行乎哉？立，則見其參於前也；在輿，則見其倚於衡也。夫然後行。」子張書諸紳。

語譯　子張問孔子如何才能行得通。孔子說：「說話誠懇信實，做事篤厚認眞，就算在異邦也可以行得通；說話不誠懇，做事不認眞，就算是在自己的家鄉，難道就行得通嗎？站著的時候，就像看到忠信篤敬這幾個字在你面前；坐車的時候，就像看到這幾個字刻在車前橫木上。能夠這樣，自然行得通了。」子張把孔子的話記在衣帶上。

注釋　①蠻貊　朱注：「蠻，南蠻。貊，北狄。」②州里　《集解》：「鄭曰：二千五百家爲州，五家爲鄰，五鄰爲里。」③參　直立。④衡　車前橫軛。⑤紳　衣帶。

———— ❈ 第六章 ❈ ————

子曰：「直哉史魚！邦有道，如矢；邦無道，如矢。君子哉蘧伯玉！邦有道，則仕；邦無道，則可卷而懷之。」

語譯　孔子說：「史魚眞是正直！國家政治清明，他像箭那麼直；國家政治昏亂，他還是像箭那麼直。蘧伯玉眞是個君子啊！國家政治清明，他就出來做官；國家政治昏亂，也可以隱退。」

❖ Chapter 4 ❖

The Master said, "May not Shun be instanced as having governed efficiently without exertion? What did he do? He did nothing but gravely and reverently occupy his royal seat."

注釋　instance: v. 引證、舉例；exertion: n. 努力。

解說　「無爲」譯爲 without exertion（不用費力），或譯爲 without overreaching。

❖ Chapter 5 ❖

5.1.　Tsze-chang asked how a man should conduct himself, so as to be everywhere appreciated.

5.2.　The Master said, "Let his words be sincere and truthful and his actions honorable and careful; -- such conduct may be practiced among the rude tribes of the South or the North. If his words be not sincere and truthful and his actions not honorable and carefull will he, with such conduct, be appreciated, even in his neighborhood?

5.3.　"When he is standing, let him see those two things, as it were, fronting him. When he is in a carriage, let him see them attached to the yoke. Then may he subsequently carry them into practice."

5.4.　Tsze-chang wrote these counsels on the end of his sash.

注釋　honorable: adj. 可敬的、有誠意的；counsel: n. 勸告；sash: n. 飾帶。

❖ Chapter 6 ❖

The Master said, "Truly straightforward was the historiographer Yu. When good government prevailed in his state, he was like an arrow. When bad government prevailed, he was like an arrow. A superior man indeed is Chu Po-yu! When good government prevails in his state, he is to be found in office. When bad government prevails, he can roll his principles up, and keep them in his breast."

注釋　①**史魚**　衛國大夫。②**矢**　箭矢。③**卷而懷之**　收而藏之。

解說　《韓詩外傳》：「昔者、衛大夫史魚病且死，謂其子曰：『我數言蘧伯玉之賢而不能進，彌子瑕不肖而不能退。爲人臣，生不能進賢而退不肖，死不當治喪正堂，殯我於室、足矣。』衛君問其故，子以父言聞，君造然召蘧伯玉而貴之，而退彌子瑕，從殯於正堂，成禮而後去。生以身諫，死以尸諫，可謂直矣。」《孔子家語・困誓》：「孔子聞之曰：古之列諫之者，死則已矣，未有若史魚死而尸諫，忠感其君者也，不可謂直乎？」

※ 第七章 ※

子曰：「可與言而不與之言，失人；不可與言而與之言，失言。知者不失人，亦不失言。」

語譯　孔子說：「可以對他說而沒有說，是錯失了好人；不可以對他說而說了，是說錯話。智者不會錯失好人，也不會說錯話。」

解說　《荀子》：「故禮恭，而後可與言道之方；辭順，而後可與言道之理；色從而後可與言道之致。故未可與言而言，謂之傲；可與言而不言，謂之隱；不觀氣色而言，謂瞽。故君子不傲、不隱、不瞽，謹順其身。」對孔子的這段話詮釋得非常生動。在工作或生活當中，確實很難掌握說話的分際。

※ 第八章 ※

子曰：「志士仁人，無求生以害仁，有殺身以成仁。」

語譯　孔子說：「志士仁人，沒有爲了生命而殘害仁德的，倒是有犧牲生命以成就仁德的。」

注釋　①**志士**　《孟子》趙注：「守義者也。」

解說　朱注：「理當死而求生，則於其心有不安矣，是害其心之德也。當死而死，則心安而德全矣。」然則什麼是「殺身成仁」呢？《正義》引焦循《雕菰樓文集》說：「殺身成仁，解者引比干之諫，夷齊之餓，固矣。然殺身不必盡刀鋸鼎鑊也。舜勤眾事而野死，冥勤其官而水死，爲民禦大災，捍大患，所謂仁也。以死勤事，即是殺身成仁。……夫聖賢之死不

注釋 straightforward: adj. 正直；historiographer: n. 歷史學家。

Chapter 7

The Master said, "When a man may be spoken with, not to speak to him is to err in reference to the man. When a man may not be spoken with, to speak to him is to err in reference to our words. The wise err neither in regard to their man nor to their words."

注釋 in reference to: 關於。

Chapter 8

The Master said, "The determined scholar and the man of virtue will not seek to live at the expense of injuring their virtue. They will even sacrifice their lives to preserve their virtue complete."

注釋 determined: adj. 堅決的。

死，審乎仁不仁，非謂仁必死也，非謂死則仁也。」根據這個解釋，鞠躬盡瘁，死而後已，也可以說是「殺身成仁」了。

※ 第九章 ※

子貢問為仁。子曰：「工欲善其事，必先利其器。居是邦也，事其大夫之賢者，友其士之仁者。」

語譯　子貢問孔子培養仁德的方法。孔子說：「工匠想要做好工作，得先有完備的工具。住在這個國家，就要為賢能的大夫做事，和有仁德的讀書人交朋友。」

解說　前面說過，「如切如磋，如琢如磨」，德行是在社會的互動裡完成的。在工作上有好長官可以學習，在生活中有好朋友可以互相砥礪，這是成就道德人格的重要資糧。

※ 第十章 ※

顏淵問為邦。子曰：「行夏之時，乘殷之輅，服周之冕，樂則韶舞。放鄭聲，遠佞人。鄭聲淫，佞人殆。」

語譯　顏淵問如何建立國家制度。孔子說：「用夏朝的曆法，坐商朝的木車，戴周朝的禮帽，採用舜時的韶樂。捨棄鄭國的音樂，遠離便佞的小人。鄭國的音樂太放縱，便佞的小人有危險。」

注釋　①為邦　錢穆：「為，創制義。」建立國家制度的意思。②行夏之時　用夏朝的曆法。當時有夏正、殷正、周正之分，夏正即現在的陰曆，合於農時，所以孔子主張行夏之時。③乘殷之輅　輅亦作路，天子所成乘之車。《集解》：「馬曰：殷車曰大輅。左傳曰：大輅越席，昭其儉也。」周制有五路，其中殷路是木車，最為儉樸。④服周之冕　冕，祭服之冠。周朝的祭服隆重而不奢侈，所以孔子主張穿周朝的祭服。⑤韶舞　韶，舜時的音樂。舞同武，指周武王的音樂。⑥放鄭聲　放，禁絕。鄭聲，鄭國的音樂。《樂記》：「鄭音好濫淫志。」⑦佞人　諂媚逢迎的人。⑧淫　過度的意思。⑨殆　危害。

解說　這裡要注意的是孔子在審度各個朝代的制度優缺點時的原則，了解孔子如

━━━━━━━━━━━━━ ⚜ **Chapter 9** ⚜ ━━━━━━━━━━━━━

Tsze-kung asked about the practice of virtue. The Master said, "The mechanic, who wishes to do his work well, must first sharpen his tools. When you are living in any state, take service with the most worthy among its great officers, and make friends of the most virtuous among its scholars."

注釋　mechanic: n. 技工；sharpen: v. 使鋒利。

━━━━━━━━━━━━━ ⚜ **Chapter 10** ⚜ ━━━━━━━━━━━━━

10.1. Yen Yuan asked how the government of a country should be administered.

10.2. The Master said, "Follow the seasons of Hsia.

10.3. "Ride in the state carriage of Yin.

10.4. "Wear the ceremonial cap of Chau.

10.5. "Let the music be the Shao with its pantomimes. Banish the songs of Chang, and keep far from specious talkers. The songs of Chang are licentious; specious talkers are dangerous."

注釋　pantomime: n. 默劇；banish: v. 放逐；specious: adj. 似是而非的；licentious: adj. 放蕩的。

解說　「韶舞」譯為 Shao with its pantomimes，單指韶樂，而不包含武樂。

何在傳統與創新之間斟酌損益。不過孔子對於詩歌和音樂的看法，始終是以道德教化爲藝術的標準，這似乎是太過狹隘了。

※ 第十一章 ※

子曰：「人無遠慮，必有近憂。」

語譯　孔子說：「如果沒有長遠的考慮，必定會有眼前的憂患。」

解說　《詩經・豳風・鴟鴞》說：「迨天之未陰雨，徹彼桑土，綢繆牖戶。」鴟鴞在還沒下雨之前，就開始修補鳥巢，我們總不能缺水了才想到要限水吧？

※ 第十二章 ※

子曰：「已矣乎！吾未見好德如好色者也。」

語譯　孔子說：「算了吧！我沒看過好德像好色的人啊！」

解說　見〈子罕篇〉。

※ 第十三章 ※

子曰：「臧文仲其竊位者與？知柳下惠之賢，而不與立也。」

語譯　孔子說：「臧文仲可以說是竊佔官位吧？他知道柳下惠的賢能，卻不能推薦他，和他同立於朝。」

注釋　①臧文仲　魯國大夫。②柳下惠　魯大夫展禽，食邑柳下，諡曰惠。③與立　並立於朝。或解釋爲不授與職位。

※ 第十四章 ※

子曰：「躬自厚而薄責於人，則遠怨矣。」

語譯　孔子說：「律己要嚴格，少責備別人，別人就不會怨恨你了。」

解說　「則遠怨矣」或解釋爲「自己心裡便沒有怨恨了」。

❋ **Chapter 11** ❋

The Master said, "If a man take no thought about what is distant, he will find sorrow near at hand."

注釋　at hand: 近在眼前。

❋ **Chapter 12** ❋

The Master said, "It is all over! I have not seen one who loves virtue as he loves beauty."

❋ **Chapter 13** ❋

The Master said, "Was not Tsang Wan like one who had stolen his situation? He knew the virtue and the talents of Hui of Liu-hsia, and yet did not procure that he should stand with him in court."

注釋　situation: n. 職業；procure: v. 謀取。

❋ **Chapter 14** ❋

The Master said, "He who requires much from himself and little from others, will keep himself from being the object of resentment."

注釋　resentment: n. 氣憤。

———————— ❖ 第十五章 ❖ ————————

子曰：「不曰『如之何、如之何』者，吾末如之何也已矣。」

語譯　孔子說：「不想想『怎麼辦，怎麼辦』的人，我也拿他沒辦法了。」

注釋　①如之何如之何　朱注：「熟思而審處之辭也。」動腦筋想想怎麼辦的意思。

———————— ❖ 第十六章 ❖ ————————

子曰：「群居終日，言不及義，好行小慧，難矣哉！」

語譯　孔子說：「和大家整天在一起，談話都不談正經事，喜歡賣弄小聰明，這種人很難了。」

注釋　①小慧　小聰明。

———————— ❖ 第十七章 ❖ ————————

子曰：「君子義以為質，禮以行之，孫以出之，信以成之。君子哉！」

語譯　孔子說：「君子以道義為做事的根本，遵循禮節去實行，以謙虛的言詞去表達，用誠實的態度去完成。這樣才是君子啊！」

注釋　①質　本質。②孫以出之　孫同遜。言詞謙遜。

———————— ❖ 第十八章 ❖ ————————

子曰：「君子病無能焉，不病人之不己知也。」

語譯　孔子說：「君子只愁自己無能，不愁別人不知道自己。」

注釋　①病　擔憂。

解說　〈憲問篇〉：「不患人之不己知，患其不能也。」意思相同。

❧ **Chapter 15** ❧

The Master said, "When a man is not in the habit of saying -- 'What shall I think of this? What shall I think of this?' I can indeed do nothing with him!"

注釋　in habit of: 習慣於。

❧ **Chapter 16** ❧

The Master said, "When a number of people are together, for a whole day, without their conversation turning on righteousness, and when they are fond of carrying out the suggestions of a small shrewdness; -- theirs is indeed a hard case."

注釋　shrewdness: n. 聰明。

❧ **Chapter 17** ❧

The Master said, "The superior man in everything considers righteousness to be essential. He performs it according to the rules of propriety. He brings it forth in humility. He completes it with sincerity. This is indeed a superior man."

注釋　bring forth: 提出來；humility: n. 謙恭。

❧ **Chapter 18** ❧

The Master said, "The superior man is distressed by his want of ability. He is not distressed by men's not knowing him."

注釋　distressed: adj. 苦惱的。

———— ✤ 第十九章 ✤ ————

子曰：「君子疾沒世而名不稱焉。」

語譯　孔子說：「死後沒有好的名聲，君子會引以為恨。」

注釋　①**疾**　苦惱。②**沒世**　死後。

解說　《史記‧孔子世家》：「子曰：『弗乎弗乎，君子病沒世而名不稱焉。吾
　　　道不行矣，吾何以自見於後世哉？』乃因史記作春秋，上至隱公，下訖哀
　　　公十四年，十二公。」孔子說這句話，是在作春秋之時。《傳習錄》：「稱
　　　字去聲讀。亦『聲聞過情，君子恥之』之意。實不稱名，生猶可補。沒則
　　　無及矣。」把「稱」解釋為「相稱」。亦通。

———— ✤ 第二十章 ✤ ————

子曰：「君子求諸己，小人求諸人。」

語譯　孔子說：「君子會處處要求自己，小人則處處要求別人。」

注釋　①**求**　責也。《集解》：「君子責己，小人責人。」

———— ✤ 第二十一章 ✤ ————

子曰：「君子矜而不爭，群而不黨。」

語譯　孔子說：「君子矜持而與人無爭，合群而不結黨營私。」

注釋　①**矜**　《集解》：「包曰：矜，矜莊也。」②**黨**　《集解》：「孔曰：黨，助
　　　也。君子雖眾，不相私助，義之與比。」偏私的意思。

解說　朱注：「莊以持己曰矜。然無乖戾之心，故不爭。和以處眾曰群。然無阿
　　　比之意，故不黨。」

———— ✤ 第二十二章 ✤ ————

子曰：「君子不以言舉人，不以人廢言。」

語譯　孔子說：「君子不會因為某人的說話好而提拔他，也不因為某人的行為有

☀ **Chapter 19** ☀

The Master said, "The superior man dislikes the thought of his name not being mentioned after his death."

☀ **Chapter 20** ☀

The Master said, "What the superior man seeks, is in himself. What the mean man seeks, is in others."

解說　「求」譯爲 seek（追求），是根據朱注的解釋。

☀ **Chapter 21** ☀

The Master said, "The superior man is dignified, but does not wrangle. He is sociable, but not a partisan."

注釋　wrangle: v. 爭吵；sociable: adj. 和善、人緣好；partisan: n.黨派觀念很強的人。

☀ **Chapter 22** ☀

The Master said, "The superior man does not promote a man simply on account of his words, nor does he put aside good words because of the man."

注釋　put aside: 忽視。

缺點而不理會他所說的話。」

注釋 ①**不以言舉人** 《集解》：「包曰：有言者不必有德，故不可以言舉人也。」
②**不以人廢言** 蔣伯潛：「芻蕘之言，聖人擇焉；故其言有可采，亦不以
其人之無可取而廢之。」

⊹ 第二十三章 ⊹

子貢問曰：「有一言而可以終身行之者乎？」子曰：「其恕乎！己
所不欲，勿施於人。」

語譯 子貢問孔子說：「有沒有一個字是可以終身奉行的？」孔子說：「那大概
只有恕吧！自己不喜歡的，不要強加在別人身上。」

注釋 ①**一言** 一個字。

解說 「己所不欲，勿施於人。」這句話也就是民主社會的行為原則：「個人的
自由以不侵犯他人的自由為前提。」所謂的恕道，只不過是凡事多為別人
想一想。

⊹ 第二十四章 ⊹

子曰：「吾之於人也，誰毀誰譽？如有所譽者，其有所試矣。斯民
也，三代之所以直道而行也。」

語譯 孔子說：「我對於別人，批評了誰？稱讚了誰？如果我稱讚了某個人，必
定是我驗證過的。這些人啊，正是夏商周三代以直道教養的啊。」

注釋 ①**誰毀誰譽** 指不隨便批評或讚美。朱注：「毀者，稱人之惡而損其真。譽
者，揚人之善而過其實。」②**斯民** 指夏、商、周三代之民。③**直道** 《正
義》：「直者，無私曲之謂。如有所譽，似偏於厚，而究其磨礪誘掖之
意，非為私曲，故曰直道。」

⊹ 第二十五章 ⊹

子曰：「吾猶及史之闕文也，有馬者借人乘之。今亡矣夫！」

 **Chapter 23**

Tsze-kung asked, saying, "Is there one word which may serve as a rule of practice for all one's life?" The Master said, "Is not RECIPROCITY such a word? What you do not want done to yourself, do not do to others."

注釋　reciprocity: n. 相互關係。

Chapter 24

24.1. The Master said, "In my dealings with men, whose evil do I blame, whose goodness do I praise, beyond what is proper? If I do sometimes exceed in praise, there must be ground for it in my examination of the individual.

24.2. "This people supplied the ground why the three dynasties pursued the path of straightforwardness."

注釋　ground: n. 理由。

Chapter 25

The Master said, "Even in my early days, a historiographer would leave a blank in his text, and he who had a horse would lend him to another to ride.

語譯　孔子說：「我還看過有史官存疑而不書，有馬的人先借給別人騎。現在沒有這種事了！」

注釋　①**猶及**　還趕得上。②**史之闕文**　《集解》：「包曰：古之良史，於書字有疑則闕之，以待知者。」

解說　《漢書‧藝文志》：「古制，書必同文，不知則闕，問諸故老，至於衰世，是非無正，人用其私。故孔子曰：『吾猶及史之闕文也，今亡矣夫！』蓋傷其浸不正。」

———————※ 第二十六章 ※———————

子曰：「巧言亂德，小不忍則亂大謀。」

語譯　孔子說：「花言巧語會使人失德，小處不能忍耐，會壞了大事。」

解說　朱注：「巧言，變亂是非，聽之使人喪其所守。小不忍，如婦人之仁、匹夫之勇皆是。」孔子非常痛恨以似是而非的言論混淆正道的人。

———————※ 第二十七章 ※———————

子曰：「眾惡之，必察焉；眾好之，必察焉。」

語譯　孔子說：「即使是大家都討厭他，也得仔細考察；即使是大家都喜歡他，也得仔細考察。」

解說　《集解》：「或眾阿黨比周，或其人特立不群，故好惡不可不察也。」這也是告訴我們要有獨立判斷的精神，不要人云亦云。

———————※ 第二十八章 ※———————

子曰：「人能弘道，非道弘人。」

語譯　孔子說：「人可以使道弘大，道不能使人弘大。」

解說　《中庸》：「苟不至德，至道不凝焉。」真理有待於人的行動才能體現，這句話看似簡單，實則寓意深遠。

Now, alas! there are no such things."

注釋　blank: n. 空白處。

✤ **Chapter 26** ✤

The Master said, "Specious words confound virtue. Want of forbearance in small matters confounds great plans."

注釋　confound: n. 混淆；forbearance: n. 自制。

✤ **Chapter 27** ✤

The Master said, "When the multitude hate a man, it is necessary to examine into the case. When the multitude like a man, it is necessary to examine into the case."

注釋　examine into: 審察。

✤ **Chapter 28** ✤

The Master said, "A man can enlarge the principles which he follows; those principles do not enlarge the man."

注釋　enlarge: v. 擴大、開闊。

---------------------------------- ✤ 第二十九章 ✤ ----------------------------------

子曰：「過而不改，是謂過矣。」

語譯　孔子說：「有過錯而不改正，這才是過失啊。」

解說　犯了錯不思改過，反而文過飾非，那麼他眞的就沒有向善的機會了。

---------------------------------- ✤ 第三十章 ✤ ----------------------------------

子曰：「吾嘗終日不食，終夜不寢，以思，無益，不如學也。」

語譯　孔子說：「我曾經整天不吃飯，整晚不睡覺，努力思考，還是沒有益處，不如求教於別人。」

解說　這裡的思考，是指「思而不學」，與其枯坐冥想，不如博文約禮。《中庸》說：「博學之，審問之，愼思之，明辨之，篤行之。」

---------------------------------- ✤ 第三十一章 ✤ ----------------------------------

子曰：「君子謀道不謀食。耕也，餒①在其中矣；學也，祿在其中矣。君子憂道不憂貧。」

語譯　孔子說：「君子致力於道德學問，而不用心於衣食生活。種田也有挨餓的時候；認眞做學問，裡頭自然有俸祿。君子只擔心道之不行，不擔心貧困。」

注釋　①餒　挨餓。

解說　當時的士大夫階級式微，而有人爲謀食而習耕，孔子這句話有勸學之意。

---------------------------------- ✤ 第三十二章 ✤ ----------------------------------

子曰：「知及之，仁不能守之，雖得之，必失之。知及之，仁能守之，不莊以涖之，則民不敬。知及之，仁能守之，莊以涖之，動之不以禮，未善也。」

語譯　孔子說：「才識足以治國，如果他的仁德不足以堅守，那麼即使得到職

✳ **Chapter 29** ✳

The Master said, "To have faults and not to reform them, -- this, indeed, should be pronounced having faults."

注釋　reform: v. 改正。

✳ **Chapter 30** ✳

The Master said, "I have been the whole day without eating, and the whole night without sleeping: -- occupied with thinking. It was of no use. The better plan is to learn."

注釋　occupied with: 忙於。

✳ **Chapter 31** ✳

The Master said, "The object of the superior man is truth. Food is not his object. There is plowing; -- even in that there is sometimes want. So with learning; -- emolument may be found in it. The superior man is anxious lest he should not get truth; he is not anxious lest poverty should come upon him."

注釋　plow: v. 用犁耕田；emolument: n. 薪俸。

✳ **Chapter 32** ✳

32.1. The Master said, "When a man's knowledge is sufficient to attain, and his virtue is not sufficient to enable him to hold, whatever he may have gained, he will lose again.

32.2. "When his knowledge is sufficient to attain, and he has virtue enough to hold fast, if he cannot govern with dignity, the people will not respect

位，也必定會失去。才識足以治國，仁德可以守之不失，如果沒有認眞對待百姓，百姓也不會尊敬他。才識足以治國，仁德可以守之不失，而且認眞對待，如果施政不合禮節，也不能說是完善啊。」

注釋　①涖之　面對百姓的意思。

　　　　　　　　　　　※ 第三十三章 ※

子曰：「君子不可小知，而可大受也；小人不可大受，而可小知也。」

語譯　孔子說：「不可以從小處去認識君子，卻可以授予他重大的任務；不可以把重大任務授予小人，卻可以從小處去認識他。」

解說　朱注：「蓋君子於細事未必可觀，而材德足以任重；小人雖器量淺狹，而未必無一長可取。」

　　　　　　　　　　　※ 第三十四章 ※

子曰：「民之於仁也，甚於水火。水火，吾見蹈而死者矣，未見蹈仁而死者也。」

語譯　孔子說：「百姓對仁的依賴，更甚於對水火的依賴。我看過跳到水火而死去的，卻沒有看過因爲行仁而死的。」

注釋　①蹈　踐踏。

　　　　　　　　　　　※ 第三十五章 ※

子曰：「當仁不讓於師。」

語譯　孔子說：「遇到行仁的事，即使是對老師，也不必謙讓。」

解說　朱注：「當仁，以仁爲己任也。雖師亦無所遜，言當勇往而必爲也。蓋仁者，人所自有而自爲之，非有爭也，何遜之有？」

him.

32.3. "When his knowledge is sufficient to attain, and he has virtue enough to hold fast; when he governs also with dignity, yet if he try to move the people contrary to the rules of propriety: -- full excellence is not reached."

注釋　contrary to: 違反。

Chapter 33

The Master said, "The superior man cannot be known in little matters; but he may be entrusted with great concerns. The small man may not be entrusted with great concerns, but he may be known in little matters."

注釋　concern: n. 事務。

Chapter 34

The Master said, "Virtue is more to man than either water or fire. I have seen men die from treading on water and fire, but I have never seen a man die from treading the course of virtue."

注釋　tread: v. 踩、前進。

Chapter 35

The Master said, "Let every man consider virtue as what devolves on himself. He may not yield the performance of it even to his teacher."

注釋　devolve on: 交給、歸於；yield: v. 放棄、讓渡。

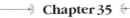

———————————— ❋ 第三十六章 ❋ ————————————

子曰：「君子貞而不諒。」

語譯　孔子說：「君子固守正道，不拘泥於小信小義。」

注釋　①**貞而不諒**　《集解》：「孔曰：貞，正。諒，信也。君子之人，正其道也。言不必小信。」

———————————— ❋ 第三十七章 ❋ ————————————

子曰：「事君，敬其事而後其食。」

語譯　孔子說：「為國君做事，要認真工作，把俸祿的事放在後頭。」

———————————— ❋ 第三十八章 ❋ ————————————

子曰：「有教無類。」

語譯　孔子說：「受教育不分階級。」

注釋　①**類**　指階級。

———————————— ❋ 第三十九章 ❋ ————————————

子曰：「道不同，不相為謀。」

語譯　孔子說：「各人道路不同，無法互相比較。」

注釋　①**謀**　商議。

解說　《正義》：「吳氏嘉賓說：『孟子曰：「伯夷、伊尹、柳下惠，三子者不同道。」道者，志之所趨舍，如出處語默之類。雖同於為善，而有不同，其是非得失，皆自知之，不能相為謀也。』……若夫『與時偕式』、『無可無不可』，夫子之謂『集大成』，安有所謂『不相謀』哉？不相謀者，道之本能，相以謀者，聖人之用。後世儒者，舉一廢百，始有異同之見，而自以為是，互相攻擊，既非聖人覆燾持載之量，亦大昧於『不相為謀』之旨。」每個人選擇進德修業的道路不同，不能比較是非得失，實則殊途

—❋ **Chapter 36** ❋—

The Master said, "The superior man is correctly firm, and not firm merely."

注釋　firm: adj. 堅定。

—❋ **Chapter 37** ❋—

The Master said, "A minister, in serving his prince, reverently discharges his duties, and makes his emolument a secondary consideration."

注釋　discharge: v. 履行；consideration: n. 考量。

—❋ **Chapter 38** ❋—

The Master said, "In teaching there should be no distinction of classes."

注釋　class: n. 階級、種類。

—❋ **Chapter 39** ❋—

The Master said, "Those whose courses are different cannot lay plans for one another."

同歸。後人用這句話做爲黨同伐異的口實，是誤解孔子的本意。

※ 第四十章 ※

子曰：「辭達而已矣。」

語譯　孔子說：「言詞只要達義就夠了。」

解說　《集解》：「凡事莫過於實，辭達則足矣，不煩文豔之辭。」

※ 第四十一章 ※

師冕見，及階，子曰：「階也。」及席，子曰：「席也。」皆坐，子告之曰：「某在斯，某在斯。」師冕出。子張問曰：「與師言之道與？」子曰：「然。固相師之道也。」

語譯　樂師冕來見孔子，走到階梯前面，孔子說：「這是階梯。」走近坐席，孔子說：「這是坐席。」大家都坐定後，孔子告訴師冕說：「某人在這裡，某人在那裡。」師冕離開後，子張問孔子說：「對樂師要這樣說話嗎？」孔子說：「是的，這就是引導樂師的方式。」

注釋　①**師冕**　《集解》：「孔曰：樂人，盲者，名冕。」古代樂師多盲者。②**相**　引導。

解說　從這些小地方可以看到孔子待人之誠懇。

---- ※ **Chapter 40** ※ ----

The Master said, "In language it is simply required that it convey the meaning."

注釋　convey: v. 傳達。

---- ※ **Chapter 41** ※ ----

41.1. The music master, Mien, having called upon him, when they came to the steps, the Master said, "Here are the steps." When they came to the mat for the guest to sit upon, he said, "Here is the mat." When all were seated, the Master informed him, saying, "So and so is here; so and so is here."

41.2. The music master, Mien, having gone out, Tsze-chang asked, saying. "Is it the rule to tell those things to the music master?"

41.3. The Master said, "Yes. This is certainly the rule for those who lead the blind."

注釋　call upon: 拜訪

季氏第十六

---◆ 第一章 ◆---

季氏將伐顓臾。冉有、季路見於孔子曰：「季氏將有事於顓臾。」
孔子曰：「求！無乃爾是過與？夫顓臾，昔者先王以為東蒙主，且
在邦域之中矣，是社稷之臣也。何以伐為？」冉有曰：「夫子欲
之，吾二臣者皆不欲也。」孔子曰：「求！周任有言曰：『陳力就
列，不能者止。』危而不持，顛而不扶，則將焉用彼相矣？且爾
言過矣。虎兕出於柙，龜玉毀於櫝中，是誰之過與？」冉有曰：
「今夫顓臾，固而近於費。今不取，後世必為子孫憂。」孔子曰：
「求！君子疾夫舍曰欲之，而必為之辭。丘也聞有國有家者，不
患寡而患不均，不患貧而患不安。蓋均無貧，和無寡，安無傾。夫
如是，故遠人不服，則修文德以來之。既來之，則安之。今由與求
也，相夫子，遠人不服而不能來也；邦分崩離析而不能守也。而謀
動干戈於邦內。吾恐季孫之憂，不在顓臾，而在蕭牆之內也。」

語譯　季氏準備要攻打顓臾。冉有、季路去見孔子說：「季氏要對顓臾用兵
了。」孔子說：「求啊！這難道不是你的過錯嗎？講到顓臾，從前先王
封為東蒙山的主祭，而且在魯國境內，也是魯國的附庸，為什麼要討伐
他呢？」冉有說：「這是季孫的主意，我們兩個家臣都不同意啊。」孔子
說：「求啊！從前周任有句話說：『擔任職務，就要盡力去做；如果不
行，就該辭去職務。』就像導盲者一樣，走路不穩的時候不去扶持他，快
要跌倒的時候不去攙扶他，那還要這個導盲者做什麼？而且你這句話也不
對啊。老虎和野牛從柵欄跑出來，龜殼和美玉在匣子裡毀壞，這是誰的責
任呢？」冉有說：「那個顓臾城牆堅固，而且離季氏的采地費邑很近。現
在不拿下來，會給後代子孫貽禍。」孔子說：「求啊！君子最討厭的，就
是捨去自己的欲望不說，另外找藉口掩飾。我聽人家說過，諸侯或卿大
夫，不要擔心貧乏，而要擔心無法各得其分；不要擔心人民太少，而要擔
心境內不安定。因為各得其分，就無所謂貧窮；和睦團結，就不嫌人口
少，境內安定，就沒有傾覆的危險。能夠做到這樣，所以假使遠方的人不
歸服，便推行禮樂政教以招徠他們。他們來歸順了，就要安頓他們。現在
仲由和冉求你們兩個人輔佐季氏，遠方的人不悅服而不能招徠他們；國家
就要分離瓦解卻無法堅守。反而想要打起內戰來。我怕季孫的憂患不在於

※ **Chapter 1** ※

1.1. The head of the Chi family was going to attack Chwan-yu.

1.2. Zan Yu and Chi-lu had an interview with Confucius, and said, "Our chief, Chi, is going to commence operations against Chwan-yu."

1.3. Confucius said, "Ch'iu, is it not you who are in fault here?

1.4. "Now, in regard to Chwan-yu, long ago, a former king appointed its ruler to preside over the sacrifices to the eastern Mang; moreover, it is in the midst of the territory of our state; and its ruler is a minister in direct connection with the sovereign: What has your chief to do with attacking it?"

1.5. Zan Yu said, "Our master wishes the thing; neither of us two ministers wishes it."

1.6. Confucius said, "Ch'iu, there are the words of Chau Zan, -- 'When he can put forth his ability, he takes his place in the ranks of office; when he finds himself unable to do so, he retires from it. 'How can he be used as a guide to a blind man, who does not support him when tottering, nor raise him up when fallen?

1.7. "And further, you speak wrongly. When a tiger or rhinoceros escapes from his cage; when a tortoise or piece of jade is injured in its repository: -- whose is the fault?"

1.8. Zan Yu said, "But at present, Chwan-yu is strong and near to Pi; if our chief do not now take it, it will hereafter be a sorrow to his descendants."

1.9. Confucius said. "Ch'iu, the superior man hates those declining to say -- 'I want such and such a thing,' and framing explanations for their conduct.

1.10. "I have heard that rulers of states and chiefs of families are not troubled lest their people should be few, but are troubled lest they should not keep their several places; that they are not troubled with fears of poverty, but are troubled with fears of a want of contented repose among the people in their several places. For when the people keep their several places, there will be no poverty; when harmony prevails, there will be

顓臾,而在於魯國國君吧。」

注釋　①顓臾　《集解》:「孔曰:顓臾,伏羲之後,風姓之國,本魯之附庸。當時臣屬魯,季氏貪其土地,欲滅而取之。」②有事　有征伐之事。③東蒙主　主祭東蒙山。蒙山在魯東,故曰東蒙。④邦域之中　在魯國境內。⑤社稷之臣　國家的臣屬。⑥夫子欲之　「夫子」指季孫。歸咎於季孫。⑦周任　古之良史。⑧陳力就列　列,位也。居其位當盡其才。⑨顛　跌倒。⑩相　扶持視障者的人叫作相。⑪兕　野牛。或說是犀牛。⑫柙　柵欄。⑬櫝　匣子。⑭固而近於費　固,城郭堅固。費音必,季氏之私邑。⑮**不患寡而患不均,不患貧而患不安**　應作「不患貧而患不均,不患寡而患不安」。《春秋繁露・度制篇》:「孔子曰:不患貧而患不均。」亦見俞樾《群經平議》。「均」不是指「平均」,而是各得其分的意思。⑯**分崩離析**　《集解》:「孔曰:民有異心曰分,欲去曰崩,不可會聚曰離析。」⑰**干戈**　戰爭。⑱**蕭牆之內**　《集解》:「蕭之言肅也。牆謂屏也。君臣相見之禮,至屏而加肅敬焉。是以謂之蕭牆。後季氏家臣陽虎,果囚季桓子。」這是說季氏之家。《正義》引方觀旭《論語偶記》的說法,認為「蕭牆」是指魯哀公。

解說　朱注:「洪氏曰:二子仕於季氏,凡季氏所欲為,必以告於夫子。則因夫子之言而救止者,宜亦多矣。伐顓臾之事,不見於經傳,其以夫子之言而止也與?」冉有和子路硬著頭皮來挨孔子一頓罵,後來季孫大概也聽說了,因而放棄攻打顓臾。「不患寡而患不均,不患貧而患不安」,這句話非常重要。

※ 第二章 ※

孔子曰:「天下有道,則禮樂征伐自天子出;天下無道,則禮樂征伐自諸侯出。自諸侯出,蓋十世希不失矣;自大夫出,五世希不失矣;陪臣執國命,三世希不失矣。天下有道,則政不在大夫。天下有道,則庶人不議。」

no scarcity of people; and when there is such a contented repose, there will be no rebellious upsettings.

1.11. "So it is. -- Therefore, if remoter people are not submissive, all the influences of civil culture and virtue are to be cultivated to attract them to be so; and when they have been so attracted, they must be made contented and tranquil.

1.12. "Now, here are you, Yu and Ch'iu, assisting your chief. Remoter people are not submissive, and, with your help, he cannot attract them to him. In his own territory there are divisions and downfalls, leavings and separations, and, with your help, he cannot preserve it.

1.13. "And yet he is planning these hostile movements within the state. -- I am afraid that the sorrow of the Chi-sun family will not be on account of Chwan-yu, but will be found within the screen of their own court."

注釋　commence: v. 開始；operation: n. 軍事作戰；preside over : 主持；territory: n. 領域；totter: v. 踉蹌；rhinoceros: n. 犀牛；tortoise: n. 龜；repository: n. 貯藏室；frame: v. 想出、編造；troubled:adj. 苦惱；lest: conj.唯恐；several: adj. 各自的；harmony: n. 和諧；scarcity: n. 匱乏；rebellious: adj. 叛亂的；upsetting: n.顛覆；remote: adj. 遙遠的；submissive: adj. 服從的；cultivate: v. 修習、培養；tranquil: adj. 平靜的；downfall: n. 沒落；hostile: adj. 敵對的；screen: n. 屏風。

解說　關於「均」這個字，字面意思是 equality，理雅各譯爲 keep their several places，並解釋爲 every one getting his own proper name and place（謂各得其分）。「龜」譯爲 tortoise，理雅各也不認爲活烏龜可以放在櫃子裡，所以懷疑是「圭」之誤。其實「龜」是指占卜用的龜殼，譯爲 tortoise shell 就可以。

Chapter 2

2.1. Confucius said, "When good government prevails in the empire, ceremonies, music, and punitive military expeditions proceed from the son of Heaven. When bad government prevails in the empire, ceremonies, music, and punitive military expeditions proceed from

語譯　孔子說：「天下太平時，所有的禮樂征伐都由天子決定；天下混亂時，則禮樂征伐就由諸侯自己作主。諸侯自己作主的，大概傳十代以後，很少有不失去政權的；由大夫作主的，傳了五代，很少有不失去政權的；如果是大夫的家臣把持國內命令，三代以後很少有不滅亡的。天下太平時，政權不會落在大夫手裡。天下太平時，老百姓也不會議論紛紛。」

注釋　①禮樂征伐自天子出　朱注：「先王之制，諸侯不得變禮樂，專征伐。」②希　稀少。③陪臣　家臣。④不議　是指沒有非議，而不是箝制言論的意思。

解說　孔子的這段話是有歷史根據的。《集解》：「孔曰：周幽王為犬戎所殺，平王東遷，周始微弱。諸侯自作禮樂，專行征伐，始於隱公。至昭公十世失政，死於乾侯矣。季文子初得政，至桓子五世，為家臣陽虎所囚。……馬曰：家臣陽虎為季氏家臣，至虎三世而出奔齊。」

※ 第三章 ※

孔子曰：「祿之去公室，五世矣；政逮於大夫，四世矣；故夫三桓之子孫，微矣。」

語譯　孔子說：「自從魯國國君失去國家政權，已經五代了；政權落在大夫手裡，也已經四代了；所以三家大夫的子孫，現在也式微了。」

注釋　①祿　百官之俸。爵祿賞罰之權。引申為政權的意思。②逮　及也。③微　式微。

解說　朱注：「魯自文公薨，公子遂殺子赤，立宣公，而君失其政。歷成、襄、昭、定，凡五公。自季武子始專國政，歷悼、平、桓子，凡四世，而為家臣陽虎所執。」

※ 第四章 ※

孔子曰：「益者三友，損者三友。友直，友諒，友多聞，益矣。友便辟，友善柔，友便佞，損矣。」

語譯　孔子說：「有益的朋友有三種，有害的朋友也有三種。與正直的人為友，

the princes. When these things proceed from the princes, as a rule, the cases will be few in which they do not lose their power in ten generations. When they proceed from the great officers of the princes, as a rule, the case will be few in which they do not lose their power in five generations. When the subsidiary ministers of the great officers hold in their grasp the orders of the state, as a rule the cases will be few in which they do not lose their power in three generations.

2.2. "When right principles prevail in the kingdom, government will not be in the hands of the great officers.

2.3. "When right principles prevail in the kingdom, there will be no discussions among the common people."

注釋 punitive: adj. 懲罰性的；expedition: n. 遠征；subsidiary: adj. 從屬的、輔助的；in the grasp of: 控制。

❈ Chapter 3 ❈

Confucius said, "The revenue of the state has left the ducal house now for five generations. The government has been in the hands of the great officers for four generations. On this account, the descendants of the three Hwan are much reduced."

注釋 revenue: n. 國家歲入；ducal: adj. 公爵的；reduced: 沒落的。

解說 「祿」譯爲 revenue（稅收），不符合原文的意思。或譯爲 the power of conferring nobility and emolument（授予爵祿之權）。

❈ Chapter 4 ❈

Confucius said, "There are three friendships which are advantageous, and three which are injurious. Friendship with the upright; friendship with the sincere; and friendship with the man of much observation: -- these are advantageous. Friendship with the man of specious airs; friendship with

與守信的人爲友，與見聞廣博的人爲友，會有好處。結交華而不實的人，結交諂媚逢迎的人，結交花言巧語的人，會有害處。」

注釋　①諒　信實。②便辟　朱注：「謂習於威儀而不直。」③善柔　朱注：「謂工於媚悅而不諒。」④便佞　朱注：「謂習於口語，而無聞見之實。」

解說　這也是耳熟能詳的句子，告訴我們交朋友要謹慎。

———— ❋ 第五章 ❋ ————

孔子曰：「益者三樂，損者三樂：樂節禮樂，樂道人之善，樂多賢友，益矣；樂驕樂，樂佚遊，樂宴樂，損矣。」

語譯　孔子說：「有益的愛好有三種，有害的愛好也有三種。喜好禮樂的節制，喜好稱道別人的好處，喜好多結交賢友，會有好處。喜歡驕縱放肆，喜歡怠墮遊蕩，喜歡飲宴耽溺，則會有害處。」

注釋　①益者三樂　「樂」音「要」。愛好。②節禮樂　得禮樂之節。③驕樂　《集解》：「孔曰：恃尊貴以自恣。」④佚遊　《集解》：「王曰：出入不節。」⑤宴樂　《集解》：「沈荒淫瀆。」耽於飲宴的意思。

———— ❋ 第六章 ❋ ————

孔子曰：「侍於君子有三愆：言未及之而言謂之躁，言及之而不言謂之隱，未見顏色而言謂之瞽。」

語譯　孔子說：「隨侍君子時容易有三種過失：沒輪到他說話卻搶著說，是輕躁；該他說話了卻不說，是隱匿；沒有看君子臉色就說話，是瞎了眼。」

注釋　①愆　過失。②躁　不安靜。③隱　隱瞞。④瞽　朱注：「無目，不能察言觀色。」

解說　這是說話的藝術，前面引述的《荀子·勸學篇》也是相同的意思。

———— ❋ 第七章 ❋ ————

孔子曰：「君子有三戒：少之時，血氣未定，戒之在色；及其壯也，血氣方剛，戒之在鬥；及其老也，血氣既衰，戒之在得。」

the insinuatingly soft; and friendship with the glib-tongued: -- these are injurious."

注釋　advantageous: adj. 有益的；injurious: adj. 有害的；specious: adj. 虛有其表的；air: n. 外表、態度；insinuatingly: adv. 諂媚地；soft: adj. 甜言蜜語的；glib-tongued: adj. 口齒伶俐的。

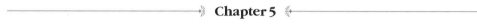
Chapter 5

Confucius said, "There are three things men find enjoyment in which are advantageous, and three things they find enjoyment in which are injurious. To find enjoyment in the discriminating study of ceremonies and music; to find enjoyment in speaking of the goodness of others; to find enjoyment in having many worthy friends: -- these are advantageous. To find enjoyment in extravagant pleasures; to find enjoyment in idleness and sauntering; to find enjoyment in the pleasures of feasting: -- these are injurious."

注釋　discriminating: adj. 有辨識力的；extravagant: adj. 奢侈的、過度的；idleness: n. 無所事事；saunter: v. 閒逛。

Chapter 6

Confucius said, "There are three errors to which they who stand in the presence of a man of virtue and station are liable. They may speak when it does not come to them to speak; -- this is called rashness. They may not speak when it comes to them to speak; -- this is called concealment. They may speak without looking at the countenance of their superior; -- this is called blindness."

注釋　liable to: 傾向於；rashness: n. 輕率；concealment: n. 隱瞞。

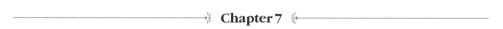
Chapter 7

Confucius said, "There are three things which the superior man guards against. In youth, when the physical powers are not yet settled, he guards

語譯　孔子說：「君子有三件事要警惕的：少年的時候，血氣還沒有穩定，小心不要耽於色慾；到壯年的時候，血氣正剛強，小心不要逞強好鬥；年老的時候，血氣衰弱，小心不要貪得無厭。」

注釋　①戒　警惕。②血氣　朱注：「血氣，形之所待以生者，血陰而氣陽也。」就是指生理特質。③得　貪得。

解說　隨著生理特質的變化，人的心理也會改變，這時候就要注意可能產生的偏差。希臘斯多噶學派主張理性自制的生活，強調心靈的寧靜以及道德的價值，可以和孔子的思想互相印證。

———※ 第八章 ※———

孔子曰：「君子有三畏：畏天命，畏大人，畏聖人之言。小人不知天命而不畏也，狎大人，侮聖人之言。」

語譯　孔子說：「君子有三件敬畏的事：敬畏天命，敬畏在上位者，敬畏聖人的話。小人不知道天命，也就無所謂敬畏，和在上位者過於狎近，戲侮聖人的話。」

注釋　①畏　敬畏。②大人　鄭注：「謂天子諸侯爲政教者。」《集解》：「大人即聖人，與天地合其德。」③狎　狎近而輕忽。④侮　輕侮。

解說　有敬畏的心，我們才找得到自己在世界裡的定位和價值。對眞理和超越者心存敬意，也就是認識自我的有限性和追尋的目標。這點非常重要。

———※ 第九章 ※———

孔子曰：「生而知之者，上也；學而知之者，次也；困而學之，又其次也；困而不學，民斯爲下矣。」

語譯　孔子說：「生下來就知道的，那是最高等的；經過學習而知道的，則是次一等；遇到困難才去學習的，更次一等；遇到困難以後還不肯學習，這種人是最下等的了。」

注釋　①困　《集解》：「困謂有所不通。」《正義》：「不通者，言心有所隔塞也。」

against lust. When he is strong and the physical powers are full of vigor, he guards against quarrelsomeness. When he is old, and the animal powers are decayed, he guards against covetousness."

注釋　guard against: 警戒、留心；settled: adj.安穩的；lust: n. 肉慾；vigor: n. 活力；quarrelsomeness: n. 好鬥；covetousness: n. 貪得無饜。

------ ※ **Chapter 8** ※ ------

8.1.　Confucius said, "There are three things of which the superior man stands in awe. He stands in awe of the ordinances of Heaven. He stands in awe of great men. He stands in awe of the words of sages.

8.2.　"The mean man does not know the ordinances of Heaven, and consequently does not stand in awe of them. He is disrespectful to great men. He makes sport of the words of sages."

注釋　in awe of: 敬畏；ordinance: n. 命令；disrespectful: adj. 無禮的；make sport of: 戲弄。

------ ※ **Chapter 9** ※ ------

Confucius said, "Those who are born with the possession of knowledge are the highest class of men. Those who learn, and so readily get possession of knowledge, are the next. Those who are dull and stupid, and yet compass the learning, are another class next to these. As to those who are dull and stupid and yet do not learn; -- they are the lowest of the people."

注釋　readily: adj. 容易的、迅速的；dull: adj. 遲鈍的；compass: v. 計畫、充分了解。

解說　比較以下的翻譯：Confucius said: "Those who are born knowing it are the best.

解說　《中庸》也說過：「或生而知之，或學而知之，或困而學之，及其知之，一也。」

------------------------------ ❋ 第十章 ❋ ------------------------------

孔子曰：「君子有九思：視思明，聽思聰，色思溫，貌思恭，言思忠，事思敬，疑思問，忿思難，見得思義。」

語譯　孔子說：「君子有九件用心思考的事：看的時候要思考是否看清楚了；聽的時候要思考是否聽明白了；思考自己的臉色是否溫和；思考自己的容貌態度是否恭敬；思考說話是否誠懇；思考做事是否認真；遇到疑惑時思考如何請教別人，忿怒的時候思考會有什麼後患；見到有利益可得時思考是否合於道義。」

注釋　①**思**　思慮。②**難**　患難。

解說　這是在日常生活裡自我反省的功夫。在待人接物的時候，多停下來想一想，行爲會更加合宜。

------------------------------ ❋ 第十一章 ❋ ------------------------------

孔子曰：「『見善如不及，見不善如探湯。』吾見其人矣，吾聞其語矣。『隱居以求其志，行義以達其道。』吾聞其語矣，未見其人也。」

語譯　孔子說：「『見到善，像是深怕趕不上似的，見到不善，像是把手探入熱湯似的趕緊避開。』我看過這樣的人，也聽過這樣的話。『避世隱居以保全自己的意志，出仕行義以成就其主張。』我聽過這樣的話，卻沒有看過這樣的人。」

注釋　①**探湯**　把手伸到熱湯裡。

Those who study to know it are next; those who are limited and yet study are next; those who are limited and do not even study are considered to be the lowest level of people."

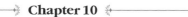

Chapter 10

Confucius said, "The superior man has nine things which are subjects with him of thoughtful consideration. In regard to the use of his eyes, he is anxious to see clearly. In regard to the use of his ears, he is anxious to hear distinctly. In regard to his countenance, he is anxious that it should be benign. In regard to his demeanor, he is anxious that it should be respectful. In regard to his speech, he is anxious that it should be sincere. In regard to his doing of business, he is anxious that it should be reverently careful. In regard to what he doubts about, he is anxious to question others. When he is angry, he thinks of the difficulties his anger may involve him in. When he sees gain to be got, he thinks of righteousness."

注釋　thoughtful: adj. 深思熟慮的、體諒的；benign: adj. 親切的；demeanor: n. 態度、表情；involve: v. 使其涉入 [into]；gain: n. 利益。

解說　「思」在這裡有三種譯法：thoughtful consideration、anxious、think of，以區別不同情境時的思考。

Chapter 11

11.1. Confucius said, "Contemplating good, and pursuing it, as if they could not reach it; contemplating evil and shrinking from it, as they would from thrusting the hand into boiling water: -- I have seen such men, as I have heard such words.

11.2. "Living in retirement to study their aims, and practicing righteousness to carry out their principles: -- I have heard these words, but I have not seen such men."

注釋　contemplate: v. 注視；shrink from: 退避；thrust: v. 插入。

❀ 第十二章 ❀

（「誠不以富，亦祇以異。」）齊景公有馬千駟，死之日，民無德而稱焉。伯夷叔齊餓於首陽之下，民到于今稱之。其斯之謂與？

語譯　孔子說：「『人不是因爲有錢才值得稱道，而是因爲他的德行不同於他人。』齊景公有四千匹馬，他死去的時候，百姓不覺得他有什麼值得稱述的。伯夷、叔齊餓死在首陽山下，老百姓到現在還稱道他們。這句話大概是這個意思吧？」

注釋　①**誠不以富，亦祇以異**　朱注：「胡氏曰：程子以爲第十二篇錯簡『誠不以富，亦祇以異』，當在此章之首。」②**千駟**　四匹馬叫作駟。千駟就是四千匹馬。

❀ 第十三章 ❀

陳亢問於伯魚曰：「子亦有異聞乎？」對曰：「未也。嘗獨立，鯉趨而過庭。曰：『學詩乎？』，對曰：『未也。』『不學詩，無以言。』鯉退而學詩。他日，又獨立，鯉趨而過庭。曰：『學禮乎？』對曰：『未也。』『不學禮，無以立。』鯉退而學禮。聞斯二者。」陳亢退而喜曰：「問一得三：聞詩，聞禮，又聞君子之遠其子也。」

語譯　陳亢問伯魚說：「你在你父親那裡有聽到什麼特別的教訓嗎？」伯魚回答說：「沒有啊！有一次，我父親獨自站在大廳，我快步走過庭院。我父親說：『學過詩沒有？』我回答說：『沒有。』他說：『不學詩就不知道如何說話。』我回去便學詩。又有一次，我父親獨自站在大廳，我快步走過庭院。我父親說：『學過禮沒有？』我回答說：『沒有。』他說：『不學禮就無法立身。』我回去便學禮。我只聽過這兩件事。」陳亢回去很高興地說：「我才問一件事，卻得到了三個道理：知道學詩的道理，知道學禮的道理，也知道君子不私厚自己的兒子。」

注釋　①**陳亢**　陳國人，字子禽。②**異聞**　異於諸子之聞。③**趨而過庭**　《正義》：「禮，臣行過君前，子行過父前，皆當徐趨，所以爲敬也。」④**無以立**　朱注：「品節詳明，而德性堅定，故能立。」指人格成熟的意思。⑤**遠**　無私厚。

❖ **Chapter 12** ❖

12.1. The Duke Ching of Ch'i had a thousand teams, each of four horses, but on the day of his death, the people did not praise him for a single virtue. Po-i and Shu-ch'i died of hunger at the foot of the Shau-yang mountains, and the people, down to the present time, praise them.

12.2. "Is not that saying illustrated by this?"

注釋　saying: n. 諺語。

❖ **Chapter 13** ❖

13.1. Ch'an K'ang asked Po-yu, saying, "Have you heard any lessons from your father different from what we have all heard?"

13.2. Po-yu replied, "No. He was standing alone once, when I passed below the hall with hasty steps, and said to me, 'Have you learned the Odes?' On my replying 'Not yet,' he added, 'If you do not learn the Odes, you will not be fit to converse with.' I retired and studied the Odes.

13.3. "Another day, he was in the same way standing alone, when I passed by below the hall with hasty steps, and said to me, 'Have you learned the rules of Propriety?' On my replying 'Not yet,' he added, 'If you do not learn the rules of Propriety, your character cannot be established.' I then retired, and learned the rules of Propriety.

13.4. "I have heard only these two things from him."

13.5. Ch'ang K'ang retired, and, quite delighted, said, "I asked one thing, and I have got three things. I have heard about the Odes. I have heard about the rules of Propriety. I have also heard that the superior man maintains a distant reserve towards his son."

注釋　hasty: adj. 匆匆；reserve: n. 節制、冷淡。

解說　《正義》：「司馬光《家範》引此文說云：『遠者，非疏遠之謂也，謂其
　　　進見有時，接遇有禮，不朝夕嘻嘻相褻狎也。』」現在許多所謂開明的父
　　　母親教育孩子的方式，大概就是和孩子「朝夕嘻嘻相褻狎也」吧？

❖ 第十四章 ❖

邦君之妻，君稱之曰夫人，夫人自稱曰小童；邦人稱之曰君夫人，
稱諸異邦曰寡小君；異邦人稱之亦曰君夫人。

語譯　國君的妻子，國君稱她爲「夫人」，她自稱爲「小童」；國人稱她爲「君
　　　夫人」，對外國人稱她爲「寡小君」，外國人稱她爲「君夫人」。

解說　小童、寡小君，都是謙稱。《禮記·曲禮》：「天子之妃曰后，諸侯曰夫人，
　　　大夫曰孺人，士曰婦人，庶人曰妻。公侯有夫人、有世婦、有妻、有妾。
　　　夫人自稱於天子曰老婦；自稱於諸侯曰寡小君；自稱於其君曰小童。」

----- ✳ **Chapter 14** ✳ -----

The wife of the prince of a state is called by him Fu Zan. She calls herself Hsiao T'ung. The people of the state call her Chun Fu Zan, and, to the people of other states, they call her K'wa Hsiao Chun. The people of other states also call her Chun Fu Zan.

陽貨第十七

---※ 第一章 ※---

陽貨欲見孔子，孔子不見，歸孔子豚。孔子時其亡也，而往拜之，遇諸塗。謂孔子曰：「來！予與爾言。」曰：「懷其寶而迷其邦，可謂仁乎？」曰：「不可。」「好從事而亟失時，可謂知乎？」曰：「不可。」「日月逝矣，歲不我與。」孔子曰：「諾，吾將仕矣！」

語譯 陽貨想要見孔子，孔子不見他。陽貨送孔子一隻（蒸熟了的）小豬。孔子趁陽貨不在家的時候，到他家去拜謝，不料在途中遇到陽貨。陽貨對孔子說：「過來，我有話跟你說。」陽貨又說：「身懷著本事而任憑國家混亂，這樣算是仁者嗎？不算吧。喜歡做官卻屢次錯過機會，這樣算是智者嗎？不算吧。日子過得很快，歲月是不會等我們的啊。」孔子說：「好，我要出來做官了。」

注釋 ①**陽貨** 陽虎，季氏家臣。崔述則認爲陽虎和陽貨是兩個人。②**歸** 即饋，贈送。③**豚** 小豬。④**時其亡** 趁他不在家的時候。⑤**塗** 路上。⑥**懷其寶而迷其邦** 朱注：「謂懷藏道德，不救國之迷亂。」⑦**亟** 屢次。⑧**諾** 好吧。

解說 關於這段插曲，《孟子·滕文公下》有較詳細的敘述：「陽貨欲見孔子而惡無禮，大夫有賜於士，不得受於其家，則往拜其門。陽貨矙孔子之亡也，而饋孔子蒸豚；孔子亦矙其亡也，而往拜之。當是時，陽貨先，豈得不見？」孔子說他要出來做官，不過沒有說要爲陽貨做事。

---※ 第二章 ※---

子曰：「性相近也，習相遠也。」

語譯 孔子說：「人的天性是相近的，因爲習染不同，便漸漸相遠了。」

注釋 ①**性** 天性。

解說 關於人性善惡的問題，有各種說法。孔子只是說，人的天性是相近的，而因爲後天環境和學習的不同而有所差異。

⁎ Chapter 1 ⁎

1.1. Yang Ho wished to see Confucius, but Confucius would not go to see him. On this, he sent a present of a pig to Confucius, who, having chosen a time when Ho was not at home, went to pay his respects for the gift. He met him, however, on the way.

1.2. Ho said to Confucius, "Come, let me speak with you." He then asked, "Can he be called benevolent who keeps his jewel in his bosom, and leaves his country to confusion?" Confucius replied, "No." "Can he be called wise, who is anxious to be engaged in public employment, and yet is constantly losing the opportunity of being so?" Confucius again said, "No." "The days and months are passing away; the years do not wait for us." Confucius said, "Right; I will go into office."

注釋　bosom: n. 胸懷。

⁎ Chapter 2 ⁎

The Master said, "By nature, men are nearly alike; by practice, they get to be wide apart."

注釋　apart: adj. 相異的。

———————————— ✦ 第三章 ✦ ————————————

子曰：「唯上知與下愚不移。」

語譯　孔子說：「只有上等的智者和下等的愚者是無法改變的。」

解說　人的天性雖然相近，但是資質則有所差別。

———————————— ✦ 第四章 ✦ ————————————

子之武城，聞弦歌之聲。夫子莞爾而笑，曰：「割雞焉用牛刀？」
子游對曰：「昔者偃也聞諸夫子曰：『君子學道則愛人，小人學道
則易使也。』」子曰：「二三子！偃之言是也。前言戲之耳。」

語譯　孔子到武城去，聽到琴瑟詠詩的聲音。孔子微笑說：「殺雞哪裡要用到
宰牛的刀呢？」子游回答說：「從前我聽老師說過：『君子學習了禮樂之
道，便懂得愛人；小人學習禮樂之道，就容易聽從教令。』」孔子說：「各
位！偃說得對。我剛才的話是開玩笑的。」

注釋　①武城　魯邑。《集解》：「孔曰：子游為武城宰。」②莞爾　微笑的樣
子。③割雞焉用牛刀　《集解》：「孔曰：言治小何須用大道。」

解說　孔子看到子游把武城這個小地方治理得很好，心裡很高興，也感嘆子游大
材小用。孔子說個笑話，子游立即予以糾正，孔子也虛心接受。老師說的
話不一定都對，要有接受批評的雅量。

———————————— ✦ 第五章 ✦ ————————————

公山弗擾以費畔，召，子欲往。子路不說，曰：「末之也已，何必
公山氏之之也。」子曰：「夫召我者而豈徒哉？如有用我者，吾其
為東周乎？」

語譯　公山弗擾佔據費邑圖謀叛變，叫孔子去，孔子準備要去。子路很不高興地
說：「沒有地方去就算了，何必要去公山氏那裡呢？」孔子說：「那來叫
我去的，難道是沒有任何理由的嗎？如果有人要用我，我或許可以使周朝
文化在東方復興吧？」

注釋　①公山弗擾　季氏家臣。史記作公山不狃。②畔　叛變。③末之也已　之，

❊ Chapter 3 ❊

The Master said, "There are only the wise of the highest class, and the stupid of the lowest class, who cannot be changed."

❊ Chapter 4 ❊

4.1. The Master, having come to Wu-ch'ang, heard there the sound of stringed instruments and singing.

4.2. Well pleased and smiling, he said, "Why use an ox knife to kill a fowl?"

4.3. Tsze-yu replied, "Formerly, Master, I heard you say, -- 'When the man of high station is well instructed, he loves men; when the man of low station is well instructed, he is easily ruled.'"

4.4. The Master said, "My disciples, Yen's words are right. What I said was only in sport."

注釋　fowl: n. 家禽、雞；in sport: 開玩笑的。

❊ Chapter 5 ❊

5.1. Kung-shan Fu-zao, when he was holding Pi, and in an attitude of rebellion, invited the Master to visit him, who was rather inclined to go.

5.2. Tsze-lu was displeased. and said, "Indeed, you cannot go! Why must you think of going to see Kung-shan?"

5.3. The Master said, "Can it be without some reason that he has invited ME? If any one employ me, may I not make an eastern Chau?"

注釋　rebellion: n. 叛亂。

往。沒有地方去就算了。④**之之** 第一個「之」是虛詞，第二個「之」字
是「前往」的意思。⑤**徒** 沒有理由的。⑥**吾其為東周乎** 《集解》：「興
周道於東方，故曰東周。」

解說　《左傳‧定公十二年》：「仲由爲季氏宰，將墮費，而不狃及叔孫輒率費
　　　人襲魯。夫子命申句須、樂頎伐之而後北，國人追之，敗諸姑蔑。不狃及
　　　輒遂奔齊。」《史記‧孔子世家》：「定公九年，陽虎奔於齊，是時孔子年
　　　五十。公山不狃以費畔季氏，使人召孔子。」孔子派兵討伐弗擾，怎麼還
　　　會爲他做事？趙翼和崔述都認爲本章不可信。《論語正義》則認爲弗擾召
　　　孔子在定公九年，和後來孔子討伐弗擾並不矛盾。

❖ 第六章 ❖

子張問仁於孔子。孔子曰：「能行五者於天下，為仁矣。」請問
之。曰：「恭、寬、信、敏、惠。恭則不侮，寬則得眾，信則人任
焉，敏則有功，惠則足以使人。」

語譯　子張向孔子問爲仁之道。孔子說：「能夠到處實踐以下五件事，便可以說
　　　是仁了。」子張請問那五件事。孔子說：「恭敬、寬厚、誠實、勤奮、慈
　　　惠。恭敬就不會受到侮慢；寬厚就可以得到大眾的擁護；誠實可以得到別
　　　人的信任；勤奮就容易成功；慈惠才能夠叫人爲你效勞。」

注釋　①**侮** 侮慢。

解說　朱注：「李氏曰：此章與六言、六蔽、五美、四惡之類，皆與前後文體大
　　　不相似。」

❖ 第七章 ❖

佛肸召，子欲往。子路曰：「昔者由也聞諸夫子曰：『親於其身為
不善者，君子不入也。』佛肸以中牟畔，子之往也，如之何！」子
曰：「然。有是言也。不曰堅乎，磨而不磷；不曰白乎，涅而不
緇。吾豈匏瓜也哉？焉能繫而不食？」

語譯　佛肸派人來召孔子，孔子想去。子路說：「從前我聽老師說過：『那個人

解說　「末由之矣」譯爲 Indeed, you cannot go，語意不明。或譯爲 Verily there is nowhere at all to go。

❊ **Chapter 6** ❊

Tsze-chang asked Confucius about perfect virtue. Confucius said, "To be able to practice five things everywhere under heaven constitutes perfect virtue." He begged to ask what they were, and was told, "Gravity, generosity of soul, sincerity, earnestness, and kindness. If you are grave, you will not be treated with disrespect. If you are generous, you will win all. If you are sincere, people will repose trust in you. If you are earnest, you will accomplish much. If you are kind, this will enable you to employ the services of others."

注釋　generosity: n. 寬大；repose: v. 寄託 [in]。

❊ **Chapter 7** ❊

7.1.　Pi Hsi inviting him to visit him, the Master was inclined to go.

7.2.　Tsze-lu said, "Master, formerly I have heard you say, 'When a man in his own person is guilty of doing evil, a superior man will not associate with him.' Pi Hsi is in rebellion, holding possession of Chung-mau; if you go to him, what shall be said?"

7.3.　The Master said, "Yes, I did use these words. But is it not said, that, if

自己做過壞事，君子就不去他的國家。佛肸佔據中牟圖謀叛亂，老師卻要去他那裡，這怎麼說得過去呢？」」孔子說：「不錯，我是說過這句話。但是我不是也說過，最堅硬的東西怎麼磨也不會薄嗎？我不是也說過，最潔白的東西怎麼染也染不黑嗎？我難道是匏瓜嗎？哪能只掛在那裡，而不給人採食呢？」

注釋　①**佛肸**　佛音必，肸音係。《集解》：「孔曰：晉大夫趙簡子之邑宰。」②**中牟**　邑名。③**磨而不磷**　磷音吝，薄也。磨而不變薄。④**涅而不緇**　涅，皂礬，染之則黑。這裡做動詞，以皂礬染物的意思。緇，黑色。⑤**匏瓜**　匏瓜味苦，人多不食。

※ 第八章 ※

子曰：「由也，女聞六言六蔽矣乎？」對曰：「未也。」「居！吾語女。好仁不好學，其蔽也愚；好知不好學，其蔽也蕩；好信不好學，其蔽也賊；好直不好學，其蔽也絞；好勇不好學，其蔽也亂；好剛不好學，其蔽也狂。」

語譯　孔子說：「仲由啊，你聽過六言六蔽嗎？」子路回答說：「沒有啊。」孔子說：「你坐下！我告訴你。喜好仁德而不好學，就會有容易受愚弄的弊病；喜好智慧而不好學，就會有放蕩不實在的弊病；喜好誠實而不好學，就會有容易受害的弊病；喜好直率而不好學，就會有說話尖刻的弊病；喜好勇敢而不好學，就會有容易作亂的弊病；喜好剛強而不好學，就會有膽大妄為的弊病。」

注釋　①**女**　同汝。②**六言**　六件事。六種美德。③**六蔽**　蔽，遮蔽。④**居**　坐下。⑤**蕩**　朱注：「謂窮高極廣而無所止。」⑥**賊**　賊害。⑦**絞**　急切而好譏刺他人。⑧**亂**　作亂。⑨**狂**　躁進。

※ 第九章 ※

子曰：「小子！何莫學夫詩？詩，可以興，可以觀，可以群，可以怨。邇之事父，遠之事君。多識於鳥獸草木之名。」

a thing be really hard, it may be ground without being made thin? Is it not said, that, if a thing be really white, it may be steeped in a dark fluid without being made black?

7.4. "Am I a bitter gourd? How can I be hung up out of the way of being eaten?"

注釋 guilty of: 犯了罪；associate with: 結交；grind: v. [ground] 研磨；steep: v. 浸泡；bitter: adj. 苦的；gourd: n. 瓜科植物。

※ **Chapter 8** ※

8.1. The Master said, "Yu, have you heard the six words to which are attached six becloudings?" Yu replied, "I have not."

8.2. "Sit down, and I will tell them to you.

8.3. "There is the love of being benevolent without the love of learning; -- the beclouding here leads to a foolish simplicity. There is the love of knowing without the love of learning; -- the beclouding here leads to dissipation of mind. There is the love of being sincere without the love of learning; -- the beclouding here leads to an injurious disregard of consequences. There is the love of straightforwardness without the love of learning; -- the beclouding here leads to rudeness. There is the love of boldness without the love of learning; -- the beclouding here leads to insubordination. There is the love of firmness without the love of learning; -- the beclouding here leads to extravagant conduct."

注釋 attach: v. 附著；becloud: v. 遮蔽；dissipation: n. 放蕩；disregard: n. 忽視；insubordination: n. 不順從；extravagant: adj. 過度的。

※ **Chapter 9** ※

9.1. The Master said, "My children, why do you not study the Book of Poetry?

9.2. "The Odes serve to stimulate the mind.

語譯　孔子說：「學生們！為什麼不研究詩呢？研究詩，可以學習譬喻於物，可以觀察時政得失，可以知道與人相處的道理，可以抒發心裡的憂愁。從近處看，可以用來照顧父母親，從遠處看，可以用來為國君做事。而且可以多認識些鳥獸草木的名稱。」

注釋　①何莫　何不。②興　《集解》：「孔曰：興，引譬連類。」③觀　《集解》：「鄭曰：觀風俗之盛衰。」④群　《集解》：「孔曰：群居相切磋。」⑤怨　《集解》：「怨刺上政。」⑥邇　近也。

解說　朱注：「詩，可以興，感發志意。可以觀，考見得失。可以群，和而不流。可以怨。怨而不怒。」

※ 第十章 ※

子謂伯魚曰：「女為周南、召南矣乎？人而不為周南、召南，其猶正牆面而立也與？」

語譯　孔子對伯魚說：「你研究過〈周南〉和〈召南〉了嗎？人如果沒有研究過〈周南〉和〈召南〉，就像是面對著牆壁站立吧？」

注釋　①周南召南　朱注：「詩首篇名。所言皆修身齊家之事。」②正牆面而立　正，向也。意即既不可見亦不可行。

※ 第十一章 ※

子曰：「禮云禮云，玉帛云乎哉？樂云樂云，鐘鼓云乎哉？」

語譯　孔子說：「儘說禮啊禮的，難道說的只是玉帛嗎？儘說樂啊樂的，難道說的只是鐘鼓嗎？」

注釋　①玉帛　《集解》：「鄭曰：玉圭璋之屬；帛，束帛之屬。」

解說　重要的是禮樂的精神，而不是器物和形式。《正義》：「敬為禮本，和為樂本也。」

9.3. "They may be used for purposes of self-contemplation.

9.4. "They teach the art of sociability.

9.5. "They show how to regulate feelings of resentment.

9.6. "From them you learn the more immediate duty of serving one's father, and the remoter one of serving one's prince.

9.7. "From them we become largely acquainted with the names of birds, beasts, and plants."

注釋　stimulate: v. 激勵、鼓舞；self-contemplation: n. 自我省思；sociability: n. 群居；immediate: adj. 鄰近的、當前的；acquainted with: 認識、精通。

解說　本章英譯是據朱注的解釋。

⁕ **Chapter 10** ⁕

The Master said to Po-yu, "Do you give yourself to the Chau-nan and the Shao-nan. The man who has not studied the Chau-nan and the Shao-nan is like one who stands with his face right against a wall. Is he not so?"

⁕ **Chapter 11** ⁕

The Master said, "'It is according to the rules of propriety,' they say. -- 'It is according to the rules of propriety,' they say. Are gems and silk all that is meant by propriety? 'It is music,' they say. -- 'It is music,' they say. Are bells and drums all that is meant by music?"

———————— ❧ 第十二章 ❧ ————————

子曰：「色厲而內荏，譬諸小人，其猶穿窬之盜也與？」

語譯　孔子說：「外表裝得很嚴厲，內心卻很軟弱，拿小人來打比方，就像是穿牆挖洞的小偷吧？」

注釋　①荏　音忍。柔弱。②穿窬　《集解》：「孔曰：穿，穿壁。窬，窬牆。」窬，挖空。或謂窬作踰，翻越的意思。

解說　皇侃疏：「小人為盜，或穿入屋壁，或踰入牆垣。當此之時，外形恆欲進為取物，而心恆畏人，常懷退走之路。是形進心退，內外相乖，如色外矜而心內柔佞者也。」

———————— ❧ 第十三章 ❧ ————————

子曰：「鄉原，德之賊也。」

語譯　孔子說：「整個鄉里都不得罪的那種好人，是敗壞道德的小人啊。」

注釋　①鄉原　原同愿，善也。一鄉都以為是好人。②賊　賊害。

解說　《孟子·盡心下》：「閹然媚於世也者，是鄉原也。」又說：「非之無舉也，刺之無刺也；同乎流俗，合乎汙世；居之似忠信，行之似廉潔；眾皆悅之，自以為是，而不可與入堯舜之道，故曰德之賊也。」偽善媚俗的人，孔子最討厭了。

———————— ❧ 第十四章 ❧ ————————

子曰：「道聽而塗說，德之棄也。」

語譯　孔子說：「把路上聽來的話在路上就說出去，是棄道德的小人啊。」

———————— ❧ 第十五章 ❧ ————————

子曰：「鄙夫！可與事君也與哉？其未得之也，患得之；既得之，患失之。苟患失之，無所不至矣。」

─────────── ⁂ **Chapter 12** ⁂ ───────────

The Master said, "He who puts on an appearance of stern firmness, while inwardly he is weak, is like one of the small, mean people; -- yea, is he not like the thief who breaks through, or climbs over, a wall?"

注釋　stern: adj. 嚴肅的。

─────────── ⁂ **Chapter 13** ⁂ ───────────

The Master said, "Your good, careful people of the villages are the thieves of virtue."

解說　「鄉原」譯爲 your good, careful people of the villages，不夠貼切。或譯爲 goodies。

─────────── ⁂ **Chapter 14** ⁂ ───────────

The Master said, "To tell, as we go along, what we have heard on the way, is to cast away our virtue."

注釋　cast away: 拋棄。

─────────── ⁂ **Chapter 15** ⁂ ───────────

15.1. The Master said, "There are those mean creatures! How impossible it is along with them to serve one's prince!

語譯　孔子說：「卑鄙的人啊！可以和他一起爲國君做事嗎？沒有得到官位時，害怕無法謀取官位；已經得到官位時，又害怕失掉官位。如果害怕失去官位，那麼他什麼事都做得出來。」

注釋　①鄙夫　朱注：「胡氏曰：志於富貴，即孔子所謂鄙夫也。」②無所不至　沒有做不出來的。

※ 第十六章 ※

子曰：「古者民有三疾，今也或是之亡也。古之狂也肆，今之狂也蕩；古之矜也廉，今之矜也忿戾；古之愚也直，今之愚也詐而已矣。」

語譯　孔子說：「古代的人有三種毛病，現在或許連這些毛病也沒有了。古代的狂者不拘小節，現在的狂者放蕩無羈；古代矜持的人有稜有角，現在矜持的人乖戾易怒；古代的愚者質樸率眞，現在的愚者詭詐虛僞。」

注釋　①疾　偏短缺失。②是之亡　亡同無。之，語助詞。是之亡，無是，沒有這些毛病。③肆　朱注：「謂不拘小節。」④廉　稜角。

※ 第十七章 ※

子曰：「巧言令色，鮮矣仁。」

解說　見〈學而篇〉。

※ 第十八章 ※

子曰：「惡紫之奪朱也，惡鄭聲之亂雅樂也，惡利口之覆邦家者。」

語譯　孔子說：「我厭惡紫色奪去朱色的光采，厭惡鄭國音樂擾亂了雅樂，厭惡花言巧語傾覆了國家。」

注釋　①惡　厭惡。②惡紫之奪朱也　《集解》：「朱，正色。紫，間色之好者，惡其邪好而奪正色。」③利口　多言少實。

15.2. "While they have not got their aims, their anxiety is how to get them. When they have got them, their anxiety is lest they should lose them.

15.3. "When they are anxious lest such things should be lost, there is nothing to which they will not proceed."

❊ Chapter 16 ❊

16.1. The Master said, "Anciently, men had three failings, which now perhaps are not to be found.

16.2. "The high-mindedness of antiquity showed itself in a disregard of small things; the high-mindedness of the present day shows itself in wild license. The stern dignity of antiquity showed itself in grave reserve; the stern dignity of the present day shows itself in quarrelsome perverseness. The stupidity of antiquity showed itself in straightforwardness; the stupidity of the present day shows itself in sheer deceit."

注釋　anciently: adv. 古代；failing: n. 缺陷；antiquity: n. 古代；high-mindedness: 高傲；quarrelsome: adj. 愛爭吵的；perverseness: n. 乖僻、固執；sheer: adj. 完全的；deceit: n. 欺騙。

❊ Chapter 17 ❊

The Master said, "Fine words and an insinuating appearance are seldom associated with virtue."

❊ Chapter 18 ❊

The Master said, "I hate the manner in which purple takes away the luster of vermilion. I hate the way in which the songs of Chang confound the music of the Ya. I hate those who with their sharp mouths overthrow kingdoms and families."

注釋　luster: n. 光澤；vermilion: n. 朱紅色；confound: v. 混淆；overthrow: v. 顛覆。

————— ❧ 第十九章 ❧ —————

子曰：「予欲無言。」子貢曰：「子如不言，則小子何述焉？」子曰：「天何言哉？四時行焉，百物生焉，天何言哉？」

語譯 孔子說：「我想不說話了。」子貢說：「老師如果不說話，那我們還傳述什麼呢？」孔子說：「天又說了些什麼呢？四季循環不已，萬物生生不息，天又說了些什麼呢？」

注釋 ①述　傳述。

解說 《正義》：「夫子本以身教，恐弟子徒以言求之，故欲無言，以發弟子之悟也。」所謂的天道，即見於自然的運行法則。《孟子·萬章上》：「天不言，以行與事示之而已矣。」《禮記·哀公問篇》：「公曰：『敢問君子何貴乎天道也？』孔子對曰：『貴其不已。如日月東西相從而不已也，是天道也；不閉其久，是天道也；無爲而物成，是天道也；已成而明，是天道也。』」

————— ❧ 第二十章 ❧ —————

孺悲欲見孔子，孔子辭以疾。將命者出戶，取瑟而歌，使之聞之。

語譯 孺悲要見孔子，孔子以生病爲理由不見他。傳命的人剛走出屋子，孔子便取瑟彈唱，讓使者聽到。

注釋 ①孺悲　魯國人。《禮記·雜記》：「恤由之喪，哀公使孺悲之孔子，學士喪禮。」②將命者　傳辭者。

解說 《集解》：「孔子不欲見，故辭之以疾。爲其將命者不知己，故歌。令將命者悟，所以令孺悲思之。」

————— ❧ 第二十一章 ❧ —————

宰我問：「三年之喪，期已久矣。君子三年不爲禮，禮必壞；三年不爲樂，樂必崩。舊穀既沒，新穀既升，鑽燧改火，期可已矣。」子曰：「食夫稻，衣夫錦，於女安乎？」曰：「安。」「女安則爲之！夫君子之居喪，食旨不甘，聞樂不樂，居處不安，故不爲也。

Chapter 19

19.1. The Master said, "I would prefer not speaking."

19.2. Tsze-kung said, "If you, Master, do not speak, what shall we, your disciples, have to record?"

19.3. The Master said, "Does Heaven speak? The four seasons pursue their courses, and all things are continually being produced, but does Heaven say anything?"

注釋　pursue: v. 追求、進行。

Chapter 20

Zu Pei wished to see Confucius, but Confucius declined, on the ground of being sick, to see him. When the bearer of this message went out at the door, the Master took his lute and sang to it, in order that Pei might hear him.

注釋　decline: v. 婉拒。

注釋　「使之聞之」譯為 in order that Pei might hear him，但是孺悲怎麼會聽得到孔子鼓瑟呢？應該是指使者（messenger）吧？

Chapter 21

21.1. Tsai Wo asked about the three years' mourning for parents, saying that one year was long enough.

21.2. "If the superior man," said he, "abstains for three years from the observances of propriety, those observances will be quite lost. If for three years he abstains from music, music will be ruined. Within a year

今女安，則為之！」宰我出。子曰：「予之不仁也！子生三年，然後免於父母之懷。夫三年之喪，天下之通喪也。予也，有三年之愛於其父母乎？」

語譯　宰我問孔子說：「守喪三年，其實一年已經夠久了。君子三年不行禮儀，禮儀將從此廢棄掉；三年不彈奏音樂，音樂會從此失傳。舊穀子吃完了，新穀子也就要收成，鑽木取火的木頭也經過一個循環，似乎一年就夠了吧。」孔子說：「服喪一年後就吃稻米穿錦衣，你覺得心安嗎？」宰我說：「心安啊。」孔子說：「你既然覺得心安，那就去做吧！君子在服喪時，正因為吃了美食不覺得好吃，聽了音樂不覺得快樂，住在家裡不覺得舒適，所以才不除喪。如果你覺得心安，就這麼去做吧！」宰我離開後，孔子說：「宰我真是不仁啊！兒子生下三年，三年後才能完全脫離父母的懷抱。服喪三年，是天下通行的喪期啊。宰我啊，難道沒有從父母那裡得到三年的愛嗎？」

注釋　①期　音基，周年。②沒　盡。③升　登收。④鑽燧改火　古代人鑽木取火，取火的木頭叫作燧，要保持不滅，必須不斷添薪，傳薪的木頭隨著四時而有不同，稱為改火。朱注：「改火，春取榆柳之火，夏取棗杏之火，夏季取桑柘之火，秋取柞楢之火，冬取槐檀之火，亦一年而周也。」⑤食夫稻　《正義》：「北方以稻為穀之貴者，故居喪不食也。」⑥衣夫錦　《正義》：「錦是有文采之衣……是未終喪皆服麻衣，無采飾，則不得衣錦可知也。」⑦旨　美味。⑧居處　居常時之處。⑨有三年之愛於其父母乎　《集解》：「孔曰：言子之於父母，欲報之德，昊天罔極，而予也有三年之愛乎？」也就是說：「予對父母的愛有三年那麼久嗎？」或解釋為「予難道沒有父母三年之愛嗎？」

解說　孔子真的很生氣了，才會對宰我說：「你既然覺得心安，那麼就去做吧。」仁者愛人，沒有發乎內心的愛，就什麼也不用說了。

---- ❖ 第二十二章 ❖ ----

子曰：「飽食終日，無所用心，難矣哉！不有博弈者乎，為之猶賢乎已。」

語譯　孔子說：「整天吃飽了不曾用心做點事，這種人很難有成就啊！不是有人

the old grain is exhausted, and the new grain has sprung up, and, in procuring fire by friction, we go through all the changes of wood for that purpose. After a complete year, the mourning may stop."

21.3. The Master said, "If you were, after a year, to eat good rice, and wear embroidered clothes, would you feel at ease?" "I should," replied Wo.

21.4. The Master said, "If you can feel at ease, do it. But a superior man, during the whole period of mourning, does not enjoy pleasant food which he may eat, nor derive pleasure from music which he may hear. He also does not feel at ease, if he is comfortably lodged. Therefore he does not do what you propose. But now you feel at ease and may do it."

21.5. Tsai Wo then went out, and the Master said, "This shows Yu's want of virtue. It is not till a child is three years old that it is allowed to leave the arms of its parents. And the three years' mourning is universally observed throughout the empire. Did Yu enjoy the three years' love of his parents?"

注釋　abstain from: 抑制、放棄；observances: 儀式、祭典；spring up: 長出來；procure: v. 取得；friction: n. 磨擦；embroider: v. 刺繡；at ease: 心安、自在；lodge: v. 住宿；universally:adv. 普遍地。

❖ Chapter 22 ❖

The Master said, "Hard is it to deal with who will stuff himself with food the whole day, without applying his mind to anything good! Are there not gamesters and chess players? To be one of these would still be better than doing nothing at all."

玩六博和弈棋的嗎?做這些總比完全不用心好吧。」

注釋　①**博弈**　博,六博。說文:「博,局戲也。六箸十二棋也。」弈,圍棋。②**賢**　勝也。③**已**　止也。

解說　《孟子·告子》:「今夫弈之為數,小數也;不專心致志,則不得也。」

—————— ❋ 第二十三章 ❋ ——————

子路曰:「君子尚勇乎?」子曰:「君子義以為上。君子有勇而無義為亂,小人有勇而無義為盜。」

語譯　子路說:「君子看重勇氣嗎?」孔子說:「君子認為道義是最可貴的。君子有勇氣而沒有道義,則會作亂,小人有勇氣而沒有道義,就會做強盜。」

解說　孔子認為所謂的「勇」,是見到應該去做的便勇於去做。《禮記·聘義》:「有行之謂有義,有義之謂勇敢。故所貴於勇敢者,貴其能以立義也;所貴於立義者,貴其有行也;所貴於有行者,貴其行禮也;故所貴於勇敢者,貴其敢行禮義也。」

—————— ❋ 第二十四章 ❋ ——————

子貢曰:「君子亦有惡乎?」子曰:「有惡:惡稱人之惡者,惡居下流而訕上者,惡勇而無禮者,惡果敢而窒者。」曰:「賜也亦有惡乎?」「惡徼以為知者,惡不孫以為勇者,惡訐以為直者。」

語譯　子貢說:「君子也有厭惡的人嗎?」孔子說:「有的:厭惡稱說他人壞處的人,厭惡在下位而毀謗長官的人,厭惡勇敢而不懂禮節的人,厭惡果敢而頑固不通的人。」孔子反問說:「賜啊,你也有厭惡的人嗎?」子貢說:「我厭惡抄襲別人而自以為聰明的人,厭惡倨傲不遜而自以為勇敢的人,厭惡揭人隱私而自以為正直的人。」

注釋　①**惡**　厭惡。②**訕**　毀謗。③**窒**　不通事理。④**徼**　音角。抄襲。或謂「徼」通「絞」,喜歡刺探別人的意思。⑤**不孫**　不遜讓。⑥**訐**　揭人隱私。

注釋　stuff with: 塡飽肚子；gamester: n. 賭徒。

⚜ **Chapter 23** ⚜

Tsze-lu said, "Does the superior man esteem valor?" The Master said, "The superior man holds righteousness to be of highest importance. A man in a superior situation, having valor without righteousness, will be guilty of insubordination; one of the lower people having valor without righteousness, will commit robbery."

注釋　esteem: v. 重視；valor: n. 勇猛；commit: v. 犯罪。

⚜ **Chapter 24** ⚜

24.1. Tsze-kung said, "Has the superior man his hatreds also?" The Master said, "He has his hatreds. He hates those who proclaim the evil of others. He hates the man who, being in a low station, slanders his superiors. He hates those who have valor merely, and are unobservant of propriety. He hates those who are forward and determined, and, at the same time, of contracted understanding."

24.2. The Master then inquired, "Ts'ze, have you also your hatreds?" Tsze-kung replied, "I hate those who pry out matters, and ascribe the knowledge to their wisdom. I hate those who are only not modest, and think that they are valorous. I hate those who make known secrets, and think that they are straightforward."

注釋　hatred: n. 討厭；proclaim: v. 宣說；slander: v. 誹謗；contracted: adj. 縮短的；pry out: 打聽出來；ascribe: v. 認爲是、歸於 [to]；valorous: adj. 英勇的。

———————— ❀ 第二十五章 ❀ ————————

子曰：「唯女子與小人為難養也，近之則不孫，遠之則怨。」

語譯　孔子說：「只有家裡的侍妾和僕人最難以相處，親近了，他們就不知道謙
　　　讓，疏遠了，他們就會怨恨你。」

注釋　①養　相處。

解說　朱注：「此小人，亦謂僕隸下人也。君子之於臣妾，莊以涖之，慈以畜
　　　之，則無二者之患矣。」蔣伯潛：「『女子小人』是指宮闈的嬪妾、奄
　　　宦，和士大夫的婢僕而言。」

———————— ❀ 第二十六章 ❀ ————————

子曰：「年四十而見惡焉，其終也已。」

語譯　孔子說：「到了四十歲還被人討厭，那麼他這輩子也就完了。」

注釋　①見惡　見惡於人。

---- 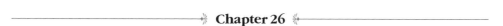 **Chapter 25** ----

The Master said, "Of all people, girls and servants are the most difficult to behave to. If you are familiar with them, they lose their humility. If you maintain a reserve towards them, they are discontented."

注釋　behave to: 對待；humility: n. 謙恭；reserve: 拘謹、冷淡；discontented: adj. 感到不滿。

---- **Chapter 26** ----

The Master said, "When a man at forty is the object of dislike, he will always continue what he is."

微子第十八

※ 第一章 ※

微子去之，箕子為之奴，比干諫而死。孔子曰：「殷有三仁焉。」

語譯　（紂王無道）微子離開他，箕子被囚為奴，比干勸諫而遭殺。孔子說：「殷代有三個仁者。」

注釋　①**微子**　紂庶兄。見紂無道，早去之。②**箕子**　紂叔父，諫紂不聽被囚，披髮佯狂為奴。③**比干**　紂叔父，諫紂被殺。

※ 第二章 ※

柳下惠為士師，三黜。人曰：「子未可以去乎？」曰：「直道而事人，焉往而不三黜？枉道而事人，何必去父母之邦。」

語譯　柳下惠擔任魯國的典獄官，被免職三次。有人對他說：「你還不可以去別的國家嗎？」柳下惠說：「我以正道做事，到哪裡去，不是都會多次被免職嗎？如果我不依正道做事，又何必離開祖國呢？」

注釋　①**士師**　典獄之官。②**黜**　貶退。

解說　朱注：「柳下惠三黜不去，而其辭氣雍容如此，可謂和矣。然其不能枉道之意，則有確乎其不可拔者。是則所謂必以其道，而不自失焉者也。」

※ 第三章 ※

齊景公待孔子，曰：「若季氏則吾不能，以季、孟之間待之。」曰：「吾老矣，不能用也。」孔子行。

語譯　齊景公接待孔子時說：「像魯國國君對待季氏那樣對待孔子，我是沒辦法，我可以用次於季氏而高於孟氏的待遇對待他。」但是他又說：「我老了，沒有什麼作為了。」於是孔子離開了齊國。

注釋　①**季孟之間**　《集解》：「魯三卿，季氏為上卿，孟氏為下卿，不用事。言待之以二者之間。」

※ **Chapter 1** ※

1.1. The Viscount of Wei withdrew from the court. The Viscount of Chi became a slave to Chau. Pi-kan remonstrated with him and died.

1.2. Confucius said, "The Yin dynasty possessed these three men of virtue."

注釋　viscount: n. 子爵；remonstrate: v. 勸告 [with]。

※ **Chapter 2** ※

Hui of Liu-hsia, being chief criminal judge, was thrice dismissed from his office. Some one said to him, "Is it not yet time for you, sir, to leave this?" He replied, "Serving men in an upright way, where shall I go to, and not experience such a thrice-repeated dismissal? If I choose to serve men in a crooked way, what necessity is there for me to leave the country of my parents?"

注釋　dismiss: v. 免職；crooked:adj. 歪斜的、不當的。

※ **Chapter 3** ※

The duke Ching of Ch'i, with reference to the manner in which he should treat Confucius, said, "I cannot treat him as I would the chief of the Chi family. I will treat him in a manner between that accorded to the chief of the Chi and that given to the chief of the Mang family." He also said, "I am old; I cannot use his doctrines." Confucius took his departure.

─────── ❀ 第四章 ❀ ───────

齊人歸女樂，季桓子受之，三日不朝，孔子行。

語譯　齊國送了許多歌妓給魯國，季桓子接受了。君臣三天不行朝禮，孔子便離開魯國。

注釋　①**女樂**　歌妓。

解說　《史記‧孔子世家》：「定公十四年，孔子年五十六，由大司寇行攝相事……於是誅魯大夫亂政者少正卯。與聞國政三月，粥羔豚者弗飾賈；男女行者別於塗；塗不拾遺；四方之客至乎邑者不求有司，皆予之以歸。齊人聞而懼，曰：『孔子爲政必霸，霸則吾地近焉，我之爲先并矣。盍致地焉？』黎鉏曰：『請先嘗沮之；沮之而不可則致地，庸遲乎！』於是選齊國中女子好者八十人，皆衣文衣而舞康樂，文馬三十駟，遺魯君。陳女樂文馬於魯城南高門外，季桓子微服往觀再三，將受，乃語魯君爲周道游，往觀終日，怠於政事。」

─────── ❀ 第五章 ❀ ───────

楚狂接輿歌而過孔子，曰：「鳳兮！鳳兮！何德之衰？往者不可諫，來者猶可追。已而，已而！今之從政者殆而！」孔子下，欲與之言。趨而辟之，不得與之言。

語譯　楚國的狂者接輿，唱著歌走過孔子的車子說：「鳳啊！鳳啊！爲什麼如此德衰？過去的無法再挽回，未來的還來得及追。算了吧，算了吧！現在從政的人都很危險的！」孔子下車想跟他說話，他卻快步走避，孔子沒辦法和他交談。

注釋　①**接輿**　楚國人。朱注：「接輿，楚人，佯狂辟世。夫子時將適楚，故接輿歌而過其車前也。」②**鳳兮！鳳兮！何德之衰？**　《集解》：「孔曰：比孔子於鳳鳥，鳳鳥待君乃見。非孔子周行求合，故曰衰。」③**已而**　罷了。④**殆**　皇侃疏：「危殆不可救復。」

解說　《莊子‧人間世》有較完整的敘述：「孔子適楚，楚狂接輿游其門曰：『鳳兮鳳兮，何如德之衰也？來世不可待，往世不可追也。天下有道，聖

Chapter 4

The people of Ch'i sent to Lu a present of female musicians, which Chi Hwan received, and for three days no court was held. Confucius took his departure.

Chapter 5

5.1. The madman of Ch'u, Chieh-yu, passed by Confucius, singing and saying, "O FANG! O FANG! How is your virtue degenerated! As to the past, reproof is useless; but the future may still be provided against. Give up your vain pursuit. Give up your vain pursuit. Peril awaits those who now engage in affairs of government."

5.2. Confucius alighted and wished to converse with him, but Chieh-yu hastened away, so that he could not talk with him.

注釋 degenerated: v. 墮落；reproof: n. 責難、歸勸；provide against: 採取預防措施；vain: adj. 徒勞無功的、空虛的；peril: n. 危險；alight: v. 下車；converse with: 交談。

人成焉；天下無道，聖人生焉；方今之時，僅免刑焉；福輕乎羽，莫之知載；禍重乎地，莫之知避；已乎已乎！臨人以德；殆乎殆乎！畫地而趨。迷陽迷陽，無傷吾行！郤曲郤曲，無傷吾足！』山木，自寇也；膏火，自煎也。桂可食，故伐之；漆可用，故割之。人皆知有用之用，而莫知無用之用也。」

───── ❧ 第六章 ❧ ─────

長沮、桀溺耦而耕，孔子過之，使子路問津焉。長沮曰：「夫執輿者為誰？」子路曰：「為孔丘。」曰：「是魯孔丘與？」曰：「是也。」曰：「是知津矣。」問於桀溺，桀溺曰：「子為誰？」曰：「為仲由。」曰：「是魯孔丘之徒與？」對曰：「然。」曰：「滔滔者天下皆是也，而誰以易之？且而與其從辟人之士也，豈若從辟世之士哉？」耰而不輟。子路行以告。夫子憮然曰：「鳥獸不可與同群，吾非斯人之徒與而誰與？天下有道，丘不與易也。」

語譯 長沮和桀溺兩個人結伴在耕地，孔子經過那裡，要子路去問渡口在哪裡。長沮說：「那在車子拉韁繩的是誰？」子路說：「是孔丘。」長沮說：「是魯國的孔丘嗎？」子路說：「是的。」長沮便說：「那麼他早就知道渡口在哪裡了吧。」子路去問桀溺，桀溺說：「你是誰？」子路說：「我是仲由。」桀溺說：「是魯國孔丘的學生嗎？」子路回答說：「是的。」桀溺說：「如洪水般的禍亂到處都是，誰能夠改變呢？而你與其跟隨到處躲著壞人的老師，為什麼不跟隨我們這些躲避俗世的人呢？」說著說著，仍然不停地在犁土覆種。子路回來告訴孔子他們所說的話。孔子悵然若失地說：「我們是無法和鳥獸共處的，我不跟世人為伍，要跟誰為伍呢？天下要是太平，我也就不必去從事改革了。」

注釋 ①**長沮、桀溺** 都是隱者。②**耦** 朱注：「並耕也。」《集解》：「鄭曰：耜廣五寸，二耜為耦。」③**津** 渡口。④**執輿** 朱注：「執轡在車也。」⑤**滔滔** 《集解》：「孔曰：滔滔，周流之貌。」洪水橫流，比喻時局不安。⑥**耰** 音優。《集解》：「覆種也。」播種後犁土覆蓋種子。⑦**憮然** 悵然。憮音五。⑧**鳥獸不可與同群** 《集解》：「孔曰：隱於山林是同群。」⑨**天下有道，丘不與易也** 朱注：「天下若已平治，則我無用變易之。正

Chapter 6

6.1. Ch'ang-tsu and Chieh-ni were at work in the field together, when Confucius passed by them, and sent Tsze-lu to inquire for the ford.

6.2. Ch'ang-tsu said, "Who is he that holds the reins in the carriage there?" Tsze-lu told him, "It is K'ung Ch'iu." "Is it not K'ung of Lu?" asked he. "Yes," was the reply, to which the other rejoined, "He knows the ford."

6.3. Tsze-lu then inquired of Chieh-ni, who said to him, "Who are you, sir?" He answered, "I am Chung Yu." "Are you not the disciple of K'ung Ch'iu of Lu?" asked the other. "I am," replied he, and then Chieh-ni said to him, "Disorder, like a swelling flood, spreads over the whole empire, and who is he that will change its state for you? Rather than follow one who merely withdraws from this one and that one, had you not better follow those who have withdrawn from the world altogether?" With this he fell to covering up the seed, and proceeded with his work, without stopping.

6.4. Tsze-lu went and reported their remarks, when the Master observed with a sigh, "It is impossible to associate with birds and beasts, as if they were the same with us. If I associate not with these people, --with mankind, -- with whom shall I associate? If right principles prevailed through the empire, there would be no use for me to change its state."

注釋　ford: n. 津渡、淺灘；rein: n. 韁繩；rejoin: v. 應答、接著說；disorder: n. 騷亂、失序；swell: v. 高漲；fall to: 開始；sigh: n. 嘆息。

為天下無道，故欲以道易之耳。」

解說　《正義》：「蓋人失意，每致寂然不動，如有所失然也。沮溺不達己意，
而妄非己，故夫子有此答也。」「鳥獸不可與同群，吾非斯人之徒與而誰
與？天下有道，丘不與易也。」對於這段話，蔣伯潛有不同的解釋：「現
在天下的人，都和鳥獸一樣，不可和他們同夥做事。長沮、桀溺是兩個有
道德的隱士。我不是和這種人相與，和誰相與呢？然而我不肯隱居者，正
因為天下無道，所以奔波勞碌，辛辛苦苦的，想把我的道，去改易天下的
無道也。若是天下有道，我也不去改易了。」可以說道盡孔子心裡的遺憾
吧。

—※ 第七章 ※—

子路從而後，遇丈人，以杖荷蓧。子路問曰：「子見夫子乎？」丈
人曰：「四體不勤，五穀不分。孰為夫子？」植其杖而芸。子路拱
而立。止子路宿，殺雞為黍而食之，見其二子焉。明日，子路行以
告。子曰：「隱者也。」使子路反見之。至，則行矣。子路曰：「不
仕無義。長幼之節，不可廢也；君臣之義，如之何其廢之？欲潔其
身，而亂大倫。君子之仕也，行其義也。道之不行，已知之矣。」

語譯　子路跟隨著孔子，遠遠落在後頭，遇到一個老頭子，用拐杖擔著竹器。子
路問他說：「你看到我的老師嗎？」那老頭子說：「你們這些人，四肢不
勞動，五穀分不清楚。誰是你的老師啊？」把拐杖插在土裡，俯身除草。
子路拱著手站在一旁。那老頭子留子路在家過夜，還殺雞做飯請子路吃，
又叫他的兩個兒子和子路見面。第二天，子路趕上孔子，便告訴孔子這件
事。孔子說：「那是個隱士。」要子路回頭去拜訪他。子路到他家，那老
頭子已經出門了。子路對他的兩個兒子說：「不出來為國家做事，是不應
該的。長幼的禮節既然不可以廢棄，又怎麼可以拋棄君臣的大義呢？為了
要潔身自愛，卻破壞了人倫的關係。君子要為國家做事，只是履行應盡的
義務而已。至於大道不行，我們早就知道了。」

注釋　①丈人　老者。②荷蓧　荷，擔負。蓧音掉，竹器。③四體不勤五穀不
分　或謂這是荷蓧丈人說他自己。《正義》引宋翔鳳《論語發微》：「『四
體不勤，五穀不分』為自述其不遑暇逸之義。故不能知孰為夫子，以答

✳ **Chapter 7** ✳

7.1. Tsze-lu, following the Master, happened to fall behind, when he met an old man, carrying across his shoulder on a staff a basket for weeds. Tsze-lu said to him, "Have you seen my master, sir?" The old man replied, "Your four limbs are unaccustomed to toil; you cannot distinguish the five kinds of grain: -- who is your master?" With this, he planted his staff in the ground, and proceeded to weed.

7.2. Tsze-lu joined his hands across his breast, and stood before him.

7.3. The old man kept Tsze-lu to pass the night in his house, killed a fowl, prepared millet, and feasted him. He also introduced to him his two sons.

7.4. Next day, Tsze-lu went on his way, and reported his adventure. The Master said, "He is a recluse," and sent Tsze-lu back to see him again, but when he got to the place, the old man was gone.

7.5. Tsze-lu then said to the family, "Not to take office is not righteous. If the relations between old and young may not be neglected, how is it that he sets aside the duties that should be observed between sovereign and minister? Wishing to maintain his personal purity, he allows that great relation to come to confusion. A superior man takes office, and performs the righteous duties belonging to it. As to the failure of right principles to make progress, he is aware of that."

子路，非以責子路也。」④植　豎立。⑤芸　除草。⑥拱　拱手，表示尊敬。⑦止　留也。⑧見　音現。引見。⑨大倫　指君臣之義。

解說　以上三章都在敘述孔子遇見隱者的故事，也突顯了孔子知其不可而為之的淑世理想。或謂接輿、長沮、桀溺，和荷蕢、晨門、荷蓧丈人一樣，都不是他們本來的名字。既然是隱者，大概也不在乎人家怎麼稱呼他們吧。

※　第八章　※

逸民：伯夷、叔齊、虞仲、夷逸、朱張、柳下惠、少連。子曰：「不降其志，不辱其身，伯夷、叔齊與！」謂：「柳下惠、少連，降志辱身矣。言中倫，行中慮，其斯而已矣。」謂：「虞仲、夷逸，隱居放言。身中清，廢中權。」「我則異於是，無可無不可。」

語譯　有德的隱者有：伯夷、叔齊、虞仲、夷逸、朱張、柳下惠、少連。孔子說：「意志不動搖，也不遭致屈辱，大概只有伯夷、叔齊吧！」又說：「柳下惠、少連，意志動搖了，也受到屈辱。但是言語合於法度，行為合於他人的期待，能如此也就算了。」又說：「虞仲、夷逸，隱居獨善，放肆直言。是能潔身自愛，而且被廢棄也是合乎時宜的。」「我則和他們不同，沒有什麼可以的，也沒有什麼不可以的。」

注釋　①逸民　《集解》：「節行超逸也。」顏師古：「有德而隱處者。」②放言　肆意直言。《集解》：「放，置也。不復言世務。」③身中清，廢中權　朱注：「隱居獨善，合乎道之清。放言自廢，合乎道之權。」④無可無不可　《集解》：「馬曰：亦不必進，亦不必退，惟義所在。」

解說　這些隱者的事蹟多數不可考。《孟子‧公孫丑上》：「可以仕則仕，可以止則止，可以久則久，可以速則速，孔子也。」

※　第九章　※

大師摯適齊，亞飯干適楚，三飯繚適蔡，四飯缺適秦。鼓方叔入於河，播鼗武入於漢，少師陽、擊磬襄，入於海。

語譯　魯國的太師摯到齊國去，亞飯干到楚國，三飯繚到蔡國，四飯缺到秦國。

注釋　fall behind: 落後；limb: n. 肢體；unaccustomed: adj. 不習慣於 [to]；toil: n. 辛苦工作；weed: v. 除草；millet: n. 稷；feast: v. 宴請；adventure: n. 奇遇；recluse: n. 隱士；set aside: 拋棄；aware of: 知道。

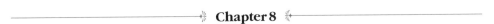

Chapter 8

8.1. The men who have retired to privacy from the world have been Po-i, Shu-ch'i, Yuchung, I-yi, Chu-chang, Hui of Liu-hsia, and Shao-lien.

8.2. The Master said, "Refusing to surrender their wills, or to submit to any taint in their persons; such, I think, were Po-i and Shu-ch'i.

8.3. "It may be said of Hui of Liu-hsia! and of Shaolien, that they surrendered their wills, and submitted to taint in their persons, but their words corresponded with reason, and their actions were such as men are anxious to see. This is all that is to be remarked in them.

8.4. "It may be said of Yu-chung and I-yi, that, while they hid themselves in their seclusion, they gave a license to their words; but in their persons, they succeeded in preserving their purity, and, in their retirement, they acted according to the exigency of the times.

8.5. "I am different from all these. I have no course for which I am predetermined, and no course against which I am predetermined."

注釋　privacy: n. 隱居；surrender: v. 放棄；submit: v. 服從、忍受；taint: n. 污點；seclusion: n. 隱遁；license: n. 放縱；exigency: n. 迫切性；predetermine: v. 預定。

Chapter 9

9.1. The grand music master, Chih, went to Ch'i.

9.2. Kan, the master of the band at the second meal, went to Ch'u. Liao, the band master at the third meal, went to Ts'ai. Chueh, the band master at the fourth meal, went to Ch'in.

打鼓的方叔住在黃河邊，搖小鼓的武住到漢水邊，少師陽和擊磬的襄則住到海濱。

注釋　①**大師**　大同太，魯國樂官之長。名摯。②**亞飯干、三飯繚、四飯缺**　飯音反。古代吃飯時演奏音樂的樂官。干、繚、缺是他們的名字。③**鼓方叔**　打鼓的方叔。④**播鼗武**　播，搖。鼗音陶，小鼓，兩旁有耳。武其名。⑤**少師陽**　樂官之佐。名陽。⑥**擊磬襄**　擊磬的樂官。名襄。

解說　朱注：「張子曰：周衰樂廢，夫子自衛反魯，一嘗治之。其後伶人賤工識樂之正。及魯益衰，三桓僭妄，自大師以下，皆知散之四方，逾河蹈海以去亂。聖人俄頃之助，功化如此。如有用我，期月而可。豈虛語哉？」

※ 第十章 ※

周公謂魯公曰：「君子不施其親，不使大臣怨乎不以。故舊無大故，則不棄也。無求備於一人。」

語譯　周公訓誡他的兒子魯公說：「君子不會輕忽他的親屬，不會使大臣抱怨不受重用。老臣故人如果沒有大過失，就不要拋棄他。不要對某個人求全責備。」

注釋　①**魯公**　周公之子伯禽。受封魯國，行前周公告誡之。②**施**　訓為「弛」，棄忘也。③**不以**　不用。④**大故**　大過。⑤**求備**　求全苛責。

解說　朱注：「胡氏曰：此伯禽受封之國，周公訓戒之辭。魯人傳誦，久而不忘也。其或夫子嘗與門弟子言之歟？」

※ 第十一章 ※

周有八士：伯達、伯适、仲突、仲忽、叔夜、叔夏、季隨、季騧。

語譯　周朝有八個賢士：伯達、伯适、仲突、仲忽、叔夜、叔夏、季隨、季騧。

注釋　①**八士**　《集解》：「周時四乳生八子，皆為顯仕，故記之爾。」一個母親生了四胎，每胎都是雙胞胎。②**伯适**　适音廓。③**季騧**　騧音瓜。

9.3. Fang-shu, the drum master, withdrew to the north of the river.

9.4. Wu, the master of the hand drum, withdrew to the Han.

9.5. Yang, the assistant music master, and Hsiang, master of the musical stone, withdrew to an island in the sea.

注釋　band: n. 樂隊；withdraw: v. 撤退。

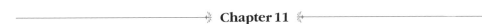

Chapter 10

The duke of Chau addressed his son, the duke of Lu, saying, "The virtuous prince does not neglect his relations. He does not cause the great ministers to repine at his not employing them. Without some great cause, he does not dismiss from their offices the members of old families. He does not seek in one man talents for every employment."

注釋　repine: v. 埋怨 [at]；cause: n. 理由、根據。

Chapter 11

To Chau belonged the eight officers, Po-ta, Po-kwo, Chung-tu, Chung-hwu, Shu-ya, Shuhsia, Chi-sui, and Chi-kwa.

子張第十九

———— ❈ 第一章 ❈ ————

子張曰:「士,見危致命,見得思義,祭思敬,喪思哀,其可已矣。」

語譯　子張說:「讀書人看到國家危難,要能夠犧牲生命,看到有利可得,要思考是否正當,祭祀時要想到莊嚴恭敬,居喪時要想到盡哀,這樣也就算是可以了。」

注釋　①**致命**　《集解》:「不愛其身。」〈憲問篇〉:「見利思義,見危授命。」

解說　《正義》引真德秀《四書集編》:「義、敬、哀皆言『思』,致命獨不言『思』者,死生之際,惟義是徇,有不待思而決也。」解釋得很好。

———— ❈ 第二章 ❈ ————

子張曰:「執德不弘,信道不篤,焉能為有?焉能為亡?」

語譯　子張說:「對德行的實踐無法擴充之,對真理的信仰不夠忠實,這種人有他算多嗎?沒有他算少嗎?」

注釋　①**執**　守也。②**弘**　大也。③**焉能為有?焉能為亡?**　《集解》:「言無所輕重。」皇侃疏:「世無此人,則不足為輕,世有此人,亦不足為重。」亡同無。

———— ❈ 第三章 ❈ ————

子夏之門人問交於子張。子張曰:「子夏云何?」對曰:「子夏曰:『可者與之,其不可者拒之。』」子張曰:「異乎吾所聞:『君子尊賢而容眾,嘉善而矜不能。』我之大賢與,於人何所不容?我之不賢與,人將拒我,如之何其拒人也?」

語譯　子夏的學生向子張問交友之道。子張說:「子夏怎麼說呢?」那學生回答說:「子夏說:『可以做朋友的就與他為伍,不可以做朋友的就拒絕他。』」子張說:「這和我聽到的不同:『君子尊敬賢者,也可以接納普通人,嘉勉好人而憐憫無能的人。』如果我是非常好的人,有什麼人不能包容的

⁕ **Chapter 1** ⁕

Tsze-chang said, "The scholar, trained for public duty, seeing threatening danger, is prepared to sacrifice his life. When the opportunity of gain is presented to him, he thinks of righteousness. In sacrificing, his thoughts are reverential. In mourning, his thoughts are about the grief which he should feel. Such a man commands our approbation indeed."

注釋　command: v. 值得；approbation: n. 嘉許。

⁕ **Chapter 2** ⁕

Tsze-chang said, "When a man holds fast to virtue, but without seeking to enlarge it, and believes in right principles, but without firm sincerity, what account can be made of his existence or non-existence?"

注釋　hold to: 信守；account: n. 重要性。

⁕ **Chapter 3** ⁕

The disciples of Tsze-hsia asked Tsze-chang about the principles that should characterize mutual intercourse. Tsze-chang asked, "What does Tsze-hsia say on the subject?" They replied, "Tsze-hsia says: 'Associate with those who can advantage you. Put away from you those who cannot do so.'" Tsze-chang observed, "This is different from what I have learned. The superior man honors the talented and virtuous, and bears with all. He praises the good, and pities the incompetent. Am I possessed of great talents and virtue? -- Who is there among men whom I will not bear with? Am I devoid of talents and virtue? -- Men will put me away from them. What have we to do with the putting away of others?"

呢？如果我是不好的人，別人會拒絕我，我怎麼還能拒絕別人呢？」

注釋　①**交**　交友之道。②**矜**　憐憫。

解說　其實他們兩個人說的都對，也都有其弊病，只是從不同的角度去解釋而已。《正義》引蔡邕《正交論》：「子夏之門人問交於子張，而二子各有所聞乎夫子。然則其以交誨也：商也寬，故告之以距人；師也褊，故告之以容眾，各從其行而矯之。若夫仲尼之正道，則汎愛眾而親仁，故非善不喜，非仁不親，交游以方，會友以仁，可無貶也。」

※ 第四章 ※

子夏曰：「雖小道，必有可觀者焉；致遠恐泥，是以君子不為也。」

語譯　子夏說：「就算小技藝，也必定有可取的地方；但是如果太過深入，恐怕會陷溺其中，所以君子不去做。」

注釋　①**小道**　才藝。②**致遠**　皇侃疏：「致，至也；遠，久也。」③**泥**　泥溺於水，不能自拔。

※ 第五章 ※

子夏曰：「日知其所亡，月無忘其所能，可謂好學也已矣。」

語譯　子夏說：「每天能夠知道原來不知道的東西，每個月不忘記複習原來會的東西，可以說是好學了吧。」

解說　皇侃疏：「日知其所亡，是知新也；月無忘所能，是溫故也。」

※ 第六章 ※

子夏曰：「博學而篤志，切問而近思，仁在其中矣。」

語譯　子夏說：「廣泛地學習，而堅守自己的志趣，有不明白的要懇切地問別人，從切近處去思考，仁德就在這裡頭了。」

注釋　①**切**　切實。②**近思**　程子：「近思者，以類而推。」

注釋 mutual: adj. 互相的；intercourse: n. 交往；advantage: v. 對……有益；bear with: 忍耐。

───────────── ☀ **Chapter 4** ☀ ─────────────

Tsze-hsia said, "Even in inferior studies and employments there is something worth being looked at; but if it be attempted to carry them out to what is remote, there is a danger of their proving inapplicable. Therefore, the superior man does not practice them."

注釋 inferior: adj. 次等的；prove: v. 證實是、成為；inapplicable: adj. 不能應用的、不適宜的。

───────────── ☀ **Chapter 5** ☀ ─────────────

Tsze-hsia said, "He, who from day to day recognizes what he has not yet, and from month to month does not forget what he has attained to, may be said indeed to love to learn."

注釋 recognize: v. 認識；attain to: 到達。

───────────── ☀ **Chapter 6** ☀ ─────────────

Tsze-hsia said, "There are learning extensivel, and having a firm and sincere aim; inquiring with earnestness, and reflecting with self-application: -- virtue is in such a course."

注釋 extensively: adv. 廣泛地；self-application: 專注。

———— ❋ 第七章 ❋ ————

子夏曰：「百工居肆以成其事，君子學以致其道。」

語譯　子夏說：「各種工人在工場製造器物，君子終身為學以成就其道。」

注釋　①肆　工場。②致　朱注：「極也。」

———— ❋ 第八章 ❋ ————

子夏曰：「小人之過也，必文。」

語譯　子夏說：「小人有了過失，必定會想辦法掩飾。」

注釋　①文　文飾。

———— ❋ 第九章 ❋ ————

子夏曰：「君子有三變：望之儼然，即之也溫，聽其言也厲。」

語譯　子夏說：「君子會給人三種印象：遠望時容貌矜莊，接近他時態度溫和，
　　　聽他說話又言辭嚴正。」

注釋　①變　不同的態度。②儼然　容貌端莊。③溫　顏色溫和。④厲　嚴正。

———— ❋ 第十章 ❋ ————

子夏曰：「君子信而後勞其民，未信，則以為厲己也；信而後諫，
未信，則以為謗己也。」

語譯　子夏說：「君子必先得到百姓的信賴以後，才會役使他們，否則他們會認
　　　為你在虐待他們；必先得到在上位者的信賴後才勸諫他，否則他會以為你
　　　在毀謗他。」

注釋　①信　取信於人。②厲　虐待。

解說　無論是對待上司或下屬，如果無法得到他們的信任，做什麼事都會被誤
　　　會。

❊ Chapter 7 ❊

Tsze-hsia said, "Mechanics have their shops to dwell in, in order to accomplish their works. The superior man learns, in order to reach to the utmost of his principles."

注釋　mechanic: n. 技工；utmost: n. 極限。

❊ Chapter 8 ❊

Tsze-hsia said, "The mean man is sure to gloss his faults."

注釋　gloss: v. 掩飾、搪塞。

❊ Chapter 9 ❊

Tsze-hsia said, "The superior man undergoes three changes. Looked at from a distance, he appears stern; when approached, he is mild; when he is heard to speak, his language is firm and decided."

注釋　undergo: v. 經歷；decided: adj. 明確的、堅決的。

❊ Chapter 10 ❊

Tsze-hsia said, "The superior man, having obtained their confidence, may then impose labors on his people. If he have not gained their confidence, they will think that he is oppressing them. Having obtained the confidence of his prince, one may then remonstrate with him. If he have not gained his confidence, the prince will think that he is vilifying him."

注釋　oppress: v. 壓迫、虐待；vilify: v. 中傷。

———— ❀ 第十一章 ❀ ————

子夏曰：「大德不踰閑，小德出入可也。」

語譯　子夏說：「人在重大的德行上不可以踰越界限，在小節上則不必太拘
　　　謹。」

注釋　①閑　朱注：「闌也，所以止物之出入。」界限、範圍的意思。②出入　出
　　　入於範圍內外。

———— ❀ 第十二章 ❀ ————

子游曰：「子夏之門人小子，當洒掃、應對、進退，則可矣。抑末
也，本之則無。如之何？」子夏聞之曰：「噫！言游過矣！君子之
道，孰先傳焉？孰後倦焉？譬諸草木，區以別矣。君子之道，焉可
誣也？有始有卒者，其惟聖人乎！」

語譯　子游說：「子夏的學生們，在洒掃、應對、進退的禮節上，那是可以的。
　　　不過這只是枝微末節而已，沒有學到根本的道理，那怎麼可以呢？」子夏
　　　聽到了說：「唉，言游錯了！君子之道，該先從哪裡教起呢？哪些是該放
　　　在後面才教的呢？就像是田圃裡的草木，要有所區分。君子的學問怎麼可
　　　以被扭曲呢？能夠循序漸進，有始有終的，大概只有聖人才做得到吧？」

注釋　①洒掃　灑水掃地。②應對　應答。③進退　《正義》：「凡摳衣趨隅，與
　　　夫正立拱手，中規中矩之節，皆幼儀所當習者。」④抑　轉折語，不過的
　　　意思。⑤末　枝末。

解說　根本的東西，往往是最難懂的。教育必須循序漸進，由淺入深。

———— ❀ 第十三章 ❀ ————

子夏曰：「仕而優則學，學而優則仕。」

⁂ **Chapter 11** ⁂

Tsze-hsia said, "When a person does not transgress the boundary line in the great virtues, he may pass and repass it in the small virtues."

注釋　transgress: v. 踰越；boundary: n. 界限、範圍；repass: v. 回頭通過。

⁂ **Chapter 12** ⁂

12.1. Tsze-yu said, "The disciples and followers of Tsze-hsia, in sprinkling and sweeping the ground, in answering and replying, in advancing and receding, are sufficiently accomplished. But these are only the branches of learning, and they are left ignorant of what is essential. -- How can they be acknowledged as sufficiently taught?"

12.2. Tsze-hsia heard of the remark and said, "Alas! Yen Yu is wrong. According to the way of the superior man in teaching, what departments are there which he considers of prime importance, and delivers? What are there which he considers of secondary importance, and allows himself to be idle about? But as in the case of plants, which are assorted according to their classes, so he deals with his disciples. How can the way of a superior man be such as to make fools of any of them? Is it not the sage alone, who can unite in one the beginning and the consummation of learning?"

注釋　sprinkle: v. 灑水；sweep: v. 掃；recede: v. 退後；accomplished: adj. 熟練的；essential: adj. 根本的、本質的；acknowledge: v. 承認；prime: adj. 首要的；deliver: v. 說教；idle about:放蕩；assort: v. 分類；consummation: n. 頂點、極致。

⁂ **Chapter 13** ⁂

Tsze-hsia said, "The officer, having discharged all his duties, should devote his leisure to learning. The student, having completed his learning, should

語譯　子夏說：「做官還有餘力的，就該做學問，做學問還有餘力的，就該去做官。」

注釋　①優　有餘。

———————————※ 第十四章 ※———————————

子游曰：「喪致乎哀而止。」

語譯　子游：「居喪只要能盡哀夠了。」

———————————※ 第十五章 ※———————————

子游曰：「吾友張也，為難能也。然而未仁。」

語譯　子游說：「我的朋友子張啊，他的成就是非常難得的。不過還沒有到達仁者的境地。」

———————————※ 第十六章 ※———————————

曾子曰：「堂堂乎張也，難與並為仁矣。」

語譯　曾子說：「子張太好高遠了，很難和他相勉為仁啊。」

注釋　①堂堂　儀表堂皇。《集解》：「言子張容儀盛，而於仁道薄也。」

———————————※ 第十七章 ※———————————

曾子曰：「吾聞諸夫子：『人未有自致者也，必也親喪乎！』」

語譯　曾子說：「我聽老師說：『人沒有自盡其心的，如果有，大概是在父母親的喪禮才會吧！』」

注釋　①自致　發乎內心而盡力去做。

———————————※ 第十八章 ※———————————

曾子曰：「吾聞諸夫子：『孟莊子之孝也，其他可能也；其不改父之臣與父之政，是難能也。』」

apply himself to be an officer."

注釋　discharge: v. 履行。

———————— ❊ **Chapter14** ❊ ————————

Tsze-yu said, "Mourning, having been carried to the utmost degree of grief, should stop with that."

———————— ❊ **Chapter 15** ❊ ————————

Tsze-yu said, "My friend Chang can do things which are hard to be done, but yet he is not perfectly virtuous."

———————— ❊ **Chapter 16** ❊ ————————

The philosopher Tsang said, "How imposing is the manner of Chang! It is difficult along with him to practice virtue."

注釋　imposing:adj. 堂皇的。

———————— ❊ **Chapter 17** ❊ ————————

The philosopher Tsang said, "I heard this from our Master: 'Men may not have shown what is in them to the full extent, and yet they will be found to do so, on the occasion of mourning for their parents.'"

注釋　to the full extent: 盡全力。

———————— ❊ **Chapter 18** ❊ ————————

The philosopher Tsang said, "I have heard this from our Master: -- 'The filial piety of Mang Chwang, in other matters, was what other men are competent

語譯　曾子說：「我聽老師說：『孟莊子的孝啊，其他方面別人還是做得到的；只有不改變父親的臣屬和施政理念，這才是難能可貴的啊。』」

解說　見〈學而篇〉：「子曰：父在，觀其志；父沒，觀其行；三年無改於父之道，可謂孝矣。」

───────── ✦ 第十九章 ✦ ─────────

孟氏使陽膚為士師，問於曾子。曾子曰：「上失其道，民散久矣。如得其情，則哀矜而勿喜。」

語譯　孟氏要陽膚做典獄官，陽膚來問曾子。曾子說：「在上位者昏亂無道，早就離心離德了。如果審訊出犯罪的事實，應該憐憫他們，不要自以為聰明而高興。」

注釋　①陽膚　曾子弟子。②散　離心離德。③情　《正義》：「情者，實也，謂民所犯罪之實也。」④哀矜　《正義》：「哀其致刑，矜其無知，或有所不得已也。《書·呂刑》云：『哀矜折獄。』」

───────── ✦ 第二十章 ✦ ─────────

子貢曰：「紂之不善，不如是之甚也。是以君子惡居下流，天下之惡皆歸焉。」

語譯　子貢說：「紂王的過錯，沒有像後世傳說的那麼過分啊。所以說君子厭惡居於卑下汙穢之處，使天下的惡名都歸到他身上。」

注釋　①下流　低窪的地方。

解說　《集解》：「孔曰：紂為不善以喪天下，後世憎甚之，皆以天下之惡歸之於紂。」

───────── ✦ 第二十一章 ✦ ─────────

子貢曰：「君子之過也，如日月之食焉：過也，人皆見之；更也，人皆仰之。」

to, but, as seen in his not changing the ministers of his father, nor his father's mode of government, it is difficult to be attained to.'"

Chapter 19

The chief of the Mang family having appointed Yang Fu to be chief criminal judge, the latter consulted the philosopher Tsang. Tsang said, "The rulers have failed in their duties, and the people consequently have been disorganized for a long time. When you have found out the truth of any accusation, be grieved for and pity them, and do not feel joy at your own ability."

注釋　disorganized: adj. 混亂失序；accusation: n. 罪狀。

Chapter 20

Tsze-kung said, "Chau's wickedness was not so great as that name implies. Therefore, the superior man hates to dwell in a low-lying situation, where all the evil of the world will flow in upon him."

注釋　wickedness: n. 邪惡；imply: v. 含義、暗示。

Chapter 21

Tsze-kung said, "The faults of the superior man are like the eclipses of the sun and moon. He has his faults, and all men see them; he changes again, and all men look up to him."

語譯　子貢說：「君子的過失啊，就像是日蝕和月蝕吧：他犯了錯，每個人都看得到；他改過的時候，每個人都仰望他。」

注釋　①食　又作蝕。②更　改過。③仰　仰望。

────────── ❋ 第二十二章 ❋ ──────────

衛公孫朝問於子貢曰：「仲尼焉學？」子貢曰：「文武之道，未墜於地，在人。賢者識其大者，不賢者識其小者，莫不有文武之道焉。夫子焉不學？而亦何常師之有？」

語譯　衛國的公孫朝問子貢說：「仲尼的學問是哪裡學來的？」子貢說：「文王、武王的禮樂典章，還沒有失傳，仍然有人記得。賢人認識那重大的東西，不賢的人只認識細節，他們都有保留文武之道。我們的老師何處不學？又哪裡有固定的老師呢？」

注釋　①公孫朝　衛國大夫。

────────── ❋ 第二十三章 ❋ ──────────

叔孫武叔語大夫於朝，曰：「子貢賢於仲尼。」子服景伯以告子貢。子貢曰：「譬之宮牆，賜之牆也及肩，窺見室家之好。夫子之牆數仞，不得其門而入，不見宗廟之美，百官之富。得其門者或寡矣。夫子之云，不亦宜乎！」

語譯　叔孫武叔在朝上對大夫們說：「子貢比仲尼還要賢能。」子服景伯把這話告訴子貢。子貢說：「拿屋子的圍牆做比喻吧，我的牆只有肩膀那麼高，人家在牆外，可以窺見家裡頭的美侖美奐。老師的圍牆有好幾仞高，如果不從大門進去，是看不見裡頭宗廟的雄偉，文武百官的人才薈萃。能夠進得大門的人太少了。也難怪武叔大夫會這麼說吧！」

注釋　①叔孫武叔　《集解》：「魯大夫叔孫州仇，武其謚。」②子服景伯　魯國大夫。③宮牆　圍牆。④仞　七尺為仞。或謂八尺，或謂五尺六寸。⑤百官　家中治事之府。

注釋　eclipse: n. 虧蝕。

❋ **Chapter 22** ❋

22.1. Kung-sun Ch'ao of Wei asked Tsze-kung, saying, "From whom did Chung-ni get his learning?"

22.2. Tsze-kung replied, "The doctrines of Wan and Wu have not yet fallen to the ground. They are to be found among men. Men of talents and virtue remember the greater principles of them, and others, not possessing such talents and virtue, remember the smaller. Thus, all possess the doctrines of Wan and Wu. Where could our Master go that he should not have an opportunity of learning them? And yet what necessity was there for his having a regular master?"

注釋　regular: adj. 固定不變的。

❋ **Chapter 23** ❋

23.1. Shu-sun Wu-shu observed to the great officers in the court, saying, "Tsze-kung is superior to Chung-ni."

23.2. Tsze-fu Ching-po reported the observation to Tsze-kung, who said, "Let me use the comparison of a house and its encompassing wall. My wall only reaches to the shoulders. One may peep over it, and see whatever is valuable in the apartments.

23.3. "The wall of my Master is several fathoms high. If one do not find the door and enter by it, he cannot see the ancestral temple with its beauties, nor all the officers in their rich array.

23.4. "But I may assume that they are few who find the door. Was not the observation of the chief only what might have been expected?"

注釋　observe: v. 評述；encompass: v. 包圍；peep: v. 窺見；fathom: n. 深度單位，約一八三公分；array: n. 列陣；assume: v. 假定、猜測。

---————— ❖ 第二十四章 ❖ —————---

叔孫武叔毀仲尼。子貢曰：「無以為也，仲尼不可毀也。他人之賢者，丘陵也，猶可踰也；仲尼，日月也，無得而踰焉。人雖欲自絕，其何傷於日月乎？多見其不知量也！」

語譯 叔孫武叔詆毀仲尼。子貢說：「這麼做是沒有用的，仲尼是沒辦法毀謗的。其他人的賢德，就像是丘陵，還可以攀越；仲尼就像是日月，是沒辦法跨越的啊。人們雖然想要背棄太陽和月亮，那對日月又有什麼傷害呢？只顯得他不自量力而已吧！」

注釋 ①絕 絕棄。②多見其不知量 只顯現他不知高低輕重。

---————— ❖ 第二十五章 ❖ —————---

陳子禽謂子貢曰：「子為恭也，仲尼豈賢於子乎？」子貢曰：「君子一言以為知，一言以為不知，言不可不慎也。夫子之不可及也，猶天之不可階而升也。夫子之得邦家者，所謂『立之斯立，道之斯行，綏之斯來，動之斯和。其生也榮，其死也哀』。如之何其可及也？」

語譯 陳子禽對子貢說：「你是太謙虛了吧，仲尼哪裡會比你賢能呢？」子貢說：「君子可以說一句話就表現出他的智慧，也可以說一句話就顯露出他的無知，所以說話不可不謹慎啊。老師的崇高不可及，就像是天空沒有階梯可以攀升。我們老師如果可以治理國家，那真是所謂的『教人民立身，人民就能夠立身，引導人民行善，人民就能夠行善，安撫百姓，百姓就來歸，使役百姓，百姓便齊心協力。生時人人都尊敬他，死時人人都哀悼他。』這樣的人如何趕得上呢？」

注釋 ①綏 安撫。②動之斯和 皇侃疏：「動謂勞役之也。悅以使民，民忘其勞。故役使之莫不和穆也。」《正義》：「動之者，以禮樂興動之也。」

解說 子貢的道德成就非常高，所以時人以為他已經超越了老師。

※ Chapter 24 ※

Shu-sun Wu-shu having spoken revilingly of Chung-ni, Tsze-kung said, "It is of no use doing so. Chung-ni cannot be reviled. The talents and virtue of other men are hillocks and mounds which may be stepped over. Chung-ni is the sun or moon, which it is not possible to step over. Although a man may wish to cut himself off from the sage, what harm can he do to the sun or moon? He only shows that he does not know his own capacity."

注釋　revile: v. 誣衊；hillock: n. 小丘；mound: n. 土堆；cut off: 斷絕關係。

※ Chapter 25 ※

25.1. Ch'an Tsze-ch' in, addressing Tsze-kung, said, "You are too modest. How can Chung-ni be said to be superior to you?"

25.2. Tsze-kung said to him, "For one word a man is often deemed to be wise, and for one word he is often deemed to be foolish. We ought to be careful indeed in what we say.

25.3. "Our Master cannot be attained to, just in the same way as the heavens cannot be gone up by the steps of a stair.

25.4. "Were our Master in the position of the ruler of a state or the chief of a family, we should find verified the description which has been given of a sage's rule: -- he would plant the people, and forthwith they would be established; he would lead them on, and forthwith they would follow him; he would make them happy, and forthwith multitudes would resort to his dominions; he would stimulate them, and forthwith they would be harmonious. While he lived, he would be glorious. When he died, he would be bitterly lamented. How is it possible for him to be attained to?"

注釋　stair: n. 樓梯；plant: v. 扶植；establish: v. 安頓；multitude: n. 群眾；resort:v. 投靠 [to]；dominion: n. 領土；stimulate: v. 鼓舞；harmonious: adj. 和諧的；lament: v. 哀悼。

◆ 第一章 ◆

堯曰：「咨！爾舜！天之曆數在爾躬。允執其中。四海困窮，天祿
永終。」舜亦以命禹。曰：「予小子履，敢用玄牡，敢昭告于皇皇
后帝：有罪不敢赦。帝臣不蔽，簡在帝心。朕躬有罪，無以萬方；
萬方有罪，罪在朕躬。」周有大賚，善人是富。「雖有周親，不如
仁人。百姓有過，在予一人。」謹權量，審法度，修廢官，四方之
政行焉。興滅國，繼絕世，舉逸民，天下之民歸心焉。所重：民、
食、喪、祭。寬則得眾，信則民任焉，敏則有功，公則說。

語譯 堯說：「唉，舜啊！天命落在你身上。你要信守著中道。如果國家民不
聊生，上天給你的俸祿也就永遠終止。」舜也以這句話交代禹。商湯說：
「我小子履，謹此以黑公牛獻祭，明白告訴光明而偉大的上帝：有罪的人
我不敢輕易赦免他們。上帝您的臣僕，我也不隱瞞他們的過失，由上帝自
己做選擇吧。我自己有過失，不要連累到百姓，百姓有罪，都歸我一個人
來承擔。」周武王得到上天的賞報，好人特別多。武王說：「我雖然有至
親，但是不如得到有仁德的人。百姓如果有過失，都由我一個人承擔。」
謹慎制定度量衡，審查各種制度，重建廢棄的官制，國家的政令就行得通
了。復興已滅亡的國家，延伸已斷絕的世代，任用有德的隱者，天下百姓
都會心悅誠服了。要重視的是：人民、糧食、喪禮、祭典。在上位者能夠
寬厚，就會得民心，言而有信，百姓就會信任他，認真做事，自然會有成
果，公正無私，就會心悅誠服。

注釋 ①咨 感嘆詞。②**曆數** 朱注：「帝王相繼之次第，猶歲時氣節之先後
也。」也就是天命的意思。③**在爾躬** 「躬」訓為「身」。或謂「在」訓
察，省察自身以承天命之謂也。④**允執其中** 允，信也。中，中道。⑤**予小
子履** 履，殷湯名。⑥**玄牡** 黑色公牛。⑦**昭** 明白。⑧**皇皇** 浩大。⑨
后帝 后，君也。《正義》：「天帝稱后者，尊之，故君之也。」⑩**簡** 選
擇。⑪**無以萬方** 以，與也。《集解》：「無以萬方，萬方不與也；萬方
有罪，我身之過。」⑫**賚** 音賴，賜予。⑬**周親** 至親。⑭**權量** 度量衡。
權，秤錘。量，斛斗。

❋ **Chapter 1** ❋

1.1. Yao said, "Oh! you, Shun, the Heaven-determined order of succession now rests in your person. Sincerely hold fast the due Mean. If there shall be distress and want within the four seas, the Heavenly revenue will come to a perpetual end."

1.2. Shun also used the same language in giving charge to Yu.

1.3. T'ang said, "I the child Li, presume to use a dark-colored victim, and presume to announce to Thee, O most great and sovereign God, that the sinner I dare not pardon, and thy ministers, O God, I do not keep in obscurity. The examination of them is by thy mind, O God. If, in my person, I commit offenses, they are not to be attributed to you, the people of the myriad regions. If you in the myriad regions commit offenses, these offenses must rest on my person."

1.4. Chau conferred great gifts, and the good were enriched.

1.5. "Although he has his near relatives, they are not equal to my virtuous men. The people are throwing blame upon me, the One man."

1.6. He carefully attended to the weights and measures, examined the body of the laws, restored the discarded officers, and the good government of the kingdom took its course.

1.7. He revived states that had been extinguished, restored families whose line of succession had been broken, and called to office those who had retired into obscurity, so that throughout the kingdom the hearts of the people turned towards him.

1.8. What he attached chief importance to were the food of the people, the duties of mourning, and sacrifices.

1.9. By his generosity, he won all. By his sincerity, he made the people repose trust in him. By his earnest activity, his achievements were great. By his justice, all were delighted.

注釋　succession: n. 繼承；distress: n. 貧苦；perpetual: adj. 永久的；charge: n. 責任；presume: v. 膽敢；myriad: adj. 無數的；offense: n. 犯罪；region: n. 地區；confer: v. 授與；discard: v. 拋棄；revive: v. 復甦；obscurity: n. 默默無聞；attach: v. 歸於。

─────────── ✦ 第二章 ✦ ───────────

子張問於孔子曰：「何如斯可以從政矣？」子曰：「尊五美，屏四惡，斯可以從政矣。」子張曰：「何謂五美？」子曰：「君子惠而不費，勞而不怨，欲而不貪，泰而不驕，威而不猛。」子張曰：「何謂惠而不費？」子曰：「因民之所利而利之，斯不亦惠而不費乎？擇可勞而勞之，又誰怨？欲仁而得仁，又焉貪？君子無眾寡，無小大，無敢慢，斯不亦泰而不驕乎？君子正其衣冠，尊其瞻視，儼然人望而畏之，斯不亦威而不猛乎？」子張曰：「何謂四惡？」子曰：「不教而殺謂之虐；不戒視成謂之暴；慢令致期謂之賊；猶之與人也，出納之吝，謂之有司。」

語譯　子張問孔子說：「如何才可以從政呢？」孔子說：「尊崇五種美德，摒除四種惡政，那就可以從政了。」子張說：「什麼是五種美德？」孔子說：「君子施惠人民，自己卻沒有破費；役使百姓，百姓卻沒有怨言；有所追求，卻不貪得；態度安舒而不驕傲；威嚴而不凶猛。」子張說：「何謂施惠而不破費？」孔子說：「看到人民有可以得利的地方，便以政令使他們獲得，這不就是施惠而不破費嗎？選擇可以役使百姓的時候去用他們，又有誰會抱怨呢？追求仁德而得到仁德，還要貪求什麼呢？無論人多人少，事大事小，君子都不敢怠慢，這不就是安舒而不驕傲嗎？君子端正衣冠，外貌莊重，使人覺得他有威儀而敬畏他，這不就是威嚴而不凶猛嗎？」子張說：「何謂四種惡政？」孔子說：「不先教育百姓，等他們犯了罪才以死刑處罰他們，這叫作殘忍；不先告誡人民，到時候又要看他們的成果，這叫作壓迫；政令延宕公布，到了期限又不通融，這叫作賊害；同樣是要給與人的，卻吝於發放，這是官僚習氣。」

注釋　①屏　摒除。②惠而不費　《集解》：「孔曰：利民在政，無費於財。」《正義》：「政在養民，故當順民之性，使之各遂其生。」③猶之　都是。④有司　官僚作風。

解說　本章詳細說明施政之道，現在的為政者要好好反省，而我們也可以據此臧否施政之良窳。

⁕ Chapter 2 ⁕

2.1. Tsze-chang asked Confucius, saying, "In what way should a person in authority act in order that he may conduct government properly?" The Master replied, "Let him honor the five excellent, and banish away the four bad, things; -- then may he conduct government properly." Tsze-chang said, "What are meant by the five excellent things?" The Master said, "When the person in authority is beneficent without great expenditure; when he lays tasks on the people without their repining; when he pursues what he desires without being covetous; when he maintains a dignified ease without being proud; when he is majestic without being fierce."

2.2. Tsze-chang said, "What is meant by being beneficent without great expenditure?" The Master replied, "When the person in authority makes more beneficial to the people the things from which they naturally derive benefit; -- is not this being beneficent without great expenditure? When he chooses the labors which are proper, and makes them labor on them, who will repine? When his desires are set on benevolent government, and he secures it, who will accuse him of covetousness? Whether he has to do with many people or few, or with things great or small, he does not dare to indicate any disrespect; -- is not this to maintain a dignified ease without any pride? He adjusts his clothes and cap, and throws a dignity into his looks, so that, thus dignified, he is looked at with awe; -- is not this to be majestic without being fierce?"

2.3. Tsze-chang then asked, "What are meant by the four bad things?" The Master said, "To put the people to death without having instructed them; -- this is called cruelty. To require from them, suddenly, the full tale of work, without having given them warning; -- this is called oppression. To issue orders as if without urgency, at first, and, when the time comes, to insist on them with severity; -- this is called injury. And, generally, in the giving pay or rewards to men, to do it in a stingy way; -- this is called acting the part of a mere official."

注釋　banish: v. 擯棄；expenditure: n. 支出；repine: v. 抱怨；covetous: adj. 貪婪的；
　　　fierce: adj. 凶猛的；derive: v. 得到、衍生出；secure: v. 順利得到；indicate:

———◈ 第三章 ◈———

子曰：「不知命，無以為君子也。不知禮，無以立也。不知言，無以知人也。」

語譯　孔子說：「不知道天命，便不能成為有德的君子。不懂得禮，便無法立身處世。不知道辨別言辭的是非，就沒辦法認識人了。」

注釋　①**知命**　知天命。《集解》：「命謂窮達之分。」②**知言**　《集解》：「聽言而別其是非。」

v. 暗示、露出；cruelty: n. 殘忍；oppression: n. 壓迫；stingy: adj. 吝嗇的。

✵ **Chapter 3** ✵

3.1.   The Master said, "Without recognizing the ordinances of Heaven, it is impossible to be a superior man.

3.2.   "Without an acquaintance with the rules of Propriety, it is impossible for the character to be established.

3.3.   "Without knowing the force of words, it is impossible to know men."

附錄
孔子年表 / 摘錄自錢穆《孔子傳》/

魯襄公二十二年	（西曆紀元前五五一年）孔子生。
魯襄公二十四年	孔子年三歲。父叔梁紇卒。
魯昭公七年	孔子年十七歲。母顏徵在卒在前。
魯昭公九年	孔子年十九歲。娶宋开官氏。
魯昭公十年	孔子年二十歲。生子鯉，字伯魚。
魯昭公十七年	孔子年二十七歲。郯子來朝，孔子見之，學古官名。其為魯之委吏乘田當在前。
魯昭公二十年	孔子年三十歲。孔子初入魯太廟當在前。琴張從遊，當在此時，或稍前。孔子至是始授徒設教。顏無繇、仲由、曾點、冉伯牛、閔損、冉求、仲弓、顏回、高柴、公西赤諸人先後從學。
魯昭公二十四年	孔子年三十四歲。魯孟釐子卒，遺命其二子及南宮敬叔師事孔子學禮。時二子年十三，其正式從學當在後。
魯昭公二十五年	孔子年三十五歲。魯三家共攻昭公，昭公奔於齊，孔子亦以是年適齊，在齊聞韶樂。齊景公問政於孔子。
魯昭公二十六年	孔子年三十六歲。當以是年返魯。
魯昭公二十七年	孔子年三十七歲。吳季札適齊返，其長子卒，葬嬴博間，孔子自魯往觀其葬禮。
魯定公五年	孔子年四十七歲。魯陽貨執季桓子。陽貨欲見孔子，當在此時。
魯定公八年	孔子年五十歲。魯三家攻陽貨，陽貨奔陽關。是年，公山弗擾召孔子。
魯定公九年	孔子年五十一歲。魯陽貨奔齊。孔子始出仕，為魯中都宰。
魯定公十年	孔子年五十二歲。由中都宰為司空，又為大司寇。相定公與齊會夾谷。

魯定公十二年	孔子年五十四歲。魯聽孔子主張墮三都。墮郈，墮費，又墮成，弗克。孔子墮三都之主張遂陷停頓。
魯定公十三年	孔子年五十五歲。去魯適衛。衛人端木賜從遊。
魯定公十四年	孔子年五十六歲。去衛過匡。晉佛肸來召，孔子欲往，不果，重返衛。
魯定公十五年	孔子年五十七歲。始見衛靈公，出仕衛，見衛靈公夫人南子。
魯哀公元年	孔子年五十八歲。衛靈公問陳，當在今年或明年，孔子遂辭衛仕。其去衛，當在明年。
魯哀公二年	孔子年五十九歲。衛靈公卒，孔子在其卒之前或後去衛。
魯哀公三年	孔子年六十歲。孔子由衛適曹又適宋，宋司馬桓魋欲殺之，孔子微服去，適陳。遂仕於陳。
魯哀公六年	孔子年六十三歲。吳伐陳，孔子去陳。絕糧於陳、蔡之間，遂適蔡，見楚葉公。又自葉返陳，自陳返衛。
魯哀公七年	孔子年六十四歲。再仕於衛，時為衛出公之四年。
魯哀公十一年	孔子年六十八歲。魯季康子召孔子，孔子返魯。自其去魯適衛，先後凡十四年而重返魯。此下乃開始其晚年期的教育生活，有若、曾參、言偃、卜商、顓孫師諸人皆先後從學。
魯哀公十二年	孔子年六十九歲。子孔鯉卒。
魯哀公十四年	孔子年七十一歲。顏回卒。齊陳恆弒其君，孔子請討之，魯君臣不從。是年，魯西狩獲麟，孔子春秋絕筆。春秋始筆在何年，則不可考。
魯哀公十五年	孔子年七十二歲。仲由死於衛。
魯哀公十六年	（西曆紀元前四七九年）孔子年七十三歲，卒。

國家圖書館出版品預行編目資料

讀論語學英語：論語中英文譯注讀本 / 理雅各（James Legge）
　英譯：林宏濤　譯注 .――二版 . ――臺北市：商周出版：家
　庭傳媒城邦分公司發行 . 2015.05
　　面：　公分 . ――

　　ISBN 978-986-272-796-6 　（精裝）

　　1. 論語　2. 注釋

121.222　　　　　　　　　　　　　　　104006256

讀論語學英語：論語中英文譯注讀本

英　　譯　　者／理雅各（James Legge）
譯　　注　　者／林宏濤
責　任　編　輯／楊如玉

版　　　　　權／翁靜如
行　銷　業　務／李衍逸、黃崇華
總　　經　　理／彭之琬
發　　行　　人／何飛鵬
法　律　顧　問／台英國際商務法律事務所　羅明通律師
出　　　　　版／商周出版
　　　　　　　　城邦文化事業股份有限公司
　　　　　　　　台北市中山區民生東路二段 141 號 9 樓
　　　　　　　　電話：(02) 2500-7008　傳眞：(02) 2500-7759
　　　　　　　　E-mail：bwp.service@cite.com.tw
　　　　　　　　Blog：http://bwp25007008.pixnet.net/blog
發　　　　　行／英屬蓋曼群島商家庭傳媒股份有限公司城邦分公司
　　　　　　　　台北市中山區民生東路二段 141 號 2 樓
　　　　　　　　書虫客服服務專線：02-25007718．02-25007719
　　　　　　　　24 小時傳眞服務：02-25001990．02-25001991
　　　　　　　　服務時間：週一至週五 09:30-12:00．13:30-17:00
　　　　　　　　郵撥帳號：19863813　　戶名：書虫股份有限公司
　　　　　　　　讀者服務信箱：service@readingclub.com.tw
　　　　　　　　城邦讀書花園：www.cite.com.tw
香港發行所／城邦（香港）出版集團有限公司
　　　　　　　　香港灣仔駱克道 193 號東超商業中心 1 樓　　E-mail:hkcite@biznetvigator.com
　　　　　　　　電話：(852) 25086231　　傳眞：(852) 25789337
馬新發行所／城邦（馬新）出版集團　【Cité (M) Sdn. Bhd. (458372U)】
　　　　　　　　41, Jalan Radin Anum, Bandar Baru Sri Petaling,
　　　　　　　　57000 Kuala Lumpur, Malaysia
　　　　　　　　電話：(603)90578822　　傳眞：(603) 90576622
　　　　　　　　email:cite@cite.com.my

封　面　設　計／王小美
排　　　　　版／豐禾設計
印　　　　　刷／高典印刷有限公司
總　　經　　銷／高見文化行銷股份有限公司　電話：(02) 26689005
　　　　　　　　傳眞：(02) 26689790　　客服專線：0800-055-365

■ 2015 年 5 月二版　　　　　　　　　　　　　　Printed in Taiwan
■ 2022 年 11 月 10 日二版 2.5 刷

定價 400 元

城邦讀書花園
www.cite.com.tw